INTRODUCTION TO
WEB DEVELOPMENT
USING

WITHDRAWN

HTML5

KRIS JAMSA, PhD, MBA

JONES & BARTLETT
LEARNING

World Headquarters
Jones & Bartlett Learning
5 Wall Street
Burlington, MA 01803
978-443-5000
info@jblearning.com
www.jblearning.com

Jones & Bartlett Learning books and products are available through most bookstores and online booksellers. To contact Jones & Bartlett Learning directly, call 800-832-0034, fax 978-443-8000, or visit our website, www.jblearning.com.

Production Credits

Chief Executive Officer: Ty Field
President: James Homer
SVP, Editor-in-Chief: Michael Johnson
SVP, Curriculum Solutions: Christopher Will
Senior Editorial Assistant: Rainna Erikson
Associate Marketing Manager: Cassandra Peterson
Editorial Management: High Stakes Writing, LLC,
    Lawrence J. Goodrich, President
Managing Editor, HSW: Ruth Walker

Copy Editor, HSW: Cynthia Hanson
Production Manager: Susan Schultz
Production Editor: Tina Chen
Rights & Photo Research Assistant: Joseph Veiga
Composition: Absolute Service, Inc.
Cover Design: Kristin E. Parker
Cover Image: © ifong/Shutterstock, Inc.
Printing and Binding: Edwards Brothers Malloy
Cover Printing: Edwards Brothers Malloy

ISBN: 978-1-4496-8654-3

Library of Congress Cataloging-in-Publication Data
Unavailable at time of printing.

6048
Printed in the United States of America
17 16 15 14 13   10 9 8 7 6 5 4 3 2 1

Debbie,
May the next 25 years be as wonderful as the first!
All my love,
Kris

Brief Contents

Contents

© Risto Viita/Shutterstock

Acknowledgments

© Risto Viita/Shutterstock

ALTHOUGH ONLY THE AUTHOR'S name appears on the cover of a book, behind the scenes, a dedicated team of editors, illustrators, proofers, page compositors, and project managers drive the book-making process and ensure the book's highest quality. For this book, I would especially like to acknowledge and thank the book's editors, Ruth Walker and Cynthia Hanson, and Larry Goodrich, president of High Stakes Writing, whose attention to detail kept the project on schedule and whose sense of humor made the project great fun. Also, Katie Dillin, who proofread much of the book, provided a sharp eye not only for grammatical errors, but also for the HTML 5 code itself! I appreciate all of your efforts and the sharing of your skills to make this a great book!

Preface

THIS BOOK EXAMINES TRADITIONAL HTML processing and all of the new HTML 5 capabilities. Each chapter is filled with hands-on examples. You will find specifics on CSS, JavaScript, and more. The following section provides a brief overview of each chapter's contents.

Chapter 1 Getting Started with HTML: Each day, users worldwide surf the Web, visiting sites that present a wide range of content using text, images, videos, and other forms of multimedia. To view Web-based content, users run a Web browser. Common Web browsers include Microsoft Internet Explorer, Google Chrome, and Mozilla Firefox. In the simplest sense, a browser knows only how to retrieve a page from a remote site (a Web server) and then to use the formatting instructions the page contains to retrieve, format, and display the needed content items, such as text, photos, and video. To create webpages, developers use the hypertext markup language (HTML). As you will learn, HTML uses special markup tags to define content formatting. One set of HTML tags may specify the text for a paragraph, another may provide specifics of a photo that is to appear on the page, and yet others to control formatting, such as the use of bold or italic fonts. Chapter 1 introduces many key HTML tags and the process of creating, editing, and uploading HTML documents.

Chapter 2 Integrating Images: Webpages make extensive use of graphics images. To place an image within an HTML page, you use the **<img>** tag. This chapter examines all aspects of webpage image use. As you will learn, using various style attributes, you have complete control over image sizing and placement. Chapter 2 examines the process of integrating photos and clip art into HTML documents.

Chapter 3 Using Hyperlinks to Connect Content: The World Wide Web is often described as a network of billions of interconnected pages of content. When viewing webpages within a browser, users click on hyperlinks to move from one document to another or from one location on page to another. A hyperlink can be text, which normally appears within the browser in blue or purple and is underlined; or the hyperlink can be a photo. To place a hyperlink within the webpages you create, you use the **<a>** and **</a>** anchor-tag pair. Chapter 3 examines the process of creating Web hyperlinks.

Chapter 4 Presenting Lists: Within a webpage, it is common to display lists of data—either numbered lists or bulleted lists. HTML provides an ordered-list tag pair, **<ol>** and **</ol>**, which you can use to create a numbered list, and an unordered-list tag pair, **<ul>** and **</ul>**, which you can use to create a bulleted list. In addition, HTML supports the **<dl>** and **</dl>** tag pair, which lets you create a definition list that consists of terms and their meanings, which you might use, for example, to create a glossary of key terms. Chapter 4 examines the process of creating HTML lists.

Chapter 5 Formatting Content with Tables: Across the Web, billions of sites present vast amounts of data, which may include numbers, text, images, or a combination of each. To organize the display of such information, Web developers make extensive use of tables. A table within a webpage consists of one or more rows, each of which contains one or more columns of data. Within each cell of a table, you can place text and images, which you can further format using additional HTML tags. In other words, you can treat each table cell as a mini-page, the format of which you can control using additional HTML tags. Chapter 5 examines the process of creating HTML tables.

Chapter 6 Getting User Input with Forms: Across the Web, sites make extensive use of forms to prompt users for information. One form might ask a user to provide a login username and password. Another form may prompt a user for register information or a credit card number, and yet another may prompt the user to enter search text. Chapter 6 examines the steps you must perform to create a form within an HTML page.

Chapter 7 Styling Content with Cascading Style Sheets: Using HTML, developers lay out content within a webpage, specifying headers, paragraphs, tables, images, and more. For years, developers would say that HTML "formats a webpage." It's preferable to say that HTML specifies the webpage elements and layout, and cascading style sheet (CSS) attributes specify the actual formatting. Chapter 7 takes a detailed look at cascading style sheets or CSS.

Chapter 8 Advanced Cascading Style Sheets: Using CSS, you can easily format the appearance of items within your page. In this chapter, you will drill down into other CSS capabilities. To start, you will define CSS classes, which group a set of style definitions you can later apply to a variety of HTML tags. Then, you will learn how to create id-based styles, which apply only to an element on your page that matches the identifier. As you will learn, CSS is very flexible and lets you combine the different style definitions you create in order to achieve your desired formatting. Chapter 8 examines advanced CSS processing.

Chapter 9 Creating Page Divisions: Since the first HTML pages began to create the Web, developers have used tables to format content. Tables have the advantage that Web browsers always seem to display them correctly. This makes the use of tables a safe design approach. Unfortunately, using a table for complex page design often leads to large and often complex amounts of HTML. As a result, such pages become harder to modify. A better approach to page layout is to use CSS and <**div**> and </**div**> tag pairs. In the simplest since, the <**div**> and </**div**> tag pair creates a container within which you can place related HTML tags for styling and positioning.

Chapter 10 JavaScript: Throughout this book's previous chapters, you have made extensive use of HTML and CSS to format and style Web-based content. To fully unlock the potential interactivity of a webpage, developers make extensive use of the JavaScript programming language. Using JavaScript, developers can change an HTML element's content, modify CSS styles, change attributes, and more. JavaScript is a programming language with which developers specify instructions the browser must perform to accomplish a specific task. What makes JavaScript unique is that the instructions are executed within the browser, a process to which developers refer to as client-side processing. Chapter 10 introduces JavaScript processing.

Chapter 11 Using the Document Object Module: A webpage consists of many types of objects: paragraphs, headings, images, lists, tables, and more. To manage the items that make up a webpage, browsers do not work in terms of individual HTML tags but rather objects. The Document Object Model, or DOM, defines the structure of a webpage in terms of objects. DOM is important beyond the developers who write the code that implement browsers, such as Internet Explorer and Google Chrome. Using JavaScript, any webpage developer can use DOM to access individual page components in order to create dynamic page content that may change based on user operations, or to perform key operations, such as validating a form's contents. Chapter 11 examines the Document Object Model.

Chapter 12 Unleashing JavaScript Using jQuery: Using JavaScript and DOM, you can perform powerful client-side processing within your webpages which access or change element settings, create animations, and more. In Chapter 12 you will learn how to leverage jQuery to simplify many JavaScript operations and to create more interactive user experiences. Do not let the name jQuery confuse you; jQuery has nothing to do with database operations. Instead, jQuery is a library of JavaScript functions your page can use to manipulate items on your webpage.

Chapter 13 Communicating with AJAX: As you have learned, when a user visits a webpage, the user's browser will request the page's HTML, CSS, JavaScript, and image files. If the user clicks on a link within the page, this process will repeat with a new page and its set of files. Web developers understand this file request model. To improve webpage processing capabilities and functionality, developers can take advantage of the fact that JavaScript can send data and request content to or from a remote server. Asynchronous JavaScript and XML, or AJAX, is a technique that developers can use to perform JavaScript-based interactions with a server. Chapter 13 examines AJAX processing.

Chapter 14 Processing JavaScript Object Notation (JSON): In this chapter, you will learn how to use a different data format from XML, JavaScript Object Notation or JSON, to exchange data. The advantage of using JSON over XML is that JSON closely resembles JavaScript, which makes it easy for your code to process. This chapter will examine several JSON-based applications.

Chapter 15 Webpage Optimization: Every day, users turn to the Web for instant information on a wide range of topics. With access to millions of webpages using only a few clicks of a mouse, users have expectations on how fast a webpage should appear. In short, users want what they want, when they want it. When websites don't meet user performance expectations, users move on. In fact, research has shown that if a webpage takes more than 2.5 seconds to load, many users won't wait, and will look elsewhere for the content they desire. This chapter looks at several steps you can take to improve your website's performance and to reduce the amount of time users must wait for a page to load.

Chapter 16 Search Engine Optimization: When it comes to promoting most websites, at least, "build it and they will come" simply doesn't work. With billions of pages of content residing on the Web, developers need to maximize a site's potential exposure. A key factor in having users find a website is having the site listed, or indexed, within search engine results. Search engine optimization (SEO) is the process developers undertake to improve their site's likelihood of appearing near the top of the search engine's results list. This chapter focuses on several SEO steps developers should perform.

Chapter 17 The Need for HTML 5: Since its origin in the late 1980s, HTML has undergone several major version upgrades. The development of HTML 5 actually began shortly after the HTML 4 release in the late 1990s. Around 2004, the Web Hypertext Application Technology Working Group (WHATWG) began working with the World Wide Web Consortium (W3C) on the HTML 5 specification. Over the years the followed, the specification was influenced by the rapid growth of mobile technologies, capabilities such as geopositioning, and greater need for user interactivity. This chapter introduces many new aspects of HTML 5.

Chapter 18 Integrating Audio and Video: With the advent of video cameras within most cell phones, it has become very easy for people to record their own videos. Thanks to sites such as You Tube, posting videos to the Web has become very easy and popular. Today, many developers want to integrate video or audio content into the webpages they create. HTML 5 was supposed to make the process very easy. Unfortunately, because not all browsers support HTML 5, and because more standardization of video file formats is needed, the process of placing videos within a webpage that all browsers can play remains challenging at best. This chapter examines the steps to perform to place video and audio within a webpage.

Chapter 19 HTML 5 Document Structure and Semantics: HTML, the hypertext markup language, had its origin from other markup languages used by publishers to format text pages. Years ago, for example, people using word-processing software actually placed special codes within their documents to turn on bolding, italics, underlining, and so on. HTML 5 continues HTML's ties to document formatting by adding tags that devices can use to specify attributes for various document-based structures, such as headers, footers, figures, captions, sidebars, and more. In addition, HTML provides several tags that provide meaning, which developers refer to as semantics, to different items on a page. Chapter 19 examines tags that support document semantics.

Chapter 20 Creating Scalable Vector Graphics Files: Throughout this book, you have extensive use of bitmap-graphics files, normally stored in the JPG file format. In this chapter, you will examine SVG graphic files, which are scalable vector graphics files. SVG graphics are powerful and flexible in that they don't lose quality if they are resized. As it turns out, an SVG file consists of XML entries that define the graphic. Across the Web, many sites offer SVG graphics that you can purchase and download and then use on your site. In addition, most vector-based drawing programs let you save the graphics you create as an SVG. Chapter 20 examines SVG image creation and HTML integration.

Chapter 21 Introducing the HTML 5 Canvas: Across the Web, users expect webpage interactivity. For years, Web developers turned to Flash-based animations to provide such user interactions. Unfortunately, not all browsers supported Flash—most specifically, those browsers running on the popular iPad and iPhone. This chapter introduces the HTML 5 canvas, which provides a region on the page within which you can display text, graphics, and animations by using JavaScript programming. The canvas is ideal for dynamic content such as charts, graphs, and animations.

Chapter 22 Advanced Canvas Programming: This chapter continues your examination of the canvas. You will learn several more advanced graphics programming techniques, such as gradients, drop shadows, moving and rotating objects, and working with pixel-based data.

Chapter 23 CSS Transformations and Rotations: Several of the books chapters examine a wide range of graphics operations—from text and image translations to rotations. With those operations in mind, it makes sense to revisit the capabilities that cascading style sheets provide to support similar text and image manipulation. This chapter examines the movement, rotation, scaling, and skewing of text and graphics using CSS.

Chapter 24 Performing CSS Transitions and Animations: Throughout this book, you will JavaScript, jQuery, and the HTML 5 canvas to create dynamic text and graphics-based animations. In this chapter you will learn how to perform animations using CSS transitions, which specify the properties you desire for an elements starting and ending states. The browser, in turn, will apply the transitions to create your animated effect. In this way, you do not need to use JavaScript or jQuery.

Chapter 25 Utilizing Web Storage: For years, to store temporary information, the only option available to most Web developers was cookies. Using a cookie, a developer could store up to 4KB of data. A website might, for example, use a cookie to track the items in a user's shopping cart from one site visit to the next, or, track the user's preferences as he or she traversed a site. HTML 5 expands beyond the storage capabilities that cookies provide to allow session-based storage and long-term storage. The session-based storage exists until the user leaves the site or closes the window. In contrast, the long-term storage persists until the user or the application deletes the data. The HTML 5 Standard states the session and long-term storage support up to 5MB. This chapter examines the Web storage capabilities.

Chapter 26 Creating Location-Aware Webpages Using Geolocation: Around the world, users now make extensive use of mobile phones and hand-held devices to access pages on the World Wide Web. Most phones now have geopositioning capabilities (GPS), which provide information about the phone's current location. Such GPS capabilities will change the way users interact with the Web. With a few clicks, a user can find nearby restaurants, retailers, and other services; they can get driving directions from their current location; and they can instantly summon a cab or emergency-service vehicle. This chapter will examine the steps you must perform to create location-aware webpages.

Chapter 27 Drag-and-Drop Processing: Today, most common applications, such as word processors, e-mail, and file utilities, support drag-and-drop operations. With HTML 5, such operations are extending to webpages. Using drag-and-drop operations within a webpage, users might drag objects that they want to purchase into a shopping cart, drag toppings onto a pizza before placing an online order, and more. In addition, users will soon be able to drag-and-drop content from an application on to a webpage, or, vice versa. This chapter examines HTML 5 drag-and-drop support.

Chapter 28 Integrating Web Workers: For years, operating systems have allowed users to run multiple programs at the same time. Today, applications also take advantage of multiple threads of execution to perform concurrent tasks. Using HTML Web workers, webpages can now use similar threads to perform concurrent processing. A webpage might, for example, use a background task to spell-check content or to parse a large collection of JSON data. Chapter 28 examines the use of Web workers.

Chapter 29 Communicating via WebSockets: Users today make extensive use of texting and instant messaging to communicate. Websites often integrate text-based chats to allow users to exchange messages with technical support staff or sales team members. To make it easier for developers to integrate such capabilities, HTML 5 introduces a Websocket application program interface (API). Admittedly, the API is still in its infancy. Over time, however, we can expect it to grow to support greater capabilities, such as peer-to-peer interactions. This chapter examines the use of Websockets for communication.

Chapter 30 HTML 5 Forms Processing: In this chapter, you will examine new form-based features provided into HTML 5. As you will learn, many of these features are still evolving; but they indicate significant capabilities for the future. That said, it is important that you test each of the features this chapter presents using a variety of browsers, to ensure that your browser provides the support that you need.

Chapter 31 Browser Identification: As the capabilities you include within a webpage increase, there may be times when you will want to determine a user's browser type, so you can process accordingly. For example, you might want to customize the code you are using to integrate video, or, you may want to format page content differently for a Web and mobile browser. This chapter examines a few techniques you can use to determine a browser's capabilities.

Getting Started with HTML

EACH DAY, USERS WORLDWIDE surf the Web, visiting sites that present a wide range of content using text, images, videos, and other forms of multimedia. To view Web-based content, users run a Web **browser**, which is a program users use to view content on the World Wide Web. Common Web browsers include Microsoft Internet Explorer, Google Chrome, and Mozilla Firefox. In the simplest sense, a browser only knows how to retrieve a page from a remote site (Web server) and then to use the formatting instructions the page contains to retrieve, format, and display the needed content items, such as text, photos, and video.

To create webpages, developers use a computer language called the **hypertext markup language (HTML)**. As you will learn, HTML uses special markup tags to define content formatting. One set of HTML tags may specify the text for a paragraph, another may provide specifics about a photo that is to appear on the page, and still others may control formatting, such as the use of bold or italic fonts. This book's chapters focus on how to use specific HTML tags to accomplish different tasks. In this chapter, you will get started with several common HTML tags that will allow you to build simple webpages.

Learning Objectives

This chapter examines how to build several simple webpages. By the time you finish this chapter, you will understand the following key concepts:

- How a Web browser downloads and processes an HTML page for display
- What the need for a Web server is

- Which Web-development software programs you can use to create webpages more easily
- How to view a site's HTML and what you can learn from doing so
- How to create your own HTML file
- How to use the HTML tags
- How Web browsers treat spacing and carriage returns
- How to create paragraphs within HTML content
- How to format text to display as bold or italic or both, and how to display document headings and horizontal rules
- Why you should avoid the use of deprecated tags
- How to display special characters within an HTML page
- How to place comments within HTML files
- How to use HTML tag attributes for greater control over your page formatting and appearance
- How to display a page title
- How to use FTP to upload files to a Web server

Understanding How a Browser Displays a Webpage

To view a webpage, a user types in its address within the browser or clicks on a link within the webpage that he or she is currently viewing. The browser, in turn, sends a message across the Internet to the corresponding website, more specifically to the **Web server** at the site, as shown in **FIGURE 1-1**. The remote Web server, in turn, listens for such requests and responds with the requested file. A Web server is a special computer on the Web; when you "browse" the Web, you're actually using your browser to request content from one or more Web servers. Web developers normally create HTML files on their own computers and then use special software, called an FTP program, to upload the files to a Web server.

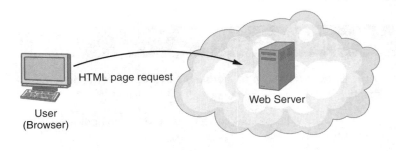

FIGURE 1-1 To display a webpage, a browser requests the page contents from a site's Web server.

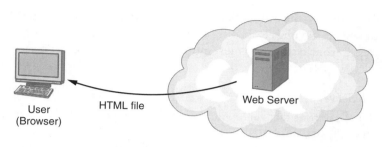

Internet

FIGURE 1-2 A Web server listens for requests from Web browsers and then returns the requested file.

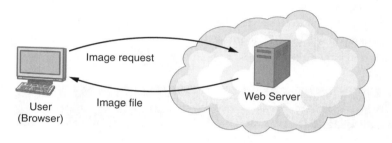

Internet

FIGURE 1-3 Most webpages reference content, such as photos, that the browser requests from the Web server.

After the Web server receives a browser's request for a page, the server returns the page's corresponding HTML content, as shown in **FIGURE 1-2**.

The browser then reads the HTML content the Web server returns and begins to format the page for display. If the HTML content references photos that are to appear on the page, the browser, as shown in **FIGURE 1-3**, sends requests to the Web server for each of the corresponding files.

After the browser receives image files from the Web server, the browser can render and display the page contents. If the user types in another Web address or clicks on a link the page contains, the process will repeat. The browser then requests the new link's HTML contents and related image files.

Understanding the Need for a Web Server

To build a webpage, you create an HTML file that specifies the page's text, images, and formatting. You will create the HTML file on your own system. Before other users can view your webpages, you must place your HTML files and related image files on a Web server. In other words, using your own computer, you can create

HTML files. You can view the contents of the files using a browser because they reside on your system. No one else can see them, however, because other users don't have access to your system. You must move the files to a Web server before others can view your pages.

Getting a Web Server

If you are building a website that you want others to view, you need a Web server. Across the Web, many sites offer Web server space free of charge. You can use such sites to host your webpages, which other users can view. Unfortunately, the free sites will integrate advertisements into your Web content, such as banners across the top of the page, that you don't want. As an alternative, you can invest about $5 a month to get your own Web server space. **TABLE 1-1** lists several companies on the Web that offer Web server space.

After you sign up for Web server space, use your computer to create your HTML files. Then you will use FTP to move the files from your system to the Web server, as shown in **FIGURE 1-4**.

TABLE 1-1 COMPANIES ON THE WEB FROM WHICH YOU CAN PURCHASE WEB SERVER SPACE	
Company	**Web Address**
Amazon.com	http://aws.amazon.com/
GoDaddy.com	http://www.godaddy.com
Bluehost.com	http://www.bluehost.com
Fatcow	http://www.FatCow.com
DreamHost	http://www.dreamhost.com

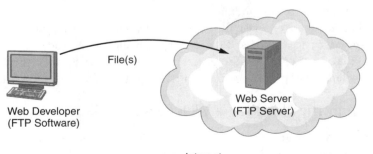

FIGURE 1-4 Using FTP software, you will upload the HTML files you create on your system to a remote Web server.

Understanding Domain Names

Each site on the Web has a unique name, called a **domain name**, such as Google.com, Yahoo.com, and Microsoft.com. If you plan to get your own Web server space, you can purchase your own domain name specific to your site. Many sites on the Web, such as GoDaddy.com, sell domain names. Expect to spend about $20. In addition, many of these sites provide server capabilities with which you can host your domain for a monthly fee. They will provide your Web server.

Web-Development Software You Can Use to Build a Webpage

As discussed, a webpage has a corresponding HTML file and possibly related images, such as photo files. To create the HTML file, you can use a free text-editing program, such as the Notepad accessory program that comes with Windows. A **text editor** lets a user edit a text file. In fact, you will use Notepad to create the HTML files presented in this chapter.

In addition to using a text editor to create HTML files, developers also use **Web-development software programs** such as DreamWeaver or Microsoft Expression Web. This special software allows a developer to create webpage content using a drag-and-drop and visual user interface.

The advantage of using a Web-development program to create your webpages is that such programs provide a more powerful editor that lets you easily position and size images, select and apply fonts and font sizes for text, and more. Then, behind the scenes, the software will create your HTML file for you. The disadvantage of using such software is that you first must buy it, and then learn how to use it. To help you get started, most of the Web-development software programs provide a free trial period. **FIGURE 1-5**, for example, illustrates the Website creation process within DreamWeaver.

TABLE 1-2 lists several Web-development software programs.

To simplify the webpage development process, several sites on the Web provide developers with the ability to create a webpage within their browser. Using such a site, you normally select your desired page layout from a template of pre-existing designs, and then type your text and upload your photos. Such sites exist primarily for users who need to create a webpage but who don't have time or a desire to learn HTML. **FIGURE 1-6**, for example, illustrates the webpage development process using Google Sites (*http://sites.google.com*).

Viewing a Site's HTML

Every page on the Web consists of HTML tags that browsers use to format and display the page contents. When you use your browser to display a webpage,

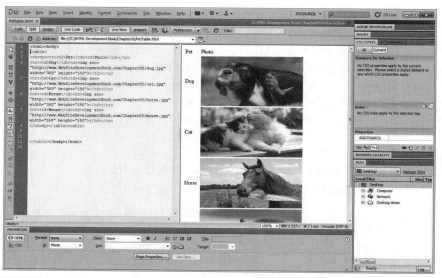

FIGURE 1–5 Using Web-development software, such as Adobe® DreamWeaver®, you can create your site design using a powerful editor.

Credit (from top): © Christian Mueller/Shutterstock; © Anastasija Popova/Shutterstock; © Melanie Hoffman/Shutterstock. Adobe product screenshot reprinted with permission from Adobe Systems Incorporated.

TABLE 1-2   COMMONLY USED WEB-DEVELOPMENT PROGRAMS

Software	Website
DreamWeaver	http://www.adobe.com/products/dreamweaver.html
Microsoft Expression Web	http://www.microsoft.com/expression/
WebPlus	http://www.serif.com/webplus/
CoffeeCup	http://www.coffeecup.com/

you can direct your browser to display the page's underlying HTML tags. Web developers often view and study a site's HTML tags to learn how the site's developers implemented a specific capability or design. **FIGURE 1-7**, for example, illustrates the Head of the Class webpage and some of the corresponding HTML tags.

TABLE 1-3 lists the steps you must perform within commonly used Web browsers to display a site's HTML source.

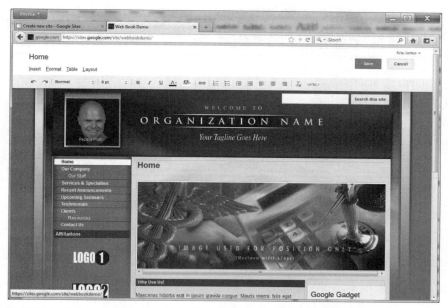

FIGURE 1-6 Several sites on the Web allow users with no knowledge of HTML to quickly design and deploy a webpage using built-in page templates.

Credit: Google and the Google logo are registered trademarks of Google Inc., used with permission.

FIGURE 1-7 Using your Web browser, you can view a site's HTML tags.

Credit: Courtesy of Head of the Class (www.theheadoftheclass.com)

TABLE 1-3 STEPS TO DIRECT A BROWSER TO DISPLAY A SITE'S HTML SOURCE	
Browser	Steps
Internet Explorer	Right click on page and select View Source
Google Chrome	Right click on page and select View Page Source
Firefox	Right click on page and select View Page Source
Opera	Right click on page and select Source
Safari	Right click on page and select View Source

Creating Your Own HTML File

To get started, use a text editor to create an HTML file that resides on your computer. Because your computer is not a Web server, only you can view your file's contents. To start, run a text editor. If you are using Windows, perform the following steps to start the Windows Notepad accessory:

1. Select the Start menu, and choose the All Programs option.
2. Within the Programs menu, click the Accessories folder.
3. Within the Accessories folder, click Notepad. Windows will start the Notepad accessory.

Within Notepad (or your text editor), type the following HTML statements:

```
<!DOCTYPE html>
<html>
<body>
Hello, HTML world!
</body>
</html>
```

Make sure you type the statements exactly as they appear here. Take your time, and double-check your work. Then use your editor to save the HTML statements to a folder on your disk with the filename Hello.html. If you are using the Windows Notepad, perform these steps to save your file:

1. Select the File menu Save As option.
2. Within the Save As dialog box, select the Save As Type pull-down list and choose All Files. If you don't do this, Notepad saves your file with the .txt file extension.
3. Within the File name field, type Hello.html.
4. Click Save.

FIGURE 1-8 Your Web browser should display this HTML file, which resides on your computer's disk.

Note: To simplify your HTML file management as you read through the chapters of this book, create a folder on your disk called HTML or HTMLBook within which you store the files that you create from this book.

To view your file's contents, open your Web browser. Within the browser's address bar, type **file://c:/** followed by the folder that contains your file and the filename Hello.html. Assuming that you stored your file with a folder named HTML, you would type:

```
file://c:/HTML/Hello.html
```

Your browser, in turn, should display your file's contents, as shown in **FIGURE 1-8**.

Remember, because the file resides on your computer's disk, and not on a Web server, other users cannot view your file.

Saving the HTML file to a folder on your disk and later displaying the file's contents is the most challenging task in Chapter 1. After you successfully display your file's contents, edit them, as shown here, by adding the word "My" before "HTML world!"

```
<!DOCTYPE html>
<html>
<body>
Hello, My HTML world!
</body>
</html>
```

Save your file's contents. Then, refresh your browser's contents. Your browser, in turn, will display your updated HTML contents, as shown in **FIGURE 1-9**.

Select names that meaningfully describe the file's contents when you name your HTML files, such as AboutUs.html or ContactUs.html. Avoid spaces within

FIGURE 1–9 After you make changes to your HTML file, you must save the file's contents, and then refresh your browser.

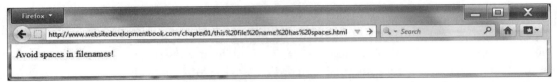

FIGURE 1–10 Avoid spaces within your HTML filenames.

your filenames. Browsers will replace the spaces with the characters **%20**, which may confuse users, as shown in FIGURE 1–10.

Understanding the HTML Tags

Now that you have successfully created, saved, and displayed an HTML file, it's time to understand the file's contents. To start, the **<!DOCTYPE html>** tag tells the browser the type of content that the file contains—its document type or DOCTYPE for short. In the past, HTML files have used a variety of more complex **<!DOCTYPE>** tags. With HTML version 5, the tag has been simplified to use just the word **html.** You should start each HTML file that you create with the following **<!DOCTYPE>** tag:

```
<!DOCTYPE html>
```

Next, the **<html>** tag marks the start of your file's HTML content. At the bottom of your file, you will see the closing **</html>** tag that marks the end of the content. The ending tag includes a slash (/) before the letters html. As you will learn, most HTML tags consist of a starting and ending tag pair. The ending tag will also have the same name as the starting tag, but the name will be preceded with a slash.

An HTML file consists of two parts: an optional header section within which you will define JavaScript program statements and cascading style sheet definitions, and a body section within which you will place the contents of your page. (A **cascading style sheet (CSS)** is a file recording style details, such as fonts and colors, that is read by browsers so that style is consistent over multiple webpages.) In the case of the file Hello.html, there is no header section; you didn't need it. The **<body>** and **</body>** tag pair enclose the page's contents.

You will make extensive use of the **<!DOCTYPE>** tag as well as the **<html>** and **<body>** tag pairs within each of the HTML files that you create.

How Web Browsers Treat Spacing and Carriage Returns

When a browser formats HTML content for display, the browser will treat spaces, tabs, and even carriage returns within your document as a single space. For example, consider the HTML file ThreeLines.html shown here:

```
<!DOCTYPE html>
<html>
<body>
First line
Second line
Third line
</body>
</html>
```

As you can see, the file uses carriage returns to place the words terms First line, Second line, and Third line on separate lines. Using your text editor, create and save the file. When you display the file's contents using your browser, it will treat the carriage returns as a space, displaying the words on one line, as shown in **FIGURE 1-11**.

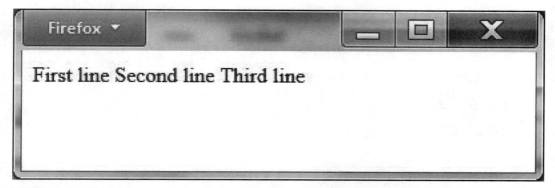

FIGURE 1-11 Web browsers treat spaces, tabs, and carriage returns within HTML content as a single space.

To direct the browser to move content to the start of a new line, you must use the HTML **
** line-break tag. You place the tag at each location within your content where you want the browser to display the content that follows at the start of a new line. The following file, LineBreak.html, illustrates the use of the **
** tag:

```
<!DOCTYPE html>
<html>
<body>
First line <br/>
Second line <br/>
Third line <br/>
</body>
</html>
```

When you save the file and view its contents, the browser will display the words on individual lines, as shown in **FIGURE 1-12**.

The **
** tag is unique in that it does not use a start and stop tag. Instead, the one tag includes the ending slash character.

Note: Use lowercase letters for your tags, **<html>**, for instance, instead of **<HTML>**, when you create your HTML files. Most browsers support lowercase, uppercase, and even mixed-case tags, such as **<HTml>**. However, standard documents that provide the HTML specifications lean toward the use of lowercase. In reality, there are likely billions of HTML documents around the Web that use uppercase tags. Browsers simply can't stop supporting uppercase tags or all of these pages would break.

FIGURE 1-12 The **
** tag directs a browser to display the content that follows at the start of a new line.

Creating Paragraphs Within HTML Content

Within many HTML documents that you create, it is common to have one or more paragraphs of text. As you have learned, using the **
** line-break tag, you can direct a browser to place the text that follows at the start of a new line. The following HTML file, LineBreaks.html, creates two paragraphs by placing the **
** tags between sections of text. The first **
** tag directs the browser to start a new line of content, and the second **
** tag creates a blank line between the text sections:

```
<!DOCTYPE html>
<html>
<body>
A man does what he must - in spite of personal con-
sequences, in spite of obstacles and dangers and
pressures - and that is the basis of all human
morality. John F. Kennedy<br/> <br/>
I do the very best I know how - the very best I
can; and I mean to keep on doing so until the end.
Abraham Lincoln
</body>
</html>
```

When you view the file's contents, the browser will display the content shown in **FIGURE 1-13**.

When using the **
** tag, we can separate text in a way that creates the appearance of paragraphs. Often, we will want to apply specific formatting to the text within paragraphs, possibly by selecting a font or a color, or by defining the line spacing. In such cases, you should use the **<p>** and **</p>** tag pair to mark

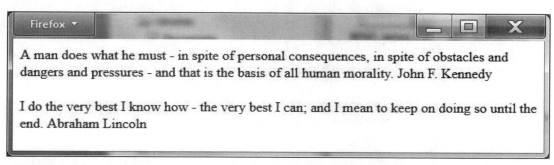

FIGURE 1-13 Use <br/> tags to separate sections of text into a paragraph-like format.

the start and end of each paragraph. The following HTML file, Paragraph.html, uses the **<p>** and **</p>** tag pair to mark each paragraph:

```
<!DOCTYPE html>
<html>
<body>
<p>Nothing can stop the man with the right mental
attitude from achieving his goal; nothing on earth
can help the man with the wrong mental attitude.
Thomas Jefferson</p>
<p>I'm not the smartest fellow in the world, but I
can sure pick smart colleagues. Franklin D.
Roosevelt</p>
</body>
</html>
```

When you view the file's contents, the browser will display the content shown in **FIGURE 1-14**. As you can see, by using the **<p>** and **</p>** tag pair, the browser places the start of each paragraph on a new line and separates each paragraph with a space.

When you place text within an HTML-based webpage, the browser automatically wraps the text to the start of the next line when the text reaches the right edge of the window. **FIGURE 1-15**, for example, illustrates the same text within several different-sized windows. As you can see, the browser wraps the text contents based on the window size.

Formatting Text

In Chapter 8, "Advanced Cascading Style Sheets," you will learn various ways to format different elements that appear within a webpage, such as paragraph text,

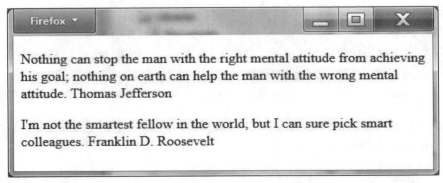

FIGURE 1-14 Using the <p> and </p> tag pair to mark the start and end of paragraph content

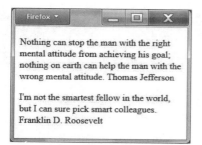 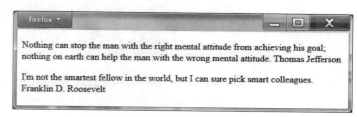

FIGURE 1–15 A browser, by default, will automatically wrap text when it reaches the right edge of the window.

headings and captions, and even images. CSS is the approved way to format a Web document. That said, there are several older HTML tags that have been around since the first version of HTML that browsers still support for formatting. Using these tags, you can make text bold, italic, and even underlined. This book will present the use of these tags because they provide you with a good way to practice using HTML to achieve formatted results. A "CSS purist" may shake his or her head in disapproval if you use the tags as opposed to CSS. But billions of HTML pages across the Web make use of the tags. You won't see browsers stop supporting these older tags any time soon, or the pages that use them would simply break.

Displaying Bold Text

Using the **** and **** tag pair, you can direct the browser to display specific text using a bold font:

```
This is not bold. <b>This is bold.</b> This is not.
```

When the browser encounters the **** tag, the browser will start its use of a bold font to display the page text. When the browser later encounters the **** stop tag, it will turn off bolding. The following HTML file, BoldText.html, illustrates the use of the **** and **** tag pair:

```
<!DOCTYPE html>
<html>
<body>
This is normal text. <b>This is bold text!</b>
This, again, is normal.
</body>
</html>
```

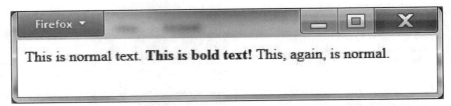

FIGURE 1-16 Using the <b> and </b> tag pair to turn the use of bold text on and off

When you view the file, the browser will display the contents shown in **FIGURE 1-16**.

Forgetting a Stop Tag

Most of the HTML tags use start and stop tag pairs. As the size and complexity of your HTML documents increase, sometimes you will make formatting errors, perhaps forgetting an ending tag or using the wrong tag. For example, the following text uses two <b> tags, as opposed to the <b> and </b> tag pair:

```
This is not bold. <b>This is bold.<b> This is still
bold due to the error.
```

When the browser encounters the first <b> tag, it will start bolding. When it encounters the second <b> tag, it will keep bolding turned on. Most browsers will then leave bolding enabled until they encounter two ending </b> tags.

The following HTML file, NoStopBold.html, shows such an HTML formatting error:

```
<!DOCTYPE html>
<html>
<body>
This is not bold. <b>This is bold.<b> This is still
bold due to the error.
</body>
</html>
```

As you can see, the file uses two <b> tags instead of the <b> and </b> tag pair. When you view the file, the browser will display the contents shown in **FIGURE 1-17**.

As you can see, once the browser turns on bolding, the file's contents never direct the browser to turn it off. When such errors occur, you must edit your HTML file, locate the errant or missing tag, correct the error, and then save the

FIGURE 1-17 Errant bolding within a webpage due to a missing **</b>** stop tag

file's updated contents. Developers refer to the process of identifying and correcting errors as debugging.

Displaying Italic Text

Using the **<i>** and **</i>** tag pair, you can direct the browser to display italic text:

```
This is not italic. <i>This is italic.</i> This
is not.
```

Like the **<b>** and **</b>** tag pair, when the browser encounters the **<i>** tag, the browser will turn on the use of an italic font. When the browser later encounters the **</i>** stop tag, it will turn off italics. The following HTML file, ItalicText.html, illustrates the use of the **<i>** and **</i>** tag pair:

```
<!DOCTYPE html>
<html>
<body>
Tact is the ability to describe others as they see
themselves. <i>Abraham Lincoln</i>
</body>
</html>
```

When you view the file, the browser will display the contents shown in **FIGURE 1-18**.

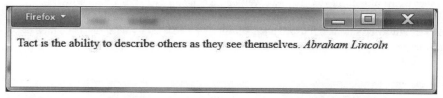

FIGURE 1-18 Using the **<i>** and **</i>** tag pair to control the use of italic text

Understanding Nested Tags

When your page formatting becomes more complex, there will be many times when you will nest one set of HTML tags inside another. For example, the following statement turns on bold and italic text:

```
<b><i>This is bold and italic.</i></b>
```

When you place one set of HTML tags inside of another, in a practice called nesting tags, you need to keep the order of your tags consistent. That is, you should close the innermost tag first. In the previous statement, the code first closes the italic tags (the innermost tags) and then the bold tag. The following statement errantly switches the tag order:

```
<b><i>This is bold and italic.</b></i>
```

Although most browsers will display the text correctly, forgiving the error, you should instead close the innermost tag first.

Displaying Document Headings

Within a webpage, depending on your design, there may be times when you want to place headings within your text, as shown in **FIGURE 1-19**.

HTML defines six tag pairs that let you create different size headings. The <**h1**> and </**h1**> tag pair creates the largest heading and the <**h6**> and </**h6**> tag

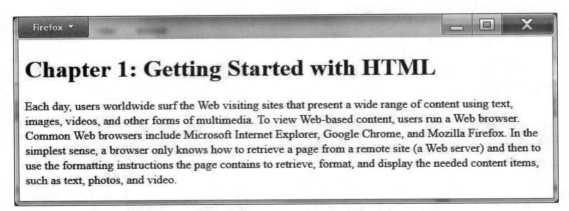

FIGURE 1-19 Using headings within an HTML page to identify text sections

pair, the smallest. The following HTML file, Headings.html, illustrates the use of each heading tag:

```
<!DOCTYPE html>
<html>
<body>
<h1>This is a Heading 1</h1>
<h2>This is a Heading 2</h2>
<h3>This is a Heading 3</h3>
<h4>This is a Heading 4</h4>
<h5>This is a Heading 5</h5>
<h6>This is a Heading 6</h6>
</body>
</html>
```

When you view the file, your browser will display the heading sizes, as shown in **FIGURE 1-20**.

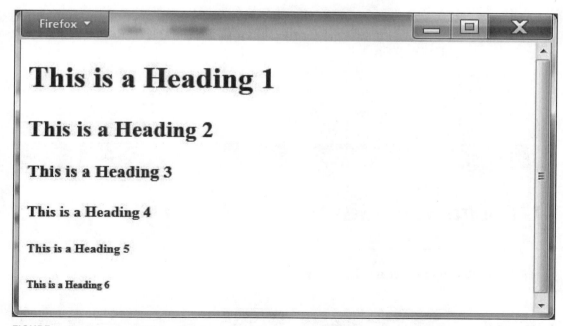

FIGURE 1-20 Using the HTML heading tag pairs **<h1>** through **<h6>**

Depending on your page design, you can use any of the heading tags to create a heading. That is, you do not have to first use **<h1>** and **</h1>** before you can use the others. Instead, you can use the heading tag that uses the font and style that best meets your page design.

Displaying a Horizontal Rule

A horizontal rule is a line the browser displays across the page, normally to divide page content. To create a horizontal rule, you use the **<hr/>** tag. The following HTML file, HorizontalRule.html, uses the **<hr/>** tag to place a horizontal rule between a heading and a paragraph text:

```
<!DOCTYPE html>
<html>
<body>
<h1>George Washington</h1>
<hr/>
<p>It is better to offer no excuse than a
bad one.</p>
</body>
</html>
```

When you display the file, the browser will display the contents shown in **FIGURE 1-21**.

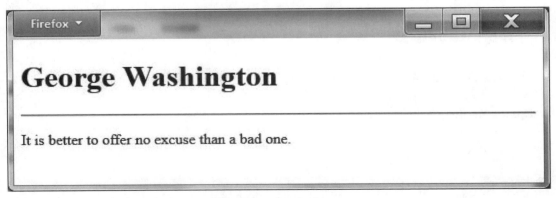

FIGURE 1-21 Using horizontal rules to separate webpage content

Understanding Deprecated Tags

Since the introduction of HTML in the late 1980s, different HTML tags have come and gone. When a tag is replaced by a newer tag or formatting capability, the older tag is called a **deprecated tag**. You should avoid the use of deprecated tags within the files that you create. Although it is unlikely, it is possible that a browser might stop supporting a deprecated tag. In reality, given there are millions of pages that use such tags, it is doubtful that a browser would not support the tags, which would essentially break the corresponding pages.

As you use different tags, note whether the tag is deprecated. Normally, a deprecated tag is your indication that there is a better way to accomplish the same result. For example, the following statement combines the **<h1>** and **<u>** tags to underline a header:

```
<h1><u>This Header Is Underlined</u></h1>
```

The **<u>** and **</u>** underline tag pair is deprecated. The preferred way to achieve such underlining is to use the text-decoration style, as shown here:

```
<h1 style="text-decoration:underline;">This Header
Is Underlined</h1>
```

Using Special Characters

HTML tags begin with the less-than symbol (<) and end within the greater-than symbol (>). Depending on your page contents, there may be times when you will use these symbols in their conventional mathematical sense, rather than as computer code, within your text:

```
1 + 2 < 5
```

When a browser encounters the less-than symbol, it assumes that an HTML tag follows. The browser will consider any text that follows the less-than symbol as the start of an HTML tag name. When the browser fails to find the ending greater-than symbol, the browser may simply ignore the text.

When you must use such symbols within your webpages, you must place special characters within your file that represent the symbol that you desire. **TABLE 1-4** presents the HTML special characters.

TABLE 1-4	SPECIAL CHARACTERS USED TO REPRESENT SYMBOLS WITHIN A WEBPAGE
Symbol	**Special Characters**
&	&amp;
>	&gt;
<	&lt;
©	&copy;
÷	&divide;
Space (non-breaking)	
™	&trade;

The following HTML file, SymbolDemo.html, illustrates the use of several of the special symbols:

```
<!DOCTYPE html>
<html>
<body>
Copyright symbol: &copy; <br/>
Trademark symbol: &trade; <br/>
Math example: 6 &divide; 2 = 3 <br/>
Three spaces   between text <br/>
</body>
</html>
```

When you view the file, the browser displays the contents shown in **FIGURE 1-22**.

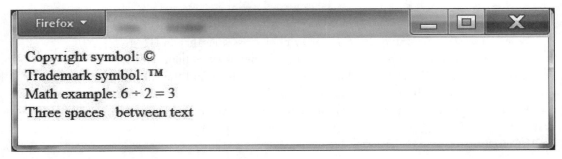

FIGURE 1-22 Displaying special symbols within a webpage

Placing Comments Within HTML Files

As your HTML files become larger and more complex, you will include CSS style definitions, JavaScript code, and so on. They may perform processing that you will want to explain to someone who is reading your HTML code; or perhaps you will want to read such comments yourself a few months or more after you create the file to help you recall the processing. For such cases, you can place comments within your HTML. To create a comment, you place text between the <!--**and** --> tags, as shown here:

```
<!-- This is a comment -->
```

When a browser examines your HTML code, the browser will simply ignore the comment text. It will not display the text. The following HTML file, CommentDemo.html, uses a comment tag to place information about the file, such as who created it, why, and when:

```
<!DOCTYPE html>
<!-- CommentDemo.html -->
<!-- Written: 9-1-2012 -->
<html>
<body>
<!-- This is a comment -->
<p>Hello, HTML World</p>
<!-- This, too, is a comment -->
</body>
</html>
```

When you view the file, the browser will display the content shown in **FIGURE 1-23**. As you can see, the browser ignores and does not display the comment text.

FIGURE 1-23   A browser will ignore the text within comment tag pairs.

Note: Users across the Web employ a wide range of browsers. Unfortunately, not all browsers behave the same way. Some browsers will display tag contents differently. You should, therefore, download and install the common browsers on your system. Then, after you create a page, test the page within each browser. You will find that you must periodically tweak your HTML in order for the page content to display correctly within each browser.

Understanding HTML Tag Attributes

To provide you with greater control over your page formatting and appearance, many tags support style attributes with values that you can specify within the tag itself to accomplish specific formatting. The following statements, for example, use the **text-align** style to center heading text within a page:

```
<!DOCTYPE html>
<html>
<body>
<h1 style="text-align:center;">Centered Header
Text</h1>
</body>
</html>
```

Throughout this book, you will make extensive use of such styles within HTML tags.

Displaying a Page Title

When you view a webpage, browsers will often display a title for the page at the top of the window or at the top of the tab. To specify your page title, use the <title> and </title> tag pair:

```
<title>This is the text for a page title</title>
```

Within your HTML file, place the **<title>** tag pair within the **<head>** and **</head>** tags, which precede the **<body>** tag. The following HTML file, TitleDemo.html, illustrates the use of the **<title>** and **</title>** tag pair:

```
<!DOCTYPE html>
<html>
```

```
<head>
<title>Hello</title>
<body>
<h1>Hello, HTML World!</h1>
</body>
</html>
```

When you view the file, the browser will display the title bar, as shown in FIGURE 1-24.

Using FTP to Upload Files to a Web Server

As you have learned, for other users to view the HTML files that you create, you must place your HTML files and any image files that you use on a Web server. To upload files from your computer to the Web server, you will use special FTP software. **File transfer protocol (FTP)** provides the rules that programs follow for uploading and download files to and from a remote server. When you purchase space on a Web server, your server provider will give you an FTP address along with an FTP username and password that you will use to connect to your site in order to upload files.

To start, you need to download and install FTP software onto your computer. Several sites around the Web offer free FTP software, trial versions of the software, or software you can buy. FIGURE 1-25, for example, shows the WS_FTP program, which you can try at no charge to get started.

To upload files to your Web server, use the FTP software first to connect to your server. To do so, provide the software with your FTP address, your FTP username, and your FTP password. In the case of FIGURE 1-25, the server disk will appear in the right half of the screen and the local disk in the left half. To upload a file or files, you simply select the folder on your machine that contains the files and then upload the files into the correct folder on your server. Most servers have

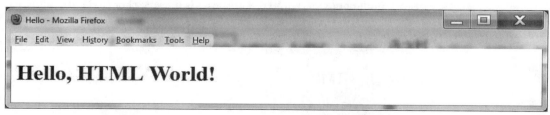

FIGURE 1-24 Using the **<title>** and **</title>** tag pair to create a page title

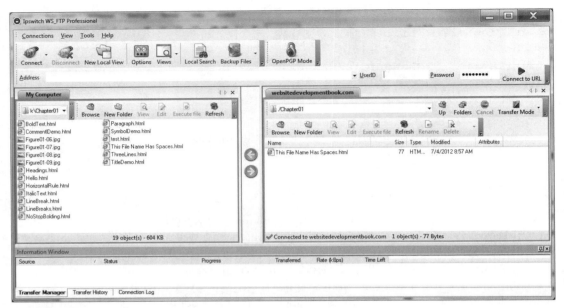

FIGURE 1-25 Using WS_FTP to upload files to a Web server
Credit: Courtesy of Ipswitch File Transfer

a folder named HTDOCS or something similar where you must place the files that you want to appear on the Web.

To move or upload a file, simply click on the file to highlight it and then click, in this case, the arrow that faces the server. The FTP software, in turn, will upload the file. The steps you perform to upload files will vary somewhat, depending on the FTP software that you select, but they will be broadly similar.

Real-World Web Design

When you use HTML, CSS, or JavaScript within your webpages, many times you will need to look up a tag definition, style attribute, or statement syntax. A site that you should bookmark for such purposes is the W3Schools' HTML tutorial at *http://w3schools.com,* as shown in **FIGURE 1-26**. The site provides detailed explanations of each HTML tag, CSS, and JavaScript.

Hands-On HTML

To view the HTML files or to experiment with the files presented in this chapter, visit this book's companion website at *http://www.websitedevelopmentbook.com/ Chapter01/TryIt.html.*

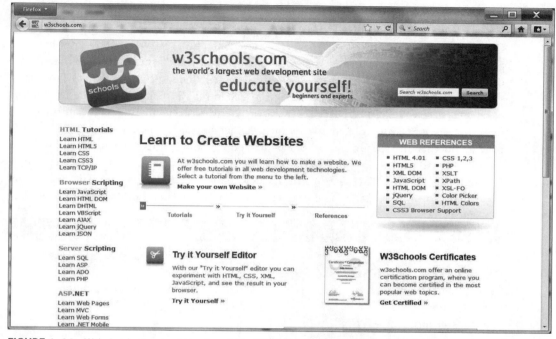

FIGURE 1-26 Web developers should bookmark the W3Schools website for Web-development tutorials and references. *Reproduced with permission of w3schools.com*

CHAPTER SUMMARY

Users make extensive use of Web browsers to view content on the Web. A browser only knows how to request a file from a remote Web server and then to use the formatting instructions the file contains to retrieve, format, and display the needed content items, such as text, photos, and video.

The pages that users view on the Web are created in HTML. To create webpages, developers use the hypertext markup language (HTML). HTML uses special markup tags to format content. One set of HTML tags may specify the title that appears in the browser window for the page, another set may specify the text for a paragraph, and another may provide specifics about a photo that is to appear on the page. This chapter introduced the process of creating simple HTML files, common HTML tags, and the file upload process that lets you move the HTML files that you create on your local PC to a Web server, which allows other users to view the content.

KEY TERMS

Browser
Cascading style sheet (CSS)
Deprecated tag
Domain name
File transfer protocol (FTP)

Hypertext markup language (HTML)
Text editor
Web-development software programs
Web server

CHAPTER REVIEW

1. Create an HTML file named HelloName.html that displays the message "Hello," followed by your name.

2. Modify the HelloName.html file you created in Question 1 to display the word "Hello" in bold and your name in italics.

3. Modify the HelloName.html to use the **\<title\>** and **\</title\>** tag pair to display the word "Hello" in the browser title bar.

4. Create an HTML file Symbols.html that illustrates the use of special symbols such as <, >, &, ®, and ±.

5. Create an HTML file named Book.html that displays the following:
   Title: Web Development with HTML 5
   Publisher: Jones and Bartlett Learning
   Author: Kris Jamsa

6. Create an HTML file that illustrates the use of the HTML comment tag pair.

7. Define and describe a deprecated HTML tag.

8. Describe why Web developers use an FTP program.

9. Research the HTML paragraph tag **\<p\>** and its style attributes. Create an HTML file named YellowParagraph.html that displays a paragraph of text with a yellow background color.

10. Create an HTML file named Nested.html that illustrates the use of nested HTML tags.

Integrating Images

WEBPAGES MAKE EXTENSIVE USE of graphics images. To place an image within an HTML page, you use the **<img>** tag. As you will learn, when using various style attributes, you have complete control over image sizing and placement.

Learning Objectives

This chapter examines all aspects of webpage image use. By the time you finish this chapter, you will understand the following key concepts:

- How to use the **<img>** tag to place an image within a webpage
- What the difference is between absolute and relative image URLs
- Why and how to specify alternative text for an image
- How to specify an image's height and width using **<img>** tag attributes
- How to center an image within a webpage
- How copyrights affect which images you can and can't use within a webpage
- What you must know about image types and file sizes
- How to optimize graphics for Web use
- How to display a page background image
- How to display an image border, and how to use the border to round image corners
- How to pad an image with pixels to provide space between the image and other page elements
- How to control image opacity
- How to align text and images
- How to position an image at a fixed location
- How to rotate an image

Placing an Image Within a Webpage

To place an image within an HTML page, you use the **<img>** tag. The **<img>** tag is unique in that it is not a tag pair. Instead, you place an ending slash within the tag immediately before the closing right bracket:

```
<img src="http://www.WebsiteDevelopmentBook/
Chapter02/dog.jpg"/>
```

When you place an **<img>** tag within an HTML file, you use the **src** attribute to specify the location of the corresponding image file. When the browser downloads and examines your file's HTML tags, the browser will then download the image from the location specified. In the case of the previous **<img>** tag, the browser will locate the image file at *http://www.websitedevelopmentbook.com/ Chapter02/dog.jpg.*

The following HTML file, FirstImage.html, uses the **<img>** tag to display a photo of a dog:

```
<!DOCTYPE html>
<html>
<body>
<img src="http://www.websitedevelopmentbook.com/
Chapter02/dog.jpg/>
</body>
</html>
```

When you view the file's contents, the browser will display the image, as shown in **FIGURE 2-1**.

FIGURE 2-1 Using the **<img>** tag to place an image within a webpage

By default, the browser will display the image inline within your existing page content. For example, the following HTML file, ImageInline.html, displays an image between two paragraphs of text:

```
<!DOCTYPE html>
<html>
<body>
<p>My German shepherd "Bo" is two years old. He
lives with us on the ranch. He likes to spend his
days at the barn with the horses and his nights
watching TV.</p>
<img src="http://www.websitedevelopmentbook.com/
Chapter02/dogsofa.jpg"/>
<p>Bo lives with four other dogs. His favorite
times of the day are breakfast and lunch.</p>
</body>
</html>
```

When you view the file's contents, your browser will display the image and text shown in **FIGURE 2-2**.

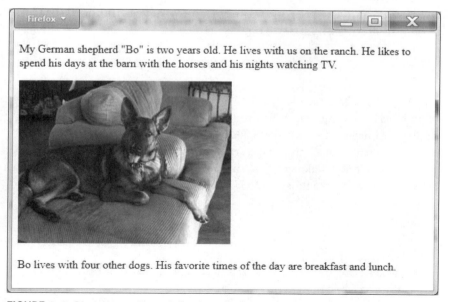

FIGURE 2-2 Displaying an image inline, between two paragraphs

FIGURE 2-3 Using multiple **<img>** tags to place several images within a webpage

Credit (from left): © Mackland/Shutterstock; © Mackland/Shutterstock; © Andraž Cerar/Shutterstock

In a similar way, the following HTML file, ThreeImages.html, uses three **<img>** tags to display photos side by side:

```
<!DOCTYPE html>
<html>
<body>
<img src="http://www.websitedevelopmentbook.com/
Chapter02/group.jpg"/>
<img src="http://www.websitedevelopmentbook.com/
Chapter02/agility.jpg/>
<img src="http://www.websitedevelopmentbook.com/
Chapter02/frisbee.jpg"/>
</body>
</html>
```

As you can see, each image file you want to place within an HTML page requires its own **<img>** tag. When you display the file's contents, the browser will display the images, as shown in **FIGURE 2-3**.

If you want to stack the images, rather than display the images side by side, you can place line-break tags **
** after each **<img>** tag as shown here in the HTML file ThreeStackedImages.html:

```
<!DOCTYPE html>
<html>
<body>
<img src="http://www.websitedevelopmentbook.com/
Chapter02/group.jpg"/><br/>
<img src="http://www.websitedevelopmentbook.com/
Chapter02/agility.jpg"/><br/>
```

```
<img src="http://www.websitedevelopmentbook.com/
Chapter02/frisbee.jpg"/><br/>
</body>
</html>
```

In this case, when you display the file's contents, the browser will stack the images, as shown in FIGURE 2-4.

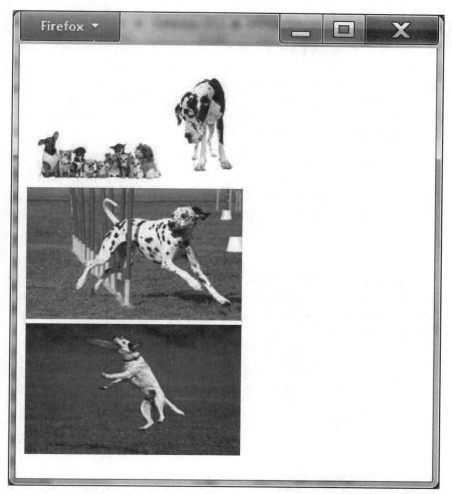

FIGURE 2-4 Using line-break tags **
** to stack images within a webpage

Credit (from top): © Mackland/Shutterstock; © Mackland/Shutterstock; © Andraž Cerar/ Shutterstock

Understanding Absolute and Relative Image URLs

When you place an **<img>** tag within an HTML file, you use the **src** attribute to tell the browser where to locate the image file. In the previous examples, absolute URLs were used to specify each image location; that is, each URL began with http:// and then specified the site holding the file as well as the path (folder location and filename) to file. An **absolute URL** is a uniform resource locator (Web address) that begins with http:// and then specifies a website, possibly a folder, and then a filename.

To better organize your files, often you will place images for your website within a specific folder. In such cases you can use a **relative URL**, which is a uniform resource locator (Web address) that is relative to the current HTML page location. The relative URL will specify the image location (rather than the complete site). Likewise, there may be times when you will simply place your image files in the same folder as the HTML file. The following HTML file, SameFolder.html, assumes that the image file Dog.jpg will reside in the same folder as the HTML file. As such, the **src** attribute within the **<img>** tag simply specifies the file name (no http://, no Web server, no file folder):

```
<!DOCTYPE html>
<html>
<body>
<img src="dog.jpg"/><br/>
</body>
</html>
```

When you view the HTML file, the browser will look for the image file in the same folder that has the HTML file. If the browser locates the image file, it will display the image within the webpage. If the browser can't locate the image, the browser will display a broken-image-link icon, as shown in **FIGURE 2-5**.

FIGURE 2-5 If a browser cannot locate the image file specified in the **src** attribute of an **<img>** link, the browser will display a broken-image-link icon.

Note: Web developers often upload an HTML file to a Web server but then forget to upload the corresponding image files. For users across the Web to be able to view the webpage with the images, the image files must reside on a Web server along with the HTML file.

The developer has organized the files by creating a subfolder named *images* beneath the folder that holds the current HTML file. The subfolder holds an image file named dog.jpg. The following contains the relevant <**img**> tag **src** attribute to locate the image:

```
<img src="images/dog.jpg"/>
```

Specifying Alternative Text for an Image

When you place an image within a webpage, you should use the <**img**> tag **alt** attribute to specify text that describes the image. If for some reason the browser can't display the image, it instead will display the alternative text, as shown in FIGURE 2-6. A **screen reader** is software that reads the contents of a webpage using a voice synthesizer. It allows users with visual disabilities to experience a webpage. Should a user with a vision disability use a screen reader to visit your webpage, it will read your alternative text to the user. The following HTML file, AltImageText.html, uses the **alt** attribute within an <**img**> tag to specify alternative image text:

```
<!DOCTYPE html>
<html>
<body>
<img src="http://www.websitedevelopmentbook.com/
Chapter02/missing.jpg" alt="Photo of a German
shepherd"/>
</body>
</html>
```

FIGURE 2-6 Some browsers will display the **alt** attribute contents if an image file is not found.

Controlling Image Height and Width

By default, when you place an image within a webpage, the browser displays the image based upon its actual size. Often, designers want to size and display an image at a specific height and width. Using the **<img>** tag **height** and **width** attributes, you can direct a browser to display an image at a specific size. The **height** and **width** attributes let you specify the size you desire in pixels or as a percentage of the page size.

The following HTML page, FixedImageSize.html, uses the **<img>** tag **height** and **width** attributes to display the same image at different fixed pixel sizes:

```
<!DOCTYPE html>
<html>
<body>
<img src="http://www.websitedevelopmentbook.com/
Chapter02/parrot.jpg" width="200" height="120"/>
<img src="http://www.websitedevelopmentbook.com/
Chapter02/parrot.jpg" width="300" height="180"/>
<img src="http://www.websitedevelopmentbook.com/
Chapter02/parrot.jpg" width="400" height="240"/>
</body>
</html>
```

When you view the file's contents, your browser will display the image sizes, as shown in **FIGURE 2-7**.

FIGURE 2-7 Using the **<img>** tag **height** and **width** attributes to display images at fixed pixel sizes
Credit: © Mayskyphoto/Shutterstock

Experiment with your browser by increasing or decreasing the browser window size. As you change the window size, the size of your images on the page won't change. That's because you have specified a fixed image size.

In contrast, the following HTML file, PercentImageSizes.html, uses the **<img>** tag **width** attribute to specify the image width as a percentage of the window size:

```
<!DOCTYPE html>
<html>
<body>
<img src="http://www.websitedevelopmentbook.com/
Chapter02/dog.jpg" width="20%"/>
<img src="http://www.websitedevelopmentbook.com/
Chapter02/dog.jpg" width="30%"/>
<img src="http://www.websitedevelopmentbook.com/
Chapter02/dog.jpg" width="40%"/>
</body>
</html>
```

Because the **<img>** tag does not specify a height, the browser proportionally will scale the height to the width. In this case, if you increase or decrease the size of your browser window, the image sizes will change, as shown in **FIGURE 2-8**.

FIGURE 2-8 Specifying image sizes as a percentage of the browser window

IMPORTANCE OF HEIGHT AND WIDTH

Even if you don't use the <img> tag **height** and **width** attributes to scale an image, and are using photo-editing software instead, you should leave the **height** and **width** attributes in your <img> tag. Some browsers, as they render the page, will use the **height** and **width** values you specify to hold space for the image. If you don't specify the **height** and **width** attributes, the browser must download the graphics file to determine the image size before it can render that part of the page. By providing the **height** and **width** attributes, you may increase the speed at which the browser can display the majority of your page content.

Using the <**img**> tag **height** and **width** attributes provides a fast way for designers to determine the image sizes they desire. After they determine the image size that they want, most designers then use photo-editing software, such as Photoshop, to physically change the image size. If you are increasing a photo's size, the photo-editing software normally will produce a better result than will a browser. If you are reducing an image's size instead, the photo-editing software can create a smaller image file, which later will download faster when a user views your webpage.

Centering an Image

As you place images within a webpage, there will be many times when you will want to center an image. For years, developers centered images by placing the <**img**> tag between the <**center**> and </**center**> tag pair. Although this technique will still work with most browsers, the <**center**> tag has been deprecated, which means browsers may not support it in the future. In Chapter 8, you will learn how to use CSS attributes to simplify image centering. For now, you can use the style attribute shown here within the file CenterImage.html, to center an image:

```
<!DOCTYPE html>
<html>
<body>
<img style="display:block; margin-left:auto;
margin-right:auto" src="http://www.website
developmentbook.com/Chapter02/cat.jpg"/>
</body>
</html>
```

FIGURE 2–9 Using a style definition to center an image within a webpage
Credit: © Marjanneke de Jong/Shutterstock

Note that the file begins with the <**DOCTYPE html**> tag, which is required for the centering to work correctly within Internet Explorer. When you view the file's contents, the browser will display the centered image, as shown in FIGURE 2–9.

Images and Copyrights

Before you place an image within a webpage, you must ensure that you have the legal right to do so. Otherwise, you may violate the rights of the owner of the image's copyright. Copyright violation is a punishable offense. As part of a lawsuit, you may also be required to pay the image owner for use of the image. If you are unsure as to whether or not you have the right to use an image, request permission in writing from the owner. If you don't have permission to use an image, do not place the image on your website. Simply finding an image on the Web doesn't give you the right to use the image. Likewise, changing the image in some way (such as cropping or sizing it) doesn't give you permission to use the image. Several sites on the Web provide images on a royalty and royalty-free basis. A **royalty-free image** is one that you can use on a webpage without having to pay the owner a fee (known as a *royalty*) each time the image is displayed. Use a search engine to search for sites, such as Shutterstock, that provide royalty-free images.

Understanding Image Types and File Sizes

As you work with images within webpages, you need to understand different image file formats, such as JPG (pronounced j-peg), GIF (pronounced jiff), and PNG (pronounced ping). Different image file formats provide different capabilities.

Most of the images on the Web use the JPG file format because it does a good job compressing images into smaller file sizes. The smaller an image's file is, the faster a browser can download the image when a user views your page.

Web designers often use GIF images for clip art illustrations that require only a few colors. GIF images can use only 256 different colors. Developers also use GIF images to store simple animated graphics as well as images that use a **transparent background**, one you can "see through," so to speak. When an image has a transparent background, rather than a white square background, when the image is displayed, the webpage background appears as the image background, and the image isn't set off with a white box around it.

The following HTML file, GIFDemo.html, uses several GIF image files that reside on this book's companion website and demonstrate GIF capabilities:

```
<!DOCTYPE html>
<html>
<body bgcolor="yellow">
<img src="http://www.websitedevelopmentbook.com/
Chapter02/Bulldog.gif"/>
<img src="http://www.websitedevelopmentbook.com/
Chapter02/Animateddog.gif"/>
<img src="http://www.websitedevelopmentbook.com/
Chapter02/DogClipArt.gif"/>
</body>
</html>
```

When you view the file's contents, the browser will display the GIF images, as shown in **FIGURE 2-10**. To allow you to see the effects of a

FIGURE 2-10 GIF images support only 256 colors, but they can be animated or use transparent backgrounds.

Credit (from left): © WilleeCole/Shutterstock; © Liusa/Shutterstock; © JungHyun Lee/Shutterstock

transparent background, the **<body>** tag sets the background color to yellow. Within the page, the **animated GIF**, which is an image file that contains a simple animation, performs and then repeats its animation. You also will see the use of a GIF with and without the use of a transparent background. The image without the transparent background is surrounded by a white box, whereas the image with the transparent background appears to sit on the webpage background.

If you are looking for animated graphics, many sites on the Web provide them. You might first start with *http://www.animationfactory.com*.

PNG image files, like GIF images, also support transparent backgrounds, but they provide an ability to display a greater number of colors.

Optimizing Graphics for Web Use

When you place an image on a webpage, the browser must download the image file before the browser can display it. The larger the size of the image file, the longer it takes to download.

To optimize your image size, and in turn, the speed of your site, you should normally save your images at 72 **dpi (dots per inch)**, which describes an image's resolution. Most digital cameras provide high-resolution images at 300 dpi. To reduce the size of image files on the Web, most Web images are 72 dpi resolution to speed up their download time. Most Web cameras initially store images at a 300 dpi resolution, which requires a much larger file. To change your image's resolution, use a photo-editing software tool such as Photoshop.

Also, as previously discussed, you should not use the **<img>** tag **height** and **width** attributes to scale your image. Instead, determine your image size, and then use the photo-editing software to scale and save your image file.

Displaying a Background Image on Your Page

Depending on your site design, there may be times when you will want to display an image background behind your page contents. Depending on the image, there may be times when you will want the browser to repeat the image completely to fill the background. In Chapter 8, you will learn how to apply different styles to specific HTML tags. The following HTML file, SmileBackground.html, uses the **<body>** tag **background-image** style to assign an image file to the page background and the **background-repeat** style to direct the browser to fill the page background with the specified image:

```
<!DOCTYPE html>
<html>
```

FIGURE 2-11 Repeating an image graphic to fill a webpage background

Credit: © Albert Ziganshin/Shutterstock

```
<head>
<style type="text/css">
<body>
{
background-image:url("http://www.WebSite
DevelopmentBook.com/Chapter02/smiley.jpg");
background-repeat:repeat;
}
</style>
</head>
</body>
</html>
```

When you view the file's contents, the browser will display the page of smiley faces, as shown in **FIGURE 2-11**. Because the images are in the background, the other content you place on the page will overwrite the content.

Controlling an Image Border

Using a border, you can place a frame around an image on a webpage. By default, images have no border. When you place images within a hyperlink as discussed in Chapter 3, "Using Hyperlinks to Connect Content," some browsers may add a border to the images. Depending on your page design, you may want to turn it off. The following HTML file, ImageBorders.html, uses the **<img>** tag **border** attribute to place various size and color borders around the webpage images:

```
<!DOCTYPE html>
<html>
```

```
<body>
<img src="http://www.WebSiteDevelopmentBook.com/
Chapter02/balloons.jpg"/>
<img src="http://www.WebSiteDevelopmentBook.com/
Chapter02/balloons.jpg" style="border:1px solid
black"/><br/>
<img src="http://www.WebSiteDevelopmentBook.com/
Chapter02/balloons.jpg" style="border:10px solid
blue"/>
<img src="http://www.WebSiteDevelopmentBook.com/
Chapter02/balloons.jpg" style="border:25px solid
green"/><br/>
</body>
</html>
```

As you can see, several of the **<img>** tags use the **border** attribute to specify the border's width, type, and color.

When you view the file's contents, your browser will display the framed images, as shown in **FIGURE 2-12**.

When you specify a border around an image, you can use the **border-radius** style to round the border corners. Unfortunately, not all browsers support the style.

FIGURE 2-12 Applying border styles to images within a webpage
Credit: © Steve Bower/Shutterstock

The following HTML file, ImageBorderRadius.html, uses the **border-radius** attribute to round the corners of several different images:

```
<!DOCTYPE html>
<html>
<body>
<img src="http://www.WebSiteDevelopmentBook.com/
Chapter02/mouse.jpg" style="border-radius:1px"/>
<img src="http://www.WebSiteDevelopmentBook.com/
Chapter02/mouse.jpg" style="border-
radius:10px"/><br/>
<img src="http://www.WebSiteDevelopmentBook.com/
Chapter02/mouse.jpg" style="border-radius:25px"/>
<img src="http://www.WebSiteDevelopmentBook.com/
Chapter02/mouse.jpg" style="border-radius:100px"/>
</body>
</html>
```

When you view the file's contents, your browser will display the images with rounded corners, as shown in FIGURE 2-13.

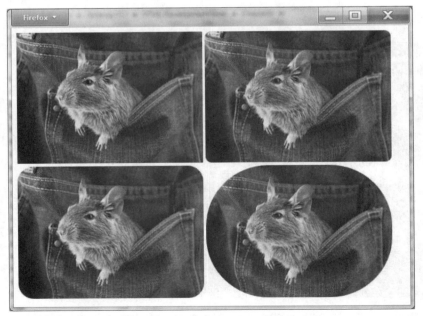

FIGURE 2-13 Using the **border-radius** attribute to round image corners
Credit: © USBFCO/Shutterstock

Padding an Image

When you place an image within a webpage, the browser, by default, will place the image inline with your existing content. Depending on your page design, there may be times when you want to separate the image from the surrounding content. In such cases, you can surround your image with "padding" space. **Image padding** is the process of placing space around an image to separate it from the content within the webpage.

The following HTML file, SixImages.html, displays two rows of three images:

```
<!DOCTYPE html>
<html>
<body>
<img src="http://www.WebSiteDevelopmentBook.com/
Chapter02/wine01.jpg" width="300" height="200"/>
<img src="http://www.WebSiteDevelopmentBook.com/
Chapter02/wine02.jpg" width="300" height=200"/>
<img src="http://www.WebSiteDevelopmentBook.com/
Chapter02/wine03.jpg" width="300"
height="200"/><br/>
<img src="http://www.WebSiteDevelopmentBook.com/
Chapter02/cigar01.jpg" width="300" height="200"/>
<img src="http://www.WebSiteDevelopmentBook.com/
Chapter02/cigar02.jpg" width="300" height="200"/>
<img src="http://www.WebSiteDevelopmentBook.com/
Chapter02/cigar03.jpg" width="300" height="200"/>
</body>
</html>
```

When you view the file's contents, the browser will display the images with only a small amount of space between them, as shown in **FIGURE 2-14**.

Using the **padding** attribute, you can surround your images with space. The following HTML file, SixPaddedImages.html, places a 10-pixel pad around each image:

```
<!DOCTYPE html>
<html>
<body>
<img src="http://www.WebSiteDevelopmentBook.com/
Chapter02/wine01.jpg" width="300" height="200"
style="padding:10px"/>
```

FIGURE 2-14 Displaying images within a webpage with no separation space

Credit (from left, top row): © Olena Mykhaylova/Shutterstock; © Michelangelo Gratton/ Shutterstock; © Gts/Shutterstock; (from left, bottom row): © Mawer/Shutterstock; © Andresr/ Shutterstock; © Marco Mayer/Shutterstock

```
<img src="http://www.WebSiteDevelopmentBook.com/
Chapter02/wine02.jpg" width="300" height="200"
style="padding:10px"/>
<img src="http://www.WebSiteDevelopmentBook.com/
Chapter02/wine03.jpg" width=300" height="200"
style="padding:10px"/><br/>
<img src="http://www.WebSiteDevelopmentBook.com/
Chapter02/cigar01.jpg" width="300" height="200"
style="padding:10px"/>
<img src="http://www.WebSiteDevelopmentBook.com/
Chapter02/cigar02.jpg" width="300" height="200"
style="padding:10px"/>
<img src="http://www.WebSiteDevelopmentBook.com/
Chapter02/cigar03.jpg" width="300" height="200"
style="padding:10px"/>
</body>
</html>
```

In this case, when you view the file's contents, your browser will display the images separated by 10 pixels on each side, as shown in **FIGURE 2-15**.

When you use the **padding** attribute, you can specify the padding in pixels, inches, centimeters, and other measurements. In addition, if you want to control

FIGURE 2-15 Using padding to separate images within a webpage

Credit (from left, top row): © Olena Mykhaylova/Shutterstock; © Michelangelo Gratton/ Shutterstock; © Gts/Shutterstock; (from left, bottom row): © Mawer/Shutterstock; © Andresr/ Shutterstock; © Marco Mayer/Shutterstock

the spacing on a specific side of the image, you can use the **padding-top**, **padding-bottom**, **padding-left**, or **padding-right** attributes.

Adjusting Image Opacity

Opacity is a measure of the amount of light that can pass through an object. Depending on your photo and webpage design, there may be times when you will want to control an image's opacity. To do so, you can use the **opacity** style.

The following HTML file, ImageOpacity.html, illustrates use of the opacity style to change the appearance of the same image:

```
<!DOCTYPE html>
<html>
<body>
<img src="http://www.WebSiteDevelopmentBook.com/
Chapter02/tiger.jpg" width="300" height="200"/>
<img src="http://www.WebSiteDevelopmentBook.com/
Chapter02/tiger.jpg" width="300" height="200"
style="opacity:0.55"/>
<img src="http://www.WebSiteDevelopmentBook.com/
Chapter02/tiger.jpg" width="300" height="200"
style="opacity:0.25"/>
</body>
</html>
```

FIGURE 2-16 Changing image opacity within a webpage
Credit: © Ipatov/Shutterstock

As you can see, the two **<img>** tags specify the opacity as decimal-based percentage values (0.25 and 0.50). When you view the file's content, the browser will display the images, as shown in **FIGURE 2-16**.

Aligning Text and Images

By default, when you place an image next to text, the text will align to the bottom right edge of the image, as shown in **FIGURE 2-17**.

Often, you will want to have the text align to the top of an image. In such cases, you can use the **float** style. The following HTML file, FloatImage.html, uses the **float** style to align text with an image. The file places the first image aligned to the left of the first paragraph and the second image aligned to the right of the second paragraph:

```
<!DOCTYPE html>
<html>
```

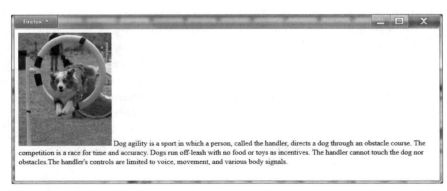

FIGURE 2-17 By default, browsers will align text to the bottom corner of an image.
Credit: © Margo Harrison/Shutterstock

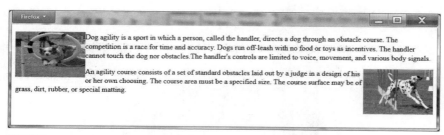

FIGURE 2-18 Using the **float** style to align text within an image

Credit: © Margo Harrison/Shutterstock; © Mackland/Shutterstock

```
<body>
<img src="http://www.WebSiteDevelopmentBook.com/
Chapter02/doghoop.jpg" width="150" height="100"
style="float:left"/><p>
Dog agility is a sport in which a person, called
the handler, directs a dog through an obstacle
course. The competition is a race for time and
accuracy. Dogs run off-leash with no food or toys
as incentives. The handler cannot touch the dog nor
obstacles. The handler's controls are limited to
voice, movement, and various body signals.</p>
<img src="http://www.WebSiteDevelopmentBook.com/
Chapter02/agility.jpg" width="150" height="100"
style="float:right"/>
<p>An agility course consists of a set of standard
obstacles laid out by a judge in a design of his or
her own choosing. The course area must be a speci-
fied size. The course surface may be of grass,
dirt, rubber, or special matting. </p>
</body>
</html>
```

When you view the file's contents, the browser will display the floating images, as shown in **FIGURE 2-18**.

Displaying an Image at a Fixed Location

Depending on your page design, there may be times when you want to control the exact location on a page where an image appears. In such cases, you can use the

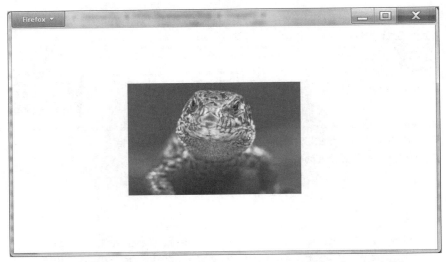

FIGURE 2-19 Using the **position** style to place an image at an absolute location within a page
Credit: © Skydie/Shutterstock

position style. The following HTML file, ImageAbsolute.html, places an image at
the pixel x, y coordinates 100, 200:

```
<!DOCTYPE html>
<html>
<body>
<img src="http://www.WebSiteDevelopmentBook.com/
Chapter02/lizard.jpg" width="300" height="200"
style="position:absolute; top:100px; left:200px"/>
</body>
</html>
```

When you view the file's contents, the browser will display the image, as
shown in **FIGURE 2-19**.

In this case, the <img> tag specified the **position:absolute** attribute to place
the image at a specific location. If you instead use **position:relative**, you can move
the image up, down, left, or right of its normal position.

In addition to specifying an image's x and y coordinates, you can use the
z-index attribute to place one image on top of another. This is called stacking the
images. The following HTML file, ImageStack.html, uses the **position** and
z-index attributes to overlap three images:

```
<!DOCTYPE html>
<html>
```

```
<body>
<img src="http://www.WebSiteDevelopmentBook.com/
Chapter02/maui01.jpg" width="300" height="200"
style="position:absolute; top: 0px; left:0px;
z-index:0"/>
<img src="http://www.WebSiteDevelopmentBook.com/
Chapter02/maui02.jpg" width="300" height="200"
style="position:absolute; top:150px; left:200px;
z-index:1"/>
<img src="http://www.WebSiteDevelopmentBook.com/
Chapter02/maui03.jpg" width="300" height="200"
style="position:absolute; top:300px; left:450px;
z-index:2"/>
</body>
</html>
```

As you can see, the **<img>** tags specify the x and y locations as **top** and **left** and the z value using **z-index**. When you view the file's contents, the browser will display the images, as shown in **FIGURE 2-20**.

FIGURE 2-20 Specifying image x, y, and z coordinates within a webpage

Credit (from left): © Alberto Loyo/Shutterstock; © Idreamphoto/Shutterstock; © EpicStockMedia/Shutterstock

Rotating an Image

By default, when you display an image within a webpage, the browser will display the image based on its original orientation. Depending on the image orientation or your page design, there may be times when you will want the browser to rotate an image on the webpage. In the past, there was a "rotation style" that was used to do this. Today, no browsers support the rotation style. Instead, different browsers use different custom tags to implement rotation. Developers, in turn, must place the corresponding tags in their HTML files for the browsers they want/need to support. Each browser, in turn, will respond only to its own tag, ignoring those tags with which it is not familiar. The following HTML file, RotateImage.html, uses the browser-specific implementations of the **rotation** style to rotate the same image by various degrees:

```
<!DOCTYPE html>
<html>
<body>
<img src="http://www.WebSiteDevelopmentBook.
com/Chapter02/wine04.jpg" width="200"
height="300"/>
<img src="http://www.WebSiteDevelopmentBook.
com/Chapter02/wine04.jpg" width="200"
height="300" style="-webkit-transform:
rotate(90deg); -moz-transform: rotate(90deg);
filter: progid:DXImageTransform.Microsoft.Basic
Image(rotation=1);"/><br/>
<img src="http://www.WebSiteDevelopmentBook.
com/Chapter02/wine04.jpg" width="200"
height="300" style="-webkit-transform:
rotate(180deg); -moz-transform: rotate(180deg);
filter: progid:DXImageTransform.Microsoft.
BasicImage(rotation=2);"/>
<img src="http://www.WebSiteDevelopmentBook.
com/Chapter02/wine04.jpg" width="200"
height="300" style="-webkit-transform:
rotate(270deg); -moz-transform: rotate(270deg);
filter: progid:DXImageTransform.Microsoft.
BasicImage(rotation=3);"/>
</body>
</html>
```

FIGURE 2-21 Rotating images within a webpage

Credit: © Marco Mega/Shutterstock

In this case, each browser recognizes its own specific style attribute and ignores those of the other browsers.

When you display the file's contents, your browser will display the rotated images, as shown in **FIGURE 2–21**. Note that to support different browsers, you must provide the browser's custom rotation tag within your HTML file.

Real-World Web Design

When you create webpages, you need to test your pages using common Web browsers, such as Internet Explorer, Chrome, Safari, and Firefox. You may even need to test various versions of the Web browsers. As you will learn, not all browsers support all CSS attributes and styles, and sometimes browsers support attributes differently.

If you are using Internet Explorer 9, for example, you can press the F12 function key to display the browser's built-in developer tools, as shown in **FIGURE 2–22**.

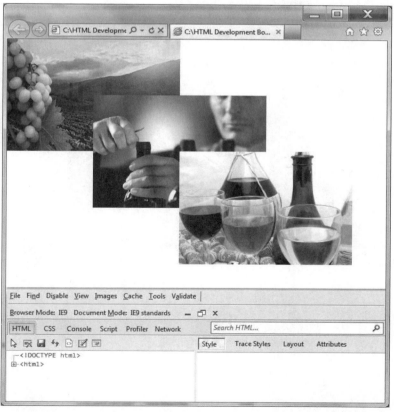

FIGURE 2–22 Taking advantage of Internet Explorer version 9 built-in developer tools

Credit: © Olena Mykhaylova/Shutterstock; © Michelangelo Gratton/Shutterstock; © Gts/Shutterstock

By selecting the Browser mode menu, you can direct Internet Explorer to behave as if it were IE version 7, IE version 8, and so on. In this way, you can quickly test your page with older versions using one browser.

Hands-On HTML

To view the HTML files or to experiment with the files presented in this chapter, visit this book's companion website at *http://www.websitedevelopmentbook.com/ Chapter02/TryIt.html*.

Chapter Summary

Across the Web, sites make extensive use of graphics images. To place an image within an HTML page, use the **<img>** tag. This chapter examined all aspects of webpage image use. As learned, when you use various style attributes, you have complete control over image sizing and placement. In addition, you learned that when you upload an HTML page to a Web server, you must also upload the corresponding graphics images. Depending on where you place the images on the server, you might use relative or absolute URLs within the **<img>** tag **src** attribute. Using various image styles, you learned how to center, border, pad, rotate, and align images.

Key Terms

Absolute URL
Animated GIF
dpi (dots per inch)
Image padding
Opacity

Relative URL
Royalty-free image
Screen reader
Transparent background

Chapter Review

1. Create an HTML file that displays the image *http://www.websitedevelopmentbook.com/Chapter02/Cat.jpg*

2. Use the HTML **<img>** tag **height** and **width** attributes within an HTML file to display the following image sized at 300 by 300: *http://www.websitedevelopmentbook.com/Chapter02/Ball.jpg*

3. Use the HTML **<img>** tag **height** and **width** attributes within an HTML file to display the following image sized at various percentages of the current browser window size: *http://www.websitedevelopmentbook.com/Chapter02/Flag.jpg*

4. Create an HTML file that centers the image at *http://www.websitedevelopmentbook.com/Chapter02/Car.jpg*

5. Create an HTML file that displays the animated GIF image *http://www.websitedevelopmentbook.com/Chapter02/Barkingdog.gif*

6. Use the **<body>** tag to fill the page background with the following image: *http://websitedevelopmentbook.com/Chapter02/BG.jpg*

7. Using image positioning, stack the following image files within a webpage:
http://www.websitedevelopmentbook.com/Chapter02/Dog01.jpg
http://www.websitedevelopmentbook.com/Chapter02/Dog02.jpg
http://www.websitedevelopmentbook.com/Chapter02/Dog03.jpg

8. Create an HTML file that displays a border around the following image, and display the image centered in the page: *http://www.websitedevelopmentbook. com/Chapter02/Dog.jpg*

9. Modify the HTML file you created in Question 8 to display the image with rounded corners.

10. Create an HTML file that rotates the following image at different angles within an HTML page: *http://www.websitedevelopmentbook.com/Chapter02/Airplane.jpg*

11. Create an HTML file that displays the following images side by side with a 20-pixel padding around the images:
http://www.websitedevelopmentbook.com/Chapter02/Dog01.jpg
http://www.websitedevelopmentbook.com/Chapter02/Dog02.jpg
http://www.websitedevelopmentbook.com/Chapter02/Dog03.jpg

12. Describe the role of the **<img>** tag **alt** attribute with respect to screen readers.

13. Create an HTML file that displays the following image using a variety of opacities: *http://www.websitedevelopmentbook.com/Chapter02/Dog.jpg*

Using Hyperlinks to Connect Content

THE WORLD WIDE WEB is often described as a network of billions of interconnected pages of content. When viewing webpages within a browser, users click on a hyperlink to move from one document to another or from one location on a page to another. A hyperlink is text or an image within a webpage that a user clicks on to jump to or display a specific page of content. To place a hyperlink within the webpages you create, use the <**a**> and </**a**> anchor tag pair.

Learning Objectives

This chapter examines hyperlinks in detail. By the time you finish this chapter, you will understand the following key concepts:

- How to use the <**a**> and </**a**> anchor tag pair to create a text-based hyperlink
- How to use the anchor tag **target** attribute to open a hyperlink in a new window
- How to use the <**a**> and </**a**> anchor tag pair to create an image-based hyperlink
- How to use absolute and relative URLs to create a hyperlink
- How to create an in-page hyperlink
- How to use the **mailto** attribute within a hyperlink to open an e-mail client
- How to create an image map

FIGURE 3-1 Using the **<a>** and **</a>** tag pair to define a hyperlink

Creating a Text-Based Hyperlink

A **hyperlink** can be a photo or text, which normally appears within the browser in blue or purple font and is underlined. To create a hyperlink within a webpage, you place the anchor tag pair **<a>** and **</a>** within your HTML file, which specifies the target content location and the text or photo that will appear on the page as a link. The following HTML file, GotoGoogle.html, creates a hyperlink to the Google website:

```
<!DOCTYPE html>
<html>
<body>
<a href="http://www.google.com">Goto Google</a>
</body>
</html>
```

To specify the target location for a hyperlink, which is the content the user views next if he or she clicks the link, use the anchor tag **href** attribute. The text that you place between the **<a>** and **</a>** tag pair will define the link, as shown in **FIGURE 3-1**.

When you view the file's content, your browser will display the text Goto Google as a hyperlink, and by default it will display the text underlined in purple. As shown in **FIGURE 3-2**, when the user clicks on the link, the browser will display the Google site's contents.

In a similar way, the HTML file SearchEngines.html uses anchor tag pairs to create hyperlinks to several commonly used search engine sites:

```
<!DOCTYPE html>
<html>
<body>
<a href="http://www.google.com">Goto Google</a><br/>
<a href="http://www.Yahoo.com">Goto Yahoo</a><br/>
```

FIGURE 3–2 Using a hyperlink to link to the Google website

Credit: Google and the Google logo are registered trademarks of Google Inc., used with permission.

```
<a href="http://www.MSN.com">Goto MSN</a><br/>
<a href="http://www.ask.com">Goto Ask</a><br/>
</body>
</html>
```

As you can see, each anchor tag pair specifies the target Web address (URL) within an **href** attribute and the link text between the **<a>** and **</a>** tags. If you view the file's contents, the browser will display the set of links, as shown in **FIGURE 3–3**.

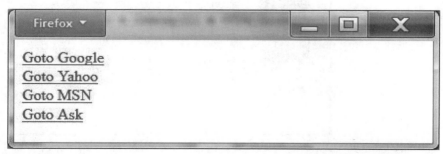

FIGURE 3–3 Using multiple anchor tags to create several hyperlinks within an HTML page

Opening a Hyperlink Within a New Window

By default, when a user clicks on a hyperlink, the browser will replace its current contents with the contents provided by the target page. Depending on your site design and the content you place within a page, there may be times when you will want the browser to open the target site content within a new window. To do so, you use the anchor tag **target** attribute to specify **target="new"** as shown in the following HTML file NewTargetWindow.html:

```
<!DOCTYPE html>
<html>
<body>
<a href="http://www.WebSiteDevelopmentBook.com"
target="new">Book's Companion Site</a><br/>
<a href="http://www.JBLearning.com"
target="new">Jones & Bartlett Learning</a><br/>
</body>
</html>
```

As shown in **FIGURE 3-4**, as users click on the hyperlinks, the browser will open a new window or tab based on the browser settings.

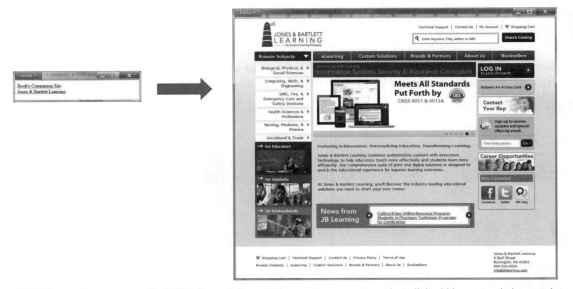

FIGURE 3-4 Use the **target="new"** attribute to direct the browser to open a target hyperlink within a new window or tab.

Using an Image as a Hyperlink

By placing text between the <a> and </a> anchor tag pair, you create a text-based hyperlink:

```
<a href="http://www.somesite.com">Hyperlink Text
</a>
```

As it turns out, you can place any HTML tags between the anchor tag pair to create a formatted hyperlink. The HTML file HeaderHyperlink.html creates a hyperlink from an <h1> and </h1> header tag pair:

```
<!DOCTYPE html>
<html>
<body>
<a href="http://www.WebSiteDevelopmentBook.com"
target="new"><h1>Book's Companion Site</h1>
</a><br/>
</body>
</html>
```

When you view the file's contents, your browser will display the header as a link, as shown in **FIGURE 3-5**.

In a similar way, the HTML file SportsLinks.html displays images of a baseball, football, basketball, and hockey puck. Each image creates a hyperlink to

FIGURE 3-5 Using HTML tags between the <a> and </a> anchor tag pair to create a formatted hyperlink

the corresponding professional sports site: NFL.com, NBA.com, MLB.com, and NHL.com:

```
<!DOCTYPE html>
<html>
<body>
<a href="http://www.mlb.com" target="new"><img
src="http://www.WebSiteDevelopmentBook.com/
Chapter03/Baseball.jpg" height="100" width="150">
</a><br/>

<a href="http://www.nba.com" target="new"><img
src="http://www.WebSiteDevelopmentBook.com/Chapter03/
Basketball.jpg" height="100" width="150"></a><br/>

<a href="http://www.nfl.com" target="new"><img
src="http://www.WebSiteDevelopmentBook.com/
Chapter03/Football.jpg" height="100" width="150">
</a><br/>

<a href="http://www.nhl.com" target="new"><img
src="http://www.WebSiteDevelopmentBook.com/
Chapter03/Hockey.jpg" height="100" width="150">
</a><br/>
</body>
</html>
```

As you can see, within each anchor tag pair the file includes an **<img>** tag, which directs the browser to use the photo as a hyperlink to the specified target page. When you view the file's contents, the browser will display the photo hyperlinks, as shown in **FIGURE 3-6**.

Using Absolute, Relative, and Page-Based Hyperlink References

As you have learned, using the anchor tag **href** attribute, you specify a hyperlink's target location. Each of the previous examples have used absolute references for the target URL. They begin with **http://** and specify a site name and, optionally, a specific folder and file within the site:

```
<a href="http://www.somesite.com">Absolute URL
Example</a>
```

FIGURE 3-6 Using an **<img>** tag within the **<a>** and **</a>** anchor tag pair to create an image hyperlink

Credit (from top): © Skizer/Shutterstock; © Razihusin/Shutterstock; © David Lee/Shutterstock; © Volkova Irina/Shutterstock.

Most websites consist of multiple pages, each of which resides within its own HTML file. Typically, each of the pages will provide links or a menu of links that allow the user to easily move between the pages. In such cases, you can place absolute URL references for each page within each file's anchor tags:

```
<a href="http://www.somesite.com/homepage.
html">Home Page</a>
<a href="http://www.somesite.com/aboutus.
html">About Us</a>
<a href="http://www.somesite.com/contactus.
html">Contact Us</a>
```

For simplicity and to make it easier to move the files to a different site later, you don't need to provide absolute URLs. Instead, you can place a relative URL within each anchor tag **href** attribute as shown here:

```
<a href="homepage.html">Home Page</a>
<a href="aboutus.html">About Us</a>
<a href="contactus.html">Contact Us</a>
```

When the browser encounters a relative URL, it will look for the specified file in a location "relative" to the current file. For the previous relative URLs, for example, the browser would look for the files in the same folder on the same server as the current HTML file.

To better understand relative hyperlink references, create the HTML file Blue.html as shown here:

```
<!DOCTYPE html>
<html>
<body bgcolor="Blue">
<a href="yellow.html" style="color:white">Yellow
</a><br/>
</body>
</html>
```

Also, because most browsers display hyperlinks in blue, which won't show up against a blue background, the anchor tag uses the **color** style to set the link text color to white. As you can see, the file uses the **<body>** tag **bgcolor** attribute to set the page background color to blue. The file contains a hyperlink to the file Yellow.html, which contains the following:

```
<!DOCTYPE html>
<html>
<body bgcolor="Yellow">
<a href="blue.html">Blue</a><br/>
</body>
</html>
```

In this case, the file uses the **bgcolor** attribute within the **<body>** tag to set the background color to yellow and an anchor tag pair to create a link to the file Blue.html.

Display one of the two files within your browser. When you click the link, the browser will display the other file. In this case, both files reside in the same folder on your hard drive, which means they are in the same relative location. The browser can then easily find each file. If you move one of the files to a different folder on your hard disks, the relative link would break because the files do not reside in the same folder.

Creating an In-Page Hyperlink

Depending on the amount of content you place within an HTML page, there may be times when you will want to create hyperlinks that point to locations within the current page. To do so, you must first identify the target locations to the browser by placing an anchor tag pair **<a>** and **</a>,** which use the **name** attribute. For example, the HTML file InsideLinks.html uses anchor tag pairs to identify three locations within the file:

```
<!DOCTYPE html>
<html>
<body>
<a href="#One">One</a>   
<a href="#Two">Two</a>   
<a href="#Three">Three</a><br/>
<a name="One"></a>
1<br/>
1<br/>
1<br/>
1<br/>
1<br/>
1<br/>
1<br/>
<a href="#One">One</a>   
<a href="#Two">Two</a>   
<a href="#Three">Three</a><br/>
<a name="Two"></a>
2<br/>
2<br/>
2<br/>
2<br/>
2<br/>
2<br/>
2<br/>
<a href="#One">One</a>   
<a href="#Two">Two</a>   
```

FIGURE 3-7 Using anchor tags to create hyperlinks to locations within the same HTML page

```
<a href="#Three">Three</a><br/>
<a name="Three"></a>
3<br/>
3<br/>
3<br/>
3<br/>
3<br/>
3<br/>
3<br/>
</body>
</html>
```

As you can see, within each anchor tag the file uses **name** attributes to identify specific locations within the file. At the top and bottom of the sections are hyperlinks the user can select that correspond to each page location. To specify that a hyperlink corresponds to a location within the current file, you include the pound sign (#) before the link name. If you view the file's contents, the browser will display the page content along with the links as shown in **FIGURE 3-7**. Make your browser window small enough to only display one section at a time, so the window will scroll. Each time you click on a link, the browser will bring the corresponding page contents into view.

Creating a Mailto Hyperlink

As you surf the Web, you will find many sites that provide a "Contact Us" link, which opens your e-mail client to allow you to send an e-mail message to the site. To create a mailto link within a webpage, place **mailto** within the anchor tag **href** attribute as shown here:

```
<a href="mailto:Name@somesite.com">Contact Us</a>
```

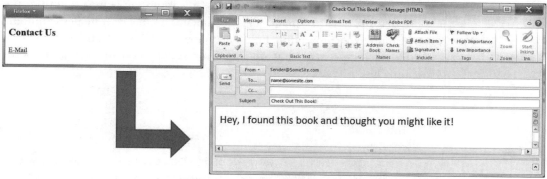

FIGURE 3-8 Using **mailto** within a **href** attribute to launch a user's e-mail client program
Credit: Used with permission from Microsoft.

Within the **mailto** text, you can specify the e-mail address of the recipient, the message subject, as well as the message text, as shown here within the file Mailto.html:

```
<!DOCTYPE html>
<html>
<body>
<h2>Contact Us</h2>
<a href="mailto:name@somesite.com?subject=Check Out
This Book!&body=Hey, I found this book and thought
you might like it!">E-Mail</a>
</body>
</html>
```

When you view the file's contents, your browser will display the link. If the user clicks on the link, the browser will open the user's e-mail client and prefill the fields as shown in **FIGURE 3-8**.

Creating an Image Map

In Chapter 2, "Integrating Images," you used the **<img>** tag to place photos within a webpage. In this chapter, you learned how to place the **<img>** tag within an anchor tag pair **<a>** and **</a>** to create a photo-based hyperlink. Depending on your page design, there may be times when you will want to create links for different parts of a photo. In such cases, you can create an **image map**, which defines coordinates within an image that a Web browser will associate with a specific Web address. If the user clicks a mouse within the coordinates, the browser will display the corresponding Web content.

In general, an image map combines an **<img>** tag, which identifies the photo to display, with a **<map>** tag, which identifies the coordinates within the image and the corresponding link. The following HTML file, ImageMap.html, creates an image map that defines four sets of coordinates and corresponding links:

```
<!DOCTYPE html>
<html>
<body>
<img src="http://www.WebSiteDevelopmentBook.com/
Chapter03/Sports.jpg" usemap="#Sports"/>
<map name="sports">
<area shape="rect" coords="1,1,200,131"
href="http://www.nhl.com"/>
<area shape="rect" coords="201,1,400,131"
href="http://www.mlb.com"/>
<area shape="rect" coords="1,132,201,262"
href="http://www.nba.com"/>
<area shape="rect" coords="201,132,400,262"
href="http://www.nfl.com"/>
</map>
</body>
</html>
```

As you can see, the **<map>** tag defines four areas (coordinates). When you display the file, your browser will display the image shown in **FIGURE 3-9**. If the user clicks on one of the corresponding areas, the browser will load the corresponding content.

Real-World Web Design

As the complexity of the sites you create increases, there may be times when your page contains a large number of links. Some are to remote content on other sites, and some are to pages on your own site. Periodically, you may need to test the links to ensure that they are working. Rather than click on each link individually, you can take advantage of the W3C link checker, which you can access at *http://validator.w3.org/checklink*. Within the page that appears in your browser, simply type the Web address of the link of which you want to test. The link-checker site, in turn, will examine your page and the links it contains, and it will provide you with a summary report.

FIGURE 3-9 Using an image map to link specific coordinates in a photo to a target location

Credit (clockwise from upper left): © Volkova Irina/Shutterstock; © Skizer/Shutterstock; © David Lee/Shutterstock; © Razihusin/Shutterstock.

Hands-On HTML

To view the HTML files or to experiment with the files presented in this chapter, visit this book's companion website at *http://www.websitedevelopmentbook.com/Chapter03/TryIt.html.*

CHAPTER SUMMARY

To make the World Wide Web, developers create HTML files that use hyperlinks to connect documents. In general, the Web is a network of billions of interconnected pages of content linked together by hyperlinks. When viewing webpages within a browser, users click on a hyperlink to move from one document to another or from one location on a page to another. A hyperlink is text or an image within a webpage that a user clicks on to jump to or display a specific page of content. To place a hyperlink within the webpages you create, use the <a> and </a> anchor tag pair.

KEY TERMS

Hyperlink
Image map

CHAPTER REVIEW

1. Using an HTML **<a>** and **</a>** anchor tag pair, create a text-based hyperlink to this book's publisher, Jones & Bartlett Learning, at *http://www.jblearning.com*.

2. Using an HTML **<a>** and **</a>** anchor tag pair, and the image file at *http://www.websitedevelopmentbook.com/Chapter03/book.jpg*, create an image-based hyperlink to this book's publisher, Jones & Bartlett Learning at *http://www.jblearning.com*.

3. Create an HTML file that illustrates the difference between relative and absolute links.

4. Create an HTML file that illustrates the use of the **mailto** attribute.

5. Modify the HTML file you created in Question 1 to open the link in a new window.

6. Create an HTML file that illustrates the use of an in-page link.

7. Using the image file *http://www.websitedevelopmentbook.com/Chapter03/Mice.jpg*, create an HTML file that uses an image map.

Presenting Lists

IT'S COMMON TO DISPLAY lists of data in a webpage—either numbered lists or bulleted lists. HTML provides an ordered-list tag pair **<ol>** and **</ol>**, which you can use to create a numbered list. It also provides an unordered-list tag pair **<ul>** and **</ul>**, which you can use to create a bulleted list. In addition, HTML supports the **<dl>** and **</dl>** tag pair, which lets you create a **definition list** that consists of terms and their meanings. You might use this list, for example, to create a glossary of key terms.

Learning Objectives

This chapter examines HTML list processing in detail. By the time you finish this chapter, you will understand the following key concepts:

- How to create an ordered list, which is sometimes called a numbered list
- How to create an unordered list, which is sometimes called a bulleted list
- How to control the appearance of the unordered list bullet
- How to use a graphic for a custom bullet
- How to position list content
- How to create a definition list consisting of terms and their meanings
- How to nest one list within another

Creating an Ordered List

An **ordered list**, sometimes called a numbered list, is useful for presenting a series of steps that the user should perform in order. To create an ordered list, you use the HTML <ol> and </ol> tag pair. The ordered list that you create will consist of two or more items. To specify each **list item**, which is an entry within an ordered or unordered list, you use the <li> and </li> tag pair. The following HTML file, OrderedList.html, creates a list of five items, as shown in FIGURE 4–1:

```
<!DOCTYPE html>
<html>
<body>
<p>To create a webpage:</p>
<ol>
<li>Draw a mockup of your page design.</li>
<li>Use photo-editing software to create the site
images.</li>
<li>Use an editor to create the HTML tags.</li>
<li>Test and modify your design.</li>
<li>Upload your HTML files and image files to a Web
server.</li>
</ol>
</body>
</html>
```

As you can see, the <ol> and </ol> tag pair groups each of the list items. Within the list, the <li> and </li> tag pair defines the specific numbered items within the list.

Formatting List Item Content

When you create an ordered or unordered list within a webpage, you use the <li> and </li> tag pair to specify each list item. When you specify a list item, you can include other HTML tags between the <li> and </li> tags to format the content.

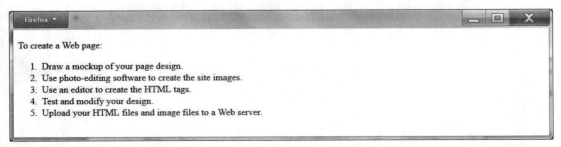

FIGURE 4–1 Using the HTML <ol> and </ol> tag pair to create an ordered list

The following HTML file, OrderedPictureList.html, for example, places an image tag within each list item to create a more visual display:

```
<!DOCTYPE html>
<html>
<body>
<p>To bake cookies:</p>
<ol>
<li>Take out the utensils you need: <br/>
<img height="100" width="200" src="utensils.jpg"/>
</li>
<li>Mix your cookie dough: <br/><img height="100"
width="200" src="dough.jpg"/></li>
<li>Put the dough on a cookie sheet: <br/>
<img height="100" width="200" src="cookiesheet.jpg"/>
</li>
<li>Bake: <br/><img height="100" width="200"
src="bake.jpg"/></li>
<li>Enjoy: <br/><img height="100" width="200"
src="enjoy.jpg"/></li>
</ol>
</body>
</html>
```

As you can see, within each list element the file uses the line break tag **
** to display the image on the line that follows the text. When you view this file's contents, your browser will display the list shown in **FIGURE 4-2**.

Changing an Ordered List's Numbering Scheme

By default, when you create an ordered list, you browser will use the numbers 1, 2, 3, and so on to precede each of the list items. Depending on your list content, there may be times when you will want to use letters or even Roman numerals for each list item. To control the type of numbering the browser uses within an ordered list, you can use the **<ol>** tag **list-style-type** attribute. The following HTML file, OrderedList Types.html, uses the attribute to display several different ordered list types:

```
<!DOCTYPE html>
<html>
<body>
Default List
<ol>
<li>Go to the grocery store</li>
```

FIGURE 4–2 Using embedded HTML tags to format list item content
Credit (from top): © Kitch Bain/Shutterstock; © Joannawnuk/Shutterstock; © Antonio Danna/ Shutterstock; © Shutterstock; © JulijaSapic_Portfolio/Shutterstock

```
<li>Get gas for the truck</li>
<li>Stop at the bank</li>
</ol>

<p>Alphabetized List</p>
<ol style="list-style-type:upper-alpha">
<li>Go to the grocery store</li>
<li>Get gas for the truck</li>
<li>Stop at the bank</li>
</ol>

<p>Roman Numeral List</p>
<ol style="list-style-type:upper-roman">
<li>Go to the grocery store</li>
<li>Get gas for the truck</li>
<li>Stop at the bank</li>
</ol>
</body>
</html>
```

FIGURE 4-3 Using the <ol> tag **list-style-type** attribute to control an ordered list's appearance

When you view the file's contents, the browser will display the list types, as shown in **FIGURE 4-3**.

Creating an Unordered List

An **unordered list**, often called a bulleted list, contains a list of items in no particular order, such as a grocery list, features for a new product, or browsers that support a particular HTML tag or tag attribute. To create an unordered list within a webpage, you use the <**ul**> and </**ul**> tag pair. To specify the items that appear within the list, you again use the <**li**> and </**li**> list item tag pair.

The following HTML file, UnorderedList.html, creates a bulleted list of HTML 5 features:

```
<!DOCTYPE html>
<html>
<body>
<p>HTML 5 Features</p>
<ul>
<li>Application caches: Think of cookies on
steroids. </li>
<li>Canvas: Create graphics and animations. </li>
<li>Geolocation: Develop location-aware
webpages.</li>
<li>Video: Embed video as easy as embedding an
image. </li>
<li>Web Workers: Supports background processing to
improve site performance. </li>
</ul>
</body>
</html>
```

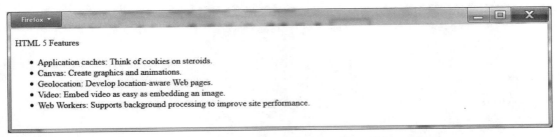

FIGURE 4-4 Using the **<ul>** and **</ul>** tag pair to create an unordered list within a webpage

As you can see, the **<ul>** and **</ul>** tag pair groups the corresponding list elements. When you display the file's contents, your browser will display the item list, as shown in **FIGURE 4-4**.

Formatting List Items Within an Unordered List

As was the case with the list items within an ordered list, when you create an unordered list, you can embed HTML tags between the **<li>** and **</li>** list item tag pair to format the list item contents. The following HTML file, Sports List.html, places **<img>** tags within each list item to create a more visual list:

```
<!DOCTYPE html>
<html>
<body>
<p>My Favorite Sports:</p>
<ul>
<li>Baseball: <br/><img height="100" width="200"
src="baseball.jpg"/></li>
<li>Football: <br/><img height="100" width="200"
src="football.jpg"/></li>
<li>Hockey: <br/><img height="100" width="200"
src="hockey.jpg"/></li>
<li>Soccer: <br/><img height="100" width="200"
src="soccer.jpg"/></li>
<li>Basketball: <br/><img height="100" width="200"
src="basketball.jpg"/></li>
</ul>
</body>
</html>
```

As you can see, each **<li>** and **</li>** tag pair includes an image followed by text. When you display the file's contents, your browser will present the list shown in **FIGURE 4-5**.

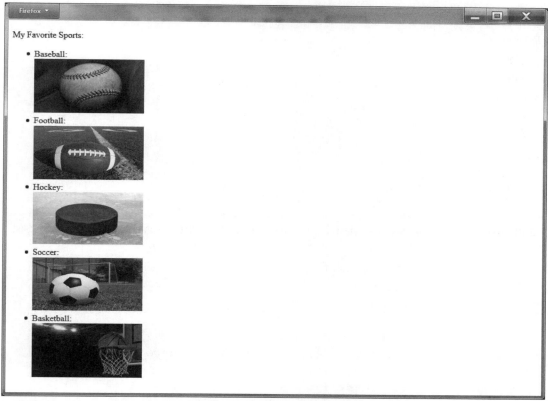

FIGURE 4-5 Embedding HTML tags within the **<li>** and **</li>** tag pair to format list items

Credit (from top): © Skizer/Shutterstock; © David Lee/Shutterstock; © Kim Reinick/Shutterstock; © Tazik13/Shutterstock; © Razihusin/Shutterstock

Controlling the Appearance of the Unordered List Bullet

By default, when you create an unordered list, the browser will precede each list item with a disc bullet. Using the **<ul>** tag **list-style-type** attribute, you can direct the browser to hide the bullet or use a circle, square, or disc to precede list items. The following HTML file, UnorderedListTypes.html, uses the **list-style-type** attribute to create lists preceded by different bullet types:

```
<!DOCTYPE html>
<html>
<body>
<p>Default Bullet:</p>
<ul>
<li>Dogs</li>
```

FIGURE 4-6 Using the **<ul>** tag **list-style-type** attribute to control the bullet appearance within an unordered list

```
<li>Cats</li>
<li>Horses</li>
</ul>

<p>Square Bullet:</p>
<ul style="list-style-type:square">
<li>Dogs</li>
<li>Cats</li>
<li>Horses</li>
</ul>

<p>Disc Bullet:</p>
<ul style="list-style-type:circle">
<li>Dogs</li>
<li>Cats</li>
<li>Horses</li>
</ul>
</body>
</html>
```

When you view the file's contents, your browser will display the lists shown in **FIGURE 4-6**.

Using a Graphic for a Custom Bullet

In addition to using the **<ul>** tag **list-style-type** attribute to select a circle, square, or disc bullet, HTML lets you specify the **<ul>** tag **list-style-image** attribute and a

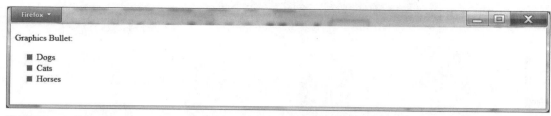

FIGURE 4-7 Using the **<ul>** tag **list-style-image** attribute to specify an image file the browser will use for each bullet within an unordered list

graphic that the browser should use for each bullet. The following HTML file, CustomBullet.html, displays a small colored square graphic as a bullet:

```
<!DOCTYPE html>
<html>
<body>
<p>Graphics Bullet:</p>
<ul style="list-style-image:url('bullet.jpg')">
<li>Dogs</li>
<li>Cats</li>
<li>Horses</li>
</ul>
</body>
</html>
```

Within the **style** attribute, you use the **url ('bullet.jpg')** to specify the image file the browser is to use for the bullet graphic. When you view the file's contents, the browser will display the list shown in **FIGURE 4-7**.

The following HTML file, LargerBullet.html, uses a slightly larger graphic as the bullet within an unordered list:

```
<!DOCTYPE html>
<html>
<body>
<p>Graphics Bullet:</p>
<ul style="list-style-image:url('pizza.jpg')">
<li>Cheese</li>
<li>Pepperoni</li>
<li>Sausage</li>
</ul>
</body>
</html>
```

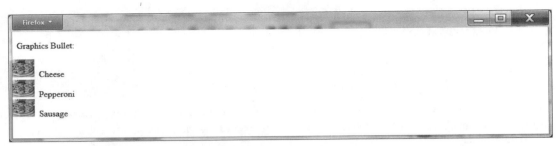

FIGURE 4-8 Using a larger graphic as a bullet within an unordered list
Credit: © Africa Studio/Shutterstock

When you view this file's contents, your browser will display the list of items shown in **FIGURE 4-8**.

Positioning List Content

By default, when you create an ordered or unordered list, the browser will indent the bullets (or numbers) and the list items, as shown in **FIGURE 4-9**.

When the text within a bulleted list or numbered list wraps, you can use the **list-style-position** attribute to control whether the bullet (or number) appears inside the text or outside the text. **FIGURE 4-9** displays two lists. Within one list, the bullets appear inside the text. In the second list, the bullet is outside the text contents.

The following HTML file, BulletListPosition.html, uses the **list-style-position** attribute **inside** and **outside** settings to control the bullet position with respect to the list content, as previously shown in **FIGURE 4-9**:

```
<!DOCTYPE html>
<html>
<body>
<p>list-style-position:inside</p>
<ul style="list-style-position:inside">
<li>When in the Course of human events, it becomes
necessary for one people to dissolve the political
bands which have connected them with another, and
to assume among the powers of the earth, the
separate and equal station to which the Laws of
Nature and of Nature's God entitle them, a decent
respect to the opinions of mankind requires that
they should declare the causes which impel them to
the separation.</li>
```

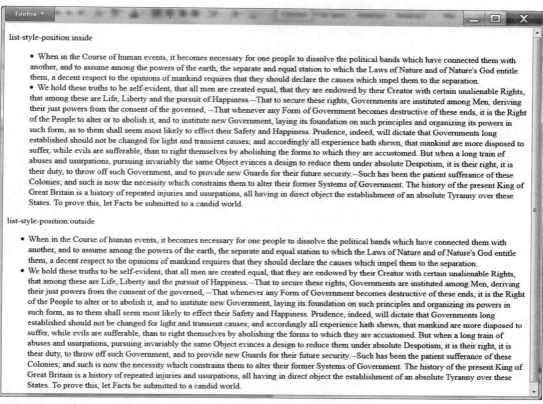

FIGURE 4-9 Using the **list-style-position** attribute to control the location of bullets in an unordered list

```
<li>We hold these truths to be self-evident, that
all men are created equal, that they are endowed by
their Creator with certain unalienable Rights, that
among these are Life, Liberty and the pursuit of
Happiness.—That to secure these rights, Governments
are instituted among Men, deriving their just
powers from the consent of the governed, —That
whenever any Form of Government becomes destructive
of these ends, it is the Right of the People to
alter or to abolish it, and to institute new
Government, laying its foundation on such princi-
ples and organizing its powers in such form, as to
them shall seem most likely to effect their Safety
and Happiness. Prudence, indeed, will dictate that
Governments long established should not be changed
```

for light and transient causes; and accordingly all
experience hath shewn, that mankind are more
disposed to suffer, while evils are sufferable,
than to right themselves by abolishing the forms to
which they are accustomed. But when a long train of
abuses and usurpations, pursuing invariably the
same Object evinces a design to reduce them under
absolute Despotism, it is their right, it is their
duty, to throw off such Government, and to provide
new Guards for their future security.—Such has been
the patient sufferance of these Colonies; and such
is now the necessity which constrains them to alter
their former Systems of Government. The history of
the present King of Great Britain is a history of
repeated injuries and usurpations, all having in
direct object the establishment of an absolute
Tyranny over these States. To prove this, let
Facts be submitted to a candid world.</li>
</ul>

<p>list-style-position:outside</p>
<ul style="list-style-position:outside">
<li>When in the Course of human events, it becomes
necessary for one people to dissolve the political
bands which have connected them with another, and
to assume among the powers of the earth, the
separate and equal station to which the Laws of
Nature and of Nature's God entitle them, a decent
respect to the opinions of mankind requires that
they should declare the causes which impel them to
the separation.</li>

<li>We hold these truths to be self-evident, that
all men are created equal, that they are endowed by
their Creator with certain unalienable Rights, that
among these are Life, Liberty and the pursuit of
Happiness.—That to secure these rights, Governments
are instituted among Men, deriving their just
powers from the consent of the governed, —That
whenever any Form of Government becomes destructive
of these ends, it is the Right of the People to

alter or to abolish it, and to institute new Government, laying its foundation on such principles and organizing its powers in such form, as to them shall seem most likely to effect their Safety and Happiness. Prudence, indeed, will dictate that Governments long established should not be changed for light and transient causes; and accordingly all experience hath shewn, that mankind are more disposed to suffer, while evils are sufferable, than to right themselves by abolishing the forms to which they are accustomed. But when a long train of abuses and usurpations, pursuing invariably the same Object evinces a design to reduce them under absolute Despotism, it is their right, it is their duty, to throw off such Government, and to provide new Guards for their future security.—Such has been the patient sufferance of these Colonies; and such is now the necessity which constrains them to alter their former Systems of Government. The history of the present King of Great Britain is a history of repeated injuries and usurpations, all having in direct object the establishment of an absolute Tyranny over these States. To prove this, let Facts be submitted to a candid world.</li>

```
</ul>
</body>
</html>
```

In a similar way, the HTML file, NumberedListPosition.html, uses the **list-style-position** attribute to control the location of the numbers within an ordered list:

```
<!DOCTYPE html>
<html>
<body>
<p>list-style-position:inside</p>
<ol style="list-style-position:inside">
<li>Take out the utensils you need: <br/>
<img height="100" width="200" src="utensils.
jpg"/></li>
<li>Mix your cookie dough: <br/><img height="100"
width="200" src="dough.jpg"/></li>
```

```
<li>Put the dough on a cookie sheet: <br/>
<img height="100" width="200" src="cookiesheet.
jpg"/></li>
<li>Bake: <br/><img height="100" width="200"
src="bake.jpg"/></li>
<li>Enjoy: <br/><img height="100" width="200"
src="enjoy.jpg"/></li>
</ol>

<p>list-style-position:outside</p>
<ol style="list-style-position:outside">
<li>Take out the utensils you need: <br/>
<img height="100" width="200" src="utensils.
jpg"/></li>
<li>Mix your cookie dough: <br/><img height="100"
width="200" src="dough.jpg"/></li>
<li>Put the dough on a cookie sheet: <br/>
<img height="100" width="200" src="cookiesheet.
jpg"/></li>
<li>Bake: <br/><img height="100" width="200"
src="bake.jpg"/></li>
<li>Enjoy: <br/><img height="100" width="200"
src="enjoy.jpg"/></li>
</ol>
</body>
</html>
```

When you display the file's content, the browser will display the lists shown in FIGURE 4-10.

Creating a Definition List

A definition list contains one or more terms and meanings. Within a webpage, you might use a definition list to create a key term glossary. To create a definition list, you use the HTML <dl> and </dl> tag pair. Between the two tags, you use the <dt> and </dt> tag pair to specify a term and the <dd> and </dd> tag pair to specify the term's meaning.

The following HTML file, DefinitionList.html, creates a glossary of the key terms presented in this chapter:

```
<!DOCTYPE html>
<html>
```

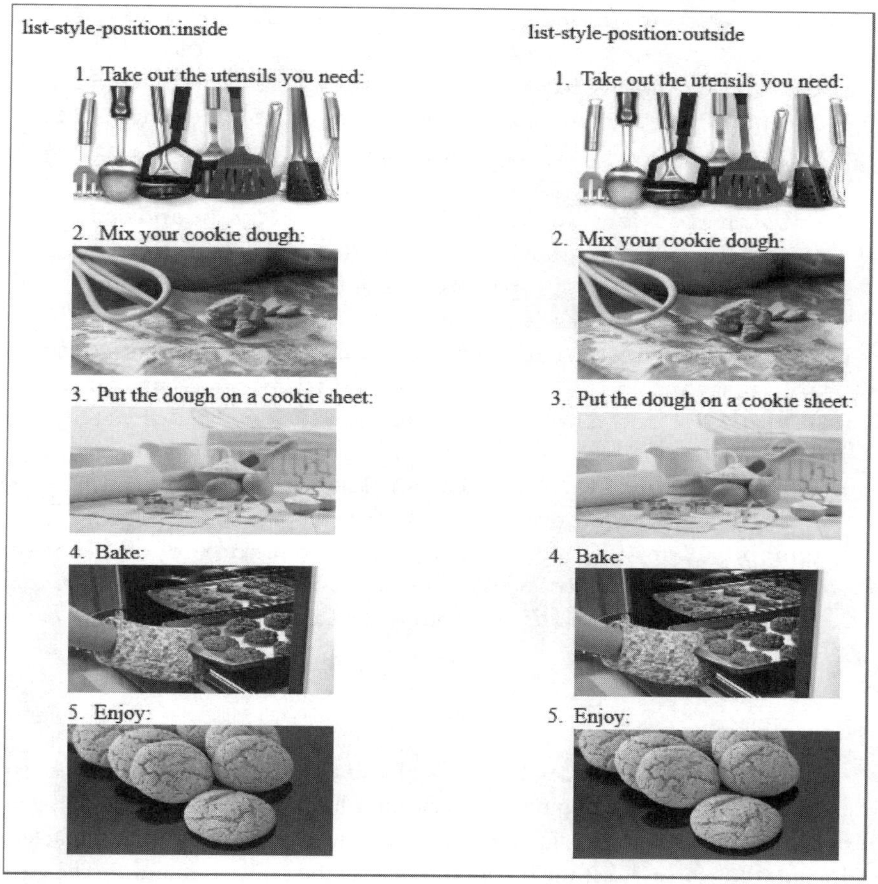

FIGURE 4-10 Using the **list-style-position** attribute to control whether a number appears inside or outside of the corresponding list item

Credit (from top): © Kitch Bain/Shutterstock; © Joannawnuk/Shutterstock; © Antonio Danna/Shutterstock; © Shutterstock; © JulijaSapic_Portfolio/Shutterstock

```
<body>
<p>Chapter Definitions</p>
<dl>
<dt>Ordered List:</dt> <dd>Also called a numbered
list; a list of items that appear in alphabetic or
numerical order. To create an ordered list in HTML,
you use the &lt;ol&gt; and &lt;/ol&gt; tag pair.</dd>
<dt>Unordered List:</dt> <dd>Also called a bulleted
list; a list of items, normally preceded by a cir-
cular bullet, that appear in no particular order.
```

```
To create an unordered list in HTML, you use the
&lt;ul&gt; and &lt;/ul&gt; tag pair.</dd>
<dt>List Item:</dt> <dd>An entry within an ordered
or unordered list. To specify a list item in HTML,
you use the &lt;li&gt; and &lt;/li&gt; tag pair.
</dd>
<dt>Lorem Ipsum:</dt> <dd>An industry-standard
placeholder (or dummy) text that graphic designers
can use within the pages they design until the
actual content is available.</dd>
<dt>Definition List:</dt> <dd>A list of terms and
their meanings. To create a definition list in
HTML, you use the &lt;dl&gt; and &lt;/dl&gt; tag
pair.</dd>
<dt>Nested List:</dt> <dd>A list of items that
appears within another list of items. To create a
nested list in HTML, you place an ordered or unor-
dered list within a &lt;li&gt; and &lt;/li&gt; tag
pair of a surrounding (outer) list.</dd>
</dl>
</body>
</html>
```

As you can see, the file uses the **<dl>** and **</dl>** tag pair to group the terms and definitions. Within the grouping tags, each entry has a term and definition. If you examine the definitions provided in the file, you will see the use of the characters **<** and **>** which direct the browser to display the symbols < and >. The goal with these definitions was to use text that displayed related HTML tags, such as <ol> and </ol> in the case of the definition for *ordered list*. Because the browser will interpret such text as HTML tags, you must use characters other than the symbols < and > to represent the less-than and greater-than characters. That's where **<** and **>** come in. When the browser encounters **<**, it will display the less-than symbol (<). When it encounters **>**, it will display the greater-than symbol (>).

When you view the file's contents, the browser will display the definition list, as shown in **FIGURE 4-11**.

As you might expect, within the **<dt>** and **<dd>** tags, you can embed other HTML tags to format your definition list content. The following HTML file, DogList.html, uses an **<img>** tag within the **<dt>** and **</dt>** tag pair to create a more visual list:

```
<!DOCTYPE html>
<html>
<body>
```

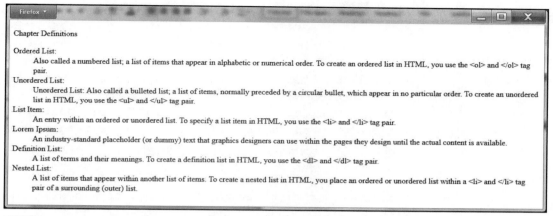

FIGURE 4-11 Using HTML to create a definition list

```
<p>Dog Breeds</p>
<dl>
<dt>Black Lab</dt><dd><img src="lab.jpg" height="160"
width="240"/><br/>The American Kennel Club (AKC)
states: "The Labrador Retriever is a strongly built,
medium-sized, short-coupled, dog possessing a sound,
athletic, well-balanced conformation that enables it
to function as a retrieving gun dog; the substance
and soundness to hunt waterfowl or upland game for
long hours under difficult conditions; the character
and quality to win in the show ring; and the temper-
ament to be a family companion. Physical features
and mental characteristics should denote a dog bred
to perform as an efficient Retriever of game with a
stable temperament suitable for a variety of
pursuits beyond the hunting environment."</dd>
<dt>Dalmatian</dt><dd><img src="dalmatian.jpg"
height="160" width="240"/><br/>The AKC states: "The
Dalmatian is a distinctively spotted dog; poised and
alert; strong, muscular and active; free of shyness;
intelligent in expression; symmetrical in outline;
and without exaggeration or coarseness. The Dalma-
tian is capable of great endurance, combined with
fair amount of speed. Deviations from the described
ideal should be penalized in direct proportion to
the degree of the deviation."</dd>
```

```
<dt>German Shepherd</dt><dd><img src="shepherd.jpg"
height="160" width="240"/><br/> The AKC states: "The
first impression of a good German Shepherd Dog is
that of a strong, agile, well muscled animal, alert
and full of life. It is well balanced, with harmo-
nious development of the forequarter and hind-
quarter. The dog is longer than tall, deep-bodied,
and presents an outline of smooth curves rather than
angles. It looks substantial and not spindly, giving
the impression, both at rest and in motion, of mus-
cular fitness and nimbleness without any look of
clumsiness or soft living. The ideal dog is stamped
with a look of quality and nobility—difficult to
define, but unmistakable when present. Secondary sex
characteristics are strongly marked, and every
animal gives a definite impression of masculinity or
femininity, according to its sex."</dd>
</dl>
</body>
</html>
```

When you display the file's contents, the browser will display the page shown in **FIGURE 4–12**.

Creating a Nested List

A **nested list** is a list that appears within the contents of another list. The following HTML file, NestedList.html, creates several nested ordered lists. Each appears within a surrounding (outer) unordered list:

```
<!DOCTYPE html>
<html>
<body>
<p>My Favorite Things:</p>
<ul>
<li>Food<ol><li>Pasta</li><li>Pizza</
li><li>Nachos</li></ol></li>
<li>Leisure<ol><li>Cigars</li><li>Wine</
li><li>Movie Night</li></ol></li>
<li>Places<ol><li>The Ranch</li><li>Palm Springs</
li><li>Vegas</li></ol></li>
</ul>
</body>
</html>
```

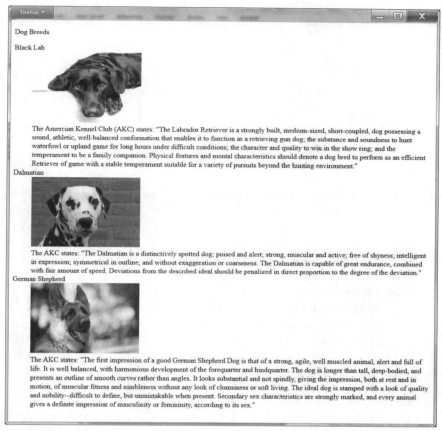

FIGURE 4-12 Using an <img> tag within an HTML definition list
Credit (from top): © Andrii Muzyka/Shutterstock; © SasPartout/Shutterstock;
© Andre Dobroskok/Shutterstock

As you can see, to create a nested list, you simply define the list as content within an <li> and </li> tag pair. When you display the file's contents, the browser will display the nested list, as shown in **FIGURE 4-13**.

Real-World Web Design

When you design webpages, there will be many times when your design precedes your content availability. Meaning, you may create a layout that you want to show to a client before the client has provided you with the text that the page will display. In such cases, you can use **lorem ipsum** text. Lorem ipsum is essentially dummy text—it is an industry standard used by graphic artists as a content placeholder. In general, it is paragraphs of Latin text.

FIGURE 4-13 Creating nested lists within a webpage

Because your clients probably don't read Latin, they will ignore the text and focus on your layout instead.

FIGURE 4-14 illustrates a simple page that uses lorem ipsum text as placeholder content. To get lorem ipsum content for use in your page design, visit the website *http://www.lipsum.com*. Within that site, you will find content that you can cut and paste into your HTML pages as needed.

Hands-On HTML

To view the HTML files or to experiment with the files presented in this chapter, visit this book's companion website at *http://www.websitedevelopmentbook.com/ Chapter04/TryIt.html*.

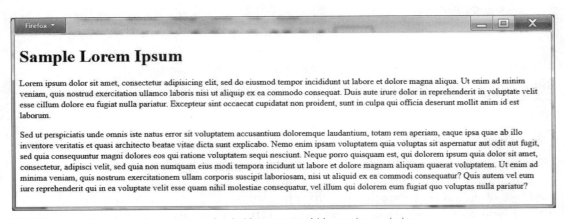

FIGURE 4-14 Using lorem ipsum text as placeholder content within a webpage design

CHAPTER SUMMARY

Across the Web, developers make extensive use of lists of data within the webpages they create—normally numbered lists or bulleted lists. A numbered list precedes the list items with a number, representing order. You might use a numbered list to present the steps a user must perform to accomplish a task. In contrast, an unordered list precedes the items with a bullet. Items in an unordered list often appear in no particular order. HTML provides an ordered-list tag pair **<ol>** and **</ol>**, which you can use to create a numbered list. It also provides an unordered-list tag pair **<ul>** and **</ul>**, which you can use to create a bulleted list. In addition, HTML supports the **<dl>** and **</dl>** tag pair, which lets you create a definition list that consists of terms and their meanings. You might use this, for example, to create a glossary of key terms.

KEY TERMS

Definition list

List item

Lorem ipsum

Nested list

Ordered list

Unordered list

CHAPTER REVIEW

1. Using the HTML **<ol>** and **</ol>** tags, create the following ordered list:

2. Using the HTML **<ul>** and **</ul>** tags, create the following unordered list:

3. Using the **<ol>** tag **list-style-type** attribute, create an ordered list that precedes each list entry with a Roman numeral.

4. Using the **<ul>** tag **list-style-type** attribute, create an unordered list that uses a square bullet.

5. Using the **<ul>** tag **list-style-image** attribute, create an unordered list that precedes each list item with a graphics image as a bullet.

6. Using the HTML **<dl>** and **</dl>** tag pair, create the following definition list:

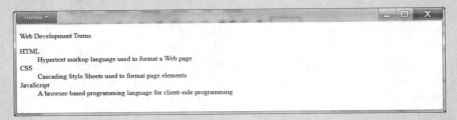

7. Using nested lists, create the following:

8. Describe lorem ipsum and explain when a graphic artist might use it.

Formatting Content with Tables

ACROSS THE WEB, BILLIONS of sites present vast amounts of data that may include numbers, text, images, or a combination of each. To organize the display of such information, Web developers make extensive use of tables. A table within a webpage consists of one or more rows, each of which contains one or more columns of data. Within each cell of a table, you can place text and images, which you can further format using additional HTML tags. In other words, you can treat each table cell as a mini page in which you can control the format using additional HTML tags.

Learning Objectives

This chapter examines HTML tables in detail. By the time you finish this chapter, you will understand the following key concepts:

- How to use the **<table>** tag to create a table within a webpage
- How to use HTML tags to format content within an HTML table
- How to embed images within an HTML table
- How to nest one table within another
- How to center a table within a page
- How to center content within a table cell
- How to align contents of a specific row or cell
- How to vertically align table row or cell contents
- How to control table cell borders
- How to control table cell spacing and padding
- How to provide a table caption
- How to provide a table heading
- How to display a table header and footer

- How to handle an unequal number of table rows and columns
- How to control a table's width and height
- How to format an entire webpage using a single table

Creating a Table Within a Webpage

A table consists of one or more rows, each of which contains one or more columns. The individual locations within a table are called cells. **FIGURE 5-1** illustrates the common table components.

To create a table using HTML, you begin with the <**table**> and <**/table**> tag pair. As discussed, a table must have at least one row. To define a row within a table, you use the <**tr**> and <**/tr**> tags. The **tr** stands for table row. Each row, in turn, must have one or more columns. To specify a column's data value, you use the <**td**> and <**/td**> tag pair. The following HTML file, TwoTableColumns.html, creates a simple table with two columns of data:

```
<!DOCTYPE html>
<html>
<body>
<table>
<tr>
<td>Column One</td>
<td>Column Two</td>
</tr>
</table>
</body>
</html>
```

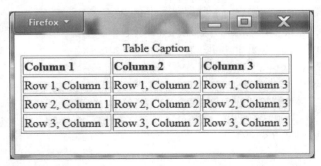

FIGURE 5-1 Tables consist of rows and columns that contain individual cells.

When you view the file's contents, the browser will display the table contents shown in **FIGURE 5-2**.

To the table to four columns of data, you simply add two more <**td**> and </**td**> tag pairs, as shown here within the file FourTableColumns.html:

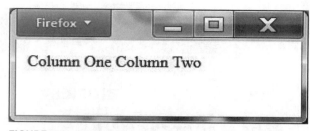

FIGURE 5-2 Displaying a table with one row and two columns

```
<!DOCTYPE html>
<html>
<body>
<table>
<tr>
<td style="color:blue">Column One</td>
<td style="color:green">Column Two</td>
<td style="color:orange">Column Three</td>
<td style="color:red">Column Four</td>
</tr>
</table>
</body>
</html>
```

In this case, to help you distinguish each column, the table uses the color attribute to set each column to a different color. When you display the file's contents, the browser will display four columns of data, as shown in **FIGURE 5-3**.

To create a table with multiple rows, you must add a <**tr**> and </**tr**> pair for each row. Then, within each <**tr**> and </**tr**> pair, you place <**td**> and </**td**> to define the column data. The following HTML file, Calories.html, uses <**tr**> and </**tr**> tags to create a multi-row table that lists calorie amounts for common foods:

```
<!DOCTYPE html>
<html>
```

FIGURE 5-3 Displaying a table with one row and four columns

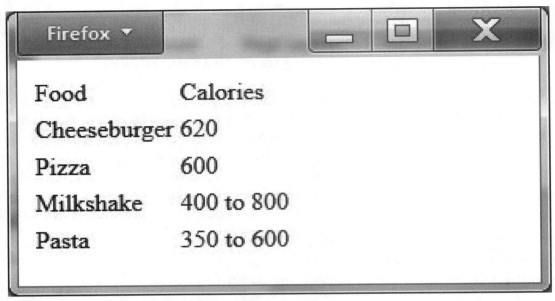

FIGURE 5-4 Using multiple **<tr>** and **</tr>** tags to create a multi-row table

```
<body>
<table>
<tr><td>Food</td><td>Calories</td></tr>
<tr><td>Cheeseburger</td><td>620</td></tr>
<tr><td>Pizza</td><td>600</td></tr>
<tr><td>Milkshake</td><td>400 to 800</td></tr>
<tr><td>Pasta</td><td>350 to 600</td></tr>
</table>
</body>
</html>
```

When you display the file's contents, the browser will display the table shown in **FIGURE 5-4**.

Formatting Content Within an HTML Table

You can think of a table cell as a miniature HTML page. That means you can use HTML tags to format the cell's contents. The following HTML file, BoldCalories.html, changes the previous HTML file's contents by bolding the number of calories within each food:

```
<!DOCTYPE html>
<html>
<body>
<table>
```

```
<tr><td>Food</td><td style="font-weight:
bold;">Calories</td></tr>
<tr><td>Cheeseburger</td><td style="font-weight:
bold;">620</td></tr>
<tr><td>Pizza</td><td style="font-weight:
bold;">600</td></tr>
<tr><td>Milkshake</td><td style="font-weight:
bold;">400 to 800</td></tr>
<tr><td>Pasta</td><td style="font-weight:
bold;">350 to 600</td></tr>
</table>
</body>
</html>
```

When you display the file's contents, the browser will display the bold text, as shown in **FIGURE 5-5**.

In a similar way, the following HTML file, CompanyLinks.html, places anchor tags **<a>** and **</a>** within table cells to create links to specific company websites:

```
<!DOCTYPE html>
<html>
<body>
```

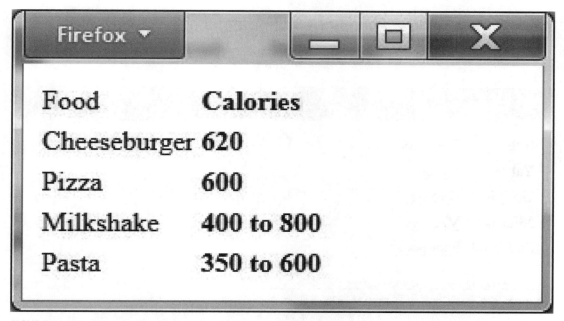

FIGURE 5-5 Embedding HTML tags within a table cell to format the cell contents

```
<table>
<tr><td>Site</td><td>Web Address</td></tr>
<tr><td>Yahoo</td><td><a href="http://www.yahoo.
com">Yahoo</a></td></tr>
<tr><td>Google</td><td><a href="http://www.google.
com">Google</a></td></tr>
<tr><td>Microsoft</td><td><a href="http://www.
microsoft.com">Microsoft</a></td></tr>
<tr><td>Facebook</td><td><a href="http://www.
facebook.com">Facebook</a></td></tr>
</table>
</body>
</html>
```

When you display the file's contents, the browser will display the company names and the clickable hyperlinks, as shown in FIGURE 5-6.

Embedding Images Within an HTML Table

Given that you can place HTML tags within a table cell, it follows that you can use the <img> tag to embed an image within a table. The following HTML file, PetTable. html, creates a table that contains text for pet types along with a corresponding photo:

```
<!DOCTYPE html>
<html>
<body>
<table>
```

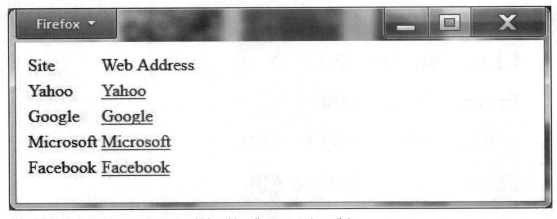

FIGURE 5-6 Embedding anchor tags within table cells to create hyperlinks

```
<tr><td>Pet</td><td>Photo</td></tr>
<tr><td>Dog</td><td><img src="http://www.WebSite
DevelopmentBook.com/Chapter05/dog.jpg" width="300"
height="150"/></td></tr>
<tr><td>Cat</td><td><img src="http://www.WebSite
DevelopmentBook.com/Chapter05/cat.jpg" width="300"
height="150"/></td></tr>
<tr><td>Horse</td><td><img src="http://www.WebSite
DevelopmentBook.com/Chapter05/horse.jpg"
width="300" height="150"/></td></tr>
<tr><td>Mouse</td><td><img src="http://www.WebSite
DevelopmentBook.com/Chapter05/mouse.jpg"
width="300" height="150"/></td></tr>
</table>
</body>
</html>
```

When you display the file's contents, the browser will display the text and images shown in **FIGURE 5-7**.

In this case, to ensure that each image displayed at a consistent size, the page used the **height** and **width** attributes. If the images were different sizes and no attributes were used, the browser, when displaying the table, would adjust the height and/or width of all of the cells as needed to the size of the largest image, as shown in **FIGURE 5-8**. As you can see, a developer has added a border to the table to make the cell size more apparent.

Note: To size the images you place within a table, you can use the **<img>** tag **height** and **width** attributes. That said, by using photo-editing software to size your images, you will optimize the image file size.

Nesting One Table Within Another

Depending on the data your webpage must display, there may be times when you will place one table within another. **FIGURE 5-9**, for example, shows the contents of the HTML file SalesData.html, which contains annual sales data for three sales people.

To nest (embed) one table within another, you simply place the inner table's contents within a table cell of an outer table. The following HTML tags implement the SalesData.html file:

```
<!DOCTYPE html>
<html>
```

FIGURE 5-7 Creating a table that contains text and graphics

Credit (from top): © Christian Mueller/Shutterstock; © Anastasija Popova/Shutterstock; © Melanie Hoffman/Shutterstock; © Eduard Kyslynskyy/Shutterstock

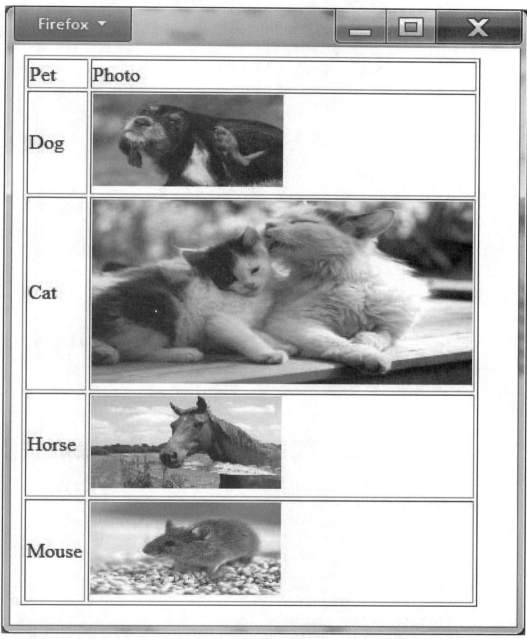

FIGURE 5–8 Unless you tell it to do otherwise (using image **height** and **width** attributes), the browser will make each table cell large enough to hold the largest cell's contents.

Credit (from top): © Christian Mueller/Shutterstock; © Anastasija Popova/Shutterstock; © Melanie Hoffman/Shutterstock; © Eduard Kyslynskyy/Shutterstock

FIGURE 5-9 Nesting one HTML table within another

```
<body>
<table>
<tr><td>Sales Member</td><td>Monthly Sales</td></tr>

<tr><td>Jim</td><td>
<table>
<tr><td>Jan</td><td>Feb</td><td>Mar</td></tr>
<tr><td>25</td><td>30</td><td>35</td></tr>
</table>
</td></tr>

<tr><td>Ted</td><td>
<table>
<tr><td>Jan</td><td>Feb</td><td>Mar</td></tr>
<tr><td>23</td><td>37</td><td>30</td></tr>
</table>
</td></tr>
```

```
<tr><td>Mary</td><td>
<table>
<tr><td>Jan</td><td>Feb</td><td>Mar</td></tr>
<tr><td>15</td><td>20</td><td>34</td></tr>
</table>
</td></tr>

<tr><td>Sara</td><td>
<table>
<tr><td>Jan</td><td>Feb</td><td>Mar</td></tr>
<tr><td>22</td><td>31</td><td>33</td></tr>
</table>
</td></tr>
</table>
</body>
</html>
```

As you can see, the HTML file places the inner table's tag definitions within the table cells of the outer table.

Centering a Table

Often, depending on your webpage design, you will want to center a table's contents within a page, as shown in **FIGURE 5-10**.

FIGURE 5-10 Centering a table's contents within a webpage

To center a table within a page, you can use the <**table**> tag **margin** style, which you set to **auto**. The following HTML file, CenterTable.html, creates the centered table previously shown in FIGURE 5-10:

```
<!DOCTYPE html>
<html>
<body>
<table style="margin: auto;">
<tr><td>Calendar</td></tr>
<tr><td>Monday: Travel to New York</td></tr>
<tr><td>Tuesday: Meeting with CNN</td></tr>
<tr><td>Wednesday: Fly to Chicago</td></tr>
<tr><td>Thursday: Bulls Game</td></tr>
<tr><td>Friday: Fly to Phoenix</td></tr>
</table>
</body>
</html>
```

Note: Many Web developers still use the <**center**> and </**center**> tag pair to center a table. Although the technique will work within most browsers, the <**center**> and </**center**> tags are deprecated, which means that in the future, a browser may not support them.

Centering Content Within a Table Cell

Just as there will be times when you want to center a table within a page, there also will be times when you will want to center the contents of a table cell within a table. You may want to center the contents vertically between the top and bottom of a cell, horizontally from between the cell's left and right edges, or both.

To control the horizontal alignment of content within a table, you can use the style value **style="text-align: center"** within the <**table**> tag as shown here, within the file TableCenterText.html:

```
<!DOCTYPE html>
<html>
<body>
<table style="text-align: center;">
<tr><td>City</td><td>Photo</td></tr>
<tr><td>Phoenix</td><td><img src="http://www.
WebSiteDevelopmentBook.com/Chapter05/Phoenix.jpg"
width="150" height="100"></td></tr>
<tr><td>San Francisco</td><td><img src="http://www.
```

```
WebSiteDevelopmentBook.com/Chapter05/SanFrancisco.
jpg" width="150" height="100"></td></tr>
<tr><td>New York</td><td><img src="http://www.
WebSiteDevelopmentBook.com/Chapter05/NewYork.jpg"
width="150" height="100"></td></tr>
</table>
</body>
</html>
```

When you display the file's contents, your browser will display the centered content, as shown in **FIGURE 5-11**.

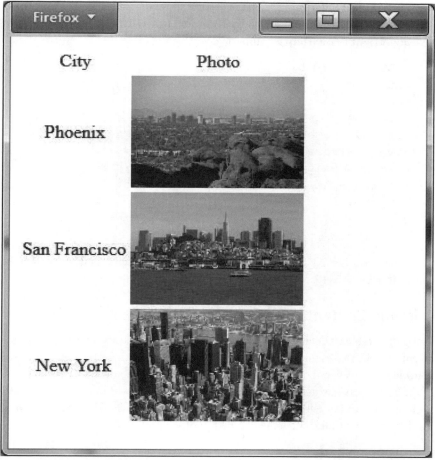

FIGURE 5-11 Centering content within a table

Credit (from top): © Alexander Morozov/Shutterstock; © Alita Bobrov/Shutterstock; © JR/Shutterstock

TABLE 5-1	VALUES FOR THE TEXT-ALIGN ATTRIBUTE TO JUSTIFY TABLE CONTENT
Value	**Meaning**
center	Center-justifies the content
inherit	Justifies content based on a surrounding element
justify	Spaces content as needed to align content to the margin
left	Left-justifies the content
right	Right-justifies the content

Using the **text-align** attribute, you can assign one of the values listed in **TABLE 5-1**. The following HTML file, TableNumbers.html, uses the **style** attribute **text-align:right** to right-justify numeric data:

```
<!DOCTYPE html>
<html>
<body>
<table style="text-align: right;">
<tr><td>Budget Item</td><td>Cost</td></tr>
<tr><td>Travel</td><td>$1535.05</td></tr>
<tr><td>Meals</td><td>$534.75</td></tr>
<tr><td>Hotel</td><td>223.33</td></tr>
</table>
</body>
</html>
```

When you display the file's content, your browser will display the data, as shown in **FIGURE 5-12**.

Aligning Contents of a Specific Row or Cell

Using the <**table**> tag **text-align** style attribute, you can specify data alignment for an entire table. Depending on your data-presentation goals, there may be times when you will want to align the data for a specific row or cell differently than the rest of the table. In such cases, you can place the **text-align** attribute within the <**tr**> or <**td**> tag to specify a row or cell's alignment. The following HTML file, TableCenterColumn.html, uses the **text-align** attribute to center photos within a table:

```
<!DOCTYPE html>
<html>
```

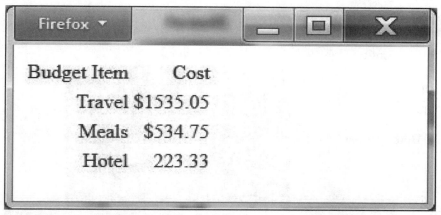

FIGURE 5-12 Right-justifying numeric data within a table

```
<body>
<table>
<tr><td>Description</td><td style="text-align:
center;">Photo</td></tr>
<tr><td>Bikes Parked</td><td style="text-align:
center;"><img src="http://www.WebSite
DevelopmentBook.com/Chapter05/bike01.jpg">
</td></tr>
<tr><td>Bike early in morning</td><td style=
"text-align: center;"><img src="http://www.
WebSiteDevelopmentBook.com/Chapter05/bike02.jpg">
</td></tr>
<tr><td>Bike rider in city</td><td style=
"text-align: center;"><img src="http://www.
WebSiteDevelopmentBook.com/Chapter05/bike03.jpg">
</td></tr>
</table>
</body>
</html>
```

As you can see, each <**td**> tag for the cells that contain photos uses the center alignment value. When you display the file's contents, the browser will display the centered photos, as shown in **FIGURE 5-13**.

Vertically Aligning Table Row or Cell Contents

Using the **text-align** style, you can justify your table, row, or cell contents. Depending on your table cell sizes, there may be times when you will want to

FIGURE 5-13 Centering the contents of specific table cells

Credit (from top): © Vitaly Titov & Maria Sidelnikov/Shutterstock; © Amy Johansson/Shutterstock; © Rikard Stadler/Shutterstock

vertically align a row or cell's contents between the cell's top and bottom edges. In such cases, you can use the **<tr>** or **<td>** tag **valign** attribute to align content to the top, middle, or bottom of a cell. The following html file, TableTextTop.html, uses the **valign** attribute to vertically align content to the top of the table cells:

```
<!DOCTYPE html>
<html>
<body>
<table>
<tr valign="top"><td>Tree Type</td><td style=
"text-align:center">Photo</td></tr>
<tr valign="top"><td>Apple</td><td><img
src="http://www.WebSiteDevelopmentBook.com/
Chapter05/apple.jpg"></td></tr>
<tr valign="top"><td>Cherry</td><td><img
src="http://www.WebSiteDevelopmentBook.com/
Chapter05/cherry.jpg"></td></tr>
<tr valign="top"><td>Orange</td><td><img
src="http://www.WebSiteDevelopmentBook.com/
Chapter05/orange.jpg"></td></tr>
</table>
</body>
</html>
```

When you display the file's contents, the browser will display the text at the top of the cell, as shown in **FIGURE 5-14**.

Controlling Table Cell Borders

Depending on your table's contents, there may be times when you want to display a border around your table and other times when you will not. **FIGURE 5-15**, for example, shows the table content with and without borders.

To control whether or not a table displays borders, you use the **border** attribute within the **<table>** tag to specify the width of the border that you desire in pixels. The **border** attribute changes only the size of the box that surrounds the table. The borders that appear between each cell will remain at one pixel. The following HTML file, BorderNoBorder.html, implements the bordered and borderless tables previously shown in **FIGURE 5-15**:

```
<!DOCTYPE html>
<html>
<body>
<table border="1">
```

FIGURE 5-14 Using the **valign** attribute to vertically align cell contents

Credit (from top): © Mazzzur/Shutterstock; © berna namoglu/Shutterstock; © chanwangrong/ Shutterstock

FIGURE 5-15 Display of a table with and without borders

```
<tr><td>1</td><td>2</td></tr>
<tr><td>3</td><td>4</td></tr>
</table><br/>

<table>
<tr><td>1</td><td>2</td></tr>
<tr><td>3</td><td>4</td></tr>
</table>
</body>
</html>
```

In this case, the browser will display a single pixel border around the outside of the table, along with single pixel rule around the cells. The two combined give the appearance of a border thicker than 1 pixel.

In a similar way, the following HTML file, BorderWidths.html, creates tables that use three different border thicknesses:

```
<!DOCTYPE html>
<html>
<body>
<table border="1">
<tr><td>1</td><td>2</td></tr>
<tr><td>3</td><td>4</td></tr>
</table><br/>
<table border="5">
<tr><td>1</td><td>2</td></tr>
<tr><td>3</td><td>4</td></tr>
```

```
</table><br/>
<table border="10">
<tr><td>1</td><td>2</td></tr>
<tr><td>3</td><td>4</td></tr>
</table>
</body>
</html>
```

As you can see, within each <table> tag, the file assigns a different pixel width of the corresponding border. When you display the file's contents, the browser will display the tables, as shown in FIGURE 5-16.

Bordering Specific Parts of a Table

By default, when you specify a table border width, the browser will place the border around the entire table and will display a thin border around each table cell. Using the <table> tag **frame** attribute, you can control the display of each side of the outer box that surrounds the table. TABLE 5-2 lists values you can assign to the **frame** attribute.

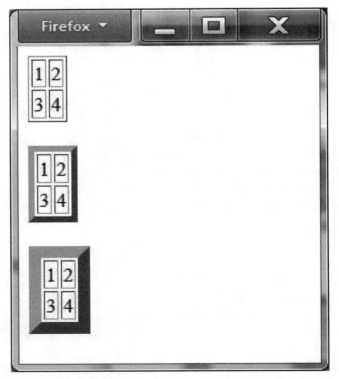

FIGURE 5-16 Using the <table> tag **border** attribute to control a table's border width

TABLE 5-2	VALUES TO ASSIGN TO THE <TABLE> TAG FRAME ATTRIBUTE TO CONTROL THE TABLE BORDER DISPLAY
Value	**Meaning**
Above	Displays the horizontal bar above the table
Below	Displays the horizontal bar below the table
Box	Surrounds the entire table
Border	Surrounds the entire table
Hside	Displays the horizontal bar above the table
Lhs	Displays the vertical bar on the left-hand side of the table
Rhs	Displays the vertical bar on the right-hand side of the table
Vside	Displays vertical bars on the right and left side of the table
Void	Removes the small border around the table cells

The following HTML file, BorderTypes.html, illustrates the use of the <**table**> tag **frame** attribute:

```
<!DOCTYPE html>
<html>
<body>
<table border="1" frame="lhs">
<tr><td>1</td><td>2</td></tr>
<tr><td>3</td><td>4</td></tr>
</table><br/>

<table border="5" frame="below">
<tr><td>1</td><td>2</td></tr>
<tr><td>3</td><td>4</td></tr>
</table><br/>

<table border="10" frame="rhs">
<tr><td>1</td><td>2</td></tr>
<tr><td>3</td><td>4</td></tr>
</table>
</body>
</html>
```

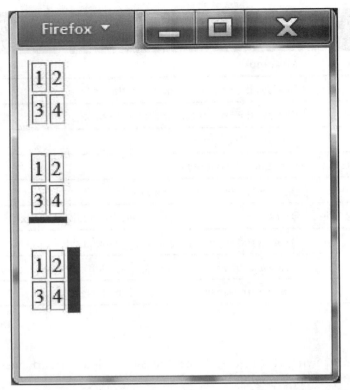

FIGURE 5-17 Using the **<table>** tag **frame** attribute to control the display of table borders

When you display the file's contents, the browser will display the table border frames, as shown in **FIGURE 5-17**.

Controlling Borders (Rules) Around Table Cells

Just as the **<table>** tag **frame** attribute lets you control the display of border lines around a table, you can use the **<table>** tag **rules** attribute to control which lines (**rules**) appear around table cells. Using the **rules** attribute, you specify one of the values listed in **TABLE 5-3** to control the display of lines around each table cell.

The following HTML file, TableCellRules.html, illustrates the use of the **<table>** tag **rules** attribute:

```
<!DOCTYPE html>
<html>
<body>
<table border="1" rules="all">
<tr><td>1</td><td>2</td></tr>
```

TABLE 5-3: VALUES TO ASSIGN TO THE <TABLE> TAG RULES ATTRIBUTE TO CONTROL THE CELL BORDER DISPLAY	
Value	Meaning
All	Displays a rule around all sides of a cell
Cols	Displays a vertical bar between cell columns
Groups	Displays lines between row or column groups
Rows	Displays a horizontal bar between cell rows

```
<tr><td>3</td><td>4</td></tr>
</table><br/>


<table border="1" rules="cols">
<tr><td>1</td><td>2</td></tr>
<tr><td>3</td><td>4</td></tr>
</table><br/>


<table border="1" rules="rows">
<tr><td>1</td><td>2</td></tr>
<tr><td>3</td><td>4</td></tr>
</table>
</body>
</html>
```

When you display the file's contents, the browser will display the table cell rules, as shown in **FIGURE 5-18**.

Controlling Table Cell Spacing and Padding

Again, depending on your webpage design, there may be times when you will want to control the amount of spacing that appears between cells in a table. You might, for example, want to separate text from one or more images. **Cell spacing**—specified by the <**table**> tag **cellspacing** attribute—defines the pixel space that appears between table cells. You use the <**table**> tag **cellspacing** attribute to specify the number of pixels you desire between cells. The following HTML file, TableCellSpacing.html, illustrates the use of the <**table**> tag **cellspacing** attribute:

```
<!DOCTYPE html>
<html>
```

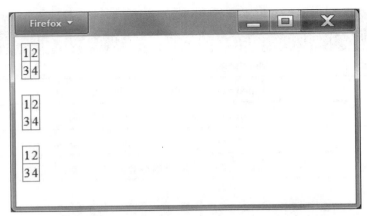

FIGURE 5-18 Using the **<table>** tag **rules** attribute to control borders around table cells

```
<body>
<h3>No Spacing</h3>
<table border="1">
<tr><td>City</td><td>Sales</td></tr>
<tr><td>Phoenix</td><td>100</td></tr>
<tr><td>San Francisco</td><td>350</td></tr>
<tr><td>New York</td><td>252</td></tr>
</table><br/>
<h3>Spacing</h3>
<table border="1" cellspacing="10">
<tr><td>City</td><td>Sales</td></tr>
<tr><td>Phoenix</td><td>100</td></tr>
<tr><td>San Francisco</td><td>350</td></tr>
<tr><td>New York</td><td>252</td></tr>
</table>
</body>
</html>
```

When you display the file's contents, the browser will display the tables, each with different cell spacing, as shown in **FIGURE 5-19**.

Related to cell spacing is the pixel padding that surrounds the contents of each table cell. By changing the **cell padding** value, you can specify, in pixels, the separation between the cell contents and the cell's surrounding border. The following HTML file, TableCellPadding.html, illustrates the use of the **<table>** tag **cellpadding** attribute:

```
<!DOCTYPE html>
<html>
<body>
```

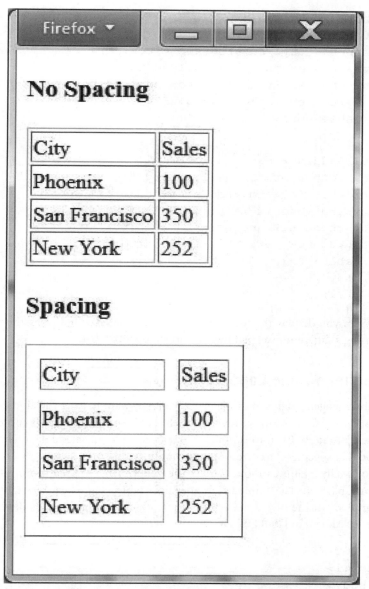

FIGURE 5–19 Using the **<table>** tag **cellspacing** attribute to control spacing between table cells

```
<h3>No Padding</h3>
<table border="1">
<tr><td>City</td><td>Sales</td></tr>
<tr><td>Phoenix</td><td>100</td></tr>
<tr><td>San Francisco</td><td>350</td></tr>
<tr><td>New York</td><td>252</td></tr>
</table><br/>


<h3>Padding</h3>
<table border="1" cellpadding="10">
<tr><td>City</td><td>Sales</td></tr>
<tr><td>Phoenix</td><td>100</td></tr>
<tr><td>San Francisco</td><td>350</td></tr>
<tr><td>New York</td><td>252</td></tr>
</table><br/>
</body>
</html>
```

When you display the file's contents, your browser will display the tables, each using a different pixel padding, as shown in **FIGURE 5–20**.

Providing a Table Caption

If your webpage contains multiple tables, you may want to assign a **table caption** —in other words, descriptive text—to each that identifies the table's contents to the user. **FIGURE 5–21**, for example, shows three tables of sales data, each with a caption that specifies the corresponding month.

To specify a table caption, you use the <**caption**> and </**caption**> tag pair. You must place the tags immediately after the <**table**> tag. The following HTML tags implement the file TableCaption.html, which creates the sales-data tables previously shown in **FIGURE 5–20**:

```
<!DOCTYPE html>
<html>
<body>
<table border="1">
<caption>January Sales</caption>
<tr><td>City</td><td>Sales</td></tr>
<tr><td>Phoenix</td><td>100</td></tr>
<tr><td>San Francisco</td><td>350</td></tr>
<tr><td>New York</td><td>252</td></tr>
</table><br/>
```

FIGURE 5-20 Using the **<table>** tag **cellpadding** attribute to specify the pixel space that separates the cell contents from the cell's surrounding border

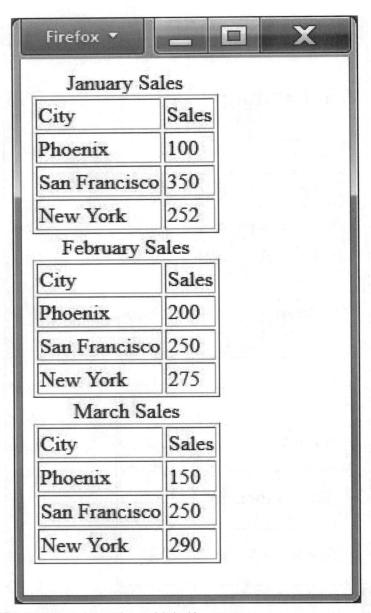

FIGURE 5-21 Using table captions to label table contents

```
<table border="1">
<caption>February Sales</caption>
<tr><td>City</td><td>Sales</td></tr>
<tr><td>Phoenix</td><td>200</td></tr>
<tr><td>San Francisco</td><td>250</td></tr>
<tr><td>New York</td><td>275</td></tr>
</table><br/>
<table border="1">
<caption>March Sales</caption>
<tr><td>City</td><td>Sales</td></tr>
<tr><td>Phoenix</td><td>150</td></tr>
<tr><td>San Francisco</td><td>250</td></tr>
<tr><td>New York</td><td>290</td></tr>
</table>
</body>
</html>
```

Providing a Table Heading

For most tables that you display within a webpage, you will want to label the table columns. For example, the HTML file, CityNewspapers.html, places a label at the top of the table columns to identify the column content, as shown in **FIGURE 5-22**.

To place a column heading above your table data, you use the **<th>** and **</th>** table heading tag pair. Normally, you specify a table heading pair for each column in your table. The following HTML tags implement the CityNewspapers.html file, previously shown in **FIGURE 5-22**:

```
<!DOCTYPE html>
<html>
<body>
<table border="1">
<caption>City Newspapers</caption>
<tr><th>City</th><th>Paper</th></tr>
<tr><td>Phoenix</td><td>Arizona Republic</td></tr>
<tr><td>San Francisco</td><td>San Francisco
Chronicle</td></tr>
<tr><td>New York</td><td>New York Times</td></tr>
</table>
</body>
</html>
```

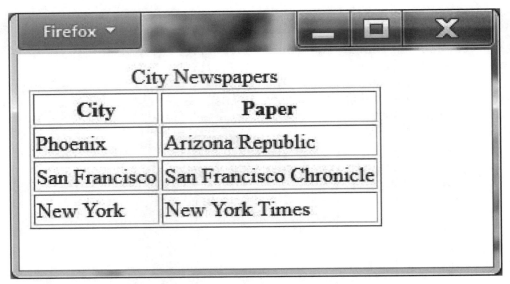

FIGURE 5-22 Using column headings to label table-column content

Displaying a Table Header and Footer

You have learned that using the **<th>** and **</th>** tag pair, you can assign **table headers** to the columns of a table that describe the column's content to a user viewing the table. Often, a table will consist of three parts, a header, body, and footer, which you may want to format differently. To help you perform such groupings, HTML supports the **<thead>**, **<tbody>**, and **<tfoot>** tag pairs. The following HTML file, TableParts.html, illustrates the use of each of these tags:

```
<!DOCTYPE html>
<html>
<body>
<table border="1">
<thead style="background: Orange"><tr><th>City
</th><th>Paper</th></tr></thead>
<tbody style="background: LightBlue">
<tr><td>Phoenix</td><td>Arizona Republic</td></tr>
<tr><td>San Francisco</td><td>San Francisco
Chronicle</td></tr>
<tr><td>New York</td><td>New York Times</td></tr>
</tbody>
<tfoot style="background: Yellow"><tr><td>Optional
Table Footer</td></tr></tfoot>
```

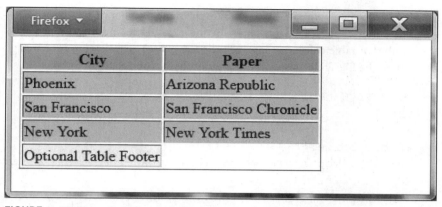

FIGURE 5-23 Using the <thead>, <tbody>, and <tfoot> tags to format a table

```
</table>
</body>
</html>
```

In this case, using the **background** style and color definitions, the file assigns a different background color to each section. When you display the file's contents, your browser will display the table components, as shown in **FIGURE 5-23**.

Handling an Unequal Number of Table Rows and Columns

Normally, when developers think of a table, they assume that each row has the same number of columns. However, depending on your data, there may be times when that is not the case, as shown in **FIGURE 5-24**.

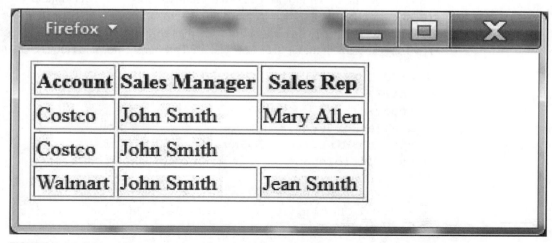

FIGURE 5-24 Table with an unequal number of columns per row

For cases when your tables do not have the same number of columns in each row, you can use the <**td**> tag **colspan** attribute. Using **colspan**, you can specify the number of table columns that a cell should span. The following HTML tags implement the file TableColspan.html previously shown in FIGURE 5-24:

```
<!DOCTYPE html>
<html>
<body>
<table border="1">
<tr><th>Account</th><th>Sales Manager</th><th>Sales
Rep</th></tr>
<tr><td>Costco</td><td>John Smith</td><td>Mary
Allen</td></tr>
<tr><td>Costco</td><td colspan="2">John Smith</
td></tr>
<tr><td>Walmart</td><td>John Smith</td><td>Jean
Smith</td></tr>
</table>
</body>
</html>
```

As you can see, the second row of the table includes a <**td**> tag, which uses the **colspan** attribute to direct the browser to use two columns for that cell.

Using the Rowspan Attribute

Just as there may be times when a table cell must span multiple columns, there may be times when a cell should span two or more rows, as shown in FIGURE 5-25.

To specify that a cell should span two or more rows, you use the <**td**> tag **rowspan** attribute to specify the number of rows the cell should span. The following HTML tags implement the file TableRowspan.html previously shown in FIGURE 5-25:

```
<!DOCTYPE html>
<html>
<body>
<table border="1">
<tr><th>Wine</th><th>Favorites</th></tr>
<tr><td rowspan="2">Pinot Grigio</td><td>Cavit</
td></tr>
<tr><td>Ecco Domani</td></tr>
<tr><td>Chardonnay</td><td>Kendall Jackson</td></tr>
<tr><td>Merlot</td><td>Robert Mondavi</td></tr>
</table>
```

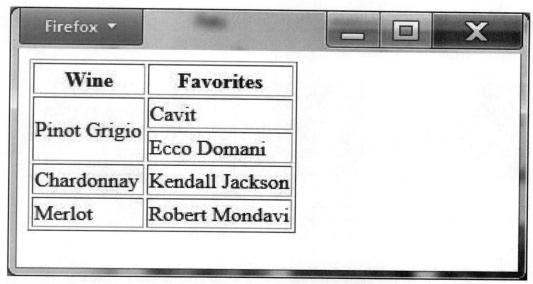

FIGURE 5-25 Using the <td> tag **rowspan** attribute to span cells over two or more rows

```
</body>
</html>
```

Revisiting Nested Tables

Using the <td> tag **rowspan** and **colspan** attributes, you can specify that a cell should span multiple rows or columns. To achieve a similar look and feel, you can also nest one table within another. The following file, TableSpanNested.html, uses **nested tables** to achieve the result previously shown in FIGURE 5-25:

```
<!DOCTYPE html>
<html>
<body>
<table border="1">
<tr><th>Wine</th><th>Favorites</th></tr>
<tr><td>Pinot Grigio</td><td><table><tr><td>Cavit</
td></tr>
<tr><td>Ecco Domani</td></tr></table></td></tr>
<tr><td>Chardonnay</td><td>Kendall Jackson</td>
</tr>
<tr><td>Merlot</td><td>Robert Mondavi</td></tr>
</table>
</body>
</html>
```

FIGURE 5-26 Highlighting a column within a table

Credit (from left): © Gts/Shutterstock; © Vaclav Volrab/Shutterstock; © Daniel Cozma/Shutterstock

As you can see, the nested table solution requires HTML code that is more difficult for another developer to understand and, ultimately, to maintain. As you develop HTML solutions, you will find that there are many ways to achieve the same result. After you implement an HTML solution, you should examine your code to determine if a simpler solution exists.

Treating One or More Columns Uniquely

Often, when you create a table, you may need to highlight one or more table columns, as shown in **FIGURE 5-26**.

To control such column highlighting, you can use the **<colgroup>** and **<col>** tag pairs. To start, the **<colgroup>** and **</colgroup>** tags group the set of columns. Within the tag pair, you place one or more **<col>** and **</col>** tag pairs that define the column formatting. The following HTML file, TableHighlightMiddle-Column.html, illustrates column formatting:

```
<!DOCTYPE html>
<html>
<body>
<table border="1" cellpadding="10" style=
"text-align:center">
<colgroup>
<col></col>
<col style="background:yellow"></col>
<col></col>
</colgroup>
<tr><th>Wine</th><th>Cigar</th><th>Pizza</th></tr>
```

```
<tr><td><img src="http://www.WebSite
DevelopmentBook.com/Chapter05/wine.jpg"/></td>
<td><img src="http://www.WebSiteDevelopmentBook.
com/Chapter05/cigar.jpg"/></td>
<td><img src="http://www.WebSiteDevelopmentBook.
com/Chapter05/pizza.jpg"/></td></tr>
</table>
</body>
</html>
```

In this case, the table has three columns. The first **<col>** and **</col>** tag pair directs the browser to display the first column using default formatting (normally white). The second **<col>** and **</col>** tag pair directs the browser to display the middle column in yellow. The third pair uses, again, the default formatting.

In a similar way, the following HTML file, FirstTwoColumnsHighlight.html, uses the **<col>** tag **span** attribute to direct the browser to highlight the first two columns:

```
<!DOCTYPE html>
<html>
<body>
<table border="1" cellpadding="10" style="text-
align:center">
<colgroup>
<col span="2" style="background:yellow"></col>
<col></col>
</colgroup>
<tr><th>Apple</th><th>Cherry</th><th>Orange</th>
</tr>
<tr><td><img src="http://www.WebSiteDevelopmentBook
.com/Chapter05/apple.jpg"/></td>
<td><img src="http://www.WebSiteDevelopmentBook.
com/Chapter05/cherry.jpg"/></td>
<td><img src="http://www.WebSiteDevelopmentBook.
com/Chapter05/orange.jpg"/></td></tr>
</table>
</body>
</html>
```

When you display the file's contents, the browser will highlight the first two columns but not the third, as shown in **FIGURE 5-27**.

FIGURE 5-27 Using the <col> tag **colspan** attribute to format two columns
Credit (from top): © Mazzzur/Shutterstock; © berna namoglu/Shutterstock; © chanwangrong/Shutterstock

Controlling a Table's Width and Height

Often, to format your page, you will need to control the size of different page elements. Using the <**table**> tag **height** and **width** attributes, you can specify a table's size in pixels or as a percentage of the current page size. The following HTML file, TableSizes.html, uses the **height** and **width** attributes to create several tables of different sizes:

```
<!DOCTYPE html>
<html>
<body>
<table border="1" height="100" width="100"
style="text-align:center">
<caption>100x100</caption>
<tr><td>1</td><td>2</td></tr>
<tr><td>3</td><td>4</td></tr>
</table>
<table border="1" height="200" width="200"
style="text-align:center">
<caption>200x200</caption>
<tr><td>1</td><td>2</td></tr>
<tr><td>3</td><td>4</td></tr>
</table>
<table border="1" height="400" width="400"
style="text-align:center">
<caption>400x400</caption><tr><td>1</td><td>2</
td></tr>
```

```
<tr><td>3</td><td>4</td></tr>
</table>
</body>
</html>
```

As you can see, within each **<table>** tag, the code specifies a height and width. When you view the file's contents, the browser will display the tables shown in FIGURE 5–28.

Revisiting Table Cell Sizes

When you specify a table's height and width, there may be times when you will also want to control the table's cell sizes. In such cases, you can use the **<td>** tag **height** and **width** attributes. Using these attributes, you specify a cell's size in pixels or as a percentage of the table size. The following HTML file, TableCell-Sizes.html, uses the **<td>** tag **height** and **width** attributes to control table cell sizes:

```
<!DOCTYPE html>
<html>
<body>
<table border="1" style="text-align:center">
<tr><td width="100" height="100">100x100</td><td
width="200" height="200">200x200</td></tr>
<tr><td width="300" height="300">300x300</td><td
width="400" height="400">400x400</td></tr>
</table>
</body>
</html>
```

Within the file, the code sets a height and width for each cell. However, because a browser must display a square or rectangular table, the browser may override a cell's width or height specifications because it must instead use the size of the row or column's highest or widest cell.

When you view the file's contents, the browser will display the table with the different cell sizes, as shown in FIGURE 5–29. As you can see, rather than display a 100×100 cell for box 1, the browser instead uses the 200 height and width of cell 2. Likewise, the browser displays cell 3 at 400 pixels high and wide as opposed to the specified 300.

Formatting an Entire Webpage Using a Single Table

HTML tables are powerful and easy to use. In fact, you can design and build a webpage using tables to control the page format. The following HTML file,

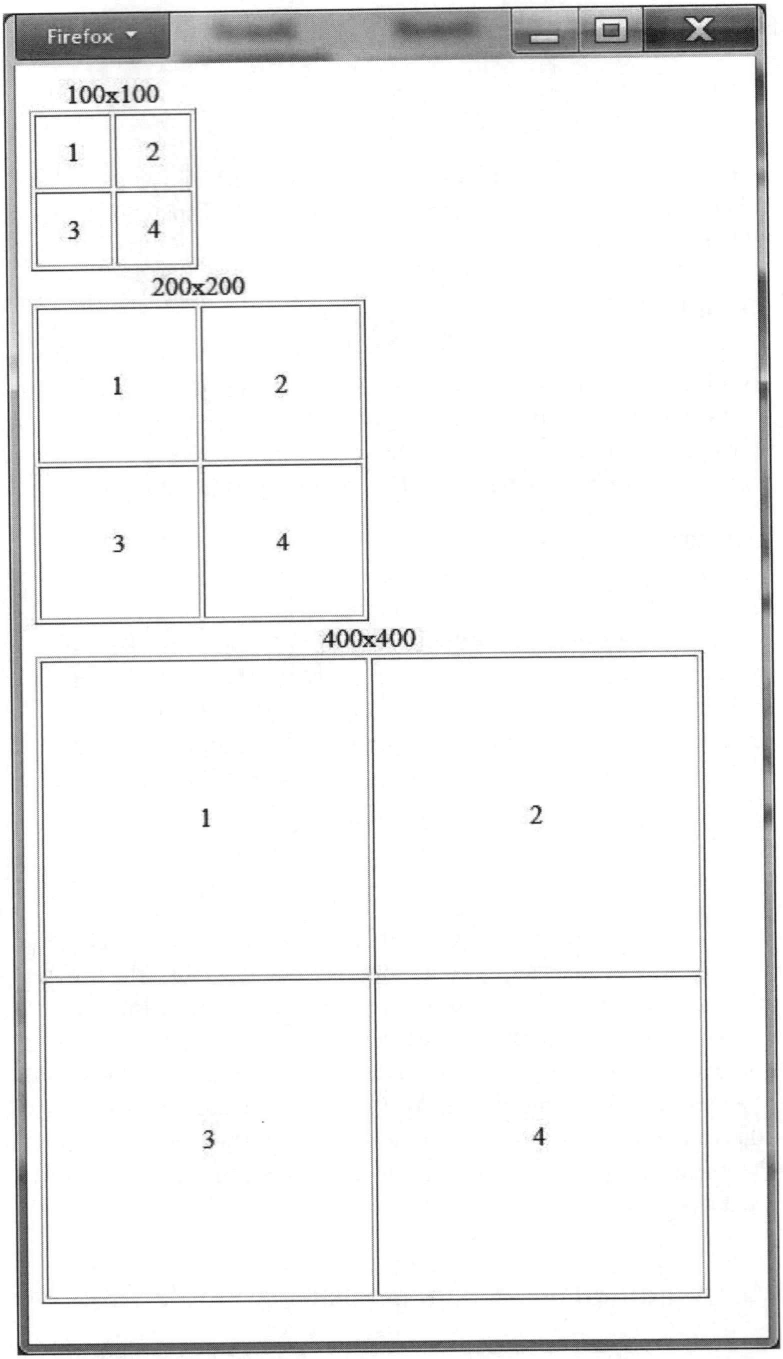

FIGURE 5-28 Using the <table> tag **height** and **width** attributes to control table sizes

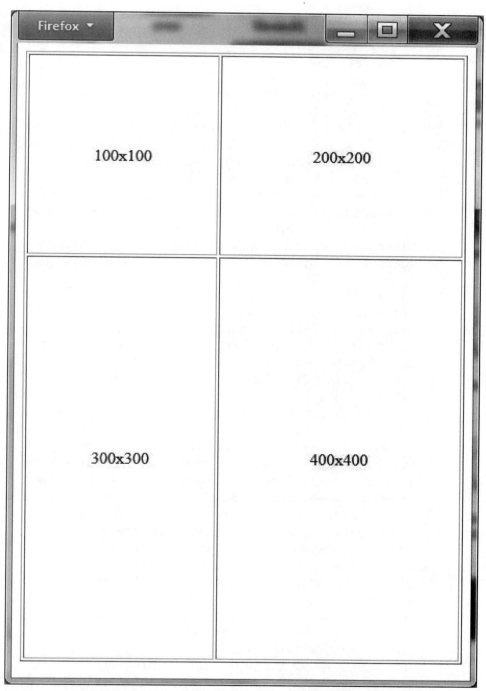

FIGURE 5-29 Using the <td> tag **height** and **width** attributes to control a table's cell sizes

PetSize.html, creates the webpage shown in **FIGURE 5-30**, which contains photos, text, and even a video. The page layout is controlled by a table:

```
<!DOCTYPE html>
<html>
<body bgcolor="lightblue">
<table border="1" style="margin:auto;
background:white; " cellpadding="10" width="800">
<tr><td style="text-align:center" colspan="2"><img
src="http://www.WebSiteDevelopmentBook.com/
Chapter05/Pets.jpg"/></td></tr>
<tr><td><p>Lorem ipsum dolor sit amet, consectetur
adipiscing elit. Suspendisse a tellus vitae quam
elementum interdum quis a massa. Etiam interdum
bibendum leo, rhoncus convallis turpis sodales
tempus. Sed eget orci ac felis mollis pretium.
Aenean et elit vitae lorem blandit aliquam et
viverra risus. In blandit, risus ac commodo
pharetra, risus magna tincidunt ante, at posuere
odio odio eu enim. Phasellus libero dui, eleifend a
eleifend eget, tempor et libero. Curabitur porta
posuere dictum. Morbi cursus nulla auctor neque
semper euismod. Nullam odio tortor, venenatis at
vehicula pulvinar, lobortis nec nisl. Nam consequat
cursus nibh quis tincidunt. Vivamus sed libero quis
mauris facilisis placerat. </p></td><td><p>Integer
et mauris massa. Praesent porttitor varius
vehicula. Lorem ipsum dolor sit amet, consectetur
adipiscing elit. Aenean aliquam ligula et risus
imperdiet vestibulum. Nullam ut metus a tellus
dignissim convallis in ac augue. Etiam fermentum
felis quis leo suscipit a scelerisque ante
imperdiet. Morbi vestibulum scelerisque viverra.
Cum sociis natoque penatibus et magnis dis
parturient montes, nascetur ridiculus mus. Aliquam
at arcu mauris. Sed est arcu, placerat feugiat
porttitor et, cursus eget nulla.</p></td></tr>
<tr><td style="text-align:center"
colspan="2"><iframe width="640" height="360"
src="http://www.youtube.com/embed/
nLuEdBr9ee4?feature=player_embedded" frameborder="0
"allowfullscreen></iframe></td></tr>
```

FIGURE 5-30 Using a table to format an HTML webpage

Credit (from top): © Eric Isselee/Shutterstock; © Dwight Smith/Shutterstock

```
  </table>
  </body>
  </html>
```

Within the file, the <**body**> tag specifies a light blue background color. The <**table**> tag, in turn, specifies the width, background color, and cell padding. The first table row uses a column with a column span of 2 to center an image. The second row uses two paragraphs of lorem ipsum text. Finally, the last row embeds a video from youtube.com.

Real-World Web Design

When you work with different HTML page elements, you will find that many allow you to specify related color values. To simplify the color-specification process, HTML predefines many color names. To view the color-name values, visit the W3Schools website at *http://www.w3schools.com/HTML/html_colornames.asp*. As shown in **FIGURE 5-31**, the site will display the predefined color names.

The following HTML file, ColorNameDemo.html, illustrates the use of color names within a variety of HTML tags:

```
<!DOCTYPE html>
<html>
<body bgcolor="blue">
<table width="800" style="background: yellow;
margin: auto; text-align:center">
<caption><h1 style="background:white">Favorite
Things</h1></caption>
<colgroup>
<col style="background: green"></col>
<col></col>
</colgroup>
<tr><th>Wine</th><th>Cigar</th></tr>
<tr><td>Cavit</td><td>Ashton</td></tr>
<tr><td><img style="border:5px solid red"
src="http://www.WebSiteDevelopmentBook.com/
Chapter05/wine.jpg"/></td>
<td><img style="border:5px solid red" src="http://
www.WebSiteDevelopmentBook.com/Chapter05/cigar.
jpg"/></td></tr>
</table>
</body>
</html>
```

When you view the file's contents, the browser will display the page with the different color components, as shown in **FIGURE 5-32**.

Hands-On HTML

To view the HTML files or to experiment with the files presented in this chapter, visit this book's companion website at *http://www.websitedevelopmentbook.com /chapter05/TryIt.html*.

FIGURE 5-31 Viewing predefined HTML color names at the W3Schools website
Reproduced with permission of w3schools.com

FIGURE 5-32 Using predefined color names within HTML page components
Credit (from left): © Gts/Shutterstock; © Vaclav Volrab/Shutterstock

CHAPTER SUMMARY

Websites make extensive use of tables to present text, images, and products, and even to format the page content itself. To create a table within a webpage, developers use the **<table>** and **</table>** tag pair. Within the table definition, the developers use the **<tr>** and **</tr>** tag pair to define a row. Each row consists of one or more cells which developers specify using the **<td>** and **</td>** tag pair. In this chapter, you made extensive use of tables to format a variety of data. As you have learned, using style attributes, you can control whether or not a table has a border, the height and width of the table and its cells, as well as the alignment. You also learned how to create a nested table, which is a table within a table.

KEY TERMS

Cell padding

Cell spacing

Nested table

Rules

Table caption

Table header

CHAPTER REVIEW

1. Using HTML **<table>** tags, create the following tables:

2. Using the **<table>** tag **frame** and **rules** attributes, create the following tables:

3. Using the **<thead>**, **<tbody>**, and **<tfoot>** tag pairs, create a table similar to the following, which assigns a different background color to each table section:

4. Using column groups, create the following table, which highlights each column.

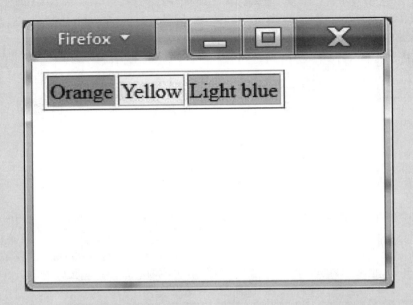

5. Create one or more HTML tables that illustrate the use of cell padding and spacing.

6. Using nested HTML tables, create the following table:

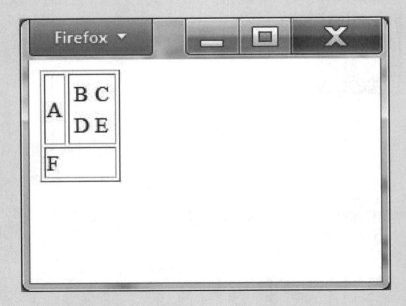

Getting User Input with Forms

ACROSS THE WEB, SITES make extensive use of forms to prompt users for information. One form might ask for a login username and password. Another form may prompt users for registration information or a credit card. Some may request search text.

Learning Objectives

This chapter examines the steps you must perform to create a form within an HTML page. By the time you finish this chapter, you will understand the following key concepts:

- How to use the **<form>** and **</form>** tag pair to create a simple form
- How to direct a form to submit data
- How to integrate content within an HTML form
- How to prompt a user for a password
- How to limit the number of characters that can be entered into a field
- How to use the **<textarea>** and **</textarea>** tag pair to prompt the user for large amounts of text within a form
- How to use the **<input>** tag to create radio buttons that simplify selection within a form
- How to use the **<input>** tag to create checkboxes to allow for selecting multiple options within a form
- How to create a pull-down list
- How to reset the contents of a form
- How to create a custom button

- How to use the **<label>** and **</label>** tag pair to label input fields
- How to direct a browser to e-mail the contents of a form
- How to use hidden fields
- How to allow a user to upload a file
- How to group related input fields within a form
- How to group related items within a pull-down list

Creating a Simple Form

To create a form within an HTML webpage, use the **<form>** and **</form>** tag pair. Within the tag pair, place labels and fields to provide input. The following HTML file, SimpleForm.html, creates a simple form that prompts the user for a name and e-mail address:

```
<!DOCTYPE html>
<html>
<body>
<form>
Name: <input type="text" name="username"/>
<br/><br/>
E-Mail: <input type="text" name="e-mail"/>
</form>
</body>
</html>
```

As you can see, the file uses standard text to prompt for the name and e-mail. Next to the text, the file uses **<input>** tags to get the user data. The file uses two line breaks between the input fields to improve the form's appearance.

When you view the file's contents, the browser will display the form's fields, as shown in **FIGURE 6-1**.

In this case, the user can enter data into the form, but that's all. The user then cannot submit the form's contents for processing. In fact, the form does not even contain a submit button.

Understanding the Form Submission Process

Normally, when a webpage displays a form, the form will contain a button the user will click to direct the browser to submit the form's contents to a remote

> Firefox ▼
>
> **Name:** [   ]
>
> **E-Mail:** [   ]

FIGURE 6–1 Using a form to prompt a webpage user for input

server. As shown in **FIGURE 6-2**, that server, in turn, processes the form's data. This often provides a new results page, which the browser displays. Such a results page is based on the processing the server performs. It might contain an order summary for an e-commerce purchase, search results in the case of a site such as Yahoo or Google, and so on.

Form processing is often called client/server processing because it requires both a client (a browser) and a remote server. As an HTML developer, use the <**form**> and </**form**> tag pair to create the client/server form. Then, you, or another developer, will use a scripting language, such as PHP, Perl, or Python, to write code for the Web server that processes the form's contents. A **script** is a set of programming instructions executed by a remote server to perform specific processing. This chapter focuses on HTML-based client-side development. The chapter presents a few simple scripts to copy onto your server.

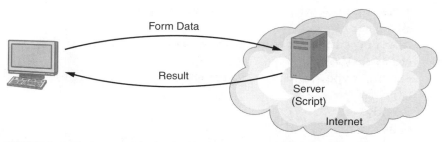

FIGURE 6–2 The browser submits the form's contents to a remote server, which, in turn, processes the data and optionally returns a results page.

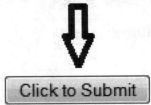

FIGURE 6-3 Customizing the text that appears within a form button

Directing a Form to Submit Data

Before a user can submit data to a remote server using an HTML form, the form must contain a button the user can click. To place a button within a form, use the **<input>** tag, as shown here:

```
<input type="submit" value="Click to Submit"/>
```

The **<input>** tag **type="submit"** attribute tells the browser to display a button. The **value** attribute specifies the text that appears within the button, as shown in **FIGURE 6-3**.

The following HTML file, NoButtonAction.html, uses the **<input>** tag to place a button within the previous form that prompts for a name and e-mail address:

```
<!DOCTYPE html>
<html>
<body>
<form>
Name: <input type="text" name="username"/>
<br/><br/>
E-Mail: <input type="text" name="e-mail"/>
<br/><br/>
<input type="submit" value="Click to Submit"/>
</form>
</body>
</html>
```

When viewing the file's contents, the browser displays the form, as shown in **FIGURE 6-4**.

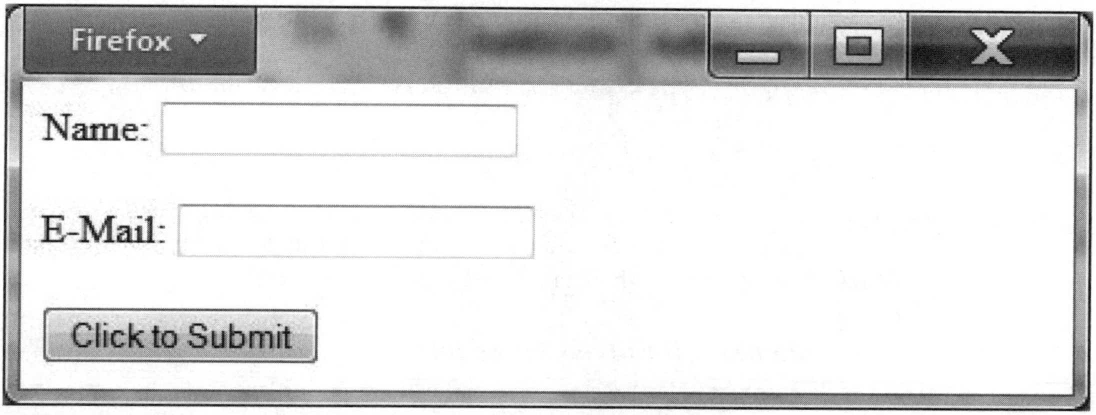

FIGURE 6-4 Displaying a button within an HTML form

If you test the NoButtonAction.html file, you will find that when you click the button, nothing happens. That's because you need to tell the form what you want it to do with the data when the button click occurs.

As discussed, when a user submits a form, the Web browser sends the form's data to a remote server for processing. The remote server, in turn, runs a script that processes the data. You can use a PHP script named FormEcho.php, which has been placed on this book's companion website at *http://www.websitedevelopmentbook. com/FormEcho.php*, to test your forms. The script simply echoes back messages that correspond to the data values it receives.

To use this script, you must modify the **<form>** tag to specify the **action** and **method** attributes, as shown here:

```
<form action="http://www.WebsiteDevelopmentBook.
com/FormEcho.php" method="post">
```

The **action** attribute specifies the script to which the browser submits the data. The **method** attribute tells the browser how to submit the data. For now, you will use "post."

The following HTML file, SubmitWithEcho.html, modifies the **<form>** tags to submit the data to a remote script:

```
<!DOCTYPE html>
<html>
<body>
<form action="http://www.WebsiteDevelopmentBook.
com/FormEcho.php" method="post">
Name: <input type="text" name="username"/>
<br/><br/>
```

```
E-Mail: <input type="text" name="e-mail"/>
<br/><br/>
<input type="submit" value="Click to Submit"/>
</form>
</body>
</html>
```

When you view the file's content and submit data, your browser displays results similar to that shown in **FIGURE 6-5**.

Examining the FormEcho.php Script

As discussed, the FormEcho.php script echoes, or displays back, the contents of the form that it receives. To create the script, use the following PHP statements:

```php
<?php
  $msg="Values submitted by the user:<br/>";
foreach($_POST as $key => $val){
    if (is_array($val)){
      $msg.="Item: $key<br>";
      foreach($val as $v){
        $v = stripslashes($v);
        $msg.=" $v<br>";
      }
```

FIGURE 6-5 Submitting a form's results to a remote script

```
    } else {
      $val = stripslashes($val);
      $msg.="$key: $val<br>";
    }
  }
  echo $msg;
?>
```

In this case, the script simply loops through the array of form data values using a **foreach** statement. If the data element is a list, the script displays the individual values.

Integrating Content Within an HTML Form

As you have learned, the HTML **<form>** and **</form>** tag pair defines the contents of a form. In general, you can place almost all other HTML tags between the tag pair to format your form's contents. The following HTML page, FavoriteFood.html, creates a form that includes graphics:

```
<!DOCTYPE html>
<html>
<body>
<form action="http://www.websitedevelopmentbook.com/FormEcho.php"
method="post">
<table>
<tr>
<td><img src="http://www.websitedevelopmentbook.com/chapter06/
Pasta.jpg" width="200" height="150"/></td>
<td><img src="http://www.websitedevelopmentbook.com/chapter06/
Pizza.jpg" width="200" height="150"/></td>
<td><img src="http://www.websitedevelopmentbook.com/chapter06/
Dessert.jpg" width="200" height="150"/></td>
</tr>
</table>
<br/>
What's Your Favorite Food: <input type="text" name="food"/>
</form>
</body>
</html>
```

When you view the file's contents, your browser will display the form field and graphics, as shown in **FIGURE 6-6**.

FIGURE 6-6 Integrating HTML content within a form
Credit (from left): © lorenzo_graph/Shutterstock; © Vima/Shutterstock; © Shebeko/Shutterstock

Prompting the User for a Password

Often, sites will use a form to prompt a user for a username and password. For security purposes, when the user types in his or her password, the password text should not appear on screen. Instead, most sites display an asterisk (*) for each character typed.

To prompt a user to enter a password, your form should use the **<input>** tag with the **type="password"** attribute:

```
Password: <input type="password"
name="userPassword"/>
```

The following HTML file, Login.html, uses a form to prompt the user for a username and password:

```
<!DOCTYPE html>
<html>
<body>
<form action="http://www.WebsiteDevelopmentBook.
com/FormEcho.php" method="post">
Username: <input type="text" name="username"/>
Password: <input type="password"
name="userPassword"/>
```

FIGURE 6-7 Using an input field to prompt the user for a password

```
</form>
</body>
</html>
```

As you can see, the username field uses an **<input>** tag with the **type="text"** attribute, whereas the **password field** (a field that displays a replacement character for each character in the password) uses **type="password."** When you view the file's contents, the browser displays the text entered for the username and asterisks for the password text, as shown in **FIGURE 6-7**.

Limiting the Number of Characters Entered

When you use a form to prompt a user for data, many times you will need to control the number of characters typed for each field. For example, if a form prompts a user for a username, it's probably unlikely that the username, even if it's a long e-mail address, needs more than 30 characters. To specify a field's character length, use the **<input>** tag **maxlength** attribute:

```
<input type="text" maxlength="30" name="username"/>
```

When you limit the number of characters for a field, you may want to specify the field's width that appears within the form. To do so, use the **size** attribute:

```
<input type="text" maxlength="30" size="30"
name="username"/>
```

The following HTML file, MaxLengthDemo.html, prompts the user for three fields: 5, 10, and 20 characters long:

```
<!DOCTYPE html>
<html>
<body>
```

FIGURE 6-8 Specifying the size of text fields within a form

```
<form action="http://www.WebsiteDevelopmentBook.
com/FormEcho.php" method="post">
Five: <input type="text" maxlength="5" size="5"/>
Ten: <input type="text" maxlength="10" size="10"/>
Twenty: <input type="text" maxlength="20"
size="20"/>
</form>
</body>
</html>
```

When you view the file's contents, the browser displays the contents shown in **FIGURE 6-8**.

Prompting the User for a Large Amount of Text

Using the <**input**> tag **type="text"** attribute, you can prompt the user for a single line of text. Many sites, however, use a form to prompt the user to enter a large amount of text, such as comments, a message, or even a multi-page résumé. For such cases, the form will use the <**textarea**> and <**/textarea**> tag pair, which allows for entering multiple lines of text. To specify the number of lines the box should consume on the form, use the **rows** attribute. To specify the box width, use the **cols** attribute.

The following HTML file, TextArea.html, creates a form that prompts the user to enter a comment:

```
<!DOCTYPE html>
<html>
<body>
<form action="http://www.WebsiteDevelopmentBook.
com/FormEcho.php" method="post">
Text Area: <textarea rows="10" cols="50">
</textarea>
```

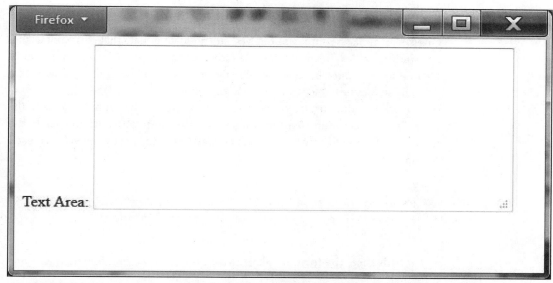

FIGURE 6-9 Using a text area to prompt a user for multiple lines of text

```
</form>
</body>
</html>
```

The form defines a box 10 lines by 50 characters wide. When you view the file's contents, the browser displays them, as shown in **FIGURE 6-9**.

If a user types more characters than the text area can store, the text will scroll within the box, allowing more input. A **text area** is the user-input control within which a user can type a large amount of text. Unlike a **textbox**, which has a fixed length, a text area supports an unlimited number of characters.

There may be times when you will want to specify the default text for a text area. To specify default text, simply place it between the **<textarea>** and **</textarea>** tags, as shown here:

```
<textarea>Default text here</textarea>
```

Limiting the Number of Characters Within a Text Area

By default, a text area can hold an unlimited number of characters. The **<textarea>** tag does not have a **maxlength** attribute. Instead, if you want to limit the number of characters, use **JavaScript**. Chapter 10, "JavaScript," examines JavaScript processing in detail.

Placing a Radio Button Within a Form

Often, a form may prompt you for "yes" or "no" data or data that corresponds to a few specific values. In such cases, use radio buttons to get the user input. **Radio buttons** are so named because, like the station buttons on the front of a radio, you can only select one choice from a group of options at a time.

To create radio buttons within an HTML form, use the **<input>** tag with the **type="radio"** attribute. Within the tag, use the **name** attribute to specify the name of a group of buttons and the **value** attribute to specify the value of each unique button:

```
Gender:
Male <input type="radio" name="gender" value="male"/>
Female <input type="radio" name="gender"
value="female"/>
```

In this case, the form displays two radio buttons, one for male and one for female.

The following HTML file, RadioButtonDemo.html, creates two sets of radio buttons—one for gender and one for PC type:

```
<!DOCTYPE html>
<html>
<body>
<form action="http://www.WebsiteDevelopmentBook.
com/FormEcho.php" method="post">
Gender:
Male <input type="radio" name="gender"
value="male"/>
Female <input type="radio" name="gender"
value="female"/>
<br/>
<br/>
PC Type:
Windows <input type="radio" name="PC"
value="Windows"/>
Mac <input type="radio" name="PC" value="Mac"/>
<br/>
<br/>
<input type="submit" value="Click to Submit"/>
</form>
</body>
</html>
```

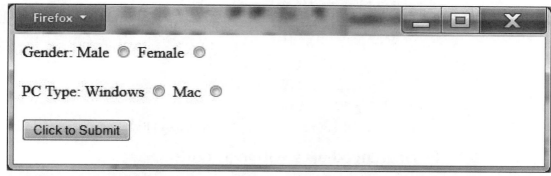

FIGURE 6-10 Displaying radio button sets within a form

The form creates two sets of radio buttons—one named gender and one named PC. The form also creates a button the user can click to submit the form's data.

When you view the file's contents, your browser will display the contents shown in **FIGURE 6-10**.

If you submit the form's contents to the remote server, the script will display output similar to that shown in **FIGURE 6-11** for the radio buttons.

Selecting a Default Radio Button

Depending on the contents your form displays, there may be times when you will want to specify default values for a group of radio buttons; that is, to specify the button that is selected by default. To do so, you must place the

FIGURE 6-11 How a remote script views radio buttons

checked attribute within the **<input>** tag for the radio button you want to select:

```
Male <input type="radio" name="gender"
value="male" checked/>
Female <input type="radio" name="gender"
value="female"/>
```

In this case, the browser will preselect the male radio button.

Placing Checkboxes Within a Form

Radio buttons exist to let a user select one value from a group of values. Often, however, a form may need to prompt users for multiple values, such as the items they want included on a pizza or a list of news topics of interest. In such cases, the form should use checkboxes.

To create a **checkbox,** a small square on a computer screen that you click on with your mouse to choose a feature, use the **<input>** tag **type="checkbox"** attribute. The following HTML file, CheckboxDemo.html, prompts the user for the pizza toppings he or she desires:

```
<!DOCTYPE html>
<html>
<body>
<form action="http://www.WebsiteDevelopmentBook.
com/FormEcho.php" method="post">
Desired Pizza Toppings:
Cheese <input type="checkbox" name="cheese"/><br/>
Pepperoni <input type="checkbox"
name="pepperoni"/><br/>
Bacon <input type="checkbox" name="bacon"/><br/>
Pineapple <input type="checkbox"
name="pineapple"/><br/>
<br/>
<br/>
<input type="submit" value="Click to Submit"/>
</form>
</body>
</html>
```

As you can see, the form uses **<input>** tags with the **checkbox** attribute. Each **<input>** tag has a unique value to specify the corresponding option.

When you view the file's contents, the browser displays the checkboxes shown in **FIGURE 6-12**.

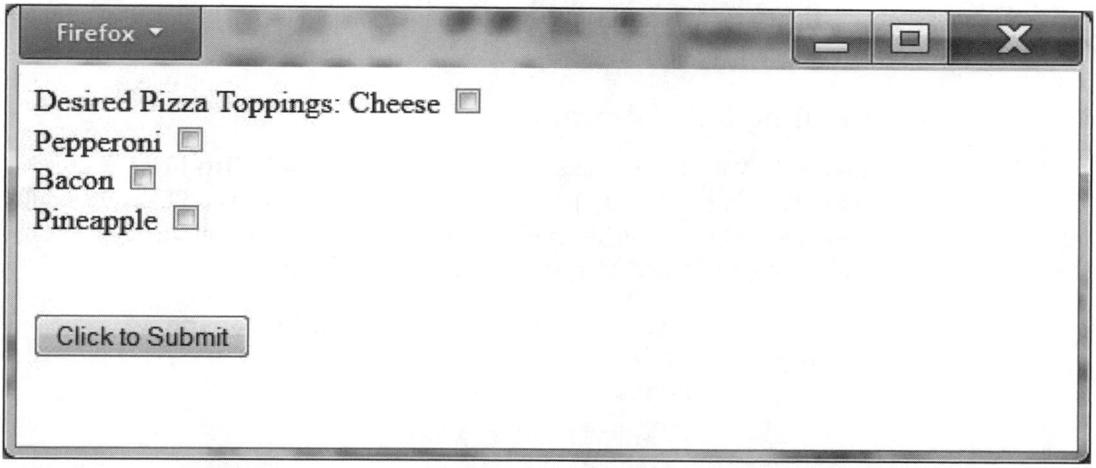

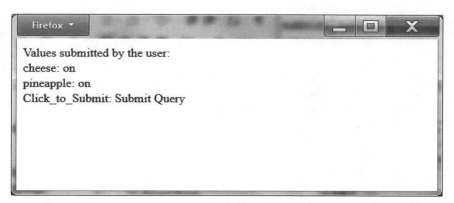

FIGURE 6-12 Using checkboxes within a form to prompt the user to select multiple options

If you submit the form's contents to the remote script, your screen will display output similar to that shown in **FIGURE 6-13** for each checkbox that is selected.

Preselecting Checkbox Fields

Again, depending on the data for which a form prompts the user, there may be times when you will want to preselect checkbox entries. In such cases, use the **<input>** tag **checked** attribute:

```
Cheese <input type="checkbox" name="cheese"
checked/><br/>
```

FIGURE 6-13 How a remote script views checkboxes

Unlike radio buttons where only one button can be selected, you can prese-lect any number of checkboxes.

Creating a Pull-Down List

Across the Web, forms make extensive use of **pull-down lists** to allow users to select data from a list of options, such as a state of residence. To create a pull-down list within a form, use the <**select**> and </**select**> tag pair to define the list and the <**option**> and </**option**> tag pair to define entries within the list:

```
Dinner Choice: <select name="DinnerChoice">
<option>Pizza</option>
<option>Pasta</option>
<option>Burgers</option>
</select>
```

In this case, the list contains three entries.

The following HTML file, PullDownListDemo.html, creates a form with two pull-down lists—one that prompts the user for a salutation and one that prompts the user for a favorite sport:

```
<!DOCTYPE html>
<html>
<body>
<form action="http://www.WebsiteDevelopmentBook.
com/FormEcho.php" method="post">
Salutation: <select name="salutation">
<option>Dr</option>
<option>Mr</option>
<option>Mrs</option>
<option>Miss</option>
<option>Ms</option>
</select>
<br/><br/>
Favorite Sport: <select name="sport">
<option>Baseball</option>
<option>Basketball</option>
<option>Football</option>
<option>Hockey</option>
<option>Soccer</option>
</select>
<br/><br/>
```

FIGURE 6-14 Displaying pull-down lists within a browser

```
<input type="submit" value="Click to Submit"/>
</form>
</body>
</html>
```

As you can see, the file uses two **<select>** and **</select>** tag pairs to create the two pull-down lists. Within each tag pair, the file uses the **<option>** and **</option>** tag pair to define a list item.

When you view the file's contents, the browser displays the pull-down lists shown in **FIGURE 6-14**. As you select a list, the browser opens the list to display its contents.

If you make some selections and then submit the form to a remote script, your screen displays output similar to that shown in **FIGURE 6-15**.

FIGURE 6-15 How a remote script views a pull-down list

FIGURE 6-16 Displaying multiple rows within a pull-down list

Controlling the Pull-Down List Size

By default, when you create a pull-down list, the browser will display only one row of data. If you want the browser to display more rows, you specify the <**select**> tag **size** attribute:

```
Salutation: <select name="salutation" size= "5">
```

In this case, the browser would display five rows within the list, as shown in **FIGURE 6-16**.

Selecting Multiple List Elements

Depending on your list's purpose, there may be times when you want to let the user select multiple choices. In such cases, use the <**select**> tag **multiple** attribute. The following HTML file uses a pull-down list within which the user can select multiple favorite sports:

```
Favorite Sport: <select name="sport[]" multiple>
<option>Baseball</option>
<option>Basketball</option>
<option>Football</option>
<option>Hockey</option>
<option>Soccer</option>
</select>
```

Note that this file includes brackets following the sport name, sport[], to tell the remote script that the value is an array. When you view the file's contents, the browser lets you select multiple sports from the list. If you submit the form's contents with selections made to the remote script, your screen displays output similar to that shown in **FIGURE 6-17**.

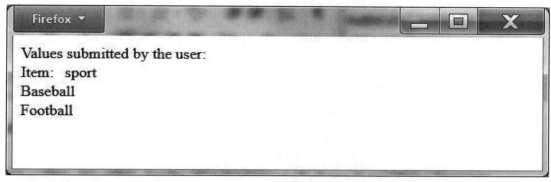

FIGURE 6-17 How a remote script views multiple values within a pull-down list

Resetting a Form's Contents

As users complete the fields within a form, sometimes they may want to start over, quickly deleting the contents entered. To assist the user in resetting the form contents, place a reset button on the form. Be careful where you add such a button. If users errantly click the button and the form resets, they will not be happy.

To create a reset button, use the **<input>** tag **type="reset"** attribute. The following HTML file, ResetDemo.html, provides a Reset button to reset a form's contents:

```
<!DOCTYPE html>
<html>
<body>
<form action="http://www.WebsiteDevelopmentBook.
com/FormEcho.php" method="post">
Name: <input type="text" name="name"/><br/>
Phone: <input type="text" name="phone"/><br/>
Programming Languages:
C <input type="checkbox" name="C"/><br/>
Java <input type="checkbox" name="Java"/><br/>
VB <input type="checkbox" name="VB"/><br/>
<br/><br/>
<input type="submit" value="Click to
Submit"/><input type="reset" value="Reset"/>
</form>
</body>
</html>
```

Experiment with the HTML file by typing text and selecting options and then clicking Reset.

Creating a Custom Button

As you have learned, using the **<input>** tag **type="submit"** attribute, you can create a button that contains specific text. Depending on your form's design, there may be times when you will want to format the button's text or even use an image for the button. In such cases, you can use the **<button>** and **</button>** tag pair:

```
<button type="submit"><b>Click Here</b></button>
```

The following HTML file, CustomButton.html, uses the **<button>** and **</button>** tag pair to use an image as a button:

```
<!DOCTYPE html>
<html>
<body>
<form action="http://www.WebsiteDevelopmentBook.
com/FormEcho.php" method="post">
<button type="submit">
<img src="http://www.WebsiteDevelopmentBook.com/
Chapter06/click.jpg" height="100" width="100"/>
</button>
</form>
</body>
</html>
```

When you view this file's contents, the browser displays the screen shown in **FIGURE 6-18**.

In addition to using the **<button>** and **</button>** tag pair, you also can display an image button using the **<input>** tag **type="image"** attribute.

Labeling Input Fields

Within a form, you will normally display a field name, which developers often call "field labels," next to the fields:

```
Name: <input type= "text" name="Username"/>
```

To simplify the labeling process, use the **<label>** and **</label>** tag pair to specify an input element's label. The **id** attribute specifies its element's unique identifier (ID).

```
<label for="firstname">First name: </label>
<input type="text" id="firstname"><br/>
```

Within the text you specify for the label, use HTML tags for formatting.

FIGURE 6-18 Using the **<button>** and **</button>** tag pair to use an image as a button
Credit: © Michael D Brown/Shutterstock

The following HTML file, LabelDemo.html, illustrates the use of the **<label>** and **</label>** tag pair:

```
<!DOCTYPE html>
<html>
<body>
<form action="http://www.WebsiteDevelopmentBook.
com/FormEcho.php" method="post">
<label for="firstname"><b>First name:</b></label>
<input type="text" id="firstname"><br/>
<label for="lastname"><b>Last name: </b></label>
<input type="text" id="lastname"><br/>
<label for="email"><i>email:</i></label>
<input type="text" id="email"><br/>
<br/><br/>
<input type="submit" value="Click to Submit"/>
</form>
</body>
</html>
```

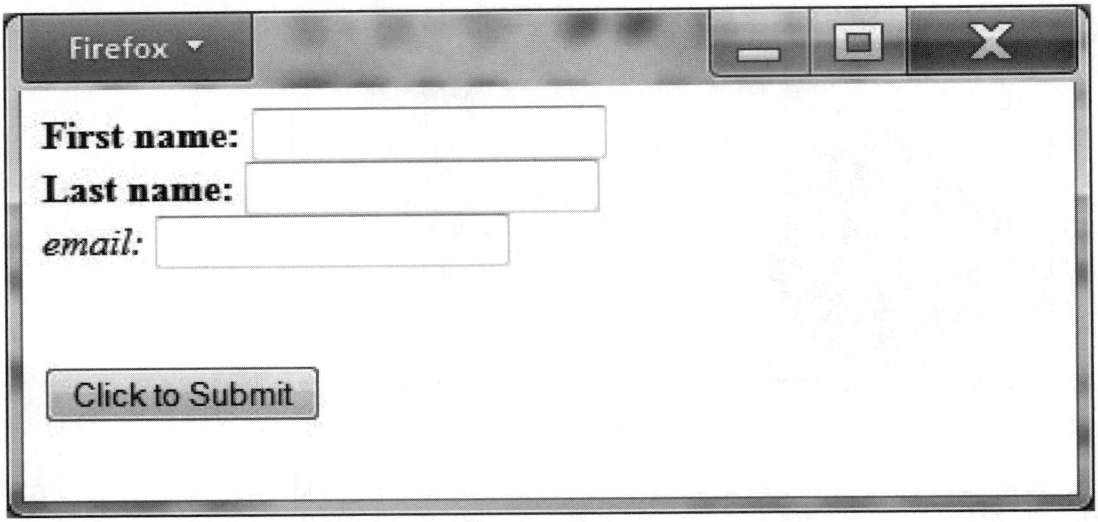

FIGURE 6-19 Assigning labels to input fields

In this case, the file uses **bold** and *italic* attributes within the label text. When you display the file's contents, the screen displays output similar to that shown in **FIGURE 6-19**.

E-mailing a Form's Contents

You have learned that when a user submits a form's contents by clicking on a submit button, the browser normally sends the contents to a remote server for processing. If you don't have a server available, you instead can direct the browser to e-mail the form's data to you. To do so, you specify **mailto:** within the form's **action** attribute along with the desired e-mail address:

```
<form action="mailto:SomeUser@SomeSite.com"
method="post">
```

The following HTML file, MailtoDemo.html, directs the browser to e-mail the form's data to SomeUser@SomeSite.com. Replace that e-mail address with your own:

```
<!DOCTYPE html>
<html>
<body>
<form action="mailto:SomeUser@SomeSite.com"
method="post">
```

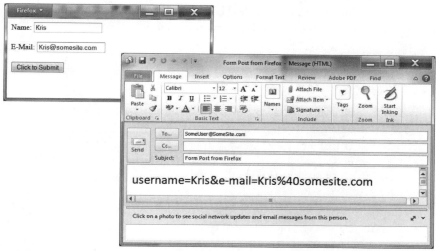

FIGURE 6-20 E-mailing a form's contents using the mailto action
Used with permission from Microsoft

```
Name: <input type="text" name="username"/>
<br/><br/>
E-Mail: <input type="text" name="e-mail"/>
<br/><br/>
<input type="submit" value="Click to Submit"/>
</form>
</body>
</html>
```

If you submit the form's contents, you should receive an e-mail with content similar to that shown in **FIGURE 6-20**.

Using Hidden Fields

When you create a form, there may be times when you want to submit data to a remote server with the form's data that was not entered by the user. Developers refer to such fields as hidden fields.

Assume, for example, that you are submitting a similar form to the same remote script from different webpages and that you want to easily track from which page the user submitted the data. In this case, you can include a hidden field within the data. To hide a field, use the **<input>** tag **hidden** attribute:

```
<input type="hidden" name="SomeField" value="55"/>
```

The following HTML file, HiddenField.html, uses two hidden fields—one to specify the server and one to specify a version number:

```
<!DOCTYPE html>
<html>
<body>
<form action="http://www.WebsiteDevelopmentBook.
com/FormEcho.php" method="post">
Name: <input type="text" name="username"/>
<br/><br/>
<E-Mail: <input type="text" name="e-mail"/>
<br/><br/>
<input type="hidden" name="someField" value="1.2"/>
<input type="submit" value="Click to Submit"/>
</form>
</body>
</html>
```

If you submit this page to the remote script, your screen will display output similar to that shown in **FIGURE 6–21**.

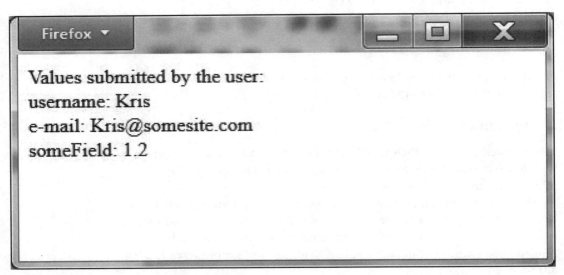

FIGURE 6–21 How a remote script views hidden fields

Allowing a User to Upload a File

Depending on your form's purpose, there may be times when you need a user to upload a file, such as a photo or resume. To do so, use the **<input>** tag **type="file"** attribute:

```
<input type="file" name="file" id="file"/>
```

In this case, the **<input>** tag will specify an **id** attribute that the remote script will use. The following HTML file, FileUpload.html, allows the user to upload a photo:

```
<!DOCTYPE html>
<html>
<body>
<form action="http://www.WebsiteDevelopmentBook.
com/Chapter06/FileUploader.php" enctype="multipart/
form-data" method="post">
File: <input type="file" name="file" id="file"/>
<input type="submit" value="Submit"/>
</form>
</body>
</html>
```

When you view the file's contents, the browser will display a screen similar to that shown in **FIGURE 6-22**.

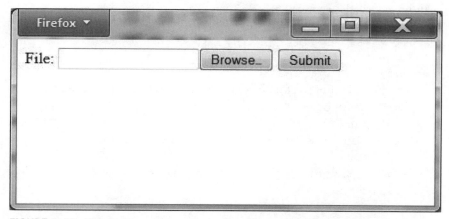

FIGURE 6-22 Allowing the user to upload a file within an HTML form

If you click the Browse button, your browser will display a dialog box where you can select the file that you want to upload.

To process a file upload requires special processing by the remote script. The following script uploads a file to the remote server and then displays the location where the file is stored:

```php
<?php
if ($_FILES["file"]["error"] > 0)
  {
  echo "Error:" . $_FILES["file"]["error"].
  "<br/>";
  }
  else
  {
  echo "Upload:" . $_FILES["file"]["name"].
"successful<br/>";
  echo "Stored in:" . $_FILES["file"]["tmp_name"];
  }
?>
```

Grouping Related Input Fields Within a Form

To improve the appearance and organization of your forms, there may be times when you will want to group related items within the form, as shown in **FIGURE 6-23**.

To group related fields, you place the field tags within the **<fieldset>** and **</fieldset>** tag pair. The following HTML file, FieldSetDemo.html, groups the fields previously shown in **FIGURE 6-23**:

```html
<!DOCTYPE html>
<html>
<body>
<form action="http://www.WebsiteDevelopmentBook.
com/FormEcho.php" method="post">
<fieldset>
Name: <input type="text" name="username"/>
<br/><br/>
E-Mail: <input type="text" name="e-mail"/>
</fieldset>
<fieldset>
Salutation: <select name="salutation">
```

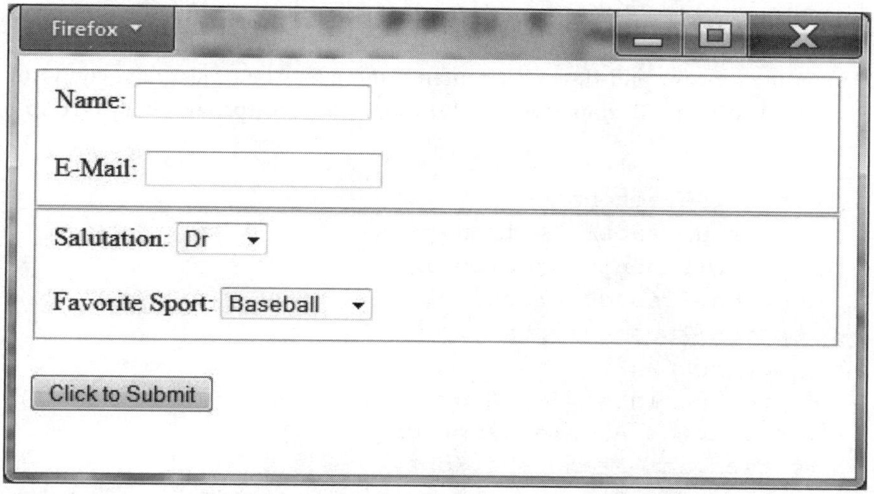

FIGURE 6-23 Grouping fields within a form

```
<option>Dr</option>
<option>Mr</option>
<option>Mrs</option>
<option>Miss</option>
<option>Ms</option>
</select>
<br/><br/>
Favorite Sport: <select name="sport">
<option>Baseball</option>
<option>Basketball</option>
<option>Football</option>
<option>Hockey</option>
<option>Soccer</option>
</select>
</fieldset>
<br/>
<input type="submit" value="Click to Submit"/>
</form>
</body>
</html>
```

As you can see, the file uses two **<fieldset>** and **</fieldset>** tag pairs to create the two groupings.

Grouping Related Items Within a Pull-Down List

Depending on your pull-down list contents, there may be times when you want to group list items. To do so, you will use the **<optgroup>** and **</optgroup>** tag pair:

```
City: <select name="cities">
<optgroup label="Arizona">
<option>Phoenix</option>
<option>Prescott</option>
<option>Tucson</option>
</optgroup>
<optgroup label="California">
<option>Los Angeles</option>
<option>San Francisco</option>
<option>San Diego</option>
</optgroup>
</select>
```

In this case, the browser will display the list's contents within groups, as shown in **FIGURE 6-24**.

The following HTML file, OptGroupDemo.html, groups different wines:

```
<!DOCTYPE html>
<html>
<body>
<form action="http://www.WebsiteDevelopmentBook.
com/FormEcho.php" method="post">
```

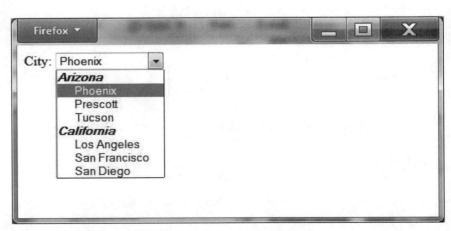

FIGURE 6-24 Grouping related items within a pull-down list

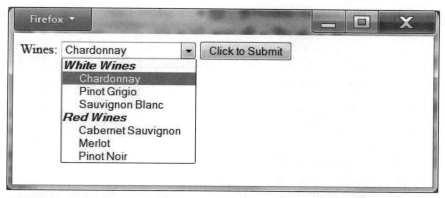

FIGURE 6-25 Grouping list items using the **<optgroup>** and **</optgroup>** tag pair

```
Wines: <select name="wine">
<optgroup label="White Wines">
<option>Chardonnay</option>
<option>Pinot Grigio</option>
<option>Sauvignon Blanc</option>
</optgroup>
<optgroup label="Red Wines">
<option>Cabernet Sauvignon</option>
<option>Merlot</option>
<option>Pinot Noir</option>
</optgroup>
</select>
<input type="submit" value="Click to Submit"/>
</form>
</body>
</html>
```

When you view the file's contents, the browser will display the grouped-list items, as shown in **FIGURE 6-25**.

Real-World Web Design

When a user submits a form, the browser sends the form's contents to a remote server. Within the remote server, the script processes the form's data. If the form is missing a field's value, meaning the user did not submit a value for a field, the script can display an error message and redisplay the form. However, using the script to test for missing fields is time-consuming because of the network traffic required to send the form contents to the server and the network messages required to display the error message.

A better solution is to use JavaScript to validate the form's user input. Because the browser processes JavaScript, you eliminate the network traffic. Chapter 10 provides examples of JavaScript form processing in detail. For now, the following HTML file, Validate.html, uses JavaScript to ensure that the user has provided a name, phone number, and e-mail address:

```html
<!DOCTYPE html>
<head>
<script>
function validateForm()
{
  if (document.forms["myForm"]["name"].value==null ||
  document.forms["myForm"]["name"].value=="")
  {
    alert("Name must be filled out");
    return false;
  }
  if (document.forms["myForm"]["phone"].value==null
  || document.forms["myForm"]["phone"].value=="")
  {
    alert("Phone must be filled out");
    return false;
  }
  if (document.forms["myForm"]["email"].value==null
  || document.forms["myForm"]["email"].value=="")
  {
    alert("Email must be filled out");
    return false;
  }
return true;
}
</script>
</head>
<html>
<body>
<form name="myForm" action="http://www.Website
DevelopmentBook.com/FormEcho.php" method="post"
onsubmit="return validateForm()">
Name: <input type="text" name="name"/><br/>
Phone: <input type="text" name="phone"/><br/>
E-mail: <input type="text" name="e-mail"/><br/>
```

```
<input type="submit" value="Click to Submit"/>
</form>
</body>
</html>
```

In this case, the JavaScript does simple testing to confirm only that the user has provided a value for each field. If the user fails to input a field's value, the JavaScript displays popup messages telling the user that he or she must enter a value for the corresponding field.

As your skills with JavaScript increase, you can use it to ensure not only that the user has provided values for each field, but also that the value he or she enters for a phone number has the correct number of digits and that the e-mail address entered is in the form *name@somesite.com*.

Hands-On HTML

To view the HTML files or to experiment with the files presented in this chapter, visit this book's companion website at *http://www.websitedevelopmentbook.com/ Chapter06/TryIt.html*.

CHAPTER SUMMARY

Depending on the processing a webpage performs, it is common for the page to require user input of some type. To perform such input operations, HTML pages use forms. Across the Web, sites use forms to prompt the user for login credentials, to request registration data, to get credit card and shipping information, and much more. In this chapter, you learned how to use the **<form>** and **</form>** tag pair to define a form and the **<input>** tag to create the most common form input fields. To perform form processing normally requires that one developer use HTML tags to create the form and that a second developer create scripts, using PHP or another scripting language, which process the data on the remote server. This chapter focused on the HTML form development process. In Chapter 7, "Styling Content with Cascading Style Sheets," you will learn how to use inline, embedded, and external CSS style definitions to format the appearance of elements on your page.

KEY TERMS

Checkbox

JavaScript

Password field

Pull-down list

Radio buttons

Script

Text area

Textbox

CHAPTER REVIEW

1. Create an HTML file that uses a form to prompt a user for his or her name, age, and favorite website. The form should submit its contents to *http://www.websitedevelopmentbook.com /FormEcho.php*.

2. Modify the HTML file you created in Question 1 to group the field elements using the **<fieldset>** and **</fieldset>** tag pair.

3. Modify the HTML file that you created in Question 1 to mail the form results to your e-mail address.

4. Create an HTML form that uses radio buttons to prompt the user for his or her favorite type of pet: dog, cat, fish, or horse. The form should submit its contents to *http://www. websitedevelopmentbook.com/FormEcho.php*.

5. Create an HTML form that prompts a user for his or her name and then lets the user paste his or her résumé into a text area. The form should submit its contents to *http://www. websitedevelopmentbook.com/FormEcho.php*.

6. Create a form that prompts a user for his or her favorite sport using a pull-down list. The list should include at least 10 sports. The form should submit its contents to *http://www. websitedevelopmentbook.com/FormEcho.php*.

Styling Content with Cascading Style Sheets

USING HTML, DEVELOPERS LAY out content within a webpage, specifying headers, paragraphs, tables, images, and more. For years, developers would say that HTML "formats a webpage." It's preferable to say that HTML specifies the webpage elements and layout, and cascading style sheet attributes specify the actual formatting. This chapter takes a detailed look at cascading style sheets, or CSS. In Chapter 8, you will continue to drill down into additional formatting capabilities. That said, you have actually been using CSS attributes throughout this book's first six chapters! You have used attributes to specify background colors, text alignment, image appearance, and more.

Learning Objectives

This chapter examines how to use cascading style sheets to format webpages. By the time you finish this chapter, you will understand the following key concepts:

- How to use the **style** attribute within an HTML tag to apply an inline style
- How to use the **<style>** and **</style>** tag pair to define embedded style definitions
- How to create an external style sheet file and use the **<link>** tag to include it within an HTML file
- Why the word "cascading" is used in the term "cascading style sheets"

Applying Inline Styles

Throughout this book, you have made use of tag attributes to control an element's appearance. For example, the following <h1> tag uses the **color** property (as defined below) to display header text in red:

```
<h1 style="color:red">This text is red
```

A **style** is a collection of formatting attributes applied to an HTML tag. Using a style for text, a developer may specify a font family, font size, text color, text alignment, and so on. Developers refer to attribute settings that appear within an HTML tag as **inline styles**. To specify inline styles, place the **style** attribute within an HTML tag, and within the **style** attribute, assign values to the desired formatting properties. With a simple HTML page, using inline styles is fine. As you will learn, as the number of pages in your website increases, the use of inline styles often leads to redundancy of effort and pages that are hard to modify.

Revisiting Inline Styles

Applying inline styles is easy. The only challenge is in knowing which **style** attributes exist. To help you get started, the W3Schools HTML tutorial website provides a complete list of CSS properties at *http://www.w3schools.com/cssref/default.asp.*

The sections that follow will help you better understand formatting performed by assigning property values to element attributes. A **property** is an attribute value within a style definition, such as **background-color** or **font-family**, to which a developer can assign a specific value.

Getting a feel for the various attributes is important because, later in this chapter, you will use the same attributes to create embedded styles as well as external CSS files. Developers use **embedded styles** to apply formatting to an entire HTML page. Developers use **external styles** to apply formatting to an entire website.

Applying Inline Styles to the <body> Tag

As you have learned, the <**body**> and </**body**> tag pair groups your entire page's HTML tags. Using inline CSS styles within the <**body**> tag, you can assign a color or image to the page background. You also can specify default settings for fonts, font colors, and so on, which the browser uses throughout the page as it displays the content.

The following HTML file, YellowBody.html, uses the **background-color** property to set the page background to yellow:

```
<!DOCTYPE html>
<html>
<body style="background-color:yellow">
```

```
<h1>Yellow Background</h1>
<hr/>
</body>
</html>
```

As you can see, to specify the inline style, you specify the **style** attribute within the tag followed by the specific property settings within quotes.

In a similar way, the following HTML file, BodyBackgroundImage.html, uses the **background-image** property to direct that the browser repeat a photo to fill the page background:

```
<!DOCTYPE html>
<html>
<body style="background-image:
url('http://www.websitedevelopmentbook.com/
chapter07/puppy.jpg')">
</body>
</html>
```

When you view the file's contents, your browser will display the contents shown in **FIGURE 7-1**.

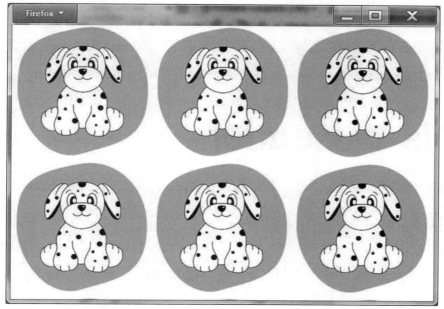

FIGURE 7-1 Using an inline CSS style to specify a page background image
Credit: © sbego/Shutterstock

When you apply CSS property settings to an HTML tag that encloses other tags, the styles you select also apply to the internal tags. For example, the following HTML file, BodyFont.html, uses CSS inline styles to select the Comic Sans MS font for the <**body**> tag. Because the <**body**> tag encloses the other tags within your file, the font becomes the default for text within nested tags:

```
<!DOCTYPE html>
<html>
<body style="font-family:'Comic Sans MS'">
<h1>This is a Header</h1>
<hr/>
<p>This is sample paragraph text!</p>
</body>
</html>
```

When you view the file's contents, the browser displays the contents shown in FIGURE 7–2.

Again, by applying the **font-family** property to the <**body**> tag, you can set the default font for all elements. Those elements, in turn, can override the font

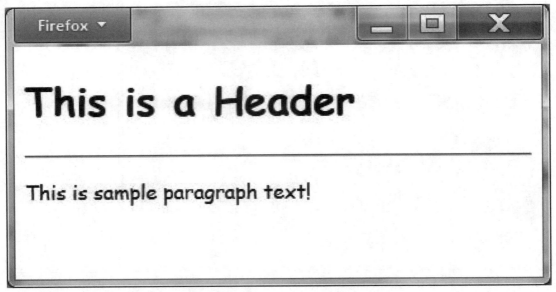

FIGURE 7–2 Using the **font-family** style attribute to specify the default font

setting by also using the **font-family** property within an inline style. For example, the following HTML file, FontOverride.html, sets the default font for the page within the **<body>** tag and then later, a paragraph tag uses an inline style to override the font setting for its text content:

```
<!DOCTYPE html>
<html>
<body style="font-family:'Comic Sans MS'">
<h1>This is a Header</h1>
<hr/>
<p style="font-family:Arial">This is sample
paragraph text!</p>
</body>
</html>
```

As you examine HTML tags, you should note the various CSS properties they support. Again, the W3Schools reference is a great resource.

The following HTML file, ImageStack.html, uses inline styles to specify the x, y, and z coordinates to position images on a page:

```
<!DOCTYPE html>
<html>
<body>
<img src="http://www.websitedevelopmentbook.com/
Chapter07/cigar.jpg" style="position:absolute;
left:400px; top:300px; z-index:1;" />
<img src="http://www.websitedevelopmentbook.com/
Chapter07/wine.jpg" style="position:absolute;
z-index:0;" />
<img src="http://www.websitedevelopmentbook.com/
Chapter07/pizza.jpg" style="position:absolute;
left:500px; top:0px; z-index:2;" />
</body>
</html>
```

As you can see, each image specifies **absolute** positioning and then specifies a left-edge position, top-edge position, and a z-index. Using the z-index value, the page stacks images on top of one another. When you view the file's contents, your browser will display the contents shown in **FIGURE 7-3**.

As you work with inline styles to format your page, you may find that you begin to repeat the same style definitions throughout the file. For example, the following HTML file, RepeatStyles.html, has three headings, three paragraphs,

FIGURE 7-3 Using CSS styles to specify image coordinates

Credit (clockwise from upper left): © bitt24/Shutterstock; © Vima/Shutterstock; © marco mayer/Shutterstock

and three images. The file applies the same styles to each element, meaning each **<h1>** tag uses the same attributes, each **<p>** tag uses the same attributes, and each **<img>** tag uses the same attributes:

```
<!DOCTYPE html>
<html>
<body>
<h1 style="color:red; font-family:arial;">Dogs</h1>
<p style="color:blue; font-decoration:italic;
text-align:left;">Dogs are great!</p>
<img style="border:0;" src="http://www.
websitedevelopmentbook.com/chapter07/dogs.jpg"/>
<h1 style="color:red; font-family:arial;">Cats</h1>
<p style="color:blue; font-decoration:italic;
```

```
text-align:left;">Cats are great!</p>
<img style="border:0;" src="http://www.
websitedevelopmentbook.com/chapter07/cats.jpg"/>
<h1 style="color:red; font-family:arial;">Horses</h1>
<p style="color:blue; font-decoration:italic;
text-align:left;">Horses are great!</p>
<img style="border:0;" src="http://www.
websitedevelopmentbook.com/chapter07/horses.jpg"/>
</body>
</html>
```

When you view the file's contents, your browser will display the content shown in **FIGURE 7-4**.

As you may start to guess, if your website has multiple pages of similar content, repeating the style definitions for each tag is time-consuming at best. Worse yet, if you decide to change an element's look and feel on your page, it requires changing every style definition throughout your files, which not only takes time, but is prone to errors.

When you need to apply the same format to each occurrence of an HTML tag throughout a page, embedded CSS styles provide the solution.

Defining Embedded Style Definitions

An inline style is so named because it appears "inline" within an HTML tag. The inline style applies only to the tag within which it appears. In contrast, an embedded style, which you will define using the **<style>** and **</style>** tag pair, will, by default, apply to all occurrences of a tag.

To define an embedded style, you place the **<style>** and **</style>** tag pair inside the **<head>** and **</head>** tag pair at the top of your file. Within the **<style>** and **</style>** tags, you will define your tag properties:

```
<head>
<html>
<style type="text/css">
/* Style Attributes Here */
</style>
</head>
```

To define styles for a specific HTML tag, specify the tag selector, which is the letter or letters that appear between the left and right brackets, followed by left and right braces that contain the property settings you desire. The following style

FIGURE 7-4 Repeating CSS property values throughout an HTML file

Credit (from top): © Marina Jay/Shutterstock; © Oksana Kuzmina/Shutterstock; © mariait/ Shutterstock

definition, for example, directs the browser to set the text color for the **<h1>** tag to blue:

```
<head>
<style type="text/css">
h1 { color:blue; }
</style>
</head>
<body>
```

Within the **<style>** tag, use the **type** attribute to tell the browser that you are specifying text values for CSS styles. As you can see, to specify a tag, you do not include the brackets, which normally enclose the tag name. Instead, you just specify, in this case, **h1** for the **<h1>** tag. Developers refer to the tag name without the brackets as a *selector*. You place the desired style property value within left and right curly braces.

Often, when assigning attributes to a tag selector, you specify values for multiple properties. To do so, separate the property settings with a semicolon, as shown here:

```
h1 { color:red; font-decoration:italic;
text-align:left; }
```

In this case, the style definition selects a red, italic font for the **<h1>** tag that uses left-justified text.

In addition, you will often define the properties for multiple elements at the same time, as shown here:

```
<style type="text/css">
h1 { color:red; font-decoration:italic;
text-align:left; }
p { color:blue; font-decoration:italic;
text-align:left; }
img { border:0; }
</style>
```

In this case, the statements specify the style properties for three tags: **h1**, **p**, and **img**.

The following HTML file, ThreeEmbeddedStyles.html, uses embedded styles to format the heading, paragraph, and image tags previously individually formatted using inline styles within the file RepeatStyles.html:

```
<!DOCTYPE html>
<html>
<head>
```

```
<style type="text/css">
h1 { color:red; font-decoration:italic;
text-align:left; }
p { color:blue; font-decoration:italic;
text-align:left; }
img { border:0; }
</style>
</head>
<body>
<h1>Dogs</h1>
<p>Dogs are great!</p>
<img src="http://www.websitedevelopmentbook.com/
chapter07/dogs.jpg"/>
<h1>Cats</h1>
<p>Cats are great!</p>
<img src="http://www.websitedevelopmentbook.com/
chapter07/cats.jpg"/>
<h1>Horses</h1>
<p>Horses are great!</p>
<img src="http://www.websitedevelopmentbook.com/
chapter07/horses.jpg"/>
</body>
</html>
```

Using the embedded styles, you need to specify the style settings only one time. The browser, in turn, will apply the styles to each occurrence of the specified HTML tag. Should you decide to change a style, perhaps changing the <h1> tag's color from red to blue, you need to change only the one style definition. In this way, you can quickly and easily make changes throughout your entire page.

Inline Styles Override Embedded Styles

When you define style properties for an HTML element using embedded styles, you set the default format for each occurrence of the tag throughout your HTML file. After you define a default style, there may be times to use a unique format for a specific tag within your page. In such cases, override the embedded style definition using an inline style.

The following HTML file, MiddleYellow.html, uses embedded styles to define the background color and font for the paragraph selector:

```
<!DOCTYPE html>
<html>
<head>
```

```
<style type="text/css">
p { color:blue; background-color:orange; }
</style>
</head>
<body>
<p>11111111</p>
<p style="background-color:yellow">2222222</p>
<p>33333333</p>
</body>
</html>
```

As you can see, the embedded style definition sets the background color for the <**p**> tag to orange. Upon examining the file's second paragraph tag, you will find that it uses an inline style to override the background color, setting it for that specific tag to a yellow background color:

```
<p style="background-color:yellow">2222222</p>
```

When you display the file's contents, the browser will display the contents shown in **FIGURE 7–5**.

The embedded style definitions set the default settings for each occurrence of an HTML tag throughout your page, making it easy to apply consistent formatting quickly across your entire page. Should you need one element, such as a paragraph, to look different from the default settings, use an inline style.

Making Quick Changes to Your Page

Using embedded styles, a developer can quickly apply the same styles to elements within an HTML file. In addition, should the developer later need to change a style definition, the one definition can be edited, and the change immediately applied throughout the page. Take time to experiment with the <**p**> tag style that appears at

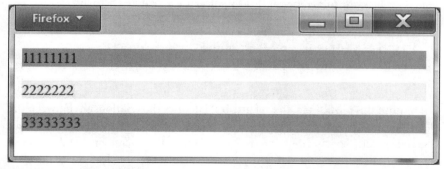

FIGURE 7–5 Using inline styles to override an embedded style

the top of the MiddleYellow.html file previously shown, perhaps changing the **back-ground-color** property from orange to white. After you save and refresh the file's contents, the browser immediately applies the change throughout your file.

Creating External Style Sheets

As you have learned, embedded styles let you control the format of HTML elements throughout your entire page. In this way, you can quickly apply or later change the entire look and feel of your page. Most websites, however, consist of multiple pages. Admittedly, you could place the same embedded style definitions at the top of each page. However, doing so requires repetitive work. Further, should you later decide to change an element's appearance, it would become necessary to edit every page's corresponding file again—which is not only time-consuming but also error-prone.

An **external style sheet** lets you place all of your CSS style definitions within one file that you then reference from within each of your HTML page files. When a page is viewed, the browser downloads and applies the style definitions provided in the corresponding CSS file. Should you later need to change a style, simply edit the CSS file, and the changes automatically apply to the pages that use the file.

To create an external style sheet file, use a text editor, just as you would to create an HTML file. Within the external style sheet file, do not use the **<style>** and **</style>** tag pair to define your style properties. Instead, simply place the definitions within the file:

```
h1 { color:red; background-color:yellow;
font-family:'Comic Sans MS'; }
p { color:blue; background-color:orange;
font-family:Arial; }
```

You should assign a meaningful name to the external style sheet file and .CSS extension, such as SiteStyle.css.

Then, within the **<head>** and **</head>** tags for each of your HTML pages, place a **<link>** tag that specifies the URL of your style sheet file. If the CSS file resides in the same folder as your HTML files, use a relative URL, such as:

```
<head>
<link rel="stylesheet" type="text/css"
href="SiteStyle.css"/>
</head>
```

Within the **<link>** tag, the **rel** attribute defines the relationship between the HTML file and the external file, which in this case, specifies that the file contains a CSS style sheet. Likewise, the **type** attribute specifies the document's Multipurpose Internet Mail Extension (MIME) type, which specifies the document's underlying format.

If the CSS file resides in a different location from your HTML files, use an absolute URL:

```
<head>
<link rel="stylesheet" type="text/css"
href="http://www.WebSiteDevelopmentBook.com/
Chapter07/SiteStyle.css"/>
</head>
```

The following CSS style sheet, SiteStyles.css, defines several styles:

```
h1 { color:red; background-color:yellow;
font-family:'Comic Sans MS'; }
p { color:blue; background-color:orange;
font-family:Arial; }
h2 { color:white; background-color:grey; }
```

Next, the files One.html, Two.html, and Three.html all use the style definitions:

```
<!DOCTYPE html>
<html>
<head>
<link rel="stylesheet" type="text/css"
href="http://www.WebSiteDevelopmentBook.com/
Chapter07/SiteStyles.css"/>
</head>
<body>
<h1>One</h1>
<h2>111</h2>
<p>One 1 One 1 One 1</p>
</body>
</html>

<!DOCTYPE html>
<html>
<head>
<link rel="stylesheet" type="text/css"
href="http://www.WebSiteDevelopmentBook.com/
Chapter07/SiteStyles.css"/>
</head>
<body>
<h1>Two</h1>
<h2>222</h2>
```

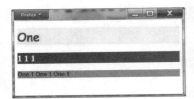  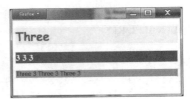

FIGURE 7-6 Using external style sheet definitions to style multiple pages

```
<p>Two 2 Two 2 Two 2</p>
</body>
</html>

<!DOCTYPE html>
<html>
<head>
<link rel="stylesheet" type="text/css"
href="http://www.WebSiteDevelopmentBook.com/
Chapter07/SiteStyles.css"/>
</head>
<body>
<h1>Three</h1>
<h2>3 3 3</h2>
<p>Three 3 Three 3 Three 3</p>
</body>
</html>
```

As you can see, each HTML file links in the external CSS file. When you view the files, each will use the style definitions, as shown in **FIGURE 7-6**.

Edit the SiteStyles.css file, and change the **h1** selector's definition as follows:

```
h1 { color:white; background-color:blue; }
```

Save the SiteStyles.css file's contents. When you later view the HTML file's One.html, Two.html, or Three.html, each immediately displays the updated style, as shown in **FIGURE 7-7**.

FIGURE 7-7 Applying a change to an external style sheet to multiple pages in one step

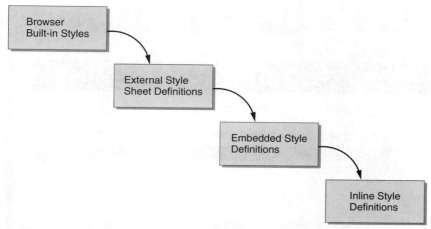

FIGURE 7-8 A browser will cascade through style definitions, applying the lowest level definition it encounters.

When your website has multiple pages, you should place most, if not all, of your style definitions in an external style sheet file.

Understanding the "Cascading" in Cascading Style Sheets

If you do not override a tag style using inline, embedded, or external style definitions, the browser will use its default (built-in) formatting for each HTML tag.

To apply styles across your entire site, use an external CSS style sheet. To change a style for a tag on a specific page, use an embedded style definition. Finally, to apply a style to a single element within a page, use an inline style.

When the browser later displays your page, it will fall through the "cascade" of style definitions, applying the lowest level definitions that it encounters, as shown in **FIGURE 7-8**.

Real-World Web Design

Web developers should keep the W3Schools.com website close at hand. Not only does the site provide a detailed coverage of HTML, it also presents the available CSS properties. In addition, the site provides a CSS validator you can use to examine the styles you define at *http://www.w3schools.com/web/web_validate.asp*.

The following CSS style sheet file, BadStyle.css, has an error within the **p** selector definition; the definition does not include a closing right brace:

```
h1 { color:white; background-color:blue; }
p { color:blue; background-color:orange;
font-family:Arial;
h2 { color:white; background-color:grey; }
```

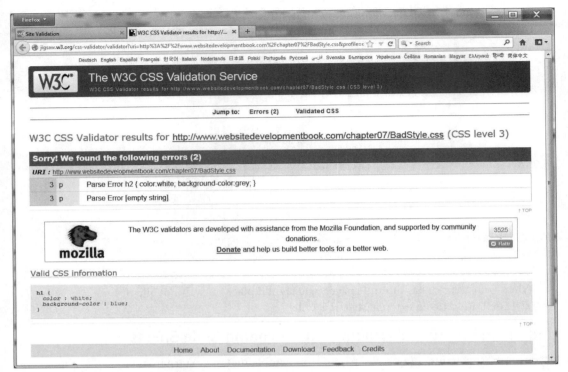

FIGURE 7-9 Using the W3C CSS Validation service to examine a CSS file
Reproduced with permission of the World Wide Web Consortium (W3C)

If you examine the file using the validator, your screen will display an error message similar to that shown in **FIGURE 7-9**, which shows the errors caused by a single missing brace.

As a rule, each time you create an external style sheet, use the validator to confirm the file's contents.

Hands-On HTML

To view the HTML files or to experiment with the files presented in this chapter, visit this book's companion website at *http://www.websitedevelopmentbook.com/ Chapter07/TryIt.html.*

CHAPTER SUMMARY

Across the Web, developers make extensive use of cascading style sheets to format elements within a webpage. By default, if a Web developer does not specify CSS attributes for an HTML element, a browser will use its own default, built-in formatting. To specify formatting using CSS, developers can use inline, embedded, and external styles. An inline style appears within an HTML element tag and affects only that occurrence of the element. An embedded style, in contrast, affects all of the corresponding tags within an HTML file. Finally, an external style sheet file defines styles that a developer can easily apply to multiple pages within a website. Using external style sheets, the developer can apply consistent styles throughout a site and easily and effectively add or modify styles. In Chapter 8, you will continue to drill down into CSS formatting capabilities.

KEY TERMS

Embedded style   Inline style
External style   Property
External style sheet   Style

CHAPTER REVIEW

1. Create an HTML file that uses inline styles and the **color** property to display **<h1>** tag contents in blue.

2. Create an HTML file that uses an inline style and the **font-family** and **font-size** properties to display a paragraph using a 14-point Arial font.

3. Create an HTML file that uses embedded style definitions to display all paragraph text in red italics at 12 points.

4. Combine embedded and inline styles to display two paragraphs in red italics text at 12 points and one paragraph at 14-point blue text.

5. Create two HTML files, Home.html and About.html, each of which uses the external style sheet definitions in a file named Custom.css (that you create) to display:

   a. Blue background

   b. Yellow heading text

   c. White paragraph text

6. Use an embedded style sheet to modify the file Home.html, which you created in Question 5, to override the **<h1>** style definition to display the text in orange.

7. Modify the Home.html file from Question 6 to add a second **<h1>** tag that displays its text in white using an inline style.

8. Use the W3School's validator at *http://www.w3schools.com/web/web_validate.asp* to validate the contents of your Custom.css file, and discuss your findings.

Advanced Cascading Style Sheets

IN CHAPTER 7, YOU LEARNED how to use cascading style sheets to format content items on your page using inline, embedded, and external style sheets. You learned how to easily format the appearance of items within your page. In this chapter, you will drill down into other CSS capabilities. To start, you will define CSS classes, which group a set of style definitions that can later be applied to a variety of HTML tags. Then, you will learn how to create an **id-based style** that applies only to an element on your page that matches the identifier. As you will learn, CSS is very flexible and lets you combine the different style definitions created to achieve your desired formatting.

Learning Objectives

This chapter examines CSS in further detail, including CSS classes and id-based styles. By the time you finish this chapter, you will understand the following key concepts:

- How to assign formatting styles to a CSS class definition
- How to define a style for multiple selectors
- How to combine style definitions
- How to create a selector-specific class definition that applies only to the specified tag
- How to assign CSS formatting styles to a name (an identifier), which can later be assigned to one specific HTML element based on the element's **id** attribute
- How to apply CSS styles to predefined pseudo classes
- How to apply CSS styles to pseudo elements

Assigning Formatting Styles to a CSS Class Definition

Using CSS, you can quickly format the appearance of specific HTML tags. The following HTML, StyleDemo.html, for example, uses embedded style definitions to format **<h1>** and **<p>** tag selectors:

```
<!DOCTYPE html>
<body>
<h1 style="color:red">Famous Quotes</h1>
<p style="font-weight:bold">Abraham Lincoln</p>
<p style="font-style:italic">Always bear in mind
that your own resolution to succeed, is more
important than any other one thing.</p>
</body>
</html>
```

When you view the file's contents, your browser will display the contents shown in **FIGURE 8-1**.

Often, there will be times when you will want to display a tag's contents differently based on the tag's context or use. For example, you might want to display your first paragraph with a bold font, a paragraph that contains a quote in italics, and other paragraphs in a standard font. In such cases, you can use CSS classes to define the formatting for each "class" of paragraph.

To define a CSS class, you specify a class name, which you define, and the corresponding attributes. You will precede the class name with a period and then place the **class** attributes within left and right braces:

```
.classname{ attributes here }
```

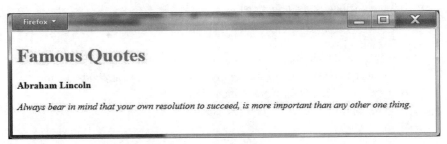

FIGURE 8-1 Using embedded style definitions to format page elements

The following statements, for example, define a class named "bold":

```
.bold
{
font-weight:bold;
}
```

In a similar way, the following statements define a quote class that uses an italic font:

```
.quote
{
font-style:italic;
}
```

After you define a class, use the **class** attribute within a tag to specify the name of the class for the attributes that you want to include. The following statement, for example, uses the **class** attribute within the **<p>** tag to apply the styles defined by the quote class:

```
<p class= "quote">Text here</p>
```

The following HTML file, CSSClassDemo.html, illustrates the use of class definitions to format different paragraphs:

```
<!DOCTYPE html>
<head>
<style type="text/css">
.bold { font-weight:bold; }
.quote { font-style:italic; }
</style>
</head>
<body>
<p>This text is normal.</p>
<p class="bold">Thomas Jefferson</p>
<p class="quote">Whenever you do a thing, act as if
all the world were watching.</p>
</body>
</html>
```

As you can see, the file defines the embedded styles within the document's **<head>** and **</head>** tag pair. Then, within the appropriate paragraph tags, the

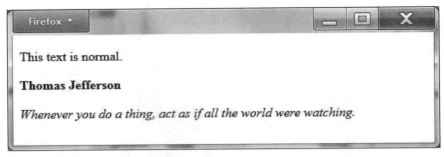

FIGURE 8-2 Using CSS styles to format paragraphs

code uses the desired **CSS class definition.** (A CSS class definition is one or more styles a Web developer assigns to a class name, which can then be applied to specific tags using the **class** attribute.)

When you view the file's contents, the browser displays the contents shown in **FIGURE 8-2**.

In a similar way, the following HTML file, HighlightTableRows.html, uses class styles to create the table shown in **FIGURE 8-3**. It uses different colors to highlight the table rows:

```
<!DOCTYPE html>
<head>
<style type="text/css">
.odd { background-color:orange; }
.even { background-color:yellow; }
</style>
</head>
<body>
<table width="500">
<tr class="odd"><td>1</td><td>1</td><td>1</td></tr>
```

FIGURE 8-3 Using CSS class definitions to format table rows

```
<tr class="even"><td>2</td><td>2</td><td>2</td></tr>
<tr class="odd"><td>3</td><td>3</td><td>3</td></tr>
<tr class="even"><td>4</td><td>4</td><td>4</td></tr>
</table>
</body>
</html>
```

As you can see, the file defines two styles: odd and even, each of which uses a different background color. Then, the file references the corresponding class name within the appropriate table rows. When you view the page contents, the browser highlights each row differently, as shown in **FIGURE 8-3**.

Defining a Style for Multiple Selectors

Often, as you format a page, you will use the same attributes for many elements, such as font or color:

```
h1 { font-family:arial; color:blue; }
h2 { font-family:arial; color:blue; }
p { font-family:arial; color:blue; }
```

In such cases, you can specify the tag selectors on one line, as shown here:

```
h1, h2, p { font-family:arial; color:blue; }
```

The following HTML file, SharedAttributes.html, applies the same attributes to several HTML tags:

```
<!DOCTYPE html>
<head>
<style type="text/css">
h1, h2, p { font-family:arial; color:blue; }
</style>
</head>
<body>
<h1>Thomas Jefferson</h1>
<h2>Books</h2>
<p>I cannot live without books.</p>
</body>
</html>
```

When you display the page contents, the browser displays the content shown in **FIGURE 8-4**.

FIGURE 8-4 Applying the same attributes to multiple HTML tags

Combining Style Definitions

As you define CSS classes, there may be times when you can combine existing class definitions to achieve the formatting you desire. In such cases, you simply specify the classes you desire within the **class** attribute:

```
<p class="bold quote">text</p>
```

The following HTML file, CombineClassDefinitions.html, uses different combinations of classes to format content within a page:

```
<!DOCTYPE html>
<head>
<style type="text/css">
.bold { font-weight:bold; }
.quote { font-style:italic; }
</style>
</head>
<body>
<p>This text is normal.</p>
<p class="bold">Abraham Lincoln</p>
<p class="quote">You cannot escape the
responsibility of tomorrow by evading
it today.</p>
<p class="quote bold">(1809 - 1865)</p>
</body>
</html>
```

As you can see, within the last **<p>** tag, the file references the **quote** and **bold** classes. When you view the file's contents, the browser displays the contents shown in **FIGURE 8-5**.

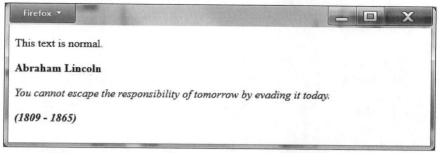

FIGURE 8-5 Combining class definitions to achieve desired formatting

Creating a Selector-Specific Class Definition

Using the **class** attribute, you can apply the styles a CSS class defines within a wide range of HTML tags:

```
<style type="text/css">
.bold { font-weight:bold; }
.quote { font-style:italic; }
.orange { color:orange; }
.blue { color:blue; }
</style>
```

As you format a page, there may be times when you will want to define specific classes that use a meaningful name, such as "center," but require different attribute settings. For example, you may want to use a class named "center," which would require different attributes for text and an image. In such cases, you can define class-specific attributes:

```
<style type="text/css">
.center { text-align:center; }
img.center { display:block; margin-left:auto;
margin-right:auto; }
</style>
```

The first class definition is generic in that it does not specify a selector. However, the second class definition, **img.center**, applies only to the <**img**> tag.

The following HTML file, CenterTextAndImage.html, uses **tag-specific classes** to format text and an image. (A tag-specific class is one whose definition applies only to a specific selector.)

```
<!DOCTYPE html>
<head>
<style type="text/css">
.center { text-align:center; }
img.center { display:block; margin-left:auto;
margin-right:auto; }
</style>
</head>
<body>
<h1 class="center">Theodore Roosevelt</h1>
<p class="center">Believe you can and you're
halfway there.</p>
<img class="center"
src="http://www.websitedevelopmentbook.com/
chapter08/apple.jpg" />
</body>
</html>
```

In this case, within each tag simply refers to **class="center"**. The browser will determine which class to apply based upon the tag. When you view the file's contents, your browser displays the content shown in FIGURE 8-6. As you can see, the browser centered the text as well as the image.

In a similar way, there may be times when you want to use most of the attributes defined in a class, but not all. For example, the following statements define a class named SiteFont, which sets the font family, color, and alignment:

```
<style type="text/css">
.SiteFont{ font-family:arial; color:blue;
text-align:left; }
</style>
```

Assume, however, that you want paragraph text to appear in red. To do so, modify the class definition specifically for the <p> element, changing or adding definitions, while leaving the remaining **class** attributes unchanged:

```
<style type="text/css">
.SiteFont{ font-family:arial; color:blue;
text-align:left; }
p.SiteFont { color:red; }
</style>
```

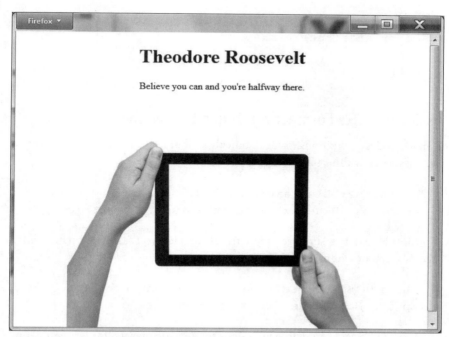

FIGURE 8-6 Using the **class="center"** tag to center text and image
Credit: © Denys Prykhodov/Shutterstock

In this case, the <p> selector inherits the properties defined in the **SiteFont** class and replaces the value assigned to the **color** property.

The following HTML file, OverrideParagraph.html, uses the SiteFont class to specify **font** attributes. The file then modifies the class definition for the <p> tag:

```
<!DOCTYPE html>
<head>
<style type="text/css">
.SiteFont { font-family:arial; color:blue;
text-align:left; }
p.SiteFont { color:red; }
</style>
</head>
<body class="SiteFont">
<h1>This uses the SiteFont definition</h1>
<p>So does this default paragraph.</p>
```

```
<p class="SiteFont">This one overrides the
color attribute.</p>
</body>
</html>
```

Assigning CSS Formatting Styles to a Name

Using CSS class definitions, you can quickly style HTML elements by referring to the class name within a **class** attribute:

```
<h1 class="BlueText">The heading content</h1>
<p class="BlueText">The paragraph content</p>
```

Most HTML tags support an **id** attribute that lets you associate a name with a specific element within your page:

```
<h1 id="SiteTitle">The heading content</h1>
<p id="Main">The paragraph content</p>
```

Just as CSS lets you define attributes for specific tags, it also lets you define attributes for a specific element id. To do so, specify the id following a pound sign (#), as shown here:

```
#idName{ style definition }
```

Defining an id-based style is similar to defining a class. However, unlike a class that you can apply to multiple tags or elements, the id-based style is specific to one element within your page.

The following HTML file, idStyle.html, defines an id-based style:

```
<!DOCTYPE html>
<head>
<style type="text/css">
.SiteFont { font-family:arial; color:blue;
text-align:left; }
#LastParagraph { color:red; }
</style>
</head>
<body class="SiteFont">
<h1>This uses the SiteFont definition</h1>
<p>So does this default paragraph.</p>
```

FIGURE 8-7 Using an id-based style definition

```
<p id="LastParagraph">This one overrides the color
attribute.</p>
</body>
</html>
```

As you can see, the last paragraph tag uses **id="LastParagraph"**. The browser, in turn, when rendering the page, uses the corresponding id-based style definition for the content. When you view the file's contents, your browser displays the page shown in **FIGURE 8-7**.

Applying CSS Styles to Predefined Pseudo Classes

Many HTML tags have an associated state. For example, a link with a mouse hovering above it or a link previously clicked on by a user might change color when subjected to these associated states. Using CSS, you can specify styles for different states. **TABLE 8-1** lists several **pseudo classes** that correspond to these different states.

TABLE 8-1   CSS STATE-BASED PSEUDO CLASSES

Pseudo Class	Description
:active	Applies to a selected link
:focus	Applies to a form element that has the keyboard focus
:hover	Applies to a link over which the mouse is hovering
:link	Applies to an unvisited link
:visited	Applies to a visited link

Within CSS, a pseudo class starts with a colon (:) followed by a name. To use a pseudo class, specify a tag name followed by the pseudo class. The following statement, for example, displays a link within a page in yellow when the user hovers the mouse over the link:

```
a:hover{ color: yellow; };
```

Likewise, this statement directs the browser to display links in red that the user previously visited:

```
a:visited { color: red; }
```

The following HTML file, PseudoLinks.html, illustrates the use of CSS pseudo classes for various link states:

```
<!DOCTYPE html>
<head>
<style type="text/css">
a:hover{ background-color:yellow; }
a:visited { background-color:red; }
a:selected { background-color:blue; }
a:link { background-color:orange; }
</style>
</head>
<body>
<a href="http://www.theheadoftheclass.com">Head of
the Class</a>
</body>
</html>
```

As you can see, the code simply applies styles to the pseudo classes for the **a** selector, just as it would for a standard CSS class definition.

In a similar way, the following HTML file, FormHighlight.html, uses the :active and :focus pseudo classes to highlight a selected form and the field within the form that has the input focus:

```
<!DOCTYPE html>
<head>
<style type="text/css">
input:focus { background-color:yellow; }
form:active { background-color:white; }
body { background-color:blue; }
</style>
```

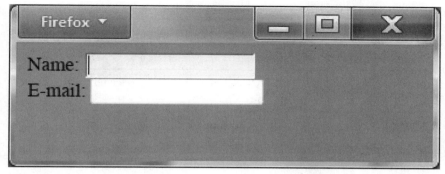

FIGURE 8-8 Using CSS pseudo classes to highlight a form and input fields

```
</head>
<body>
<form>
Name: <input type="text" name="Username"/><br/>
E-mail: <input type="text" name="email"/>
</body>
</html>
```

When you view the file's contents and click on a field within the form, the browser changes the form and field's colors, as shown in **FIGURE 8-8**.

TABLE 8-2 defines additional CSS pseudo classes.

The following HTML file, OtherPseudoClasses.html, illustrates the use of the several pseudo classes, which **TABLE 8-2** defines:

```
<!DOCTYPE html>
<head>
<style type="text/css">
p:first-child { background-color: yellow; }
p { background-color: white; }
:not(p) { background-color: orange }
li:first-of-type { font-size:200%; }
</style>
</head>
<body>
<p>This is the first paragraph within the body.</p>
<ol>

<li>This is the first list element.</li>
<li>Second list element</li>
```

TABLE 8-2   CSS POSITION-BASED PSEUDO CLASSES

Pseudo Class	Description
:checked	Selects every checked item—such as selected checkboxes within a form
:disabled	Selects the disabled elements—such as the disabled elements within a form
:empty	Selects an empty element of the selector type
:first-child	Selects the first child of every parent element, such as the first paragraph within a **<body>** or **<div>** tag or first **<li>** within an ordered, or numbered, list
:first-of-type	Selects the first element that is the first of that type of element within a parent—such as the first table or first image
:enabled	Selects the enabled elements—such as the elements within a form
:last-child	Selects the element that is the last of that type of element within a parent—such as the last image
:last-of-type	Selects the last of that type of element within a parent—such as the last table or last image
:not(selector)	Selects every item that is not specified selector type
:nth-child(n)	Selects the element that is the nth element of that type of element within a parent—such as the 3rd table or 2nd image
:nth-last-child(n)	Selects the element that is the nth element from the last of that type of element within a parent—such as the 3rd from the last table or 2nd from the last image
:only-of-type	Selects the element that is the only of that type of element within a parent—such as the only table or only image
:root	Selects the root element within the document
::selection	Selects user-selected text
:target	Selects the element that is a target of a URL anchor

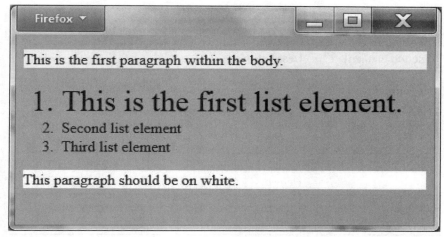

FIGURE 8-9 Using CSS pseudo codes to format specific page elements

```
<li>Third list element</li>
</ol>
<p>This paragraph should be on white.</p>

</body>
</html>
```

In this case, the code assigns the first paragraph a yellow background, other paragraphs a white background, and any element that is not a paragraph an orange background. In addition, the code assigns the first list element a font that is 200 percent larger than normal. When you view the file's contents, the browser displays the contents shown in **FIGURE 8-9**.

Applying CSS Styles to Pseudo Elements

As you have learned, CSS pseudo classes let you specify formatting for dynamic elements within a page based on states as well as elements based upon the document structure. In addition, CSS defines **pseudo elements** that are not position- or state-based, which you can use to specify formatting. **TABLE 8-3** describes the pseudo elements.

The following HTML file, BigFirstLetter.html, uses the **:first-letter** pseudo element to display a large font for the first letter of the paragraph:

```
<!DOCTYPE <html>
<head>
<style type="text/css">
```

TABLE 8-3	CSS PSEUDO ELEMENTS
Pseudo Element	**Description**
:first-letter	Applies to the first letter of a block element, such as a paragraph.
:first-line	Applies to the first line of a block element, such as a paragraph.
:after	Applies to the space that immediately follows an element.
:before	Applies to the space that immediate precedes an element.

```
p:first-letter
{
font-size:300%;
color:Blue;
}
</style>
</head>
<body>
<p>It is better to be alone than in bad company.</p>
<p>George Washington</p>
</body>
</html>
```

As you can see, to use the **:first-letter** pseudo element with a page, simply specify the tag selector followed by the pseudo element, and then define the corresponding styles.

When you view the file, your browser will display the contents shown in **FIGURE 8-10**.

Real-World Web Design

Across the Web, developers have a wide-ranging set of skills. When companies look for a developer, it is often hard to determine the developer's level of knowledge. If you are learning HTML and CSS on your own, and you don't have a corresponding degree in Web development and design, one way to confirm your skills is through certification. This book has repeatedly referred you to the

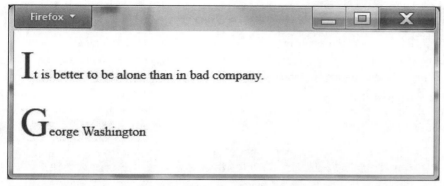

FIGURE 8-10 Using the **:first-letter** pseudo element to display a large first letter at the start of a paragraph

W3Schools.com website for references on a variety of HTML and CSS topics. The W3Schools.com site is well-respected within the Web development community. The site provides certificate programs on HTML, CSS, JavaScript, jQuery, and more. For more information on the certification process, visit: *http://www .w3schools.com/cert/default.asp.*

Hands-On HTML

To view the HTML files or to experiment with the files presented in this chapter, visit this book's companion website at *http://www.websitedevelopmentbook.com/ Chapter08/TryIt.html.*

Chapter Summary

Across the Web, developers make extensive use of cascading style sheets to format the appearance of objects within an HTML page. In this chapter, you learned how to create CSS class definitions, which you can then apply to specific HTML tags using each tag's **class** attribute. You also learned how to define selector-specific classes and id-based classes. In addition, you learned that CSS defines pseudo classes that correspond to an object's state or position, such as when a mouse hovers over an object or an object is the first element in a list.

Key Terms

CSS class definition

Id–based style

Pseudo class

Pseudo element

Tag-specific classes

Chapter Review

1. Create and apply a CSS class named BigBlue, which selects a large, blue-colored font.

2. Create and apply a CSS class named YellowBackground that selects a yellow background. Apply the class to your HTML file's body tag.

3. Create an ordered list that uses both the BigBlue and YellowBackground styles that you created in Questions 1 and 2.

4. Create a paragraph-specific class named BigBlue that you created in Question 1, which uses the Arial font. Show the use of the standard and class-specific classes within your HTML file.

5. Create an HTML file that illustrates the use of the **:first–letter** and **:first–line** pseudo elements.

6. Create an HTML file that illustrates the use of the **:after** and **:before** pseudo elements.

7. Create an HTML file that illustrates the use of the **:checked**, **:enabled**, and **:disabled** pseudo classes.

Creating Page Divisions

© Risto Viita/Shutterstock

chapter

9

SINCE THE FIRST HTML pages began to create the Web, developers have used tables to format content. Tables are advantageous because Web browsers always seem to display them correctly—making the use of tables a safe design approach. Unfortunately, using a table for complex page design often leads to large and often complex amounts of HTML. As a result, such pages become harder to modify.

A better approach to page layout is to use CSS and **<div>** and **</div>** tag pairs. In the simplest sense, the **<div>** and **</div>** tag pair creates a container where you can place related HTML tags for styling and positioning.

Learning Objectives

This chapter examines the use of page division tags in detail. By the time you finish this chapter, you will understand the following key concepts:

- How to use tables to format text and images within an HTML page
- How to create a page division using the **<div>** and **</div>** tag pair
- How to use page divisions to create columns
- How to use tables to format content
- How to create fixed-size content

FIGURE 9-1 Using HTML tables to format content
Credit: © Eric Isselee/Shutterstock

Using Tables to Format Text and Images

Chapter 5, "Formatting Content with Tables," examined the use of tables in detail. At that time, you learned that by using tables, you can format text and images, as shown in **FIGURE 9-1**.

The following HTML file, TableDemo.html, creates the output shown in **FIGURE 9-1**:

```
<!DOCTYPE html>
<html>
<body bgcolor="lightblue">
<table border="1" style="margin:auto;
background:white;" cellpadding="10" width="800">
<tr><td style="text-align:center" colspan="2">
<img src="http://www.WebSiteDevelopmentBook.com/
Chapter09/Pets.jpg"/></td></tr>
<tr><td><p>Loremipsum dolor sit amet, consectetura-
dipiscingelit. Suspendisse a tellus vitae quam
elementuminterdumquis a massa. Etiaminterdumbiben-
dumleo, rhoncusconvallisturpissodales tempus.
```

```
Sedegetorci ac felismollispretium. Aeneanetelit
vitae loremblanditaliquam et viverrarisus. In
blandit, risus ac commodopharetra, risus magna tin-
cidunt ante, at posuereodioodioeuenim. Phasellusli-
bero dui, eleifendaeleifendeget, temporetlibero.
Curabiturportaposueredictum. Morbicursusnullaauc-
torneque semper euismod.Nullamodiotortor, venenatis
at vehiculapulvinar, lobortisnecnisl. Nam conse-
quatcursusnibhquistincidunt. Vivamussedliberoquis-
maurisfacilisisplacerat.</p></td>
<td><p>Integer etmaurismassa. Praesentporttitorvari-
usvehicula. Loremipsumdolorsitamet,consecteturadipis
cingelit. Aeneanaliquam ligula etrisusimperdietves-
tibulum. Nullamutmetus a tellusdignissimconvallis in
ac augue. Etiamfermentumfelisquisleosuscipit a
scelerisque ante imperdiet. Morbivestibulumsceleris-
queviverra. Cum sociisnatoquepenatibusetmagnis dis
parturient montes, nasceturridiculus mus. Aliquam at
arcumauris. Sedestarcu, placeratfeugiatporttitoret,
cursusegetnulla.</p></td></tr>
</table>
</body>
</html>
```

As you can see, the table defines two rows—the first row has one cell and the second row has two.

Creating Page Divisions

Using the **<div>** and **</div>** tag pair, you can define a container for styling related components in the HTML page. The following HTML file, SimpleDiv.html, uses a **<div>** and **</div>** tag pair to group two paragraphs to which it assigns a blue background and white text:

```
<!DOCTYPE html>
<html>
<body>
<p>This is paragraph 1</p>
<div style="background:blue; color:white;">
<p>This is paragraph 2</p>
<p>This is paragraph 3</p>
</div>
```

FIGURE 9-2 Using the **<div>** and **</div>** tag pair to group paragraph tags for styling

```
<p>This is paragraph 4</p>
</body>
</html>
```

In this case, the code groups paragraphs 2 and 3 within a page division. Within the **<div>** tag, the code uses an inline style to define the division's formatting.

When you view the file's contents, the browser will display the output shown in **FIGURE 9-2**.

Using Page Divisions to Create Columns

As you have learned in Chapter 5, by using the **height** and **width** attributes, you can control the size of tables and columns. In a similar way, using CSS, you can specify the width of **page divisions,** which are webpage containers where a developer can place and style related HTML tags. The following HTML file, Three-Columns.html, uses CSS styles to create **Start**, **Middle**, and **End** classes that the file then applies to three **<div>** and **</div>** tag pairs to create columns, as shown in **FIGURE 9-3**.

FIGURE 9-3 Creating columns (containers) for HTML content within a page

The following statements implement the ThreeColumns.html file:

```
<!DOCTYPE html>
<html>
<head>
<style type="text/css">
.Start { background-color:red; width:200px;
height:200px; position:absolute;left:0px; top:0px; }
.Middle { background-color:white; width:200px;
height:200px; position:absolute;left:200px;
top:0px; }
.End { background-color:blue; width:200px;
height:200px; position:absolute;left:400px;
top:0px; }
</style>
</head>
<html>
<body>
<div class="Start"></div>
<div class="Middle"></div>
<div class="End"></div>
</body>
</html>
```

In this case, the style applied to each division specifies the background color and absolute page locations.

As discussed, the <**div**> and <**/div**> tag pair creates a container for other HTML tags. The following HTML file, AddTextToColumns.html, assigns lorem ipsum text to each page division. To separate the text between columns, the file creates a **pad** class that uses the **margin** attribute to provide spacing, which the file then applies to each paragraph:

```
<!DOCTYPE html>
<html>
<head>
<style type="text/css">
.Start { background-color:red; width:200px;
height:200px; position:absolute;left:0px;
top:0px; }
.Middle { background-color:white; width:200px;
height:200px; position:absolute;left:200px;
top:0px; }
.End { background-color:blue; width:200px;
```

```
height:200px; position:absolute;left:400px;
top:0px; }
.pad { margin: 0px 10px 10px10px; }
</style>
</head>
<html>
<body>
<div class="Start"><p class="pad">Loremipsum dolor
sit amet, consecteturadipisicingelit, sed do eius-
modtemporincididuntutlabore et dolore magna aliqua.
Utenim ad minim veniam, quisnostrud exercitation
ullamcolaborisnisiutaliquip ex eacommodoconsequat.
</p></div>
<div class="Middle"><p class="pad">Sedutperspiciati
sundeomnisistenatus error sitvoluptatemaccusantium-
doloremquelaudantium, totam rem aperiam, eaqueipsa
quae abilloinventoreveritatiset quasi architecto-
beatae vitae dicta suntexplicabo.</p></div>
<div class="End"><p class="pad">Atveroeosetaccusa
mus et iustoodiodignissimosducimus qui blanditiis-
praesentiumvoluptatumdelenitiatquecorrupti quos
dolores et quasmolestiasexcepturisintoccaecaticu-
piditate non provident, similiquesunt in culpa
qui</p></div>
</body>
</html>
```

When you view the file's contents, the browser displays the contents shown in **FIGURE 9-4**.

Using Tables to Format Content

As discussed, Web developers often use tables to format content. The following HTML file, DivFormat.html, formats the contents identically to the table previously shown in **FIGURE 9-1**:

```
<!DOCTYPE html>
<html>
<head>
<style type="text/css">
.CenterAll { width:800px; margin-left: auto;
margin-right: auto; }
```

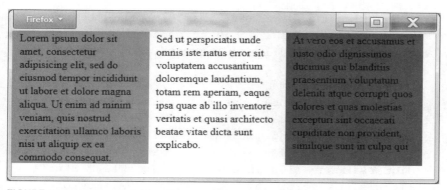

FIGURE 9-4 Using page divisions to separate text columns

```
.Outer { background-color:white; width:800px;
text-align:center; border:1px solid black; }
.Column { width:400px; text-align:left;
float:left; }
.Clear { clear: both; }
.pad { margin:5px 5px 5px5px; }
</style>
</head>
<html>
<body bgcolor="lightblue">
<div class="CenterAll">
<div class="Outer">
<div style="border:1px solid black;">
<img src="http://www.WebSiteDevelopmentBook.com/
Chapter09/Pets.jpg"/>
</div>
<div class="Column">
<p class="pad">Loremipsum dolor sit amet, consecte-
turadipiscingelit. Suspendisse a tellusvitae quam
elementuminterdumquis a massa. Etiaminterdumbiben-
dumleo, rhoncusconvallisturpissodales tempus. Sede-
getorci ac felismollispretium. Aeneanetelit vitae
loremblanditaliquametviverrarisus. In blandit,
risus ac commodopharetra, risus magna tincidunt
ante, at posuereodioodioeuenim. Phaselluslibero
dui, eleifendaeleifendeget, temporetlibero.
Curabiturportaposueredictum. Morbicursusnullaauc-
torneque semper euismod. Nullamodiotortor,
```

```
venenatis at vehiculapulvinar, lobortisnecnisl.
Nam consequatcursusnibhquistincidunt. Vivamussedli-
beroquismaurisfacilisisplacerat.</p>
</div>
<div class="Column">
<p class="pad">Integer etmaurismassa. Praesentport-
titorvariusvehicula. Loremipsumdolorsitamet, con-
secteturadipiscingelit. Aeneanaliquam ligula
etrisusimperdietvestibulum.Nullamutmetus a tellus-
dignissimconvallis in ac augue. Etiamfermentumfe-
lisquisleosuscipit a scelerisque ante imperdiet.
Morbivestibulumscelerisqueviverra. Cum sociisnato-
quepenatibusetmagnis dis parturient montes, nascet-
urridiculus mus. Aliquam at arcumauris. Sedestarcu,
placeratfeugiatporttitor et, cursusegetnulla.</p>
</div>
<div class="clear"></div>
</div>
</div>
</body>
</html>
```

At first glance, you may be thinking tables are a good solution! The file, in this case, uses several containers. The first, to which the file assigns the **CenterAll** class, centers the contents on the page. The second, to which the file assigns the **Outer** class, creates a box around the image and text, which defines the width and sets the background color. To create the columns, the Column class uses the **float:left** attribute, which directs the browser to continue to try to move items next to one another. You will note near the bottom of the file that the division using the **Clear** class, which clears the **float** attribute, turns off floating.

Creating Fixed-Size Content

Across the Web, many developers will create fixed-size content that does not change in size with respect to changes in size with the browser window. Developers use such a fixed-size page to maintain a consistent page appearance across different screen resolutions.

For example, the following HTML file, FixedSize.html, displays content that does not change as the browser window changes. **FIGURE 9-5** illustrates the content at different window sizes.

The following statements implement the FixedSize.html file:

```
<!DOCTYPE html>
<html>
```

FIGURE 9-5 Displaying fixed-size content that does not change with the browser window size
Credit: © Gts/Shutterstock

```
<body>
<img src="http://www.WebSiteDevelopmentBook.com/
Chapter09/wine.jpg"/>
</body>
</html>
```

In this case, each division uses a fixed-size height and width. In contrast, the following HTML file, DynamicSize.html, uses an image height and width that is 100 percent of the window size. As a result, the image scales with the window, as shown in **FIGURE 9-6**:

```
<!DOCTYPE html>
<html>
<body>
<img src=http://www.WebSiteDevelopmentBook.com/
Chapter09/wine.jpg height="100%" width="100%"/>
</body>
</html>
```

Finally, the HTML file, ThreeColumnsFloat.html, changes the three-column text example presented earlier in this chapter to scale the column content based on the window size:

```
<!DOCTYPE html>
<html>
<head>
<style type="text/css">
```

FIGURE 9-6 In this example, where image height and width are 100 percent of window size, the image scales with the window.

Credit: © Gts/Shutterstock

```
.Start { background-color:red; width:20%;
height:100%; float:left; }
.Middle { background-color:white; width:20%;
height:100%; float:left; }
.End { background-color:blue; width:20%;
height:100%; float:left; }
.pad { margin: 0px 10px 10px10px; }
</style>
</head>
<html>
<body>
<div class="Start"><p class="pad">Loremipsum dolor
sit amet, consecteturadipisicingelit, sed do eius-
modtemporincididuntutlabore et dolore magna aliqua.
Utenim ad minim veniam, quisnostrud exercitation
ullamcolaboris nisi utaliquip ex eacommodoconse-
quat.</p></div>
<div class="Middle"><p class="pad">Sedutperspiciati
sundeomnisistenatus error sit voluptatemaccusan-
tiumdoloremquelaudantium, totam rem aperiam,
eaqueipsa quae abilloinventoreveritatiset quasi
architectobeatae vitae dicta suntexplicabo.
```

FIGURE 9-7 Using dynamic-content sizing to adjust the page-content appearance as the window size changes

```
</p></div>
<div class="End"><p class="pad">Atveroeosetaccusa
mus et iustoodiodignissimosducimus qui blanditiis-
praesentiumvoluptatumdelenitiatquecorrupti quos
dolores et quasmolestiasexcepturisintoccaecaticu-
piditate non provident, similiquesunt in culpa
qui</p></div>
</body>
</html>
```

FIGURE 9-7 illustrates the page contents at different window sizes.

Real-World Web Design

In Chapter 2, "Integrating Images," you learned how to use x, y, and z coordinates to stack images, as shown in **FIGURE 9-8**.

Depending on your page design, there may be times when you want to stack text content, as shown in **FIGURE 9-9**.

The following HTML file, StackText.html, creates and positions three page divisions to stack the text content, as shown in **FIGURE 9-9**:

```
<!DOCTYPE html>
<head>
<style type="text/css">
.Start { background-color:red; width:200;
height:200; position:absolute; top:100; left:100;
z-index=0; }
```

FIGURE 9-8 Using x, y, and z coordinates to position images on a page
Credit (from left): © Alberto Loyo/Shutterstock; © Idreamphoto/Shutterstock; © EpicStockMedia/Shutterstock

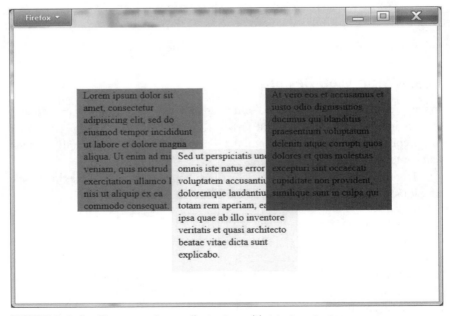

FIGURE 9-9 Stacking x, y, and z coordinates to position text content on a page

```
.Middle { background-color:yellow; width:200;
height:200; position:absolute; top:200; left:250;
z-index=1; }
.End { background-color:blue; width:200;
height:200; position:absolute; top:100; left:400;
z-index=2; }
.pad { margin: 0px 10px 10px10px; }
</style>
</head>
<html>
<body>
<div class="Start"><p class="pad">Loremipsum dolor
sit amet, consecteturadipisicingelit, sed do eius-
modtemporincidididuntutlabore et dolore magna aliqua.
Utenim ad minim veniam, quisnostrud exercitation
ullamcolaboris nisi utaliquip ex eacommodoconse-
quat.</p></div>
<div class="Middle"><p class="pad">Sedutperspiciati
sundeomnisistenatus error sit voluptatemaccusan-
tiumdoloremquelaudantium, totam rem aperiam,
eaqueipsa quae abilloinventoreveritatiset quasi
architectobeatae vitae dicta suntexplicabo.
</p></div>
<div class="End"><p class="pad">Atveroeosetaccusa
mus et iustoodiodignissimosducimus qui blanditiis-
praesentiumvoluptatumdelenitiatquecorrupti quos
dolores et quasmolestiasexcepturisintoccaecaticu-
piditate non provident, similiquesunt in culpa
qui</p></div>
</body>
</html>
```

As you can see, the file simply specifies the x, y, and z coordinates for the divisions that contain each section of text. In this way, the text positioning becomes as easy as positioning the images.

Hands-On HTML

To view the HTML files or to experiment with the files presented in this chapter, visit this book's companion website at *http://www.websitedevelopmentbook.com/ Chapter09/TryIt.html.*

CHAPTER SUMMARY

For years, developers made extensive use of tables to format content within a webpage. Developers argue that the use of tables for formatting is safe because browsers, all browsers, render the content correctly. Unfortunately, the use of tables for content formatting, particularly nested tables, can lead to code that is difficult to maintain and possibly large in size, which increases download times.

As an alternative formatting technique, developers are moving to page divisions, which are essentially webpage containers that can group related HTML tags for styling and positioning. To create such containers, developers use the <**div**> and </**div**> tag pair. This chapter examined various uses of the tags to format content. In Chapter 10, "JavaScript," you will examine the JavaScript programming language and ways you can use it to increase the capabilities of your webpages.

KEY TERMS

Page divisions

CHAPTER REVIEW

1. Create an HTML page that uses three page divisions to format text and photo content (three photos and three paragraphs) with different backgrounds and colors.

2. Create an HTML file that uses page divisions to stack a text division with an image division.

3. Create an HTML file that uses page divisions to create three colored columns. The columns should change size as the window size changes.

4. Create an HTML file that displays three partially stacked colored page divisions in such a manner that part of each division shows. When the user clicks the mouse on a division, that division should move to the top of the stack.

JavaScript

© Risto Viita/Shutterstock

chapter

10

THROUGHOUT THIS BOOK'S PREVIOUS chapters, you made extensive use of HTML and CSS to format and style Web-based content. To fully unlock the potential interactivity of a webpage, developers make extensive use of the JavaScript programming language. Using JavaScript, developers can change an HTML element's content, modify CSS styles, change attributes, and more. JavaScript is a programming language where developers specify instructions the browser must perform to accomplish a specific task. What makes JavaScript unique is that the instructions are executed within the browser, a process referred to by developers as client-side processing.

Learning Objectives

This chapter examines the JavaScript programming language. By the time you finish this chapter, you will understand the following key concepts:

- How to place JavaScript code within an HTML file by using the **<script>** and **</script>** tag pair
- How to correct the cause of errors created when a programmer violates the syntax of JavaScript code
- How to use JavaScript operators to perform common arithmetic operations, such as addition, subtraction, multiplication, and division
- How JavaScript allows programmers to define and use variables to allow programs to store information as they execute
- How JavaScript's case sensitivity can lead to errors that are difficult to correct
- How to comment or document code to explain the processing it performs

- How JavaScript supports conditional processing via the **if–else** and **switch** statements to allow programs to make decisions
- How to repeat one or more statements, known as iterative processing, with JavaScript code
- How to use JavaScript functions to break tasks into smaller pieces to simplify large programming tasks
- How to use JavaScript events, such as user mouse or keyboard operations
- How to store multiple values within a single variable using an **Array** object
- How to use JavaScript objects
- How to create a link using an external JavaScript file

Getting Started With JavaScript

To place JavaScript programming instructions within an HTML file, developers normally place the <**script**> and </**script**> tag pair within the head section of the HTML file. The following HTML file, FirstJavaScript.html, places a single JavaScript statement that displays a dialog box with the message "Hello, JavaScript!" This is shown in **FIGURE 10–1**.

```
<!DOCTYPE html>
<html>
<head>
<script>
alert('Hello, JavaScript!');
</script>
</head>
<body>
</body>
</html>
```

In this case, when the browser loads the HTML file, the browser will execute the JavaScript statement **alert('Hello, JavaScript!');** this directs it to display the dialog box.

JavaScript <script> Tags the Old-Fashioned Way

In the previous example, the HTML file placed a <**script**> and </**script**> tag pair within the document's head section. The <**script**> tag is HTML 5 format. As you

FIGURE 10-1 Using JavaScript to display a dialog box to the user

examine older JavaScript code within HTML files, you will encounter **<script>** tags in the following form:

```
<script type="text/javascript">
// code here
</script>
```

In this case, the **type="text/javascript"** attribute tells the browser that the script that follows will be JavaScript. Although this format still works, HTML 5 has simplified it, making JavaScript the default scripting language.

Looking at a Second Example

A **program** is a list of instructions that tells the computer how to perform a specific task. When using JavaScript, use program statements to specify the instructions that you desire. In JavaScript, statements will normally end with a semicolon (;). The following HTML file, SecondJavaScript.html, has two statements. The first uses the built-in JavaScript **alert** function to say "Hello." The second performs similar processing to say "JavaScript World!":

```
<!DOCTYPE html>
<html>
<head>
<script>
```

```
alert('Hello');
alert('JavaScript World!');
</script>
</head>
<body>
</body>
</html>
```

In this case, **alert** is the name of programming statements built into JavaScript that display a dialog box with the specified message. Developers refer to a collection of statements that perform a specific task as a function. Using the **alert** function, you specify the message you want it to display within single or double quotes contained within the parentheses that follows the **alert** function name.

Note that each JavaScript statement in the previous example ends with a semicolon. In the simplest sense, the semicolon tells the browser where the first statement ends and the second begins.

Understanding Syntax

Every language, including English, French, Spanish, and even JavaScript, has a **syntax** that specifies the rules for the language. In English, for example, a sentence ends with a period, exclamation mark, or question mark. Likewise, a sentence starts with a capital letter. When you write JavaScript code, you need to follow the JavaScript language rules. Otherwise, a syntax error will occur. Depending on the browser, the browser may display an error message indicator or it may simply stop executing the script. As the developer, you need to find and correct the cause of the error.

The following HTML file, JavaScriptSyntaxError.html, has an error. It does not provide a closing quote after the message that the **alert** function is to display:

```
<!DOCTYPE html>
<html>
<head>
<script>
alert('Hello');
alert('JavaScript World!');
</script>
</head>
<body>
</body>
</html>
```

Experiment with this HTML file using different browsers to see how each handles the error. Then, correct the error by placing a quote at the end of the message, and save the file's contents. When you refresh the file, the message box should occur.

When using JavaScript, syntax errors occur—they are simply a fact of a programmer's life. When such an error occurs, you need to locate the cause and correct it.

Using JavaScript Operators

When programming, you often need to perform arithmetic operations, such as addition, subtraction, and multiplication. To help you perform such operations, JavaScript provides the set of operators defined in **TABLE 10-1**.

The following HTML file, MathOps.html, demonstrates the use of several JavaScript arithmetic operators:

```
<!DOCTYPE html>
<html>
<head>
<script>
alert(3+4);
alert(3*4);
alert(3/4);
</script>
</head>
<body>
</body>
</html>
```

TABLE 10-1 JAVASCRIPT ARITHMETIC OPERATORS

Operator	Purpose	Description
+	Addition	Adds to values or concatenates two strings
-	Subtraction	Subtracts two values
*	Multiplication	Multiplies two values
/	Division	Divides two values
%	Modulus	Divides two values, and returns the remainder
++	Increment	Adds one to a variable
—	Decrement	Subtracts one from a variable

In this case, the file uses three separate **alert** dialog boxes to display the math results. When you view the file's contents, the browser displays an **alert** message box for each result. When you click "OK" in response to one dialog box, the page then displays the next.

Storing Data in JavaScript Variables

As you write program instructions, even for simple tasks, it is common to need to temporarily store values that your instructions will later use. Programmers store such temporary values using named locations in memory called variables. In the simplest sense, a **variable** is the name of a storage location in memory. In other programming languages, you have to provide specifics about the memory location, such as the size of the value the location will hold as well as the type of value, such as a number, date, or sequence of characters. JavaScript, in contrast, is a "loosely typed" programming language, which means you simply need to specify a variable name, but not a related data type. To declare a JavaScript variable, use the **var** keyword followed by a variable name. A **keyword** is a word reserved by a programming language that has special meaning to the language and cannot be used for a variable name. The following statement creates a variable named **message**:

```
var message;
```

When you declare a variable, choose a name for the variable that describes the content it will store. Avoid names such as **A**, **B**, or **C** because they do not give another programmer who is reading your code any information about the value the variable stores. In contrast, names such as **Username**, **OrderDate**, or **GraphicsFile** are much more meaningful.

When you declare variables within JavaScript, the names of several variables can be specified within one statement:

```
var Username, OrderDate, GraphicsFile;
```

Or you can individually declare each variable:

```
var Username;
var OrderDate;
var GraphicsFile;
```

JavaScript is a "forgiving" programming language. If you forget to declare a variable, JavaScript creates one for you when it encounters the first occurrence of an unknown name. As a best practice, however, declare each variable before using it.

JavaScript Is Case Sensitive

When you create JavaScript instructions, keep in mind that JavaScript is case sensitive. This means JavaScript considers uppercase and lowercase letters as different. To JavaScript, **alert** is different from **Alert**. The following HTML file, JSError.html, does not display a dialog box, because JavaScript does not recognize **Alert** with an uppercase **A**:

```
<!DOCTYPE html>
<html>
<head>
<script>
Alert('Hello');
</script>
</head>
<body>
</body>
</html>
```

To correct the program error, replace the uppercase letter **A** with a lowercase **a**.

Assigning a Value to a Variable

As you have learned, a variable defines a storage location in memory for storing values as a program's instructions execute. To create a variable within JavaScript, use the **var** keyword to specify the variable's name.

After you declare a variable, use the equal sign, which is the JavaScript assignment operator, to assign a value to the variable:

```
var Age;
Age = 21;
```

In this case, the code used two statements to declare and then to initialize the variable **Age**. Both operations also can be performed in one statement, as shown here:

```
var Age = 21;
```

When you assign a value to a variable, the type of value you assign may differ. The following statements assign an integer, a floating-point, and a character-string value to different variables:

```
var Age = 21;
var Salary = 35000.00;
var Name = 'Jane Doe';
```

As you can see, the variable **Age** is assigned the integer value 21. An integer value is essentially a counting number. The following statement assigns the value 35000.00 to the variable **Salary**. Developers refer to numbers with a decimal point as a floating-point number. Finally, the last statement assigns a name, contained in single quotes, to the variable **Name**. Programmers refer to characters contained between quotes as a string.

The following HTML file, ShowVariables.html, assigns values to three variables and then displays each variable's value using an **alert** dialog box:

```
<!DOCTYPE html>
<html>
<head>
<script>
var Age = 21;
var Salary = 35000.00;
var Name = 'Jane Doe';
alert(Age);
alert(Salary);
alert(Name);
</script>
</head>
<body>
</body>
</html>
```

Within the code, Age, Salary, and Name are variables which contain a value. To reference the value a variable stores, you simply use the variable name. That's why there are no single quotes around the names within the alert statements. The file uses the assignment operator to assign values to each variable. After you assign a value to a variable, when you use the variable's name within your code, JavaScript retrieves the variable's value from memory and substitutes that value for the name.

When you view the file's contents, the browser displays the dialog boxes, as shown in **FIGURE 10-2**.

Single Quotes Versus Double Quotes

A character string is a sequence of characters enclosed within quotes. In JavaScript, you can use either single or double quotes to group the characters. However, you must use the quotes consistently; that is, if you start with a single quote, you must end with a single quote:

```
var Firstname = 'Kris';
var Lastname = "Jamsa";
```

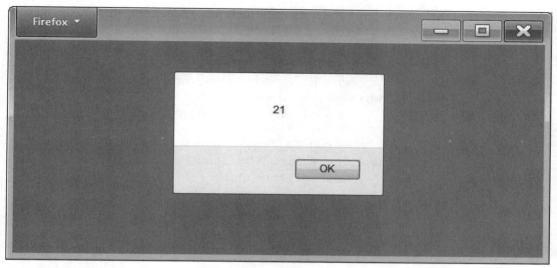

FIGURE 10-2 Using **alert** dialog boxes to display variable values

Breaking a Character String

When you work with long character strings in JavaScript, there may be times you will want to wrap the string to the start of the next line to improve the readability of your code. To do so, you have two choices. First, break the string into multiple strings and use the string concatenation operator, also known as the plus sign, to combine the strings:

```
alert('This is a very long string' +
' that wraps to the second line');
```

Second, you can use the backslash character (\) to wrap the content:

```
alert('This is a very long string \
that wraps to the second line');
```

Commenting JavaScript Code

When developers specify program statements, they need to comment or document their code to explain the processing that it performs. To comment your JavaScript code, use two techniques. First, you can comment one line at a time, by placing double slashes:

```
var Age = 21; // Assume the user is 21 years old
```

When JavaScript encounters the double slashes that start the comment, it ignores the characters that follow, up to the end of the line. That assumes they are simply messages to other programmers who are reading the program statements.

Many programmers place several lines of comments at the start of their code to explain who wrote the code, when, and why:

```
// Written by: Kris Jamsa
// Written: 09/30/13
// Purpose: Prompt the user for his or her age and
display appropriate content
```

The second way to comment JavaScript code is to use the /* and */ comment tag pair. When JavaScript encounters the characters /*, it ignores the characters that follow until it encounters the characters */.

```
/*
   Written by: Kris Jamsa
   Written: 09/30/13
   Purpose: Prompt the user for his or her age and
   display appropriate content
*/
```

When searching for errors within your code, there may be times you will want to disable statements until you can find the one causing the error. To do so, precede the statements with a comment. In the following statements, for example, only the **alert** function will execute. JavaScript ignores the first two statements because of the comments:

```
// var Age;
// Age = 21;
alert('Past the variable declaration');
```

Making Decisions Within JavaScript Code

When programs execute statements from the first statement to the last, they perform what is called sequential processing. For programs to perform meaningful work, they often need to make decisions. For example, if a user is 21 years of age or older, a webpage may display different content than it would for a younger user. To perform such decision-making processing, JavaScript supports **conditional processing**. This means JavaScript lets programs make decisions using the **if**, **if-else**, and **switch** statements.

When you use an **if** statement within your code, you specify a condition that, when true, directs JavaScript to execute the statement or statements that follow it:

```
if (SomeConditionIsTrue)
  statement;
if (SomeOtherConditionIsTrue)
{
  statement01;
  statement02;
}
```

When JavaScript must execute only one statement when a condition is true, simply specify the statement immediately after the **if** statement. If JavaScript must execute multiple statements when the condition is true, group the statements within left and right braces{}.

The following HTML file, AgeTest.html, creates a variable named Age. The code then prompts the user to enter an age by displaying a dialog box using the **prompt** function. The statement then uses an **if-else** statement to test if the user's age is greater than or equal to 21 and displays a message accordingly:

```
<!DOCTYPE html>
<html>
<head>
<script>
var Age;
Age = prompt('Enter an Age');
if (Age >= 21)
  alert('This Bud's for you!');
else
  alert('No Bud's for you!');
</script>
</head>
<body>
</body>
</html>
```

In this case, if the user enters an age of 21 or older, the **if** statement's condition will evaluate as true, and JavaScript will execute the statement that follows. If, instead, the user enters an age younger than 21, the **if** statement's condition will be false, which directs JavaScript to execute the statement that follows the **else**.

TABLE 10-2	THE JAVASCRIPT COMPARISON OPERATORS
Operator	**Description**
==	Tests if two values match
!=	Tests if two values do not match
>	Tests if a value is greater than another
<	Tests if a value is less than another
>=	Tests if a value is greater than or equal to another
<=	Tests if a value is less than or equal to another
===	Tests if two objects have the same value and type
!==	Tests if two objects differ by type or value

JavaScript Comparison Operators

When you perform tests within JavaScript **if** statements, you often need to compare one value with another, possibly to determine if the values are equal, one value is greater than or less than the other, and so on. To perform such operations, use the JavaScript comparison operators, defined in TABLE 10-2.

JavaScript Logical Operators

When you use the **if** statement within JavaScript code to implement conditional processing, there will be many times when you must consider more than one condition. For example, if the user has a pet and that pet is a dog, then display a photo of a dog on the page. To perform tests that require more than one condition, use the JavaScript logical operators, described in TABLE 10-3.

TABLE 10-3	THE JAVASCRIPT LOGICAL OPERATORS
Operator	**Description**
&&	Performs a logical and operation
||	Performs a logical or operation
!	Performs a logical not operation

JavaScript "if" Statements and Indentation

To make program statements easier to read, developers normally indent statements that follow an **if** or **else** statement:

```
if (condition)
  statement; // Note the indentation
if (condition)
  statement;
else
  statement;
if (condition)
  {
    statement01;
    statement02;
  }
```

JavaScript and Whitespace

To improve the visual appearance of their code, which makes the code easier to read, JavaScript developers often use extra space characters and blank lines. Developers refer to spaces and blank lines as **whitespace**. The following statements illustrate the use of whitespace to improve readability:

No Whitespace	With Whitespace

`var age,name,email;`
 	
`age=21;`
`name='Smith';`
`e-mail='Smith@somesite.`
`com';`
`if(age>=21) alert('This`
`Bud's for you');`
`else alert('No Bud's`
`for you');`
	`var age, name, email;`
	
	`age = 21;`
	`name = 'Smith';`
	`e-mail = 'Smith@somesite.`
	`com';`
	
	`if (age >= 21)`
	`  alert('This Bud's for`
	`  you');`
	`else`
	`  alert('No Bud's for`
	`  you');`

Using the JavaScript switch Statement

When you perform conditional processing, there may be times when you compare a variable with multiple values using **if-else** statements and then process accordingly. For example, the following statements test to determine a user's pet type:

```
if (pet == 'dog')
  alert('Dogs are great');
else if (pet == 'cat')
  alert('Cats are great');
else if (pet == 'fish')
  alert('Fish are great');
else if (pet == 'horse')
  alert('Horses are great');
```

When you compare a variable with a series of values in this way, you can take advantage of the JavaScript **switch** statement, which examines a value and then chooses a matching value:

```
switch (pet) {
case 'dog':   alert('Dogs are great');
              break;
case 'cat':   alert('Cats are great');
              break;
case 'fish':  alert('Fish are great');
              break;
case 'horse': alert('Horses are great');
              break;
default: alert('You should get a pet!');
```

In this case, JavaScript will examine the value of the variable **pet**. If the value is "dog," the code will execute the corresponding statements. Likewise, if the value is "cat," the **switch** statement will perform the cat-based statements. Note the use of the **break** statement. When the **switch** statement encounters a match, by default, JavaScript not only executes the statements for that match but for all of the conditions that follow. The **break** statement tells JavaScript that you have performed the processing you desire, and that it should continue its processing with the first statement that follows the **switch** statement. Also note the use of the **default** option. If JavaScript does not find a match within the entries, it executes the statements associated with the **default**.

Using the JavaScript Conditional Operator

Often, your code examines a condition and then uses an **if-else** statement to assign a value to a variable:

```
If (pet == 'dog')
  treat = 'bone';
```

```
else
  treat = 'cookie';
```

To simplify such operations, JavaScript provides a conditional operator that takes the form:

```
(condition) ? TrueResult: FalseResult;
```

Consider the following statement, which is equivalent to the previous **if-else** statements:

```
treat = (pet == 'dog') ? 'bone': 'cookie';
```

In this case, JavaScript will examine the condition (**pet ==‘dog’**). If the condition is true, JavaScript will assign to the variable **treat** the value "bone." If, instead, the pet is not a dog, Javascript will assign to the variable **treat** the value "cookie."

Repeating One or More Statements

In addition to letting JavaScript code make decisions, your code often needs to repeat one or more statements a specific number of times or as long as a condition is met. To allow you to perform such repetitive processing, which developers refer to as **iterative processing**, JavaScript provides the statements described in **TABLE 10-4**.

TABLE 10-4   JAVASCRIPT ITERATIVE STATEMENTS

Statement	Purpose

for loop
for (i = 0; i< 10; i++)
    alert(i);
	Repeats one or more statements a specific number of times

while loop while (i< 100) ++i;	Repeats one or more statements as long as a specified condition is true

do-while loop
do {
    alert(i);
} while (i< 100);
	Executes a loop's statements at least one time, and then repeats the statements if a condition is true

for/in loop
for (property in object)
    alert(property);
	Loops through an object's properties

The **for** loop is the most commonly used JavaScript iterative statement. It lets your code repeat one or more statements a specific number of times. The following loop consists of four parts: an initialization, test, increment, and statements to execute:

```
for (initializationPart; testCondition;
incrementPart)
statementsToExecute;
```

Consider the following loop:

```
for (i = 0; i< 5; ++i)
  alert(i);
```

As it starts, the **for** loop, in this case, initializes the variable **i** with the value 0. The loop then tests the variable's value to see if it is less than 5. If so, the loop executes the **alert** statement, which displays the variable's value. Then, the loop increments the variable's value and repeats the test. If the value is still less than 5, the processing repeats. When the variable eventually equals, the loop's condition will return false, which ends the loop. JavaScript then continues its processing with the first statement that follows the loop.

The following HTML file, ForLoopDemo.html, integrates this loop into an HTML page:

```
<!DOCTYPE html>
<html>
<head>
<script>
var i;
for (i = 0; i< 5; i++)
  alert(i);
</script>
</head>
<body>
</body>
</html>
```

When you view the file's contents, the browser displays **alert** dialog boxes for the values 0, 1, 2, 3, and 4.

Using JavaScript Functions

To program large or complex tasks, programmers often break the tasks into smaller pieces, which they can implement using a group of related statements called a function. In the simplest sense, a function contains the statements for a set of instructions that accomplish a specific task. To create a function within JavaScript, developers use the keyword **function** followed by the function name and parentheses, which specify values passed to the function, called parameters. The developer then groups the function statements within left and right braces:

```
functionSomeFunctionName(parameter01, parameter02)
{
// function statements
}
```

The following function, SayHello, displays the word "Hello" to the user:

```
functionSayHello()
{
  alert('Hello');
}
```

In this case, the **SayHello** function does not receive any parameter values. However, you must still include the parentheses following the function name.

In a similar way, the following function, **ShowMessage**, displays a specific message that the function receives as a parameter:

```
functionShowMessage(message)
{
  alert(message);
}
```

When a function receives a parameter value, it uses the name specified between the parentheses that follow the function name as the name of a variable that stores the parameter. Within the function code, you can treat the name as a variable.

Programmers refer to the process of using a function as "calling the function." To call a function, specify the function name within your code, including the parentheses and any parameters. The following HTML file, UseFunctions.html, creates the SayHello and ShowMessage functions and then calls them:

```
<!DOCTYPE html>
<html>
<head>
```

```
<script>
function SayHello()
{
  alert('Hello');
}
function ShowMessage(message)
{
  alert(message);
}
SayHello();
ShowMessage('I like Java!');
</script>
</head>
<body>
</body>
</html>
```

As you can see, after the code defines the functions, it calls them by simply referring to the function names. The **SayHello** function does not receive parameters, but you need to still include the empty parentheses after its name.

Using JavaScript Events

Often, when you use JavaScript within a webpage, you will call specific functions as different events occur, such as a user clicking on a button, the page loading, or even at specific timer intervals. To help you perform such processing, JavaScript lets you detect and respond to a wide range of events, as discussed in TABLE 10-5.

The following HTML file, ProcessEvents.html, calls the **SayHello** function when the page loads and the **ShowMessage** function when the user clicks the page button:

```
<!DOCTYPE html>
<html>
<head>
<script>
function SayHello()
{
  alert('Hello');
}
function ShowMessage(message)
{
```

TABLE 10-5   EVENTS DEFINED BY JAVASCRIPT

Event	Trigger
onafterprint	Triggered after the document is printed
onbeforeprint	Triggered before the document is printed
onbeforeunload	Triggered before the document is unloaded
onblur	Triggered when the element loses focus
onchange	Triggered when the value of the element is changed
onclick	Triggered when a user clicks on the element
oncontextmenu	Triggered when a context menu is triggered
ondblclick	Triggered when a user double-clicks the element
ondrag	Triggered when an element is dragged
ondragend	Triggered at the end of a drag operation
ondragenter	Triggered when an element is dragged to a valid drop target
ondragleave	Triggered when an element leaves a valid drop target
ondragover	Triggered when an element is being dragged over a valid drop target
ondragstart	Triggered at the start of a drag operation
ondrop	Triggered when a dragged element is being dropped
onerror	Triggered when an error occurs
onfocus	Triggered when the element gets focus
onformchange	Triggered when a form changes
onforminput	Triggered when a form gets user input
onhaschange	Triggered when the document has changed
oninput	Triggered when an element gets user input
oninvalid	Triggered when an element is invalid

continues

TABLE 10-5   EVENTS DEFINED BY JAVASCRIPT, continued

Event	Trigger
onkeydown	Triggered when a user is pressing a key
onkeypress	Triggered when a user presses a key
onkeyup	Triggered when a user releases a key
onload	Triggered after the page is finished loading
onmessage	Triggered when the message is triggered
onmousedown	Triggered when a mouse button is pressed down on an element
onmousemove	Triggered when the mouse pointer moves over an element
onmouseout	Triggered when the mouse pointer moves out of an element
onmouseover	Triggered when the mouse pointer moves over an element
onmouseup	Triggered when a mouse button is released over an element
onmousewheel	Triggered when the mouse wheel is being rotated
onoffline	Triggered when the document goes offline
ononline	Triggered when the document comes online
onpagehide	Triggered when the window is hidden
onpageshow	Triggered when the window becomes visible
onpopstate	Triggered when the window's history changes
onredo	Triggered when the document performs a redo
onreset	Triggered when a form's Reset button is clicked
onresize	Triggered when the browser window is resized
onscroll	Triggered when an element's scrollbar is being scrolled

continues

TABLE 10-5 EVENTS DEFINED BY JAVASCRIPT, continued	
Event	**Trigger**
onselect	Triggered when text is selected in an element
onstorage	Triggered when a Web storage area is updated
onsubmit	Triggered when a form is submitted
onundo	Triggered when the document performs an undo
onunload	Triggered when a page is unloaded or the browser window is closed

```
    alert(message);
  }
</script>
</head>
<body onload="SayHello()">
<button onclick="ShowMessage('Clicked!')">Click
Here</button>
</body>
</html>
```

As you can see, when the page loads, the browser calls the **SayHello** function. Likewise, using the **onclick** event, the browser calls the **ShowMessage** function when you click the button.

Returning a Value from a Function

Often, a function will perform its processing and then return a result. The following function, MinValue, compares the two values it receives as parameters and then returns the smaller of the two:

```
functionMinValue(A, B)
{
  if (A < B)
    return(A);
  else
    return(B);
}
```

In this case, the **MinValue** function receives two parameters. When a function receives multiple parameters, you separate the parameters with a comma. The following HTML file, UseReturn.html, creates and then calls the **MinValue** function. The code displays the value the number returns within an **alert** dialog box:

```
<!DOCTYPE html>
<html>
<head>
<script>
function MinValue(A, B)
{
  if (A < B)
    return(A);
  else
    return(B);
}
</script>
</head>
<body>
<button onclick="alert(MinValue(5, 2))">Click
Here</button>
</body>
</html>
```

The page contains a button that, when clicked, the browser calls the **MinValue** function passing to the function the values 5 and 2. The function then determines and returns the smaller of the two values, which the page displays using the **alert** function.

Declaring Variables Within a Function

As you create functions to perform specific tasks, many times the functions will need variables to store specific information while the function's code executes. In such cases, simply declare the variables following the function name:

```
functionSomeFunction()
{
var Name, Age, Email;
}
```

Variables defined within a function are called **local variables** in that their values, and even the fact that they exist, are only known to that function. Other functions you create, for example, would not know about the variables **Name**, **Age**, and **Email** defined in the **SomeFunction** code just shown.

In contrast to a local variable that is known only to the function within which it is declared, a **global variable** is known to every function in a file. To create a global variable, declare the variable outside of a function:

```
var TitleGlobalVariable = 'HTML 5 Web Development';
functionShowBook()
{
  alert(TitleGlobalVariable);
}
```

In this case, the code declares the global variable **TitleGlobalVariable** the value of which will be known to every function in the file. As a general rule, limit the use of global variables because of the risk of inadvertent errors, which can be difficult to detect and correct. They occur when a function with access to the global variable changes the variable's value in some way.

Storing Multiple Values in an Array

As you have learned, a variable lets your code temporarily store values in memory as the code executes. Depending on the processing your page performs, there may be times when your code needs to store multiple related values, such as a set of recommended links, a set of photos, a set of e-mail addresses, and so on. In such cases, use an **array** variable to store the multiple values. Think of an array as the name of a group of related storage locations. To specify which location in the array you desire, use an index value. The first item in the array is at the index value 0. The second is at index 1, the third at index 2, and so on. To specify an index, place the corresponding value with left and right brackets following the array name. For example, the following statements test to see if the first value in an array named **Student** contains the name "Smith":

```
if (Student[0] == 'Smith')
  alert('Some message');
```

To create an array variable, create an **Array** object, as shown here:

```
var Names = new Array();
```

After you declare an array variable, assign values to the indexed locations:

```
Names[0] = 'Smith';
Names[1] = 'Jones';
Names[2] = 'Davis';
```

JavaScript also lets you initialize an array as you declare the variable, as shown here:

```
var Names = new Array['Smith', 'Jones', 'Davis'];
```

Finally, you can use this syntax to declare and initialize an array:

```
var Names = ['Smith', 'Jones', 'Davis'];
```

The following HTML file, ArrayDemo.html, initializes an array of names and then uses a **for** loop to display the array values by calling the **alert** method:

```
<!DOCTYPE html>
<html>
<head>
<script>
function ShowArray()
{
  var Names = ['Smith', 'Jones', 'Davis'];
    var i;
  for (i = 0; i<Names.length; ++i)
    alert(Names[i]);
}
</script>
</head>
<body>
<button onclick="ShowArray()">Click Here</button>
</body>
</html>
```

When viewing the file's contents, the loop displays an **alert** dialog box for each name. The **for** loop, in this case, uses the array **length** property to determine the number of elements in the array.

Using JavaScript Objects

JavaScript is an object-oriented programming language that lets you use an object to store data as well as functions that operate on the data. To better understand JavaScript object processing, consider the built-in JavaScript **Date** object, which can be used to determine the current date and time. To start, use the JavaScript **new** operator to create a variable of the **Date** type:

```
var dateVariable = new Date();
```

Objects can store one or more values, called properties, and one or more functions, called methods. You access both the properties and methods using the JavaScript dot operator:

```
alert(dataVariable.toString());
```

The following HTML file, ShowDateTime.html, uses the **Date** object to display the current system date and time:

```
<!DOCTYPE html>
<html>
<head>
<script>
function ShowDateTime()
{
  var dateVariable = new Date();
  alert(dateVariable.toString());
}
</script>
</head>
<body>
<button onclick="ShowDateTime()">Click Here
</button>
</body>
</html>
```

When you view the file's contents, the browser displays an **alert** dialog box with the system date and time.

TABLE 10-6 lists other objects that are built into JavaScript.

In addition to using the built-in JavaScript objects, you can create your own objects. Assume that you want to create a **Student** object that contains a name, age, and GPA. To start, you must create a function that is named the same as your object, such as **Student**. The function will receive a parameter for each value the object stores. The **Student** function, therefore, will receive a name, age, and GPA parameter. Within the function, use the "this" object reference to assign the parameter values to the object fields, as shown here:

```
function Student(Name, Age, GPA)
{
this.Name = Name;
this.Age = Age;
this.GPA = GPA;
}
```

TABLE 10-6   JAVASCRIPT BUILT-IN OBJECTS

JavaScript Object	Purpose
Array	Creates an object capable of storing multiple values
Boolean	Stores a value as true or false
Date	Creates an object that provides access to the system date and time
Math	Provides a variety of constant definitions and methods for common arithmetic operations
Number	Stores a number as a 64-bit value with related properties and methods
RegExp	Provides routines for manipulating regular expressions
String	Provides an object capable of storing a character string with related string-manipulation methods

After you define the function, you can create objects using the **new** operator:

```
var someStudent = new Student('Smith', 21, 3.5);
var anotherStudent = new Student('Jones', 20, 3.3);
```

After you assign values to an object, you can use the dot operator to access an object's fields:

```
alert(anotherStudent.Name);
```

The following HTML file, CreateShowObject.html, creates a **Student** object that uses an **alert** dialog box to display the student fields:

```
<!DOCTYPE html>
<html>
<head>
<script>
function Student(Name, Age, GPA)
{
```

```
      this.Name = Name;
      this.Age = Age;
      this.GPA = GPA;
    }
    function ShowStudents()
    {
      var someStudent = new Student('Smith', 22, 3.15);
      alert(someStudent.Name);
      alert(someStudent.Age);
      alert(someStudent.GPA);
    }
</script>
</head>
<body>
<button onclick="ShowStudents()">Click Here
</button>
</body>
</html>
```

In this case, when the user clicks the page's button, the browser calls the **ShowStudents** function, which creates and displays a student.

Using an External JavaScript File

Throughout this chapter, you have used the **<script>** and **</script>** tag pair to place JavaScript statements within a page. Often, developers have a collection of JavaScript routines they use in many pages. Rather than copy the code into each file, the developers link an external file using a statement similar to the following:

```
<script src="someFile.js'></script>
```

In this case, the code links in a file named someFile.js. External JavaScript files normally use the .js file extension. Within the file, simply place your Java-Script statements without the **<script>** and **</script>** tag pair.

Real-World Web Design: Form Validation

In Chapter 6, "Getting User Input with Forms," you learned that webpages that perform form processing normally call a JavaScript function to validate that a user has provided values for each form field before the browser submits the form to the remote-server script. In this way, if the user has omitted the field, your code can notify the user and give him or her an opportunity to provide the data and not waste time sending the errant form across the network.

The JavaScript function that validates the form will return the value **true,** if the user has provided values for all required fields, or **false,** otherwise. That's how the browser knows whether it should send the data to the remote script or wait.

The following HTML file, SimpleForm.html, displays a form with three fields. When the user clicks the submit button, the browser calls the **ValidateForm** function. If the function returns **true,** the browser sends the data to the remote script:

```
<!DOCTYPE html>
<html>
<head>
<script>
function ValidateForm()
{
  if (document.forms["myForm"]["name"].value==null
  || document.forms["myForm"]["name"].value=="")
    {
      alert("Name must be filled out");
      return false;
    }
  if (document.forms["myForm"]["phone"].value==null
|| document.forms["myForm"]["phone"].value=="")
    {
      alert("Phone must be filled out");
      return false;
    }
  if (document.forms["myForm"]["email"].value==null
  || document.forms["myForm"]["email"].value=="")
    {
      alert("Email must be filled out");
      return false;
    }
  return true;
}
</script>
</head>
<html>
<body>
<form name="myForm" action="http://www.WebsiteDe-
velopmentBook.com/FormEcho.php" method="post"
```

```
onsubmit="return ValidateForm()" >
Name: <input type="text" name="name" /><br/>
Phone: <input type="text" name="phone" /><br/>
E-mail: <input type="text" name="email" /><br/>
<input type="submit" value="Click to Submit" />
</form>
</body>
</html>
```

As you can see, within the file, the **ValidateForm** function checks each field's value. If a field does not have a value, the function displays an error message using an **alert** dialog box and returns **false**. If, after checking all fields, the form is valid, the function returns **true**.

Hands-On HTML

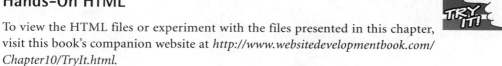

To view the HTML files or experiment with the files presented in this chapter, visit this book's companion website at *http://www.websitedevelopmentbook.com/ Chapter10/TryIt.html*.

CHAPTER SUMMARY

JavaScript is a programming language used to automate tasks within a webpage and improve the page's interactivity. What makes JavaScript unique is that the browser executes the JavaScript statements. As such, developers refer to JavaScript programming as client-side programming. This chapter introduced the JavaScript programming language. You will make extensive use of JavaScript throughout this book's chapters to access page elements, manipulate CSS, program the HTML 5 canvas, and more. Chapter 11, "Using the Document Object Model," examines the DOM, which programmers can use with JavaScript to access elements contained within a webpage.

KEY TERMS

Array

Conditional processing

Global variable

Iterative processing

Keyword

Local variable

Program

Syntax

Variable

Whitespace

CHAPTER REVIEW

1. Create an HTML file that uses an **alert** dialog box to display the message "Hi There!" when the page loads.

2. Create an HTML file that creates a variable named **TestScore**. Use a **prompt**-function dialog box to ask the user to specify a value for the variable. Then, use a series of **if-else** statements to display the corresponding grade based on the following:

   90 to 100: A

   80 to 89: B

   70 to 79: C

   60 to 69: D

   Below 60: F

3. Create an HTML file that uses a **for** loop to display the letters of the alphabet within **alert** dialog boxes.

4. Create an HTML file that displays the current system date and time within an **alert** dialog box as the page loads.

5. Create an HTML file that uses an array to store links for your three favorite websites. Use a **for** loop to display each link URL within an **alert** dialog box.

6. Create an HTML file that uses a function, which you create, named **Max** that returns the larger of two values.

7. Compare and contrast global and local variables, and provide a JavaScript example.

8. Create an HTML form, and use JavaScript to validate the fields.

9. Research the JavaScript **String** object, and discuss the capabilities it provides. Include examples of the object's use.

10. Create an HTML file that creates a **Dog** object that includes a breed, name, and age. Assign values to the object, and then use an **alert** dialog box to display each field's value.

Using the Document Object Model

A WEBPAGE CONSISTS OF many types of objects: paragraphs, headings, images, lists, tables, and more. To manage the items that make up a webpage, browsers do not work in terms of individual HTML tags but, rather, objects. The **Document Object Model (DOM)** defines the structure of a webpage in terms of objects. DOM is important beyond the developers who write the code that implements browsers, such as Internet Explorer and Google Chrome. Using JavaScript, any webpage developer can use DOM to access individual page components to create dynamic page content that may change based on user operations or to perform key operations, such as validating a form's contents.

Learning Objectives

This chapter examines the Document Object Model. By the time you finish this chapter, you will understand the following key concepts:

- How the Document Object Model defines the structure of a webpage in terms of objects
- How by using common DOM mouse events, such as **mouseover** or **mouseout**, your pages can respond to specific user mouse operations
- How to use frame-based events to control the look and feel of a document
- How using an object's **innerHTML** attribute allows you to access the nested HTML tags because many HTML tags enclose other HTML tags
- How to use the **document** object itself
- How to perform still more operations with DOM using other objects, such as the **window**, **navigator**, **history**, **screen**, and **location** objects, to use JavaScript code within your page

A Closer Look at Objects

An object, in the simplest sense, is a "thing." With respect to an HTML page, an object might be a paragraph, image, or table. All things have attributes, and the same is true for DOM objects. A paragraph, for example, has related text; an image has a corresponding source URL; a table might have a height and width.

In addition to attributes, the browser associates different events with objects, such as a mouse entering a table, hovering over an image, and so on. The sections that follow use different JavaScript functions to leverage object attributes and in the process change a webpage's behavior.

From a Web developer's perspective, it is less important to know the specifics of DOM than how it is possible to leverage DOM to perform common operations. This chapter focuses on the common operations. That said, if you want to drill deeper into DOM, the W3C website, at *http://www.w3.org/DOM/*, shown in **FIGURE 11-1,** provides details on the DOM specification.

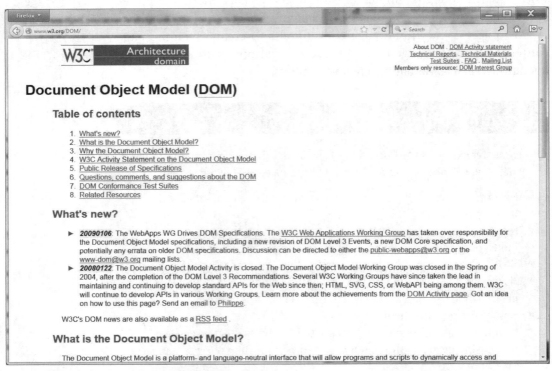

FIGURE 11-1 The W3C website provides specifics on the Document Object Model.

Reproduced with permission of the World Wide Web Consortium (W3C)

Common DOM Mouse Events

DOM defines several mouse and keyboard events that you can use to change your page's processing. The following HTML file, MouseOver.html, uses the DOM **mouseover** and **mouseout** events to change the image it displays when the user rolls the mouse onto and off the image:

```
<!DOCTYPE html>
<html>
<head>
<script>
function imageDog()
  {
  var ImageObject = document.getElementById("DogCat");

  ImageObject.src = "http://www.websitedevelopment
  book.com/Chapter11/Dog.jpg";
  }

function imageCat()
  {
  var ImageObject = document.getElementById("DogCat");

  ImageObject.src = "http://www.websitedevelopment
  book.com/Chapter11/Cat.jpg";
  }
</script>
</head>

<body>
<img id="DogCat" onmouseover="imageCat()"
onmouseout="imageDog()"
src="http://www.websitedevelopmentbook.com/
Chapter11/Dog.jpg" >
</body>
</html>
```

As you can see, the file uses the Dog.jpg image. Within the **<img>** tag, the file uses the **onmouseover** and **onmouseout** events to call JavaScript functions that use the **getElementByID** method to get the **image** object and then to assign a new image URL to the object. When you view the file's contents, the browser will display the starting image. If you roll your mouse over the image, it will change, as shown in **FIGURE 11-2**.

FIGURE 11-2 Using DOM mouse events to create dynamic page content
Credit (from left): © jurra8/Shutterstock; © dinadesign/Shutterstock

In a similar way, the following HTML file, MouseOverParagraph.html, performs similar processing, but by using text as opposed to an image:

```
<!DOCTYPE html>
<html>
<head>
<script>
function greenText()
  {
  var paragraphObject = document.
  getElementById("Paragraph");
  paragraphObject.style.color = 'yellow';
  }

function blueText()
  {
  var paragraphObject = document.
  getElementById("Paragraph");

  paragraphObject.style.color = 'blue';
  }
</script>
</head>
```

FIGURE 11-3 Using DOM mouse events to dynamically change the appearance of text within an HTML page

```
<body>
<p id="Paragraph" style="color:blue"
onmouseover="greenText()" onmouseout="blueText()">
Paragraph text
</p>
</body>
</html>
```

In this case, the code still uses the **onmouseover** and **onmouseout** events. Within the JavaScript event handlers, the code uses the DOM **style** class **color** property to set the paragraph text color.

If you view the file's contents, your browser will illustrate the dynamic processing, as shown in **FIGURE 11-3**.

Taking Advantage of Frame-Based Events

In addition to having mouse-based events, DOM provides frame-based events that you can use to control your document's look and feel. For example, your page contents might use a different font size as the user increases or decreases the browser window size.

The following HTML file, WindowSize.html, displays an **alert** dialog box each time the user sizes the window. Depending on the speed at which you move the window, the browser may trigger multiple **onresize** events for one sizing operation:

```
<!DOCTYPE html>
<html>
<body onresize="alert('Resize Operation')">
<img src="http://www.websitedevelopmentbook.com/
Chapter11/dog.jpg" id="Dog">
</body>
</html>
```

Using an Object's InnerHTML Attribute

Many HTML tags have content, called **innerHTML**, that exists between the starting and ending tags. The **<body>** and **</body>** tag pair's **innerHTML**, for example, contains your webpage's entire content. The following HTML file, ShowParagraph.html, uses a message box to display the **innerHTML** of the document's middle paragraph:

```
<!DOCTYPE html>
<html>
<body>
<p>Paragraph one</p>
<p id="middleParagraph">Paragraph two</p>
<p>Paragraph three</p>
<button onclick="alert(document.getElementById
('middleParagraph').innerHTML);">
Show innerHTML
</button>
</body>
</html>
```

The HTML file, in this case the **<button>** tag, detects the **onclick** event and directly calls the **alert** function to display the element's **innerHTML**.

When you view the file's contents, the browser displays the page shown in **FIGURE 11-4**. If you click on the **Show innerHTML** button, the page displays an alert window that contains the paragraph's **innerHTML**.

In addition to letting you display an element's **innerHTML**, you can also use JavaScript to change it. The following HTML file, EnglishHindi.html, displays a

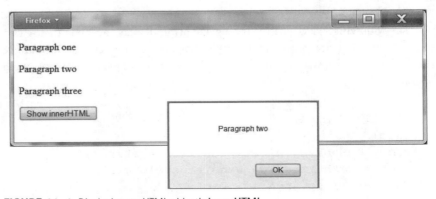

FIGURE 11-4 Displaying an HTML object's **innerHTML**

paragraph in English by default. When you roll your mouse over the paragraph, the page changes the content to Hindi:

```
<!DOCTYPE html>
<html>
<script>
function toHindi()
  {
  var paragraphObject = document.getElementById
  ("Paragraph");

  paragraphObject.innerHTML = "गर्भावस्थाक आमतौर पर 9
महीयने (40 ससाॅह) तक चलती है, जिसे आपकी पिछली माहवारी की
तारीख से गिना जाता है। अपनी सटीक नियत तिथि का अनुमान लगाने के
लिए (लगभग 2 ससाकह तक सटीक) अपनी पिछली माहवारी की तारीख से
आरंभ करें और उसमें 280 दिन";
  }

function toEnglish()
  {
  var paragraphObject = document.getElementById
  ("Paragraph");

  paragraphObject.innerHTML = "Pregnancy normally
lasts 9 months (40 weeks), calculated from the date
of your last menstrual period. To estimate
(accurate to about 2 weeks) your due date, start
with the date of your last menstrual cycle and then
add 280 days.";
  }

</script>
<body>
<p id="Paragraph" onmouseover="toHindi()" onmouseout
="toEnglish()">Pregnancy normally lasts 9 months
(40 weeks), calculated from the date of your last
menstrual period. To estimate (accurate to about
2 weeks) your due date, start with the date of your
last menstrual cycle and then add 280 days.</p>
</body>
</html>
```

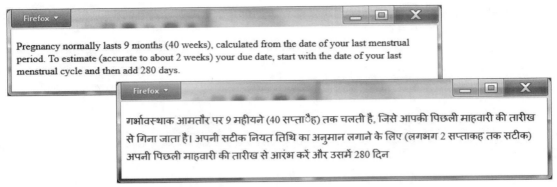

FIGURE 11-5 Using JavaScript to change an element's **innerHTML**

As you can see, the **<p>** tag detects the **onmouseover** and **onmouseout** events and calls functions that assign either English or Hindi to the paragraph's **innerHTML** property.

If you view the file's contents, the browser displays the English text to start. When you roll your mouse over the paragraph, the page changes the content to Hindi, as shown in **FIGURE 11-5**.

Using the Document Object

One of the most commonly used objects within the Document Object Model is the **document** object itself. Each page that the browser loads becomes a **document** object. The document, in turn, holds the other page elements. Using JavaScript, developers use the **document** object's **write** and **writeln** methods to write content to the document. The difference between the two functions is that **writeln** includes a carriage return and line feed after the text. As a page loads, a developer might, for example, determine which browser the user is using and write browser-specific code to the page.

The following HTML file, DocumentWriteline.html, uses JavaScript and the **document.writeln** method to write the message "Hello, DOM" to the screen as the page loads:

```
<!DOCTYPE html>
<html>
<body>
<script>
document.writeln("Hello, DOM");
</script>
<p>Other document content</p>
</body>
</html>
```

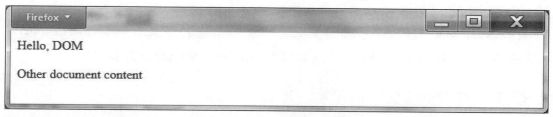

FIGURE 11-6 Using the **document.writeln** method to write content to the current page

As you have learned, when a browser loads a page, the browser executes specified JavaScript statements. In this case, the **document.writeln** statement directs the browser to write a message to the current webpage. If you view this file's contents, the browser displays the content, as shown in **FIGURE 11-6**.

When you use the **document.writeln** method, you write content to the current HTML page. The browser, in turn, examines and displays that content. If you include HTML tags within that content, the browser uses the tags to format the content. For example, the following HTML file, BoldWriteline.html, changes the previous **document.writeln** statement to bold the word "Hello" in the message:

```
<!DOCTYPE html>
<html>
<body>
<script>
document.writeln("<b>Hello</b>, DOM");
</script>
<p>Other document content</p>
</body>
</html>
```

If you view the file's contents using your browser, the browser displays the contents shown in **FIGURE 11-7**.

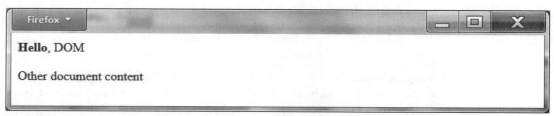

FIGURE 11-7 Using **document.writeln** to write HTML tags and content to the current page

Sun Oct 07 201208:50:26 GMT-0700 (US Mountain Standard Time)

Other document content

FIGURE 11–8 Writing dynamic content, such as the date and time, to the current document

The following HTML file, WriteDateTime.html, uses the **document.writeln** statement to write the current date and time to the document:

```
<!DOCTYPE html>
<html>
<body>
<script>
document.writeln(new Date().toDateString() + new
Date().toTimeString());
</script>
<p>Other document content</p>
</body>
</html>
```

When you view the file's contents, the browser displays content similar to that shown in **FIGURE 11–8**.

Still More Operations to Perform with DOM

This chapter's goal was to get you started with different types of operations you can perform using DOM. The W3Schools website provides additional JavaScript examples at *http://www.w3schools.com/jsref/default.asp.*

In addition to letting JavaScript developers access DOM object attributes and events, browsers also let them retrieve information and events related to the current window, the browser itself, the screen, the user's browser history, and specifics about the current page location (URL).

Using the Window Object

Using the **window** object, you can determine the window's current coordinates relative to the screen, the height and width of the window's inner contents, and more. The following HTML file, WindowInfo.html, uses a message box to display specifics about the current window. In this case, the page displays a **Window Information** button that, when clicked, directs the file to display a message box with the window's specifics:

```
<!DOCTYPE html>
<html>
<body>
<script>
alert("Top: " + window.screenY + " Window.left: "
+ window.screenX + " Inner Height: "
+ window.innerHeight + " Inner Width: "
+ window.innerWidth);
</script>
</body>
</html>
```

As you can see, the **alert** method combines text output with the values for various **window** object properties.

When you view the file's contents and click the button, the page displays the message box containing the window's specifics, as shown in **FIGURE 11-9**.

The following HTML file, PrintWindow.html, uses a **window** object **print** method to print the window contents. In this case, the window displays a button the user can click to trigger the print operation:

```
<!DOCTYPE html>
<html>
<body>
<img src="http://www.websitedevelopmentbook.com/
Chapter11/Dog.jpg" >
<br/>
```

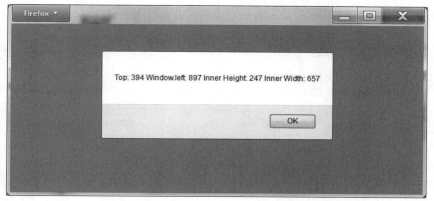

Top: 394 Window.left: 897 Inner Height: 247 Inner Width: 657

OK

FIGURE 11-9 Using the **window** object to get information on the browser window

FIGURE 11-10 Using the **window.print** method to print a webpage's contents
Credit: © jurra8/Shutterstock

```
<button onclick="window.print()">Print Window</button>
</body>
</html>
```

In this case, the **<button>** tag detects the **onclick** event and simply calls the **window.print** method. If you view the file's contents using the Firefox browser, your screen displays output similar to that shown in **FIGURE 11-10**.

Using the Screen Object

As you have learned, using the **window** object, you can determine specifics about the current browser window. In a similar way, using the **screen** object, you can determine the size of the screen that is displaying the current window. The following HTML file, ScreenInfo.html, uses a message box to display the current screen settings:

```
<!DOCTYPE html>
<html>
<body>
```

```
<script>
alert("Width: " + screen.width + " Height: "
+ screen.height + " Colors: " + screen.colorDepth);
</script>
</body>
</html>
```

As you can see, the page simply uses an **alert** message box to display specifics about the **screen** object. When you view the file's contents, your screen displays coordinates similar to those shown in **FIGURE 11-11**.

Using the Navigator Object

Despite the generic nature of HTML, there may be times when you need to perform some browser-specific processing. In such cases, use the **navigator** object to determine the current browser. The following HTML file, BrowserName.html, retrieves the **navigator** object and then uses it to determine the name of the current browser, which it displays using a message box:

```
<!DOCTYPE html>
<html>
<body>
<script>
alert(navigator.appName);
</script>
</body>
</html>
```

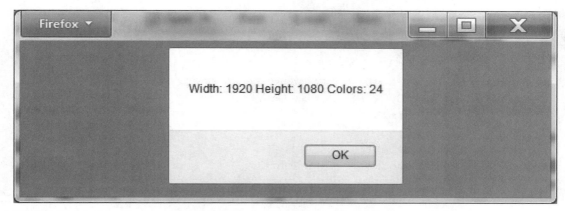

FIGURE 11-11 Using the **screen** object to determine specifics about the current screen display

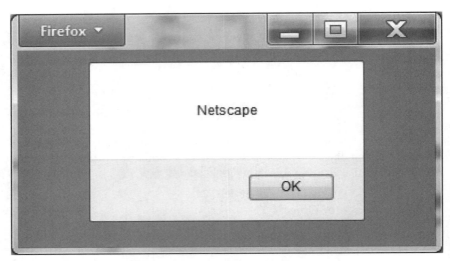

FIGURE 11-12 Displaying browser specifics using the **navigator** object

When you view the file's contents, your screen will display a message box similar to that shown in **FIGURE 11-12**.

Using the History Object

As you surf the Web, your browser tracks the sites that you visit within its history list. Using the **history** object, your pages can query the number of sites in the history list and even direct the browser to load a specific page from the history, such as page 2 or page 3. Your webpage cannot, however, actually view specifics about a page in the list (that is, it cannot determine the URL). Instead, the page can only direct the browser to load a page from its position in the history list.

The following HTML file, HistoryDemo.html, uses the **history** object to determine the number of items in the history list. Then, the file creates a pull-down list from which the user can load a specific page:

```
<!DOCTYPE html>
<html>
<head>
<script>
function changeContent()
{
  var value = document.getElementById('PullDown')
  .value;
```

```
    history.go(value);
}
</script>
</head>
<body>
<select id="PullDown" onchange="changeContent();"
style="width:100;">
<script>
for (i = 0; i < history.length; i++)
{
  document.writeln("<option value=" + i + ">" + i
  + "</option>");
}
</script>
<select>
</body>
</html>
```

In this case, the code uses a JavaScript **for** loop to build a pull-down list with numbers that correspond to pages in the **history** object. When you view the file's contents, the browser will display content similar to that shown in FIGURE 11-13. When the user selects a page, the page uses the **history.go** method to load that page.

Using the Location Object

The **location** object lets you get information about a page's URL, such as the domain name, file path, or the search query appended to the end of the URL, such as *http://www.somesite.com/file.html?someQuery=value.*

FIGURE 11-13 Providing a user with access to the browser's history list

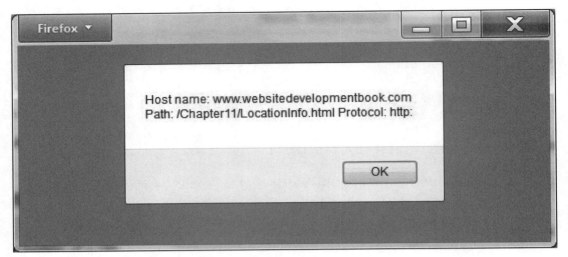

FIGURE 11-14 Using the **location** object to determine file specifics

The following HTML file, LocationInfo.html, uses a message box to display information about the current page URL:

```
<!DOCTYPE html>
<html>
<body>
<script>
alert("Host name: " + location.host + " Path: "
+ location.pathname + " Protocol: "
+ location.protocol);
</script>
</body>
</html>
```

When you view the file's contents, your browser displays content similar to that shown in **FIGURE 11-14**.

Real-World Web Design

Throughout this chapter, you examined a wide range of objects. As shown in **FIGURE 11-15**, the W3Schools website provides detailed documentation on the DOM objects as well as the JavaScript objects. As you work with various objects within your HTML pages, you may want to keep open a W3Schools window with the object's specifics.

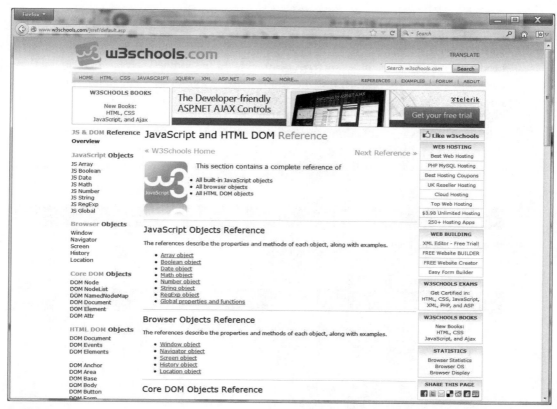

FIGURE 11-15 The W3Schools site provides detailed documentation on DOM and JavaScript objects.
Reproduced with permission of w3schools.com

Hands-On HTML

To view the HTML files or to experiment with the files presented in this chapter, visit this book's companion website at *http://www.websitedevelopmentbook.com/ Chapter11/TryIt.html*.

CHAPTER SUMMARY

To render a webpage, a browser treats the elements that make up the page, such as paragraphs, headings, images, lists, tables, and so on, as objects. In the simplest sense, an object is a thing consisting of attributes, events, and operations. One object may be a paragraph, one an image, one a table, and so on. To access such objects within a webpage, browsers use the Document Object Model, or DOM. This chapter introduced the Document Object Model. As you learned, using JavaScript within your webpage, you can use DOM to access individual page components to create dynamic page content that your page can change based on operations the user performs. You can also use DOM objects to perform key operations, such as validating a form's contents.

KEY TERMS

Document Object Model (DOM)
InnerHTML

CHAPTER REVIEW

1. Create an HTML file that displays paragraph text in white on a blue background. If the user moves the mouse over a paragraph, reverse the colors, displaying blue text on a white background.

2. Create an HTML file that uses the DOM to swap the contents of one paragraph with the contents of a second paragraph each time the user clicks a button.

3. Create an HTML file that uses **document.writeln** when a page loads to display the information in the **navigator** object within the page content.

4. Create an HTML file that uses the **history** object to reload the previous page contents each time the file's page loads. The file should use the **<body>** tag **onload** event to detect the page load option.

5. Create an HTML file that moves the current window from the top-left corner to the top-right corner, to the bottom-right corner, and to the bottom-left corner in a cyclic pattern every 10 seconds.

Unleashing JavaScript Using jQuery

IN THE LAST TWO chapters, you examined JavaScript and the Document Object Model (DOM). Using JavaScript and DOM, you can perform powerful client-side processing within your webpages that access or change element settings, create animations, and more. In this chapter, you will learn how to leverage jQuery to simplify many JavaScript operations and create more interactive user experiences. Do not let the name jQuery confuse you. It has nothing to do with database operations. Rather, **jQuery** is a library of JavaScript functions your page can use to manipulate items on your webpage.

Learning Objectives

This chapter examines common jQuery functions. By the time you finish this chapter, you will understand the following key concepts:

- How to integrate the jQuery library into an HTML page
- How to implement jQuery syntax
- How to use jQuery to fade an element out of or into a page
- How to use jQuery to hide or show an element
- How to use jQuery to slide a page division
- How to use jQuery to animate an object
- How to use jQuery to access HTML or CSS elements within a page

Integrating the jQuery Library

JQuery is a library of routines your pages can call using JavaScript. You access it much as you would an external JavaScript file. Developers integrate jQuery into the pages they create in two ways. First, the developers often download the jQuery library from the jQuery.com website, shown in **FIGURE 12-1**.

After they download the jQuery library file, the developers then place a copy of the file into the folder that contains a page's HTML files. Then they link to the file within their page using a statement such as:

```
<script src="jquery.js"></script>
```

The second way developers integrate jQuery into their code, and the method used throughout this chapter's example programs, is to link the jQuery file from an existing site on the Web. In this book's examples, the code will link to the jQuery file on this book's companion website using the following statement:

```
<script src="http://www.websitedevelopmentbook.com/
chapter12/jquery.js"></script>
```

Note: From the jQuery.com website, download the jQuery library in source code format or an obfuscated format that downloads faster within your programs. If you are creating real-world programs, use the smaller and faster obfuscated form.

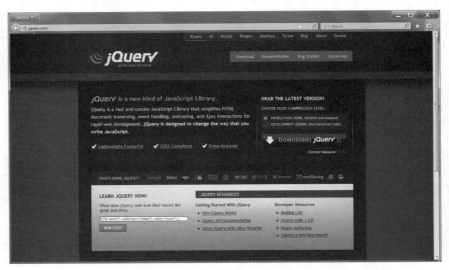

FIGURE 12-1 Developers download the jQuery library from the jQuery.com website.
Reproduced with permission of the jQuery Foundation (www.jquery.com)

The jQuery Syntax

To use jQuery, you generally specify an element on your page and the operation you want to perform on the element. The general jQuery syntax is:

```
$(elementSelector).action();
```

The **elementSelector** corresponds to a selector you would use with cascading style sheets. Consider the following examples:

```
$(this).fadeOut();            // fades out the current
                              element
$("div").fadeOut();           // fades out all div
                              elements
$(".classname").fadeOut();    // fades out elements
                              that use the specified
                              CSS class
$("#elementID").fadeOut();    // fades out the element
                              with the id elementID
```

The following HTML file, FirstjQuery.html, illustrates the use of jQuery. The page first displays a photo of pets. Then, the page fades the photo to reveal the underlying page of content, as shown in **FIGURE 12-2**:

```
<!DOCTYPE html>
<html>
<head>
<script src="http://www.websitedevelopmentbook.com/
chapter12/jquery.js"></script>
<script>
function HideImage()
{
  $("#Pets").fadeOut(8000);
}
</script>
</head>
<body onload="HideImage()">
<img id="Pets" src="http://www.websitedevelopment
book.com/chapter12/Pets.jpg"
style="position:absolute; top:0px; left:0px;
z-index:1;"
width="650px" height="425px"/>
<div id="PageContent" style="position:absolute;
```

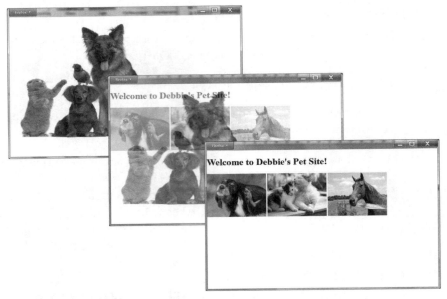

FIGURE 12-2 Using jQuery to fade out an image to reveal page content

Credit (from top): © Eric Isselee/Shutterstock; © Christian Mueller/Shutterstock; © Anastasija Popova/Shutterstock; © Melanie Hoffman/Shutterstock

```
top:0px;left:0px">
<h1>Welcome to Debbie's Pet Site!></h1>
<img src="http://www.websitedevelopmentbook.com/
chapter12/dog.jpg" width="200px" height="150px"/>
<img src="http://www.websitedevelopmentbook.com/
chapter12/cat.jpg" width="200px" height="150px"/>
<img src="http://www.websitedevelopmentbook.com/
chapter12/horse.jpg" width="200px" height="150px"/>
</div>
</body>
</html>
```

As you can see, the file uses a **z-index** value of 1 to place the large pet image over the **PageContent** page division. When the page loads, it calls the **HideImage** function, which fades the image over an eight-second period, displaying the underlying content.

JQuery Fade Operations

The previous file used the jQuery **fadeOut** method to slowly fade an image out of view. JQuery actually provides four functions that control element fading, as discussed in **TABLE 12-1**.

TABLE 12-1	JQUERY FUNCTIONS THAT CONTROL ELEMENT FADING	
Name	**Purpose**	**Sample**
fadeIn	Fades an object into view	$(element).fadeIn(speed, callback function)
fadeOut	Fades an object out of view	$(element).fadeOut(speed, callback function)
fadeToggle	Fades an object in or out of view based on its current setting	$(element).fadeToggle(speed, callback function)
fadeTo	Fades an object to a specified opacity	$(element).fadeTo(speed, opacity, callback function)

The following HTML file, jQuerySlideShow.html, uses jQuery to display a series of photos, much like a slide show. The page will display each photo for a few seconds and then fade the photo out to reveal a new photo. The page will repeat this process to display all of the images, at which point it repeats the process:

```
<!DOCTYPE html>
<html>
<head>
<script src="http://www.websitedevelopmentbook.com/
chapter12/jquery.js"></script>
<script>
function FadeImage(I)
{
var Image = '#'+I;
$(Image).fadeIn();
$(Image).fadeOut(5000, function()
{ FadeImage((I == 1) ? 3: I-1); });
}
</script>
</head>
<body onload="FadeImage(3);">
<img id="1" src="http://www.websitedevelopmentbook.
com/chapter12/maui01.jpg"
style="position:absolute; left:0; top:0;
z-index:1;" />
<img id="2" src="http://www.websitedevelopmentbook.
com/chapter12/maui02.jpg"
```

FIGURE 12-3 Using jQuery to implement a slide show

Credit (from top): © EpicStockMedia/Shutterstock; © idreamphoto/Shutterstock; © Alberto Loyo/Shutterstock

```
style="position:absolute; left:0; top:0;
z-index:2;"/>
<img id="3" src="http://www.websitedevelopmentbook.
com/chapter12/maui03.jpg"
style="position:absolute; left:0; top:0;
z-index:3;"/>
</body>
</html>
```

As you can see, the page uses **z-index** values to originally stack the photos. When the page loads, it calls the function **FadeImage** with a value that corresponds to the **id** of the top image. The function first calls the **FadeIn** function to make sure the photo is visible in case it was previously faded out. Then, the function fades the image over a five-second period. When the fade out operation completes, it calls back the function for the next image. After the last image, the image with the **id** of 1 fades out, and the function calls itself back with the **id** of the top image (3).

When you view the page contents, the browser will cycle through the images, as shown in **FIGURE 12-3**.

Hiding and Showing Page Elements

Depending on the processing your page performs, there may be times when you will want to hide one or more elements or show previously hidden elements.

In such cases, use the jQuery **hide** and **show** methods. The format of the **hide** method is:

```
$(elementSelector).hide(speed, callback);
```

The function's **speed** and **callback** parameters are optional. You can specify the **speed** as "slow" or "fast" or in terms of milliseconds. The **callback** parameter specifies a function that jQuery will call after it completes the **hide** operation. In a similar way, the format for the **show** function is:

```
$(elementSelector).show(speed, callback);
```

The following HTML file, TicTacToeInterface.html, displays a tic-tac-toe board. The user can click on the location, and the board will display a large X or O as appropriate. The page simply displays the user choices. It does not implement the tic-tac-toe logic needed to play a game against the computer:

```
<!DOCTYPE html>
<html>
<head>
<script src="http://www.websitedevelopmentbook.com/
chapter12/jquery.js"></script>
<script>
var move = 'O';
varSpaceOpen = [0,0,0,0,0,0,0,0,0];

function ShowMove(location)
{
  if (SpaceOpen[location-1] == 1)
    return;
  else
    SpaceOpen[location-1] = 1;

  if (move == 'X')
    {
      Image = '#' + location + "x";
      $(Image).show();
      move = 'O';
    }
  else
  {
    Image = '#' + location + "o";
    $(Image).show();
    move = 'X';
```

```
    }
  }
  function HideImage(Image)
  {
    $(Image).hide();
  }

</script>
</head>
<body>
<div style="background-color: yellow; width:125px;
height:125px; position:absolute; top:0px; left:0px"
id="1" onclick="ShowMove(this.id)">
<img id="1o" src="o.jpg" style="z-index:0;"
onload="HideImage(this)"/>
<img id="1x" src="x.jpg" style="position:absolute;
top:0px; left:0px; z-index:1;"
onload="HideImage(this)"/>
</div>

<div style="background-color: orange; width:125px;
height:125px; position:absolute; top:0px;
left:125px" id="2" onclick="ShowMove(this.id)">
<img id="2o" src="o.jpg" style="z-index:0;"
onload="HideImage(this)"/>
<img id="2x" src="x.jpg" style="position:absolute;
top:0px; left:0px; z-index:1;"
onload="HideImage(this)"/>
</div>

<div style="background-color: yellow; width:125px;
height:125px; position:absolute; top:0px;
left:250px" id="3" onclick="ShowMove(this.id)">
<img id="3o" src="o.jpg" style="z-index:0;"
onload="HideImage(this)"/>
<img id="3x" src="x.jpg" style="position:absolute;
top:0px; left:0px; z-index:1;"
onload="HideImage(this)"/>
</div>

<div style="background-color: orange; width:125px;
height:125px; position:absolute; top:125px;
```

```
left:0px" id="4" onclick="ShowMove(this.id)">
<img id="4o" src="o.jpg" style="z-index:0;"
onload="HideImage(this)"/>
<img id="4x" src="x.jpg" style="position:absolute;
top:0px; left:0px; z-index:1;"
onload="HideImage(this)"/>
</div>

<div style="background-color: yellow; width:125px;
height:125px; position:absolute; top:125px;
left:125px" id="5" onclick="ShowMove(this.id)">
<img id="5o" src="o.jpg" style="z-index:0;"
onload="HideImage(this)"/>
<img id="5x" src="x.jpg" style="position:absolute;
top:0px; left:0px; z-index:1;"
onload="HideImage(this)"/>
</div>

<div style="background-color: orange; width:125px;
height:125px; position:absolute; top:125px;
left:250px" id="6" onclick="ShowMove(this.id)">
<img id="6o" src="o.jpg" style="z-index:0;"
onload="HideImage(this)"/>
<img id="6x" src="x.jpg" style="position:absolute;
top:0px; left:0px; z-index:1;"
onload="HideImage(this)"/>
</div>

<div style="background-color: yellow; width:125px;
height:125px; position:absolute; top:250px;
left:0px" id="7" onclick="ShowMove(this.id)">
<img id="7o" src="o.jpg" style="z-index:0;"
onload="HideImage(this)"/>
<img id="7x" src="x.jpg" style="position:absolute;
top:0px; left:0px; z-index:1;" onload="HideImage
(this)"/>
</div>

<div style="background-color: orange; width:125px;
height:125px; position:absolute; top:250px;
left:125px" id="8" onclick="ShowMove(this.id)">
<img id="8o" src="o.jpg" style="z-index:0;"
```

```
    onload="HideImage(this)"/>
    <img id="8x" src="x.jpg" style="position:absolute;
    top:0px; left:0px; z-index:1;"
    onload="HideImage(this)"/>
    </div>

    <div style="background-color: yellow; width:125px;
    height:125px; position:absolute; top:250px;
    left:250px" id="9" onclick="ShowMove(this.id)">
    <img id="9o" src="o.jpg" style="z-index:0;"
    onload="HideImage(this)"/>
    <img id="9x" src="x.jpg" style="position:absolute;
    top:0px; left:0px; z-index:1;"
    onload="HideImage(this)"/>
    </div>

    </body>
    </html>
```

In this case, the page defines nine page divisions to match the nine board positions. Within each division, the page loads and then hides an image of an X and an O. Later, when the user clicks on a location, the page checks if that image is already filled, and if not, depending on the current move, displays an X or O image, as shown in **FIGURE 12–4**.

Using jQuery to Slide Content

When pages need to display large amounts of content, Web developers can use jQuery to let users slide open or closed regions on the screen display to maximize the use of limited screen real estate. To perform such operations, jQuery provides the slide functions, as described in **TABLE 12–2**.

FIGURE 12–4 Using jQuery to display Xs and Os on a tic-tac-toe board

TABLE 12-2   JQUERY SLIDE FUNCTIONS

Name	Purpose	Syntax
slideUp	Slides a division closed	$(element).fadeslideUp(speed, callback function)
slideDown	Slides a division open	$(element).fadeslideDown(speed, callback function)
slideToggle	Toggles the division open or closed based on its current setting	$(element).fadeslideToggle(speed, callback function)

The following HTML file, jQueryQuoteGuess.html, displays several quotes within bars on the screen. Next to each quote are buttons that users can use to reveal a photo of the person who made the quote and later to hide the person's photo, as shown in **FIGURE 12-5**:

```
<!DOCTYPE html>
<html>
<head>
```

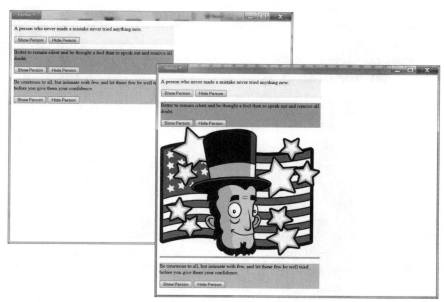

FIGURE 12-5 Using jQuery to slide open and closed the content regions on the page
Credit: © Cory Thoman/Shutterstock

```
<script src="http://www.websitedevelopmentbook.com/
chapter12/jquery.js"></script>
<script>

function CloseSlide(Division)
{
  Division = '#'+Division;
  $(Division).slideUp();
}
function OpenSlide(Division)
{
  Division = '#'+Division;
  $(Division).slideDown();
}

</script>
</head>
<body>
<div style="background-color:yellow; width:500px;
height=500px;" id="1">
<div style="width:500px; height=50px;" id="1a">
<p>A person who never made a mistake never tried
anything new.</p>
<button onclick="OpenSlide('1b')">Show Person
</button>
<button onclick="CloseSlide('1b')">Hide Person
</button>
</div>
<div style="width:500px; height=450px;" id="1b">
<img src="einstein.jpg" onload="CloseSlide('1b')"/>

</div>
</div>

<div style="background-color:orange; width:500px;
height=500px;" id="2">
<div style="width:500px; height=50px;" id="2a">
<p>Better to remain silent and be thought a fool
than to speak out and remove all doubt.</p>
<button onclick="OpenSlide('2b')">Show Person
</button>
<button onclick="CloseSlide('2b')">Hide Person
```

```
</button>
</div>
<div style="width:500px; height=450px;" id="2b" >
<img src="lincoln.jpg" onload="CloseSlide('2b')"/>
</div>
</div>

<div style="background-color:lightblue;
width:500px; height=500px;" id="3">
<div style="width:500px; height=50px;" id="3a">
<p>Be courteous to all, but intimate with few, and
let those few be well tried before you give them
your confidence.</p>
<button onclick="OpenSlide('3b')">Show Person
</button>
<button onclick="CloseSlide('3b')">Hide Person
</button>
</div>

<div style="width:500px; height=450px;" id="3b">
<img src="washington.jpg"
onload="CloseSlide('3b')"/>
</div>
</div>
</body>
</html>
```

In this case, the page creates one large division for each quote. Then, within that division, the page creates a division that has the quote and buttons as well as a division that opens and closes to hide and reveal the image.

Creating jQuery Animations

Using jQuery, combine techniques presented in this chapter along with object positioning to create animations. To support such operations, use the jQuery **animate** function:

```
$(elementSelector).animate({params},speed,
callback);
```

The **animate** method lets you specify ending parameter values for the object, such as an ending color or ending position. The following HTML file,

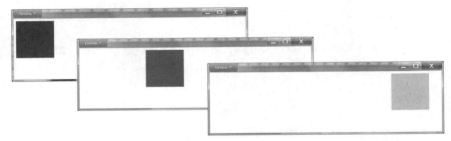

FIGURE 12-6 Using jQuery to slide an object across a window

SimplejQueryAnimation.html, slides a box across a window, reducing the object's opacity as it moves, as shown in **FIGURE 12-6**:

```
<!DOCTYPE html>
<html>
<head>
<script src="http://www.websitedevelopmentbook.com/
chapter12/jquery.js"></script>
<script>
function SlideBox(Division)
{
  Division = '#'+Division;
  $(Division).animate({ left:'600px',
  opacity: '0.2' }, 5000);
}

</script>
</head>
<body onload="SlideBox('1')">
<div style="width:125px; height:125px; background-
color:blue; position:absolute; left:0px" id="1">
</div>
</body>
</html>
```

To create the animation, the page creates a division with a blue background, which it will move. To animate an object, set the **position** attribute. After the page loads, it calls the **SlideBox** function, which uses the jQuery **animate** method to start the animation. In this case, the animation specifies the ending location, opacity, and a speed of five seconds.

The following HTML file, SlideForever.html, modifies the previous file slightly to use callback functions. Each time jQuery slides the box across the page, the callback function starts the object moving back in the opposite direction. In this way, the box will slide forever:

```
<!DOCTYPE html>
<html>
<head>
<script src="http://www.websitedevelopmentbook.com/
chapter12/jquery.js"></script>
<script>

function SlideBox(Division)
{
  $(Division).animate({ left:'600px',
  opacity: '0.2' }, 5000, function ()
  { SlideBack(Division) });
}
function SlideBack(Division)
{
  $(Division).animate({ left:'10px',
  opacity: '1.0' }, 5000, function ()
  { SlideBox(Division) });
}

</script>
</head>
<body onload="SlideBox('#1')">
<div style="width:125px; height:125px;
background-color:blue; position:absolute;
left:10px" id="1"></div>
</body>
</html>
```

Finally, the HTML file, RevealImage.html, creates an animation that reveals a photo image, as shown in **FIGURE 12-7**:

```
<!DOCTYPE html
<html>
<head>
<script src="http://www.websitedevelopmentbook.com/
chapter12/jquery.js"></script>
<script>
function RevealImage(Image)
{
```

FIGURE 12-7 Using jQuery to reveal a photo image
Credit (from top): © Gts/Shutterstock

```
    $(Image).animate({ opacity: '1.0' }, 5000);
}

</script>
</head>
<body onload="RevealImage('#1')">
<img id="1" src="wine.jpg" width="450"
height="300"
style="position:absolute; opacity:0.0;"/>
</body>
</html>
```

In this case, the page sets the image's original opacity to 0.0. Then, after the page loads, it calls the **RevealImage** function, which changes the opacity to 1.0 over a five-second period.

Using jQuery to Access HTML and CSS Settings

In Chapter 11, "Using the Document Object Model," you examined the DOM. To help you perform DOM-based operations, jQuery provides the functions specified in **TABLE 12-3**.

TABLE 12-3   JQUERY DOM-BASED FUNCTIONS

Name	Purpose	Syntax
text	Returns or sets the text context	($element).text()
html	Returns or sets the HTML context	($element).html()
val	Returns or sets the value of form fields	($element).val()

The following HTML file, jQueryDOMDemo.html, illustrates the use of the **jQuery html** method to assign the **<img>** tag for a page division:

```
<!DOCTYPE html>
<html>
<head>
<script src="http://www.websitedevelopmentbook.com/
chapter12/jquery.js"></script>
<script>
function DisplayImage(Pet)
{
  if (Pet == 'Dog')
    $('#ImageSpace').html('<img src="dog.jpg"/>');
  else
    $('#ImageSpace').html('<img src="cat.jpg"/>');
}
</script>
</head>
<body>
<div id="ImageSpace" style="width:1200;
height:400">
</div>
<br/>
<button onclick="DisplayImage('Dog')">Dog</button>
<button onclick="DisplayImage('Cat')">Cat</button>
</body>
</html>
```

As you can see, when the user clicks a button, the page calls the **DisplayImage** function with the desired pet type. Then the function uses the html method to assign the corresponding image, as shown in **FIGURE 12-8**.

FIGURE 12-8 Using jQuery to perform DOM-based operations
Credit (from top): © Christian Mueller/Shutterstock; © Anastasija Popova/Shutterstock

Adding or Removing Page Elements

As your webpages become more complex, there may be times when you will add or remove elements from the page dynamically, using JavaScript. In such cases, you can use the jQuery methods listed in **TABLE 12-4**.

The following HTML file, ImageAddRemove.html, adds five images to a page division, one image at a time. Then, the page reverses the processing, removing one image at a time. The page repeats its processing indefinitely:

```
<!DOCTYPE html>
<html>
<head>
<script src="http://www.websitedevelopmentbook.com/
chapter12/jquery.js"></script>
<script>

var Images = ['<img id="0" src="wine.jpg"
              width="200" height="150"/>',
```

TABLE 12-4: JQUERY METHODS FOR ADDING OR REMOVING PAGE ELEMENTS

Name	Purpose	Syntax
after	Inserts elements after the specified element	$(element).after(SomeString);
append	Appends elements at the end of the specified element	$(element).append(SomeString);
before	Inserts elements before the specified element	$(element).before(SomeString);
prepend	Inserts elements at the start of the specified element	$(element).prepend(SomeString);
empty	Removes child elements from the specified element	$(element).empty();
remove	Removes the select element and its child elements	$(element).remove();

```
'<img id="1" src="cigar.jpg"
 width="200" height="150"/>',
'<img id="2" src="pizza.jpg"
 width="200" height="150"/>',
'<img id="3" src="pasta.jpg"
 width="200" height="150"/>',
'<img id="4" src="dessert.jpg"
 width="200" height="150"/>'];

var i = 0;
var AddImageTimer;
var RemoveImageTimer;

function AddImage(Division)
{
  if (i == 0)
    {
      AddImageTimer = setInterval(function()
      { AddImage(Division) }, 1000);
      $("button").hide();
```

```
      }
   if (i<Images.length)
     {
       $(Division).append(Images[i]);
       i = i + 1;
     }
   else
     {
       i = i - 1;
       clearInterval(AddImageTimer);
       RemoveImage(Division);
     }
}

function RemoveImage(Division)
{
  if (i == (Images.length-1))
    RemoveImageTimer = setInterval(function()
    { RemoveImage(Division) }, 1000);

  if (i>= 0)
    {
       ImageId = '#'+i;
       $(ImageId).remove();
       i = i - 1;
     }
   else
     {
       i = 0;
       clearInterval(RemoveImageTimer);
       AddImage(Division);
     }
}

</script>
</head>
<body>
<div id="ImageSpace" style="width:1200;
height:400"></div><br/>
<button onclick="AddImage('#ImageSpace')">
Add Images</button></body>
</html>
```

FIGURE 12-9 Using jQuery to add and remove images from a page
Credit (from top): © Gts/Shutterstock; © marco mayer/Shutterstock; © Vima/Shutterstock; © lorenzo_graph/Shutterstock; © Shebeko/Shutterstock

To perform its processing, the code uses a JavaScript timer to call either the AddImage or RemoveImage functions every second. After all the images have been displayed, the page clears the AddImage timer and creates a new timer to remove images. To actually add the images, the code uses the jQuery **append** method. To remove an image, the code uses the jQuery **remove** method.

When you view the file's contents, the browser will display the images, as shown in **FIGURE 12-9**.

JQuery CSS Operations

As you have learned, Web developers make extensive use of CSS to format content on a webpage. Using jQuery, you can easily add, remove, or modify CSS definitions using the functions listed in **TABLE 12-5**.

The following HTML file, jQueryCSSDemo.html, illustrates the use of the **CSS** function to change a page's appearance. Using buttons on the page, you can toggle between the displays shown in **FIGURE 12-10**:

```
<!DOCTYPE html>
<html>
<head>
<script src="http://www.websitedevelopmentbook.com/
chapter12/jquery.js"></script>
<script>
function DisplayImage(Size)
```

TABLE 12-5: JQUERY CSS-BASED FUNCTIONS

Name	Purpose	Syntax
addClass	Adds one or more classes to the selected element	$(element).addClass(classString);
css	Sets or returns an element's CSS property	$(element).css('width', 400);
removeClass	Removes one or more classes from the selected element	$(element).removeClass(classString);
toggleClass	Adds or removes a class if it is missing or present	$(element).toggleClass(classString);
width	Returns an element's width	$(element).width()
height	Returns an element's height	$(element).height()
innerWidth	Returns an element's inner width	$(element).innerwidth()
innerHeight	Returns an element's inner height	$(element).innerHeight()
outerWidth	Returns an element's outer width	$(element).outerWidth()
outerHeight	Returns an element's outer height	$(element).outerHeight()

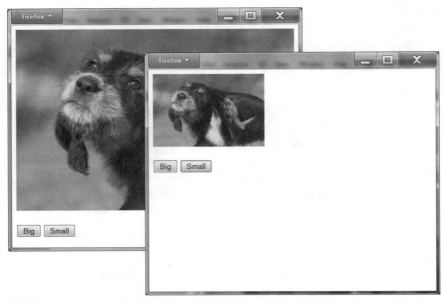

FIGURE 12-10 Using jQuery to change CSS settings to dynamically change a page display
Credit (from top): © Christian Mueller/Shutterstock

```
{
  if (Size == 'Big')
    $('#DogImage').css("width", "400px",
    "height", "300px");
  else
    $('#DogImage').css("width", "200px",
    "height", "150px");
}
</script>
</head>
<body>
<div style="width:600; height:400">
<img id="DogImage" src="dog.jpg" />
</div>
<br/>
<button onclick="DisplayImage('Big')">Big</button>
<button onclick="DisplayImage('Small')">Small
</button>
</body>
</html>
```

When the user clicks the big or small buttons, the page will call the **DisplayImage** function, which sets the **width** and **height** attributes.

JQuery AJAX Operations

In Chapter 13, "Communicating with AJAX," you will learn how to use Asynchronous JavaScript with AJAX to communicate with a remote server. To simplify AJAX operations, jQuery provides several functions you can use. After you complete Chapter 13, you should review the jQuery reference with respect to AJAX operations.

Real-World Web Design

JQuery provides powerful functions to improve your webpage's user interaction. As you work with jQuery, test-drive the examples presented at the W3Schools website at *http://www.w3schools.com/jquery/default.asp*, shown in **FIGURE 12-11**. In addition, you should keep the jQuery.com website readily available as a reference.

Hands-On HTML

To view the HTML files or to experiment with the files presented in this chapter, visit this book's companion website at *http://www.websitedevelopmentbook.com/Chapter12/TryIt.html*.

FIGURE 12–11   JQuery sample applications at the W3Schools website

Reproduced with permission of w3schools.com

CHAPTER SUMMARY

JQuery provides a library of functions you can use to improve a user's experience with your webpage. For example, using jQuery you can hide or show elements on a page, fade items in or out of view, slide open or closed page divisions, and set or retrieve HTML and CSS elements and attributes. This chapter examined common jQuery operations. In Chapter 13, "Communicating with AJAX," you will learn how to use JavaScript to send and receive data from a remote server.

KEY TERMS

JQuery

CHAPTER REVIEW

1. Create an HTML file that slides a photo back and forth across a window.

2. Create an HTML file that expands an image size when the user hovers a mouse over the image, which returns to normal size after the user moves the mouse off the image.

3. Use the jQuery HTML-based methods to create a page that changes the photo shown every five seconds.

4. Create an HTML file that uses a slide operation to reveal photos. The page shown opens the slide on a button click and then closes the slide with the next click. When the user clicks the button again, the page should reveal a new image.

Communicating with AJAX

© Risto Viita/Shutterstock

AS YOU HAVE LEARNED, when you visit a webpage, your browser requests the page's HTML, CSS, JavaScript, and image files. If you click on a link within the page, this process repeats with a new page and its set of files. Web developers understand this file request model. To improve webpage processing capabilities and functionality, developers can take advantage of the fact that JavaScript can send data and request content to or from a remote server. Asynchronous JavaScript and XML, or AJAX, is a technique that developers can use to perform JavaScript-based interactions with a server.

Learning Objectives

This chapter examines AJAX in detail. By the time you finish this chapter, you will understand the following key concepts:

- How AJAX, or Asynchronous JavaScript and Extensible Markup Language, provides a way for a browser to send and receive requests from a remote server
- How using AJAX is a three-step process: The browser sends a request, receives a response, and then processes the result
- How JavaScript code uses the **XMLHttpRequest** object to perform an AJAX request
- What happens when a page makes an AJAX request
- How to send data to a server for storage within a database where the AJAX request interacts with a remote script on the server

How AJAX Helps JavaScript Communicate with Servers

Asynchronous JavaScript and XML (AJAX) provides a way for JavaScript to send data to and receive data from a server. (XML stands for Extensible Markup Language.) A good example of the use of AJAX is the Google search engine. When you use Google, the page, as shown in **FIGURE 13-1**, provides you with suggested queries as you type. As it turns out, each time you type a letter, the site uses AJAX to send your current text to the server, which, in turn, sends back the recommended queries. The process is that fast!

The Three-Step AJAX Process

In general, to use AJAX, a site performs a three-step process. First, something happens on the page to trigger the need for an AJAX operation, such as a keyboard input or a mouse-click operation—in other words, an event. The page, in turn, uses JavaScript to send a message to a remote server. The server, in turn, processes the request and sends back a response to the page. The page processes the response and updates the page content, as shown in **FIGURE 13-2**.

Understanding the XMLHttpRequest Object

The key player within the AJAX process is the **XMLHttpRequest** object. As its name suggests, it creates an HTTP-based request for XML data. It's that simple. The following HTML file, AJAXDemo.html, uses an **XMLHttpRequest** object to

FIGURE 13-1 Using AJAX to interact with a Web server

Google and the Google logo are registered trademarks of Google Inc., used with permission.

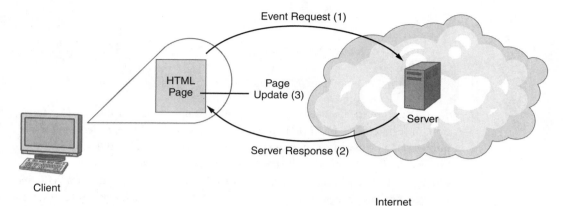

FIGURE 13-2 The three-step process to perform an AJAX operation

send a request to this book's companion website to return the file **quotes.txt**, which the page then displays:

```
<!DOCTYPE html>
<html>
<head>
<script>

var xmlhttp;
function AJAXDemo()
{
  xmlhttp = new XMLHttpRequest();
  xmlhttp.onreadystatechange = HandleData;

  xmlhttp.open("GET","quotes.txt", true);

  xmlhttp.send();
}

function HandleData()
{
  if (xmlhttp.readyState==4 && xmlhttp.status==200)
    {
      alert(xmlhttp.responseText);
    }
}
```

```
</script>
</head>
<body onload="AJAXDemo();">
</body>
</html>
```

In this case, the file calls the **AJAXDemo** function after the page loads. That function, in turn, creates an **XMLHttpRequest** object, which it uses to request the file **quotes.txt**. As you can see, the function specifies **HandleData** as the **callback** function, which the browser will call after the server sends the results. Within the **callback** function, the code checks the return status values. The value 4 stands for requests received and ready for processing, and 200 stands for OK. When a successful result is returned, the function displays it using an **alert** dialog box. You can run the file directly from *http://www.websitedevelopmentbook.com/Chapter13/AJAXDemo.html*.

When you view the page contents, the browser will connect to the remote site and download the file using AJAX, displaying the content, as shown in **FIGURE 13-3**.

When a Page Makes a Request

The "A" in AJAX stands for asynchronous. **Asynchronous** means "not occurring at the same time." An exchange of letters through postal mail, for instance, is an

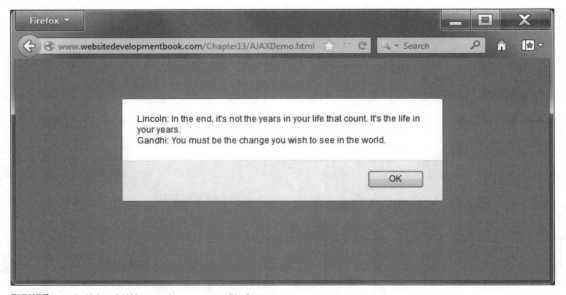

FIGURE 13-3 Using AJAX to retrieve a quote file from a remote server

example of asynchronous communication, unlike, say, a conversation in person or over the phone. What, in general, the "A" in AJAX means is that the browser sends a request to the server, which in turn performs some processing, for which it will "get back" to the page in the future. When you perform asynchronous operations, you do not know how long the operation will take or when the server will get back.

In other words, the browser sends a request to the server and then resumes whatever it was doing. When the server response comes back, the browser stops what it is doing and processes the response. For this process to work, the browser defines a JavaScript function, called a "**callback** function," which it executes when the server response comes in. The following HTML file, ServerTime.html, uses the **XMLHttpRequest** to request the server's current time by calling the script GetTime.php:

```
<!DOCTYPE html>
<html>
<head>
<script>

var xmlhttp;
function AJAXDemo()
{
  xmlhttp = new XMLHttpRequest();
  xmlhttp.onreadystatechange = HandleData;

  xmlhttp.open("GET","GetTime.php", true);
  xmlhttp.send();
}

function HandleData()
{
  if (xmlhttp.readyState==4 && xmlhttp.status==200)
    {
      alert(xmlhttp.responseText);
    }
}

</script>
</head>
<body onload="AJAXDemo();">

</body>
</html>
```

As you can see, the **open** function simply refers to the GetTime.php, which in turn simply returns the system date. The following PHP script implements GetTime.php:

```php
<?php
 $my_t=getdate(date("U"));
 print("$my_t[hours]:$my_t[minutes]");
?>
```

A Second Example

Using AJAX, your page can request a text file, as just shown. The following HTML file, ThumbNails.html, displays three thumbnail images. When you hover the mouse over a thumbnail, the page uses AJAX to request HTML content specific to the thumbnail from a remote server, which it displays on the page:

```html
<!DOCTYPE html>
<html>
<head>
<script>

var xmlhttp;
function AJAXData(DataRequest)
{
  xmlhttp = new XMLHttpRequest();
  xmlhttp.onreadystatechange = HandleData;

  xmlhttp.open("GET",DataRequest, true);
  xmlhttp.send();
}

function HandleData()
{
  if (xmlhttp.readyState==4 && xmlhttp.
    status==200)
    {
      alert(xmlhttp.responseText);
    }
}

</script>
</head>
```

```
<body>
<img src="cigar.jpg" width="300" height="200"
onmouseover="AJAXData('cigars.txt');"/>

<img src="wine.jpg" width="300" height="200"
onmouseover="AJAXData('wine.txt');"/>

<img src="pizza.jpg" width="300" height="200"
onmouseover="AJAXData('pizza.txt');"/>
</body>
</html>
```

The page in this case detects the **mouseover** events for each image and passes to the **AJAXData** function the name of a corresponding text file, which the AJAX returns from the server. When the page receives the data, it displays it using an **alert** dialog box.

When you view the file's contents, the browser displays a page similar to that shown in **FIGURE 13-4**.

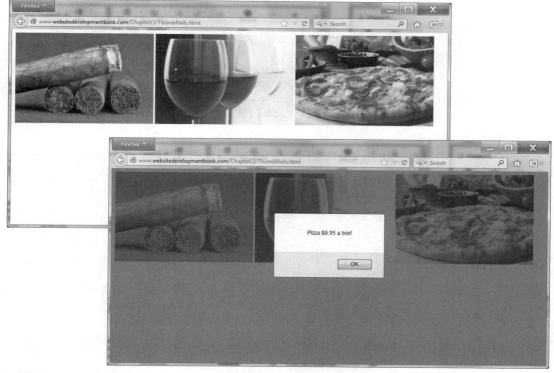

FIGURE 13-4 Using AJAX to retrieve HTML-specific content from a remote server

Credit (from top): © Vaclav Volrab/Shutterstock; © Gts/Shutterstock; © Daniel Cozma/Shutterstock

Submitting Data to a Remote Server

In the previous examples, you have used AJAX to send requests to a server. Depending on your page's processing, there may be times when a page needs to send data to a server for storage within a database. In such cases, the AJAX request would interact with a remote script on the server. The following HTML file, EchoUppercase.html, sends data to a server script on this book's companion website. The script could store data within a database. In this case, the server simply echoes the content the page sends back in uppercase, which the page then displays:

```html
<!DOCTYPE html>
<html>
<head>
<script>

var xmlhttp;
function EchoUppercase(DataString)
{
  xmlhttp = new XMLHttpRequest();
  xmlhttp.onreadystatechange = HandleData;

  xmlhttp.open("GET","Echo.php?src="+DataString,
  true);
  xmlhttp.send();
}

function HandleData()
{

  if (xmlhttp.readyState==4 && xmlhttp.status==200)
    {
      alert(xmlhttp.responseText);
    }
}

</script>
</head>
<body>
Type text: <input id="UserInput" type="text"/>
<button onclick="EchoUppercase(document.
getElementById('UserInput').value);">Click Here</
button>
</body>
</html>
```

In this case, when the user clicks the button, the code calls the **EchoUppercase** function. This specifies the name of a remote script, in this case Echo.php, and a query string that contains the query variable name **src** and the string, to convert to uppercase.

The following PHP implements the Echo.php script:

```php
<?php
  echo strtoupper($_GET["src"]);
?>
```

Receiving XML-Based Data

The following HTML file, AnimalsAJAX.html, displays thumbnails of a dog, a cat, and a horse. When a user clicks the dog, the page sends a request to the server for a specific XML file. In this case, the page simply displays the XML. The page could, however, parse the XML to access the individual fields:

```html
<!DOCTYPE html>
<html>
<head>
<script>

varxmlhttp;
function GetXMLData(DataString)
{
  xmlhttp = new XMLHttpRequest();
  xmlhttp.onreadystatechange = HandleData;

  xmlhttp.open("GET",DataString, true);
  xmlhttp.send();
}

function HandleData()
{
  if (xmlhttp.readyState==4 && xmlhttp.status==200)
    {
      varxmlDoc = xmlhttp.responseText;
      alert(xmlDoc);
    }
}

</script>
</head>
<body>
```

FIGURE 13-5 Using AJAX to request XML-based data
Credit (from left): © Christian Mueller/Shutterstock; © Anastasija Popova/Shutterstock; © Melanie Hoffman/Shutterstock

```
<img src="dog.jpg" width="300" height="200"
onclick="GetXMLData('dogs.xml');"/>

<img src="cat.jpg" width="300" height="200"
onclick="GetXMLData('cats.xml');"/>

<img src="horse.jpg" width="300" height="200"
onclick="GetXMLData('horses.xml');"/>
</body>
</html>
```

When you view the file's contents, the browser will display the contents, as shown in **FIGURE 13-5**.

Real-World Web Design

The following HTML file, StatesHint.html, illustrates how Google does its search engine hints. The page displays a prompt for the user to type a state name. As the user types, the page uses AJAX to send the current state content to a remote-server script. This, in turn, returns the name of the closest matching state, which the page then displays as a hint:

```
<!DOCTYPE html>
<html>
<head>
```

```
<script>

var xmlhttp;
function GetState(DataString)
{
  xmlhttp = new XMLHttpRequest();
  xmlhttp.onreadystatechange = HandleData;

  xmlhttp.open("GET","State.php?src="+DataString,
  true);
  xmlhttp.send();
}

function HandleData()
{
  if (xmlhttp.readyState==4 && xmlhttp.status==200)
    {
      document.getElementById('hint').innerHTML =
      xmlhttp.responseText;
    }
}

</script>
</head>
<body>
State: <input id="UserInput" type="text"
onkeyup="GetState(getElementById('UserInput').
value);"/>
<div id="hint"></div>
</body>
</html>
```

As you can see, the code detects the **onkeyup** event and then sends the current value of the input field to the PHP script. The PHP script then compares the characters entered so far with known state spellings, returning the complete state name for a match.

When you view the file's contents, the page displays hints as you type the state names, as shown in FIGURE 13-6.

The following code implements the States.php script. As you can see, the script only supports a few states:

```
<?php
  $str = strtoupper($_GET["src"]);
```

FIGURE 13-6 Using AJAX to provide user-input hints

```
if ($str === ")
    echo ";
elseif (strpos('ARIZONA', $str) === 0)
    echo 'Arizona';
elseif (strpos('ALABAMA', $str) === 0)
    echo 'Alabama';
elseif (strpos('ARKANSAS', $str) === 0)
    echo 'Arkansas';
elseif (strpos('CALIFORNIA', $str) === 0)
    echo 'California';
elseif (strpos('NEW YORK', $str) === 0)
    echo 'New York';
else
    echo";
?>
```

Hands-On HTML

To view the HTML files or to experiment with the files presented in this chapter, visit this book's companion website at *http://www.websitedevelopmentbook.com/ Chapter13/TryIt.html.*

CHAPTER SUMMARY

To improve webpage processing capabilities and functionality, developers can take advantage of the fact that JavaScript can send data and request content to or from a remote server. Asynchronous JavaScript and XML, or AJAX, is a technique that developers can use to perform JavaScript-based interactions with a server. This chapter examined AJAX and presented several common operations. You will revisit AJAX in Chapter 14, "Processing JavaScript Object Notation (JSON)," when you use AJAX to request data from a remote server that is stored in the JSON data format.

KEY TERMS

Asynchronous
Asynchronous JavaScript and XML (AJAX)

CHAPTER REVIEW

1. Create an HTML file that uses the Echo.php script to convert characters the user types within an **<input>** tag to uppercase.

2. Research AJAX on the Web. Discuss three or more applications that use AJAX.

3. Complete the file AnimalsAJAX.html presented in this chapter to parse the XML data it receives.

Processing JavaScript Object Notation (JSON)

IN CHAPTER 13, "COMMUNICATING with AJAX," you learned how to use JavaScript and AJAX to send and receive information to and from a remote server. Using AJAX, developers often retrieve XML data, which they then allow JavaScript to parse to accomplish a specific task. In this chapter, you will learn how to use a different data format from XML, the JavaScript Object Notation or JSON, to exchange data. The advantage of using JSON over XML is that JSON closely resembles JavaScript, which makes it easy for your code to process.

Learning Objectives

This chapter will examine several JSON-based applications. By the time you finish this chapter, you will understand the following key concepts:

- How JSON provides a format for defining objects
- How to create an object using JSON
- How to create an array of objects using JSON

Getting Started with JSON

JavaScript, as you have learned, makes extensive use of objects. Using **JavaScript Object Notation (JSON)**, you can store data in a format that aligns with the JavaScript object format. For example, assume that you have a **Student** object with a **studentID**, **name**, and **GPA** field. Using the JSON format, you can represent the fields and values as follows:

```
Student = {"StudentID" : "12345", "Name" : "Smith",
"GPA" : "3.5" };
```

As you can see, JSON specifies a field name followed by a colon (:), followed by a value. Using JSON, you separate fields using a comma.

The following HTML file, JSONDemo.html, creates a **Student** object and then displays each of the object fields using an **alert** dialog box:

```
<!DOCTYPE html>
<html>
<head>
<script>
function ShowStudent()
{
  var Student = {"StudentID" : "12345", "Name" :
  "Smith", "GPA" : "3.5" };

  alert("Student: " + Student.StudentID + " " +
  Student.Name + " " + Student.GPA);
}
</script>
</head>
<body onload="ShowStudent()">
</body>
</html>
```

As you can see, the file uses the JSON format to initialize a variable named **Student**, which it then displays within an **alert** dialog box. When you view the file's contents, the browser displays the contents shown in **FIGURE 14-1**.

Using JSON to Create an Object

The following HTML file, JSONWebSite.html, uses JSON to create a **website** object that contains a name and URL:

```
<!DOCTYPE html>
<html>
```

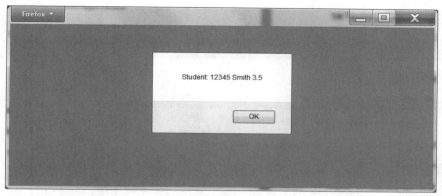

FIGURE 14-1 Using JSON to initialize a JavaScript object

```
<head>
<script>
var
  WebSite = { "Name" : "Head of the Class",
      "URL" : "http://www.theHeadoftheclass.com" };

function InitButton()
{
  document.getElementById("WebButton").innerHTML =
  WebSite.Name;
}

function OpenSite()
{
  window.open(WebSite.URL);
}

</script>
</head>
<body onload="InitButton()">
<button id="WebButton" onclick="OpenSite()">
</button>
</body>
</html>
```

The page then uses the object to create a button that contains the object name and which links to the corresponding URL if the button is clicked. In this case, the page uses JSON to initialize the **website** object's two fields.

FIGURE 14-2 Using JSON to create a **website** object
Courtesy of Head of the Class (www.theheadoftheclass.com)

When you view the file's contents, the page displays the button. If the user clicks on the button, the page opens a window with the corresponding site, as shown in **FIGURE 14-2**.

Creating an Array of Objects

The previous examples have used JSON to create individual objects. Using JSON, you can also create an array of objects. The following statements, for example, create an array of objects that correspond to popular software companies:

```
var
  Companies = [{ "Name" : "Microsoft",
  "Founder" : "Gates and Allen", "Headquarters" :
  "Redmond, WA" },
    { "Name" : "Facebook", "Founder" : "Zuckerberg",
    "Headquarters" : "Palo Alto, CA" },
    { "Name" : "Oracle", "Founder" : "Ellison",
    "Headquarters" : "Redwood Shores, CA"
}];
```

Next, the following HTML file, UseJSONArray.html, uses the JSON array to build buttons on the page for each company. When the user clicks on a button, the page displays an **alert** dialog box with information about the corresponding company, as shown in **FIGURE 14-3.**

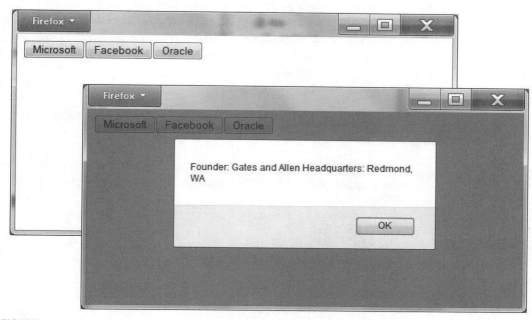

FIGURE 14-3 Using JSON to build an array of data

```
<!DOCTYPE html>
<html>
<head>
<script>
var
  Companies = [{ "Name" : "Microsoft", "Founder" :
  "Gates and Allen", "Headquarters" :
  "Redmond, WA" },
    { "Name" : "Facebook", "Founder" : "Zuckerberg",
    "Headquarters" : "Palo Alto, CA" },
    { "Name" : "Oracle", "Founder" : "Ellison",
    "Headquarters" : "Redwood Shores, CA"
}];

function InitButtons()
{
  var i;
  var currentHTML;

  for (i = 0; i < Companies.length; i++)
  {
```

```
        currentHTML = document.getElementById("thePage").
        innerHTML;document.getElementById("thePage").
        innerHTML = currentHTML + "<button onclick=
        'ShowCompany(" + i + ")'>" + Companies[i].Name
        + "</button>";
    }
}

function ShowCompany(i)
{;
    alert("Founder: " + Companies[i].Founder + "
    Headquarters: " + Companies[i].Headquarters);
}

</script>
</head>
<body id="thePage" onload="InitButtons()">
</body>
</html>
```

Real-World Web Design: Using JSON to Exchange Information

The power of JSON is in exchanging information. In Chapter 13, you learned how to use AJAX to retrieve a file from a server. The following HTML file, JSON-Quotes.html, uses AJAX to retrieve a text file from a server that contains JSON content. The page uses the JavaScript **eval** function to create objects from the file's JSON and then uses the objects to create buttons that correspond to each quoted person. When the user clicks on a button, the file displays the corresponding quote and information, as shown in **FIGURE 14-4.**

```
<!DOCTYPE html>

<html>
<head>
<script>
varxmlhttp;
var Quotes;

function loadJSON()
{
xmlhttp = new XMLHttpRequest();
xmlhttp.onreadystatechange = HandleData;
```

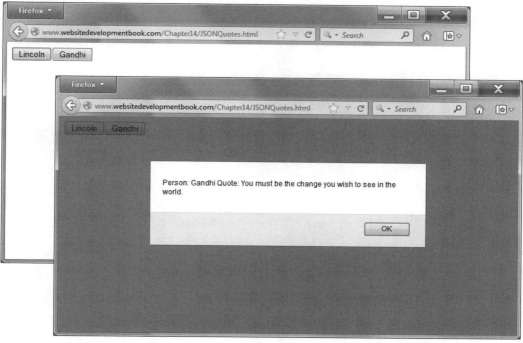

FIGURE 14-4 Retrieving and processing a JSON file

```
xmlhttp.open("GET","http://www.website
developmentbook.com/Chapter14/Quotes.txt", true);
xmlhttp.send();
}

function HandleData()
{
  if (xmlhttp.readyState==4 &&xmlhttp.status==200)
  {
    Quotes = eval('(' + xmlhttp.responseText +
    ')');
    InitButtons();
  }
}

function InitButtons()
{
    var i;
    var currentHTML;
```

```
for (i = 0; i<Quotes.Messages.length; i++)
{
  currentHTML = document.getElementById("thePage").
  innerHTML;document.getElementById("thePage").
  innerHTML = currentHTML +
    "<button onclick='ShowQuote(" + i +
    ")'>" + Quotes.Messages[i].Name + "</button>";
}
}

function ShowQuote(i)
{
  alert("Person: " + Quotes.Messages[i].Name + "
  Quote: " + Quotes.Messages[i].Quote);
}

</script>
</head>
<body id="thePage" onload="loadJSON();">
</body>
</html>
```

In this case, the JSON file will have the following format:

```
{ Messages : [ { "Name" : "Lincoln", "Quote" :"In
the end, it's not the years in your life that
count. It's the life in your years." },
    { "Name" : "Gandhi", "Quote" :"You must be the
change you wish to see in the world."
}]
}
```

Hands-On HTML

To view the HTML files or to experiment with the files presented in this chapter, visit this book's companion website at *http://www.websitedevelopmentbook.com/ Chapter14/TryIt.html*.

CHAPTER SUMMARY

Using tools such as AJAX, sites can query servers for specific data. Normally, servers respond to such queries by providing data in XML format. In this chapter, you learned to use the JSON data format. JSON is very similar to JavaScript and easy for your programs to integrate. In Chapter 15, "Webpage Optimization," you will learn several techniques to optimize your webpage performance.

KEY TERMS

JavaScript Object Notation (JSON)

CHAPTER REVIEW

1. Create an HTML file that uses the JSON syntax to create a **Pet** object that has a breed, name, and age. Use an **alert** dialog box to display specifics about the pet.

2. Use AJAX to request the JSON file Pets.txt from *http://www.websitedevelopmentbook.com/Chapter14/Pets.txt.* The file contains information on a variety of pets. Use a series of **alert** dialog boxes to display the information.

3. Research the Web, and create a list of pros and cons for using JSON as opposed to XML for data-transfer operations.

Webpage Optimization

EVERY DAY, USERS TURN to the Web for instant information on a wide range of topics. With access to millions of webpages using only a few clicks of a mouse, users have expectations for how fast a webpage should appear. In short, users want what they want when they want it. When websites don't meet user performance expectations, users move on. In fact, research has shown that if a webpage takes more than 2.5 seconds to load, many users won't wait and will look elsewhere for the content they desire.

Learning Objectives

This chapter examines several steps you can take to improve your website's performance and reduce the amount of time users must wait for a page to load. By the time you finish this chapter, you will understand the following key concepts:

- How to test your webpage performance
- How browser and server interactions affect performance
- How to design your site's home page to reduce HTTP-based file requests
- What impact image file size and resolution have on download times
- How to reduce JavaScript download overhead by obfuscating your code
- How using multiple servers for different resource types may load-balance resource requests
- How to improve download performance for text-based content by directing the server to compress the content using gzip
- How to improve download performance by combining external references files

Testing Webpage Performance

Across the Web, several sites exist that you can use to test a webpage's performance (download speed). **TABLE 15-1** lists several of these sites.

The following HTML file, TestSpeed.html, contains references to several graphics, an audio clip, and a video clip:

```
<!DOCTYPE html>
<html>
<body>
<img src="http://www.WebSiteDevelopmentBook.com/
Chapter02/maui01.jpg"/><br/>
<img src="http://www.WebSiteDevelopmentBook.com/
Chapter02/maui02.jpg"/><br/>
<img src="http://www.WebSiteDevelopmentBook.com/
Chapter02/maui03.jpg"/><br/>


<audio controls="controls">
<source src="http://www.WebsiteDevelopmentBook.com/
Chapter18/Rock.mp3" type="audio/mp3"/>
<source src="http://www.WebsiteDevelopmentBook.com/
Chapter18/Rock.ogg" type="audio/ogg"/>
</audio><br/>
```

TABLE 15-1 SITES ON THE WEB THAT DEVELOPERS CAN USE TO TEST WEBPAGE PERFORMANCE

Company Name	Web Address
Pingdom	http://tools.pingdom.com/fpt/
iWebTool	http://www.iwebtool.com/speed_test/
Website Optimization	http://www.websiteoptimization.com/services/analyze/
Webpage Test	http://www.webpagetest.org/
UpTrends	http://www.uptrends.com/aspx/free-html-site-page-load-check-tool.aspx
WebSitePulse	http://www.websitepulse.com/help/tools.php

```
<video autoplay="autoplay" controls="controls">
<source src="http://www.WebsiteDevelopmentBook.com/
Chapter18/Cigar.mp4" type="video/mp4"/>
<source src="http://www.WebsiteDevelopmentBook.com/
Chapter18/Cigar.ogg" type="video/ogg"/>
<source src="http://www.WebsiteDevelopmentBook.com/
Chapter18/Cigar.flv" type="video/flv"/>
<source src="http://www.WebsiteDevelopmentBook.com/
Chapter18/Cigar.webm" type="video/webm"/>
<source src="http://www.WebsiteDevelopmentBook.com/
Chapter18/Cigar.mov" type="video/mov"/>


Video Tag Not Supported
</video>
</body>
</html>
```

As **FIGURE 15-1** shows, when this code was submitted to the Pingdom website for an analysis of download speed, the page took more than 2.5 seconds to load.

FIGURE 15–1 Using the Pingdom website to test a page's download performance
Reproduced with permission of Pingdom

Revisiting Browser and Server Interactions

As you have learned, when a user selects a webpage for display, the browser requests that the corresponding Web server provide the requested HTML page, as shown in **FIGURE 15–2**.

After the browser receives the HTML file, it will parse the file's contents and send additional requests to the server for image files, cascading style sheets, or JavaScript files, videos, audios, and so on.

To improve performance, Web browsers do not process file downloads sequentially. That is, the browser can request several files from the server at the same time, as shown in **FIGURE 15–3**, as opposed to waiting for one file to download before requesting another.

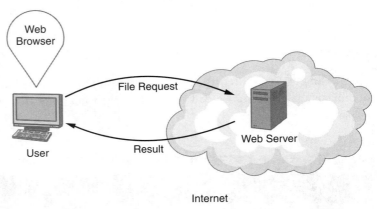

FIGURE 15–2 A browser and server interact to request and retrieve an HTML file.

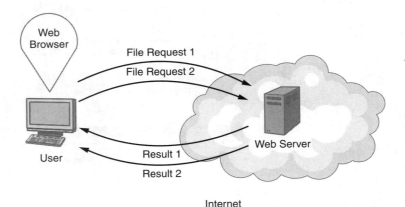

FIGURE 15–3 A browser may initiate several file download operations that occur in parallel.

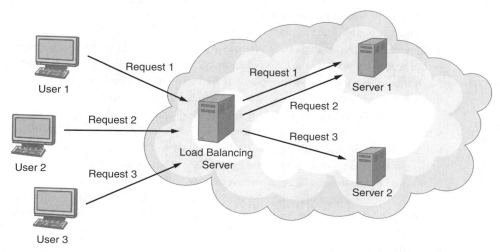

FIGURE 15-4 To handle a large number of requests, many sites use load-balancing servers that hand off requests to a variety of servers.

The number of parallel download operations the browser can perform at one time varies, depending on the browser a user is using.

Across the Web, many sites, such as Amazon, eBay, Facebook, and YouTube, experience millions of page requests per minute. Behind the scenes, to handle so many requests, the sites use one or more load-balancing servers that hand off the requests to other servers that actually provide the requested resources, as shown in **FIGURE 15-4**.

Reducing Home Page HTTP-Based File Requests

Although Internet download speeds continue to increase, browser HTTP-based file requests continue to take time and create overhead during a webpage download. Since users desire that a page download in 2.5 seconds or less, you should design your site's home page to reduce file requests.

As you consider the items to include on your home page, you may choose to move large images or videos from the home page to a secondary page where the user pursuing specific content may be more patient with the page download speed. As you experiment with your webpage design, use the sites listed in **TABLE 15-1** to test your download speed.

Reducing Your Image Resolution

An image's **resolution** specifies the number of pixels per inch that file uses to represent the image. In general, the higher the resolution, the sharper the image quality. Unfortunately, the higher the image resolution, the larger the image file, and the longer the file's download time.

Users often place photos on the Web that they have taken using a digital camera (or phone camera). Most digital cameras create image files with 300 DPI (dots per inch) resolution. Depending on the photo's size, the file that stores the image may easily exceed several megabytes in size. To reduce image file sizes, most graphic artists target a 72 DPI resolution for the files they place on the Web. Before you release a webpage for use, make sure you use photo-editing software to reduce your graphics to 72 DPI.

As discussed in Chapter 2, "Integrating Images," using the <**img**> tag **height** and **width** attributes, you can specify the size at which a browser displays an image. When you use the **height** and **width** attributes, the browser will scale an image up or down as necessary for display. However, the image file size will not change. If you use the attributes to scale down a larger image, your page will experience unnecessary over-view because the image file is larger than you need. Rather than use the height and width tags to change the display of the image, you should use photo-editing software to size the image to the **height** and **width** you desire, and to change the image's file size so that you have a resolution of 72 DPI.

The following HTML file, LargeImage.html, uses the <**img**> tag **height** and **width** attributes to scale down a 300 DPI (1000 × 600) image to 500 × 300:

```
<!DOCTYPE html>
<html>
<body>
<img src="http://www.WebSiteDevelopmentBook.com/
Chapter15/ItalyBig.jpg" height="300"
width="500"/><br/>
</body>
</html>
```

When the file is submitted to the Pingdom analyzer, the file download time requires 5.14 seconds, as shown in **FIGURE 15-5**.

In contrast, the following file, SmallImage.html, uses a photo that has been scaled to 500 × 300 at 72 DPI. When the file is submitted to Pingdom, the file download time requires 3.65 seconds, as shown in **FIGURE 15-6**.

```
<!DOCTYPE html>
<html>
<body>
<img
src="http://www.WebSiteDevelopmentBook.com/
Chapter15/ItalySized.jpg"/><
br/>
</body>
</html>
```

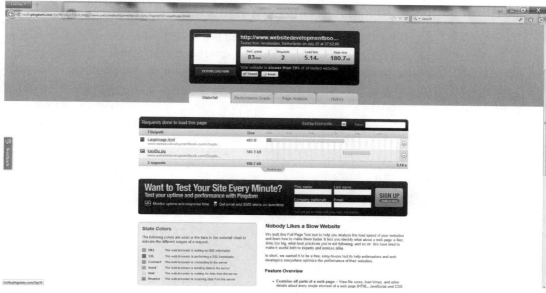

FIGURE 15-5 Download time for a 1000 × 600 image at 300 DPI

Reproduced with permission of Pingdom

FIGURE 15-6 Download time for a 500 × 300 image at 72 DPI

Reproduced with permission of Pingdom

Reducing JavaScript Download Overhead

In Chapter 10, "JavaScript," you learned how to embed JavaScript code within an HTML page as well as how to use an external JavaScript file within a webpage. Although JavaScript can enhance a page's capabilities, the JavaScript code itself will increase the HTML file's download time.

To reduce JavaScript overhead, Web developers often compress (abbreviate) their JavaScript code through a process called obfuscation. For example, the following HTML file, ImageGallery.html, uses JavaScript to cycle the display of several images:

```
<!DOCTYPE html>
<html>
<body onload="startPix()">
<img id="ChangingPix"
src="http://www.WebSiteDevelopmentBook.com/
Chapter02/maui03.jpg"/>

<SCRIPT LANGUAGE="JavaScript">
<!—Begin
vartimeDelay = 5; // change delay time in seconds

var Pix = new Array
(
"http://www.WebSiteDevelopmentBook.com/Chapter02/
maui01.jpg",
"http://www.WebSiteDevelopmentBook.com/Chapter02/
maui02.jpg",
"http://www.WebSiteDevelopmentBook.com/Chapter02/
maui03.jpg"
);

varhowMany = Pix.length;
timeDelay *= 1000;

varPicCurrentNum = 0;
varPicCurrent = new Image();
PicCurrent.src = Pix[PicCurrentNum];

function startPix() {
setInterval("slideshow()", timeDelay);
}
```

```
function slideshow() {
PicCurrentNum++;
  if (PicCurrentNum == howMany) {
PicCurrentNum = 0;
}


PicCurrent.src = Pix[PicCurrentNum];
document.getElementById("ChangingPix").src =
PicCurrent.src;
}
// End -->
</script>
</body>
</html>
```

The JavaScript code, in this case, requires about 625 characters, which is about 86 percent of the file's size.

Using the JavaScript Obfuscator Website (*http://javascript-obfuscator.com/*), shown in **FIGURE 15-7**, the Web developer can easily obfuscate the JavaScript code, reducing it in this case by 21 percent:

```
<SCRIPT LANGUAGE="JavaScript"><!--Begin
vartimeDelay=5;var Pix=new Array("http://www.WebSite
DevelopmentBook.com/Chapter02/maui01.jpg","http://
www.WebSiteDevelopmentBook.com/Chapter02/maui02.
jpg","http://www.WebSiteDevelopmentBook.com/
Chapter02/maui03.jpg");var howMany=Pix.
length;timeDelay*=1000;var PicCurrentNum=0;var
PicCurrent=new Image();PicCurrent.
src=Pix[PicCurrentNum];function startPix(){setInterv
al("slideshow()",timeDelay)}function slideshow(){Pic
CurrentNum++;if(PicCurrentNum==howMany){PicCurrent
Num=0}PicCurrent.src=Pix[PicCurrentNum];document.
getElementById("ChangingPix").src=PicCurrent.src}
</script>
```

The obfuscated code still performs the same processing, but it is much smaller. However, the obfuscated code is harder to read and understand than the original code.

Several sites on the Web will perform similar processing to reduce the size of your page's cascading style sheet definitions.

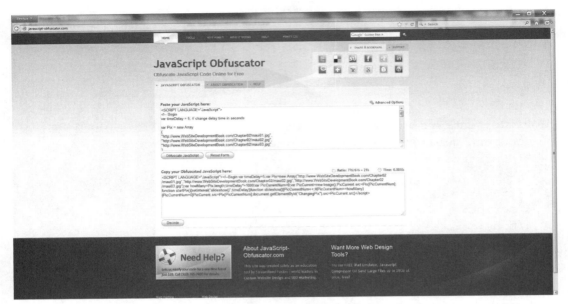

FIGURE 15-7 Using the JavaScript Obfuscator website to obsfucate JavaScript code
Reproduced with permission of Streamlined Fusion

Move JavaScript Code to the Bottom of the Page

Depending on the processing your JavaScript code performs, you may improve the page download performance by moving the script near the bottom of your page. When many browsers encounter JavaScript code, they will temporarily block parallel downloads until they have processed the code. As a result, the download performance slows down. If you are using JavaScript code that does not impact the page rendering, meaning your code does not use **document.write**, move the code near the bottom of your page, and then test your site performance.

Using Multiple Servers

As discussed, behind the scenes, many sites use load-balanced servers to process browser requests. In a similar way, developers sometimes use different servers to hold different resource types, such as one server for images, one for videos, and one for CSS and JavaScript files. The following HTML file, SameServer.html, uses the same server to process requests for all resources:

```
<!DOCTYPE html>
<html>
<body>
<img src="http://www.WebSiteDevelopmentBook.com/
Chapter02/maui01.jpg"/><br/>
```

```
<img src="http://www.WebSiteDevelopmentBook.com/
Chapter02/maui02.jpg"/><br/>
<img src="http://www.WebSiteDevelopmentBook.com/
Chapter02/maui03.jpg"/><br/>


<audio controls="controls">
<source src="http://www.WebsiteDevelopmentBook.com/
Chapter18/Rock.mp3" type="audio/mp3"/>
<source src="http://www.WebsiteDevelopmentBook.com/
Chapter18/Rock.ogg" type="audio/ogg"/>
</audio><br/>


<video autoplay="autoplay" controls="controls">
<source src="http://www.WebsiteDevelopmentBook.com/
Chapter18/Cigar.mp4" type="video/mp4"/>
<source src="http://www.WebsiteDevelopmentBook.com/
Chapter18/Cigar.ogg" type="video/ogg"/>
<source src="http://www.WebsiteDevelopmentBook.com/
Chapter18/Cigar.flv" type="video/flv"/>
<source src="http://www.WebsiteDevelopmentBook.com/
Chapter18/Cigar.webm" type="video/webm"/>
<source src="http://www.WebsiteDevelopmentBook.com/
Chapter18/Cigar.mov" type="video/mov"/>
Video Tag Not Supported
</video>
</body>
</html>
```

When you use the Pingdom site to evaluate the page, you will find that the download takes 2.12 seconds. In contrast, the following HTML file, Multiple-Servers.html, requests different resources from different servers:

```
<!DOCTYPE html>
<html>
<body>
<img src="http://www.class-files.com/WebSite
DevelopmentBook.com/Chapter02/maui01.jpg"/><br/>
<img src="http://www.class-files.com/WebSite
DevelopmentBook.com/Chapter02/maui02.jpg"/><br/>
<img src="http://www.class-files.com/WebSite
DevelopmentBook.com/Chapter02/maui03.jpg"/><br/>
```

```
<audio controls="controls">
<source src="http://www.CloudBookContent.com/
WebsiteDevelopmentBook.com/Chapter18/Rock.mp3"
type="audio/mp3"/>
<source src="http://www.CloudBookContent.com/
WebsiteDevelopmentBook.com/Chapter18/Rock.ogg"
type="audio/ogg"/>
</audio><br/>


<video autoplay="autoplay" controls="controls">
<source src="http://www.WebsiteDevelopmentBook.com/
Chapter18/Cigar.mp4" type="video/mp4"/>
<source src="http://www.WebsiteDevelopmentBook.com/
Chapter18/Cigar.ogg" type="video/ogg"/>
<source src="http://www.WebsiteDevelopmentBook.com/
Chapter18/Cigar.flv" type="video/flv"/>
<source src="http://www.WebsiteDevelopmentBook.com/
Chapter18/Cigar.webm" type="video/webm"/>
<source src="http://www.WebsiteDevelopmentBook.com/
Chapter18/Cigar.mov" type="video/mov"/>
Video Tag Not Supported
</video>
</body>
</html>
```

In this case, using the Pingdom site to evaluate the page, the download takes less than one second.

Depending on your site's traffic load, you may find that using multiple servers in this way improves performance. The downside of using multiple servers in this way is that the browser must look up each server's Internet Protocol (IP) address. To do so, the browser must send each server's domain name to a domain name server (DNS), which, as shown in **FIGURE 15-8**, returns the server's IP address. The process, called a DNS lookup operation, adds overhead to the page loading time.

Consider a Content Delivery Network

Depending on the location of your server as well as the location of the user browsing your site, your page's download time will differ. For a user across the world, for example, the content must travel through many more network hops than it would for a user down the street. To reduce such network overhead, many

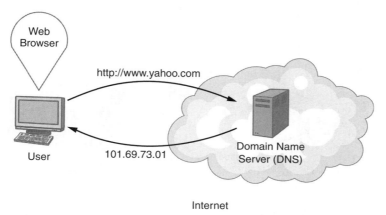

FIGURE 15-8 Before a browser can request resources from a server, the browser must determine the server's IP address.

sites use content-delivery networks. A **content delivery network** is a collection of servers distributed either across the country or around the globe, depending on your needs. The content delivery networks are high-performance servers that can deliver content quickly. To use such a server, you would acquire space, upload your content, and then refer to the server within your HTML page.

Compressing Text-Based Content

Depending on the number of HTML tags, CSS style definitions, and amount of JavaScript code a file uses, a file can have a considerable amount of text-based content, which browsers must download. To reduce the overview of such text-based content, you can direct your Web server to compress using the gzip compression. Most browsers understand gzip and uncompress the content on the fly, as shown in **FIGURE 15-9**.

When a browser first connects to a remote Web server, the browser informs the server about the capabilities it supports. If the browser supports gzip compression, the server can compress text-based content. If the browser does not support gzip, the server will simply download the uncompressed text. Depending on the Web server you are using, the steps you must perform to enable the use of gzip compression will differ. After you enable the gzip capability, the server will use the compression whenever possible for future download requests.

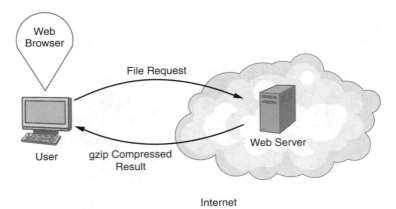

FIGURE 15-9 Reducing download times by directing a Web server to compress text-based content into a gzip compressed format, which a browser can then uncompress

Improving Download Performance

As you have learned, when your site uses JavaScript or CSS, you can use one or more external file references to integrate content into your HTML file. If you can combine multiple files into one, you may improve the download performance.

Move CSS Definitions to the Top of Your Page

As your browser downloads your HTML content, the browser will use CSS style definitions to begin to render the page. To improve page-loading performance, you should place your CSS definitions at the top of your page. Otherwise, to avoid having to re-render content, the browser may stop the rendering process until it has encountered all of your CSS definitions.

Avoiding Redirects

When Web developers release new sites, they often place a redirect within the page of an old site that directs the browser to automatically move the user to the new site. Although such redirects are convenient for the developers, they introduce a level of additional HTTP requests that add overhead to the downloading process. As such, you should try to avoid or at least reduce such redirects within your pages.

Controlling Browser Caching

As you know, after you download an HTML page and the corresponding resource files, such as images, your browser will normally cache the contents in a temporary storage location on your disk. If you later return to the site, your browser can use the cached content as opposed to downloading the files from the Web server. The browser can retrieve the cached-page content much more quickly, which improves the user's experience.

Behind the scenes, the browser examines each page's cache settings. Developers will sometimes disable caching to ensure the user must always retrieve the most recent content from the server. Other developers will direct the browser to check whether or not the server has a more current version of the content, and if so, to download it. Unfortunately, checking for updated content also takes time and adds overhead.

If your page has static content that will not change, you can use a metadata tag to set your page's expiration date to a date far into the future. If a page has expired, the browser will request new content from the server. If the page has not expired, the browser can use the cached content. The following HTML file, NeverChanges.html, uses the <**meta**> tag to set the page's expiration date to 12-31-2031:

```
<!DOCTYPE html>
<head>
<META HTTP-EQUIV="EXPIRES" CONTENT="Fri, 31 Dec
2031 11:59:59 GMT">
</head>
<html>
<body>
<img src="http://www.WebSiteDevelopmentBook.com/
Chapter02/maui01.jpg"/><br/>
<img src="http://www.WebSiteDevelopmentBook.com/
Chapter02/maui02.jpg"/><br/>
<img src="http://www.WebSiteDevelopmentBook.com/
Chapter02/maui03.jpg"/><br/>
</body>
</html>
```

Real-World Web Design

Depending on the Web operations you perform, there may be times when you need to know your IP address or specifics about your browser settings. In such cases, you can use the What's My IP site at *http://www.whatsmyIP.org*, shown in **FIGURE 15-10**.

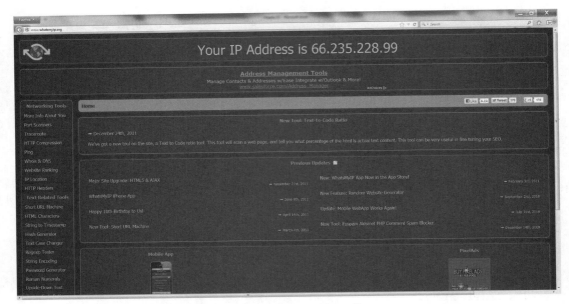

FIGURE 15-10 Determining your computer's IP address using whatsmyIP.org

Reproduced with permission of WhatsMyIP.org

FIGURE 15-11 Displaying specifics about your browser at whatsmyIP.org

Reproduced with permission of WhatsMyIP.org

CHAPTER SUMMARY

As users move from site to site across the Web, they have expectations with respect to each site's performance. As a general rule, your site should download in less than 2.5 seconds. If users have to wait beyond a few seconds for your page, many will move on to other sources of content. As you design your webpages, you need to keep performance in mind. Across the Web, there are several sites you can use to test your page performance.

Ways you can improve your site's performance include:

- Moving images, videos, and audios from your home page to a secondary page
- Reducing image size and resolution
- Using load-balancing servers—to respond to requests by using multiple servers for different content types
- Directing your server to use gzip compress for text-based content
- Setting the cache expiration date to a date far in the future for static content

KEY TERMS

Content delivery network
Resolution

CHAPTER REVIEW

1. Create an HTML file that uses at least five images, and then use the sites listed in **TABLE 15-1** to test your page performance. Do the sites provide a consistent result?

2. Use the site http://javascript-obfuscator.com/ to obfuscate JavaScript code within a webpage. Discuss how the process changes the page's download time. Is the time savings worth the loss of code readability?

3. Research the HTML **\<meta\>** tag. Using a **\<meta\>** tag, turn off caching for a webpage.

4. Using the What's My IP site, determine your PC's IP address and browser specifics.

Search Engine Optimization

WHEN IT COMES TO promoting websites, for most sites, at least, "If you build it, they will come" simply doesn't work. With billions of pages of content residing on the Web, developers need to maximize a site's potential exposure. A key factor in having users find a website is having the site listed, or indexed, within search engine results. **Search engine optimization (SEO)** is the process developers undertake to improve their site's likelihood of appearing near the top of the search engine's results list.

Learning Objectives

This chapter examines several SEO steps developers should perform. By the time you finish this chapter, you will understand the following key concepts:

- How to monitor your site's traffic
- What the pros and cons of keyword advertising within a search engine to drive traffic are
- How search engines use robots to index site content
- What the role of metadata keywords within a webpage is
- What the role is of the **<title>** and **<img>** tags
- How to increase your site's credibility by increasing the number of sites linking into it
- How to select a good domain name
- How to control well-behaved search engine robots
- How to create an XML-based site map
- How to specify canonicalization
- How to redirect to a new page

Tracking Your Network Traffic

Before you can measure the effectiveness of your SEO efforts, you should start tracking your site's network traffic to establish a baseline. Several sites across the Web provide historical data and estimates on site traffic. For example, **FIGURE 16-1** shows the Alexa.com rating for this book's publisher, Jones & Bartlett Learning. Other sites you may want to use for tracking traffic include GoogleRankings.com and TrafficEstimate.com. As you make changes to your site's SEO settings, you can use such sites to monitor the changes' impact on user traffic.

Sites such as Alexa.com provide traffic estimates. If you want to monitor exact traffic patterns, consider installing and using analytic software that you can find at Alexa.com or that Google Analytics provides at *http://www.google.com/analytics/* or Seomoz at *http://www.seomoz.org/*. Such software normally requires that you insert a small piece of JavaScript code into your page, which reports traffic information back to a database. Later, you can use the site's reporting data to view information about your site traffic.

Finding Ad Revenue: Pros and Cons of Two Approaches

Search engine companies, such as Google, Yahoo, Ask, and Bing, are businesses with the goal of making money. Each of these search engines allows you to

FIGURE 16-1 Using the Alexa.com site to monitor site traffic
© 2013, Alexa Internet (www.alexa.com)

FIGURE 16-2 Paying for placement within a search engine's search results

Reproduced with permission of Yahoo! Inc. © 2013 Yahoo! Inc. YAHOO! and the Yahoo! logo are registered trademarks of Yahoo! Inc.

"purchase" keywords for your site. Your site can appear within the search engine results for a user search for terms you have "bought." **FIGURE 16-2**, for example, shows the search results on Yahoo.com for the keyword "education." At the top of the page and along the right-hand side of the page, you can see "Sponsored links," for which companies have paid to be present within the search results.

Paying for keyword placement within a search engine's results can be an effective way for companies to drive traffic to their site. Normally, it does not cost the company anything to appear within the search results list. Instead, the companies will pay the search engine a fee each time a user clicks on their link—a process called pay per click (PPC).

Unfortunately, depending on the keywords you desire, the **cost per click (CPC)** can become expensive—ranging from a few cents to tens of dollars per click! To create a keyword-based advertising campaign, you normally select your keywords and a maximum bid amount for each. In addition, you tell the search engine how much you are willing to spend each day. **FIGURE 16-3**, for example, shows an advertising dashboard within Google AdWords that specifies keywords and related bidding amounts.

Optimizing Your Page Keywords So Robots Can Find Them

To locate content within the billions of pages that make up the World Wide Web, search engines use special programs called **robots** to scour your pages

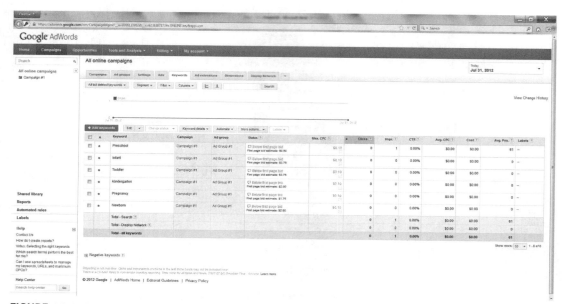

FIGURE 16-3 Keywords and bidding amounts within Google AdWords
Google and the Google logo are registered trademarks of Google Inc., used with permission.

to determine the content the pages present. Conceptually, you can think of the search engine as launching millions of robots, as shown in **FIGURE 16-4**.

In actuality, however, the robots never leave the search engine site, nor do they travel to your server. Instead, the robots reside on the search engine and

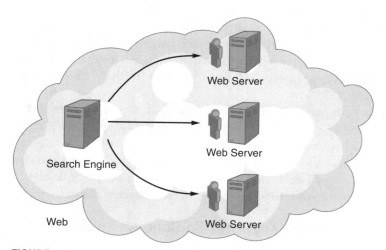

FIGURE 16-4 Search engines locate content on the Web using special programs called robots, which scour webpages.

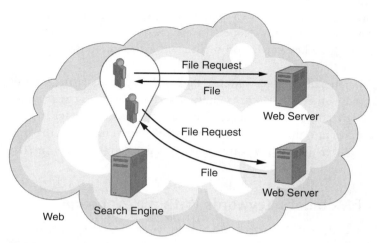

FIGURE 16-5 Robots actually reside on the search engine servers and request pages from across the Web.

request pages from your site, as shown in **FIGURE 16-5**. After the robots retrieve a page, they examine the page content and index keywords accordingly.

As a Web developer, you will normally want the robots to correctly identify your site content and the corresponding pages. That way, you can ensure your site's placements within search engine results. To assist the robots, many developers place keywords, called metadata, within **<meta>** tags that reside within each page of website content. The following HTML file, MetaDemo.html, illustrates the use of the <**meta**> tag to specify a page's keywords:

```
<!DOCTYPE html>
<html>
<head>
<meta name="description" content="Place a
meaningful site description here that contains
good keywords">
<meta name="keywords" content="web development,
HTML 5,coding,JavaScript,CSS">
</head>
<body>
Page Content Here
</body>
</html>
```

As you can see, the file uses two metadata tags. The first uses the name **description** and should contain a concise overview of the page contents. The second uses the name **keywords** and includes the site's comma-separated keywords.

In general, you should place <**meta**> tags with keywords at the start of each HTML page you create. Unfortunately, search engines may or may not use your metadata content. In the past, sites have used <**meta**> tags to mislead search engines into thinking the site provided content on topics the sites did not present. Over time, many search engines began to ignore the <**meta**> tag contents.

The Role of Metadata Keywords Within a Webpage

To help you select the best keywords and bids for your site, Google provides a keyword tool that shows the number of clicks you can expect to receive at different cost-per-click rates, as shown in **FIGURE 16–6**. Using the tool, you can estimate your needed budget and the potential effectiveness of your marketing efforts.

When a robot examines your site contents, the robot may evaluate the words within your content to determine the page's overall focus. Although you

FIGURE 16–6 Using the Google keyword tool to assist in determining advertising budgets and effectiveness
Google and the Google logo are registered trademarks of Google Inc., used with permission.

FIGURE 16-7 Measuring a site's keyword density
Reproduced with permission of davidnaylor.co.uk

may believe that your page focuses on a specific topic, an analysis of the words within your page, which is what a robot will do, may indicate otherwise. To better understand your site's keyword focus, you should use Naylor's keyword tool at *http://tools.davidnaylor.co.uk/keyworddensity/*. As shown in **FIGURE 16-7**, the site provides you with a summary of the words used throughout your content. Depending on your goals, you may choose to add additional keywords related to your primary topic.

The Role of the <title> and <img> Tags

After you place meaningful <**meta**> tags within your webpages, you should then use a <**title**> tag to assign a meaningful title to your page. Then, for each <**img**> tag, make sure you provide descriptive text within the corresponding **alt** attribute. As robots examine your page contents, they may use these tags to help determine the content the page presents.

Building Credibility Through Incoming Links

One of the ways to increase your site's credibility is to grow the number of sites that link into it. If you examine the Alexa screen previously shown in **FIGURE 16-1**, you will see that Alexa tracks "Reputation," which corresponds to the number of sites that link in. To increase the number of sites that link to yours, consider exchanging advertisements with other sites in a process in which you both display each other's ad at no cost. You might also ask related bloggers to include links to your site or possibly to exchange ads. Lastly, you should leverage social media sites, such as Facebook, Digg, Pinterest, and others, to post links to your pages.

Selecting a Good Domain Name

With most of the "great" domain names already taken, selecting a "good" domain name can be a challenging task. When you choose a domain name, try to avoid special characters, such as hyphens, or names similar to existing sites. Depending on your website potential, you may want to bid on an existing domain name through a bidding site, such as *https://www.auctions.godaddy.com,* shown in **FIGURE 16–8**.

Creating a Well-Behaved *Robots.txt* File

As you have learned, a robot is a special program that search engines run to scour your webpage content in search of topics it can index. Developers consider robots that perform such search engine indexing as "good" robots. Unfortunately, there are other types of "bad" robots that scour webpages in pursuit of e-mail addresses and other content that can later be used by spammers.

The bottom line with respect to robots, both good and bad, is that there really is no way to prevent them from examining your publicly accessible Web content.

FIGURE 16–8 Many sites across the Web hold auctions where you can purchase domain names owned by others. Reproduced with *permission of Go Daddy. © 2013 Go Daddy Operating Company, LLC.*

Before a well-behaved robot will search your site, the robot will normally look for a robots.txt file on your Web server. You can use this file to control which directories the robot searches and indexes. The badly behaved robots, however, simply ignore your robots.txt file.

The following robots.txt file directs robots not to browse any directories:

```
User-agent: *
Disallow: /
```

In this case, the asterisk following the **User-agent** entry is a wild card that states the settings that follow are for all browsers. The **Disallow** entry specifies the site's root, which essentially disables all child directories, too.

Normally, you will want robots to examine your content so they can index it within a search engine. You may, however, have one or more directories that have content you don't want the robots to examine. The following robots.txt file, for example, directs robots to ignore the images and videos directories:

```
User-agent: *
Disallow: /images
Disallow: /videos
```

Using the Rel="nofollow" Attribute

In addition to using the robots.txt file to control robot processing of your site's pages, you can also use the <a> tag **rel="nofollow"** attribute to tell robots not to include specific hyperlinks within the site's rating:

```
<a href="http://www.somelink.com" rel=
"nofollow">Link</a>
```

Creating an XML-Based Site Map

When search engine robots "crawl" your site's pages, most will use the content of an XML-based site map file you can create by hand or by using any of a myriad of site map tools available on the Web. XML is the extensible markup language developers use to package data in a meaningful way. In the case of a site map, the XML files contain metadata entries that provide specifics about the different links the developer wants a search engine robot to index. In general, using a site map, you can tell a robot a page's relative importance compared with other pages on the site as well as how often the page's content changes. **TABLE 16-1** describes the tags commonly used within an XML site map file.

TABLE 16-1   COMMON ENTRIES WITHIN AN XML SITE MAP FILE

Site Map Tag	Optional/ Required	Purpose
\<urlset\>	Required	Groups all URL entries within the site map
\<url\>	Required	Groups items for a specific URL
\<loc\>	Required	Specifies the page URL of the page, including the protocol, such as http or https
\<lastmod\>	Optional	The date that the file was last modified in the format YYYY-MM-DD
\<changefreq\>	Optional	Specifies how often the page may change: • always • hourly • daily • weekly • monthly • yearly • never
\<priority\>	Optional	Specifies the page's relative importance within the site ranging from 0.0 to 1.0, with 1.0 being the most important. The default value is 0.5.

The following XML file, Sitemap.xml, illustrates the use of the XML site map entries:

```
<?xml version="1.0" encoding="UTF-8"?>
<urlsetxmlns="http://www.sitemaps.org/schemas/
sitemap/0.9">
<url>
<loc>http://www.somesite.com/</loc>
<lastmod>2012-07-04</lastmod>
<changefreq>daily</changefreq>
<priority>0.7</priority>
</url>
<url>
```

```
<loc>http://www.somesite.com/fliers/</loc>
<changefreq>weekly</changefreq>
</url>
<url>
<loc>http://www.somesite.com/photos/</loc>
<lastmod>2012-12-25</lastmod>
<changefreq>weekly</changefreq>
</url>
<url>
<loc>http://www.somesite.com/audios/</loc>
</url>
</urlset>
```

In this case, the first two lines specify the XML document specifics and the site map protocol. As you can see, the **<urlset>** and **</urlset>** tag pair groups the individual **<url>** entries.

After you create the Sitemap.xml file, you can validate the file's contents using a site map validator, such as that shown in **FIGURE 16–9**.

Next, you must inform search engines about your site map file. Some search engines will let you submit the file directly. For example, to submit your site map

FIGURE 16–9 Validating the contents of a Sitemap.xml file
Reproduced with permission from XML-Sitemaps.com

file to Google.com, you can use the Google Webmaster Tools, which you can access at *http://www.google.com/webmaster/tools/*. In addition to submitting the file to search engines, place an entry within your robots.txt file that tells robots the location of your site map:

```
User-agent: *
Disallow: /SomeFolder
sitemap: http://www.somesite.com/Sitemap.xml
```

Specifying Canonicalization

Depending on the software you use to create your site or the subtle differences in page content that you use for different user types, there may be times when two or more pages are essentially the same. Unfortunately, when robots search your page content, they may index each of the similar pages, which may later confuse search engine users.

Canonicalization is a term used to describe the process of converting data into one standard form. With respect to webpages, canonicalization means having one standard page. If your site has similar pages, and you want search engines to index only a specific page, place a <**link**> tag with the **rel="canonical"** attribute at the top of similar pages that specify the page you want the robots to index, as shown here:

```
<!DOCTYPE html>
<html>
<head>
<link rel="canonical" href="http://www.somesite.
com/primaryLink.html>
</head>
<body>
Page Content Here
</body>
</html>
```

In this case, the <**link**> tag specifies that the primaryLink.html file is the one the search engine should index.

Using 301 Redirects

As your website's contents evolve, there may be times when you move or rename one or more files. Unfortunately, a search engine may have previously indexed the file, which means users will encounter errors when they click on the search engine link. To avoid such errors, redirect references to the old page to a new page using a process called a 301 redirect. The 301 is an HTTP status value that tells the requesting browser that the page has moved.

Depending on the Web server you are using, the steps you must perform to redirect one page to another will differ. If your Web server supports PHP, you can use the following code snippet to redirect one page to another:

```
<?
Header( "HTTP/1.1 301 Moved Permanently" );
Header( "Location: http://www.somesite.com/
newlocation/" );
?>
```

Real-World Web Design

Web developers often are interested in search engine optimization because they want to drive traffic to a site to increase product exposure and sales or to drive advertising revenue. Creating a site that drives advertising revenue can be hard at best. Sites cannot make money until they have advertisers, and advertisers will not sign up with a site until it has considerable traffic.

As an alternative means of advertising, Web developers often turn to advertising networks, such as Google Adsense, as a source of ads. Unfortunately, such an **ad network** often does not pay as well as traditional advertisers—however, it provides a start.

Advertisers normally pay for ads in one of two ways. The first is called "cost per impression" and is based on the display of the ad. Usually, advertisers will pay for such "impressions" on the basis of **cost per thousand impressions**, known as CPM. Rates for CPM-based ads can range from less than a dollar to more than $20, depending on the product and demographic audience. Assuming a $5 CPM and daily traffic of 10,000 users, the ad revenue would become:

```
Revenue = (views)(rate)/1000

        = (10,000)($5)/1000

        = $50 a day
```

As you might guess, for an advertiser, simply displaying ads within a page already filled with other ads may not be the most cost-effective way to advertise. As an alternative, many advertisers will place ads on a cost-per-click basis. This means they don't pay for the display of the ad, but pay only when a user clicks on the ad. Assuming the advertiser pays $0.03 per click and the site has 1,000 clicks a day, the revenue would become:

```
Revenue = (clicks)(rate)

        = (1,000)($0.03)

        = $30 a day
```

For information on placing Google Adsense ads within your webpages, visit *http://www.google.com/adsense/*. When you sign up with an ad network, the network will provide you with HTML or JavaScript code that you insert within your webpage, which will display a text- or image-based ad and direct user clicks to specific advertising content. The ad network will embed special codes within the ad so that it can distinguish your site from another.

Hands-On HTML

To view the HTML files or to experiment with the files presented in this chapter, visit this book's companion website at *http://www.websitedevelopmentbook.com/Chapter16/TryIt.html*.

CHAPTER SUMMARY

Across the Web, users often find a site's content through a related search engine query. Search engine optimization is the process Web developers perform to increase a site's ranking within a search engine's query results. This chapter examined techniques developers should perform to optimize their site rankings. In addition, the chapter examined ways developers can monitor their site traffic to better understand the effectiveness of their SEO operations. Finally, the chapter looked at ways a developer might advertise or integrate advertisements into a webpage.

KEY TERMS

Ad network

Canonicalization

Cost per click (CPC)

Cost per thousand impressions (CPM)

Robots

Search engine optimization (SEO)

CHAPTER REVIEW

1. Using Alexa.com, measure and describe the user traffic for three of your favorite websites.

2. Research current keyword advertising rates at various search engines for keywords of interest to you.

3. Create an HTML file named DemoTags.html that uses a **<meta>** tag to describe keywords specific to a site of interest to you.

4. Create a robots.txt file that directs a robot not to browse the audio, photos, and private directories.

5. Create an XML-based Sitemap.xml that illustrates the use of the common site map tags.

6. Assuming a site has 1 million hits a day, determine the potential revenue for an $8 CPM ad.

The Need for HTML 5

© Risto Viita/Shutterstock

17

SINCE ITS ORIGIN IN the late 1980s, HTML has undergone several major version upgrades. The development of HTML 5 actually began shortly after the HTML 4 release in the late 1990s. Around 2004, the **Web Hypertext Application Technology Working Group (WHATWG)** began working with the **World Wide Web Consortium (W3C)** on the HTML 5 specification. Over the years that followed, the specification was influenced by the rapid growth of mobile technologies, capabilities such as geopositioning, and greater need for user interactivity. While this chapter introduces HTML 5, the chapters that follow examine the specific capabilities in detail.

Learning Objectives

This chapter examines HTML 5. By the time you finish this chapter, you will understand the following key concepts:

- How HTML 5 is a step in the HTML evolutionary process
- How HTML 5 introduces support for mobile devices, such as geopositioning
- How HTML 5 makes it easier for developers to integrate video and audio into a webpage
- How HTML 5 provides a canvas region within a webpage where developers can use JavaScript to code dynamic graphics operations
- How HTML 5 provides session-based storage and longer-term storage, using 5MB capacity objects that are similar in concept to client-side cookies

- How HTML 5 supports drag-and-drop operations to improve the user interface
- How HTML 5 provides support for multitasking within a webpage through the use of JavaScript code that implements a specific task
- How HTML 5 provides support for WebSockets, which support text-based communication between users within a webpage
- How HTML 5 provides support for new tags, which provide greater document-like structure and data semantics

Understanding the Need for HTML 5

HTML, as you have learned, is the hypertext markup language developers use to create webpages. Since HTML Version 1, developers have made enhancements to HTML by adding tags, removing or deprecating other tags, adding properties, and so on. In this way, HTML 5 is, in one sense, simply a step in the evolutionary process of HTML. That said, HTML 5 supports some very powerful new capabilities, which the sections that follow will introduce.

Support for Mobile Devices

Today, use of the World Wide Web on mobile devices is exploding. HTML 5 was designed with mobile phones and hand-held tablet devices in mind. For example, using HTML 5, developers can create animations that previously required the use of Flash technology, which many hand-held devices do not support. In addition, HTML 5 provides support for geopositioning, which applications can use to determine a user's location and provide "location aware" content, such as driving directions or advertisements for nearby restaurants and retailers. Chapter 26, "Creating Location-Aware Webpages Using Geolocation," examines the creation of location-aware Web applications.

Improved Support for Video and Audio

Websites today make extensive use of media, such as videos and audio podcasts. For years, to simplify the process of working with video, developers simply uploaded their videos to sites such as YouTube and then embedded links to those videos into the pages they created. In this way, the developers shifted the underlying complexity of video integration to YouTube.

HTML provides more support and new tags for video and audio. Chapter 18, "Integrating Audio and Video," examines HTML 5 support for video and audio in

FIGURE 17–1 HTML 5 provides support for video and audio webpage integration.
Credit: © bullet74/Shutterstock

detail. As you will learn, HTML 5 makes video and audio processing better, but not perfect. Integrating video into pages that support a wide range of browsers can still be challenging. **FIGURE 17–1** shows a video window playing within an HTML 5 webpage.

Canvas Programming

As webpages become more complex, Web developers need a way to create dynamic graphics, such as dashboards, charts, and animations. As shown in **FIGURE 17–2**, HTML 5 provides a canvas region that JavaScript programmers can use for the display of 2-D images, photos, and text. Chapter 21, "Introducing the HTML 5 Canvas," introduces the canvas and programming developers can

FIGURE 17-2 The HTML 5 canvas provides a region on a page where JavaScript can display dynamic graphics.

perform to common graphics operations. Chapter 22, "Advanced Canvas Programming," looks at advanced graphics programming, such as translations, rotations, gradients, and drop shadows.

Enhanced Client-Side Storage Capabilities

For years, developers made extensive use of client-side cookies to store information about user preferences, shopping-cart entries, and more. Using cookies, websites can store up to 4KB of data. HTML 5, on the other hand, provides the ability for users to store much, much more data, up to 5MB using a **sessionStorage** object and a **localStorage** object. The **sessionStorage** object stores data for the duration of a user's session interaction with a page. The **localStorage** object stores data until the application or the user deletes the object. Chapter 25, "Utilizing Web Storage," examines the HTML 5 client-side storage capabilities in detail.

Support for Drag-and-Drop Operations

Web developers should always look for ways to improve a site's user interface and opportunities for a more natural interaction. To that end, HTML 5 provides, as shown in **FIGURE 17-3**, support for drag-and-drop operations. Using a drag-and-drop operation, for example, your webpage might allow a user to drag items into a shopping cart.

Multitasking with Web Workers

As you know, operating systems, such as Windows, allow users to run multiple programs at the same time. Many of the programs can perform their processing in the background, while the user works actively with a different window.

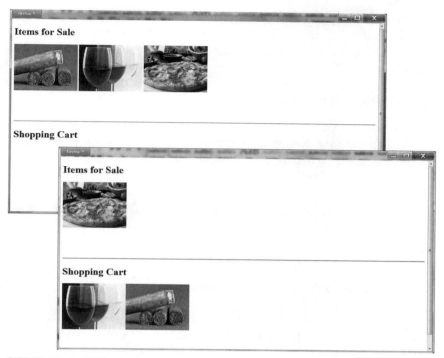

FIGURE 17-3 HTML 5 supports drag-and-drop operations.
Credit (from left): © Vaclav Volrab/Shutterstock; © Gts/Shutterstock; © Daniel Cozma/Shutterstock

Depending on the processing a webpage performs, there may be times when you will need the page to perform background processing, such as updating images while users perform other tasks on the page. To perform such background tasks within a webpage, you can use HTML 5 Web workers. Chapter 28, "Integrating Web Workers," presents the use of Web workers. As you will learn, a Web worker, in the simplest sense, is a JavaScript routine the browser runs as a background task.

Communication with WebSockets

Across the Internet, users make extensive use of texting and instant messaging to perform text-based communication with other users. To help Web developers integrate such chat capabilities into the webpages they create, HTML 5 supports the use of WebSockets. Chapter 29, "Communicating via WebSockets," illustrates socket use.

HTML 5 Document Structure and Page Semantics

Many HTML pages now display content similar in form to a document's structure, which means the pages have a header, content, a footer, figures, sidebars, and more. To make it easy for developers to format such content consistently, HTML 5 provides several new document-structure tags as well as several new semantic tags, which Chapter 19, "HTML 5 Document Structure and Semantics," examines in detail.

Real-World Web Design

As briefly discussed, the Web Hypertext Application Technology Working Group was a key player in the development of the HTML 5 specification. Take time to monitor the group's Wikis, forums, and specification notes at the WhatWG.org website, shown in **FIGURE 17-4**.

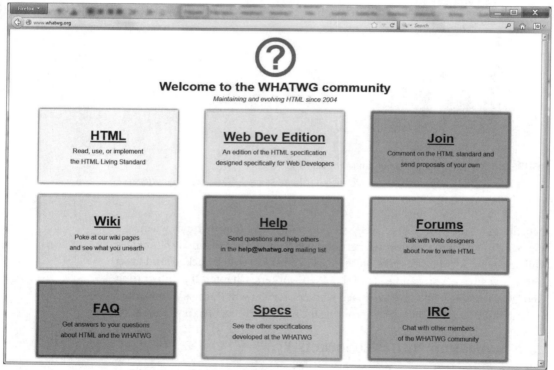

FIGURE 17-4 The WhatWG.org website monitors HTML 5 specification issues.
Courtesy of www.whatwg.org

Hands-On HTML

To view the HTML files or to experiment with the files presented in this chapter, visit this book's companion website at *http://www.websitedevelopmentbook.com/Chapter17/TryIt.html*.

CHAPTER SUMMARY

HTML 5 is the newest evolution of the hypertext markup language that developers use to create webpages. HTML 5, like most major releases of HTML, adds some new tags while deprecating others. Some of the key features of HTML 5 include improved support for video and audio integration, tags to assist in formatting document-like pages that use headers, footers, and sidebars, support for drag-and-drop operations, text-based communication, and multitasking through the use of Web workers. In the chapters that follow, you will examine these capabilities in detail.

KEY TERMS

Web Hypertext Application Technology Working Group (WHATWG)

World Wide Web Consortium (W3C)

CHAPTER REVIEW

1. Research WHATWG and W3C. Then compare and contrast the two organizations.
2. Research HTML 5, and write and discuss the new tags that HTML 5 introduces.
3. Research HTML 5, and write and discuss the tags that HTML 5 deprecates.

Integrating Audio and Video

WITH THE ADVENT OF video cameras within most cell phones, it has become very easy for people to record their own videos. Thanks to sites such as YouTube, posting videos to the Web has become very easy and popular. Today, many developers want to integrate video or audio content into the webpages they create. HTML 5 was supposed to make the process very easy. Unfortunately, because not all browsers support HTML 5, and because more standardization of video file formats is needed, the process of placing videos within a webpage that all browsers can play remains challenging at best.

Learning Objectives

The chapter examines the steps to perform to place video and audio within a webpage. By the time you finish this chapter, you will understand the following key concepts:

- How the HTML 5 **<video>** and **</video>** tag pair can be used to include a video file within a webpage
- How to add video controls with the **controls** attribute
- How video files can be saved in a variety of file formats, which not all browsers support
- How to support common browsers by providing multiple video file formats, such as streaming versus downloaded video, within your webpage
- How to control your video size with the **height** and **width** attributes
- How developers can optimize video quality or the video file size by compressing video using different formats called codecs

- How to support the **<video>** and **</video>** tag pair with older browsers by embedding video within your webpage using the **<embed>** or **<object>** tags
- How to buffer video to play it without a downloading delay
- How to display a default image until a video starts to play
- How to loop a video
- How YouTube can handle the details
- How to provide multiple audio file formats within your webpage to support common browsers
- How to embed audio within your webpage using the **<embed>** or **<object>** tags because older browsers do not support the **<audio>** and **</audio>** tag pair
- How to use a link to an audio file
- How to control background audio

Using HTML 5 Video Within a Webpage

To simplify the process of placing a video clip within a webpage, HTML 5 provides the **<video>** and **</video>** tag pair. In the ideal sense, using the **<video>** tag is similar to placing an image within a page. Use the **<video>** tag **src** attribute to specify the location of the video file:

```
<video src="http://www.WebSiteDevelopmentBook.com/
Chapter18/Cigar.mp4"></video>
```

The following HTML file, FirstVideo.html, places the video file Pizza.mp4 within a webpage. The file uses the **autoplay** attribute to automatically start the video when the page loads:

```
<!DOCTYPE html>
<html>
<body>
<h1>Pizza!</h1>
<video src="http://www.WebSiteDevelopmentBook.com/
Chapter18/Pizza.mp4" autoplay="autoplay"></video>
</body>
</html>
```

The process appears easy enough. Unfortunately, the video file specified uses the MP4 video format, and not all browsers support MP4. The browsers that do will play the video. The browsers that do not may ignore the video, display a broken-link icon, or display a message stating that the video format is not supported. You can also include text between the <**video**> and </**video**> tags that directs the browser to display a message if it does not support the tags.

Your solution to the video-format problem is to create multiple formats of the same video and then to use multiple <**source**> and </**source**> tag pairs within the <**video**> and </**video**> tag pair to specify the location of each. When a browser later examines the <**video**> tag, the browser will select and play the source file that matches the format it supports.

The following HTML file, MultipleVideoSources.html, uses a <**source**> tag to specify the location of an MP4 file and <**source**> tags to specify the location of additional video files, each of which support a specific format:

```
<!DOCTYPE html>
<html>
<body>
<h1>Wine!</h1>
<video autoplay="autoplay">
<source src="http://www.WebsiteDevelopmentBook.com/
Chapter18/Wine.mp4" type="video/mp4"/>
<source src="http://www.WebsiteDevelopmentBook.com/
Chapter18/Wine.ogg" type="video/ogg"/>
<source src="http://www.WebsiteDevelopmentBook.com/
Chapter18/Wine.flv" type="video/flv"/>
<source src="http://www.WebsiteDevelopmentBook.com/
Chapter18/Wine.webm" type="video/webm"/>
<source src="http://www.WebsiteDevelopmentBook.com/
Chapter18/Wine.mov" type="video/mov"/>

Video Tag Not Supported
</video>
</body>
</html>
```

In this case, within each <**source**> tag, the **type** attribute specifies each video's format. Using the **type** attribute, a browser can determine which video format it supports and should display the video, as shown in **FIGURE 18-1**.

TABLE 18-1 lists common video **type** attribute values.

By default, if you simply specify the **autoplay** attribute, most browsers will automatically start the video when the webpage loads. However, to ensure that all browsers automatically start the video, specify **autoplay="autoplay"** within the <**video**> tag. If you do not want the video to start automatically, omit the **autoplay** attribute or use **autoplay=""**.

FIGURE 18-1 Using multiple video formats to provide support for various Web browsers
Credit: © bullet74/Shutterstock

TABLE 18-1   COMMON VIDEO-TYPE FORMATS

File Format	Type Attribute
.MP4	video/mp4
.OGG	video/ogg
.FLV	video/flv
.MOV	video/mov
.Webm	video/webm

Adding Video Controls

When you use the <**video**> tag to insert a video within a webpage, the browser, by default, will display the video within a box without video controls (buttons for play, pause, stop, and so on). To direct the browser to display such controls, include the **controls** attribute within the <**video**> tag. Again, to specifically include the controls within all browsers, specify **controls="controls"**. Likewise, to disable the display of such controls, use **controls=""**.

The following HTML file, VideoControls.html, uses the **controls** attribute to enable video controls:

```
<!DOCTYPE html>
<html>
<body>
<h1>Cigars!</h1>
<video autoplay="autoplay" controls="controls">
<source src="http://www.WebsiteDevelopmentBook.com/
Chapter18/Cigar.mp4" type="video/mp4"/>
<source src="http://www.WebsiteDevelopmentBook.com/
Chapter18/Cigar.ogg" type="video/ogg"/>
<source src="http://www.WebsiteDevelopmentBook.com/
Chapter18/Cigar.flv" type="video/flv"/>
<source src="http://www.WebsiteDevelopmentBook.com/
Chapter18/Cigar.webm" type="video/webm"/>
<source src="http://www.WebsiteDevelopmentBook.com/
Chapter18/Cigar.mov" type="video/mov"/>

Video Tag Not Supported
</video>
</body>
</html>
```

When you view the file's contents, the browser will display the video with control buttons, as shown in **FIGURE 18-2**.

Saving Video Files

To support all browsers, save your video in a variety of file formats. If you plan to integrate video into webpages on a regular basis, purchase a good video-conversion software program. Many such programs are available on the Web that differ in price and the number of video formats they support.

FIGURE 18-2 Using the **<video>** tag **controls** attribute to direct a browser to display video controls

Credit: © Rekindle Photo and Video/Shutterstock

Streaming Versus Downloaded Video

In general, there are two video types: streaming and downloaded. A **streaming video** can start playing after the browser downloads part of the video (enough video to get started). A **downloaded video**, in contrast, must download completely to the user's system before it can play. Depending on the video's size (a video file can become large quickly), a downloaded video may force the user to wait a considerable amount of time before it begins to play. This does not provide a good user experience.

Some **video file formats**, which are file types that specify how a video was saved, support streaming, and others do not. The common streaming video file formats include: WebM (Google), MP4, Ogg, MOV (Quicktime), RM (Real Media), and FLV (Flash video). When you place a video file within a webpage, use a streaming video file format.

Controlling Your Video File Size

When you place a video file within a webpage, the browser will, by default, display the video at the size the video was saved, which is often 320x240 or 640x480. Depending on your webpage design, you may want to specify the video's height and width. To do so, use the **<video>** tag **height** and **width** attributes. The following HTML file, VideoSizes.html, places the same video within a page at two different sizes:

```
<!DOCTYPE html>
<html>
<body>
<h1>Sleepy Dog!</h1>
<video autoplay="autoplay" controls="controls"
height="240" width="320">
<source src="http://www.WebsiteDevelopmentBook.com/
Chapter18/Dog.webm" type="video/webm"/>
<source src="http://www.WebsiteDevelopmentBook.com/
Chapter18/Dog.ogg" type="video/ogg"/>
<source src="http://www.WebsiteDevelopmentBook.com/
Chapter18/Dog.mp4" type="video/mp4"/>
<source src="http://www.WebsiteDevelopmentBook.com/
Chapter18/Dog.flv" type="video/flv"/>
<source src="http://www.WebsiteDevelopmentBook.com/
Chapter18/Dog.mov" type="video/mov"/>

Video Tag Not Supported
</video>
<br/>
<video autoplay="autoplay" controls="controls"
height="480" width="640">
<source src="http://www.WebsiteDevelopmentBook.com/
Chapter18/Dog.ogg" type="video/ogg"/>
<source src="http://www.WebsiteDevelopmentBook.com/
Chapter18/Dog.mp4" type="video/mp4"/>
<source src="http://www.WebsiteDevelopmentBook.com/
Chapter18/Dog.flv" type="video/flv"/>
<source src="http://www.WebsiteDevelopmentBook.com/
Chapter18/Dog.webm" type="video/webm"/>
<source src="http://www.WebsiteDevelopmentBook.com/
Chapter18/Dog.mov" type="video/mov"/>

Video Tag Not Supported
</video>
</body>
</html>
```

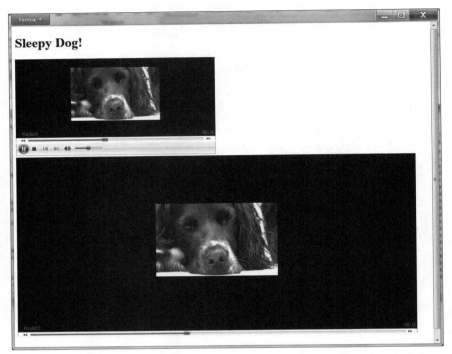

FIGURE 18-3 Using the **<video>** tag **height** and **width** attributes to control a video's size
Credit: © Christa DeRidder/Shutterstock

When you view the file's contents, the browser will display the videos, as shown in **FIGURE 18-3**.

Understanding Video Codecs

A video file is essentially a big collection of ones and zeros that define the pictures that make up the video as well as the audio. To improve the quality of the video and audio or to speed up the video download, apply different compression formats to a video file. Developers refer to these formats as **codecs**. There are a variety of codecs you can use when you save a video file. The three most common codecs are H.264, Theora, and V8. Unfortunately, not all browsers support all of these.

Supporting Older Browsers

As if providing multiple video file formats were not work enough, when you integrate video into a webpage, you also need to provide a solution for browsers that do not support the **<video>** and **</video>** tag pair. For years, to place video within a webpage, developers used the **<embed>** and **</embed>** tag pair and the **<object>** and

</**object**> tag pair. The two tags were needed because, as you might guess, some browsers supported the <**embed**> tags and other browsers supported <**object**>.

The following HTML file, OldStyleVideo.html, illustrates the use of the two tags to display video within a webpage:

```
<!DOCTYPE html>
<html>
<body>
<h1>Parrot!</h1>
<embed src="http://www.WebSiteDevelopmentBook.com/
Chapter18/Parrot.mp4" height="240" width="320">
</embed>
<object src="http://www.WebSiteDevelopmentBook.com/
Chapter18/Parrot.mp4" height="240" width="320">
</object>
</body>
</html>
```

As you can see, to support a wider range of browsers, the code includes both the <**embed**> and <**object**> tags.

To provide support for older browsers, you need to include the tags within your <**video**> and </**video**> tag pair. The following HTML file, SupportAllVideo. html, provides tags that should support the common browsers:

```
<!DOCTYPE html>
<html>
<body>
<h1>Horses!</h1>
<video autoplay="autoplay">
<source src="http://www.WebsiteDevelopmentBook.com/
Chapter18/Horse.mp4" type="video/mp4"/>
<source src="http://www.WebsiteDevelopmentBook.com/
Chapter18/Horse.ogg" type="video/ogg"/>
<source src="http://www.WebsiteDevelopmentBook.com/
Chapter18/Horse.flv" type="video/flv"/>
<source src="http://www.WebsiteDevelopmentBook.com/
Chapter18/Horse.webm" type="video/webm"/>
<source src="http://www.WebsiteDevelopmentBook.com/
Chapter18/Horse.mov" type="video/mov"/>
<embed src="http://www.WebSiteDevelopmentBook.com/
Chapter18/Horse.mp4" height="240" width="320">
</embed>
```

```
<object src="http://www.WebSiteDevelopmentBook.com/
Chapter18/Horse.mp4" height="240" width="320">
</object>
</video>
</body>
</html>
```

Directing the Browser to Start Buffering Video

When a browser downloads an HTML page, it examines the HTML tags and begins to download related files, such as photos on the page. If your webpage contains a video that you do not want to start automatically after the page loads but that you think the user will ultimately start, you can direct the browser to start downloading and buffering the video file. In this way, when the user later starts the video, the browser can begin to play it without a downloading delay.

To direct the browser to begin buffering video, use the <**video**> tag **preload** attribute. If the video is set to **autoplay**, the browser automatically begins to buffer the video and ignores the **preload** attribute.

Displaying a Default Image Until a Video Starts to Play

Depending on the first frames within a video file, the image that appears within the video box when a browser loads, but does not autoplay, may not be the image you want to appear on your page. Using the <**video**> tag **poster** attribute, you can specify an image the browser should display within the video box. The following HTML file, VideoPoster.html, illustrates the use of the **poster** attribute:

```
<!DOCTYPE html>
<html>
<body>
<h1>Clouds!</h1>
<video controls="controls" poster="http://www
.WebSiteDevelopmentBook.com/Chapter18/clouds.jpg">
<source src="http://www.WebsiteDevelopmentBook.com/
Chapter18/Clouds.mp4" type="video/mp4"/>
<source src="http://www.WebsiteDevelopmentBook.com/
Chapter18/Clouds.ogg" type="video/ogg"/>
<source src="http://www.WebsiteDevelopmentBook.com/
Chapter18/Clouds.flv" type="video/flv"/>
<source src="http://www.WebsiteDevelopmentBook.com/
Chapter18/Clouds.webm" type="video/webm"/>
```

FIGURE 18-4 Using the **<video>** tag **poster** attribute, you can specify what image the browser displays within the video box before the user begins to play the video.
Credit: © Ultra HD/Shutterstock

```
<source src="http://www.WebsiteDevelopmentBook.com/
Chapter18/Clouds.mov" type="video/mov"/>
</video>
</body>
</html>
```

When you view the file, your browser will display the image shown in **FIGURE 18-4** within the video box until the user plays the video.

Looping a Video

Depending on your video content, there may be times when you want the video to repeat, endlessly, while the webpage is open. In such cases, use the **<video>** tag **loop** attribute. The following HTML file, VideoLoop.html, sets the **loop** attribute to **true**, which directs the browser to continuously play the video content:

```
<!DOCTYPE html>
<html>
<body>
```

```
<h1>Hiker!</h1>
<video autoplay="autoplay" loop="true">
<source src="http://www.WebsiteDevelopmentBook.com/
Chapter18/Hiker.mp4" type="video/mp4"/>
<source src="http://www.WebsiteDevelopmentBook.com/
Chapter18/Hiker.ogg" type="video/ogg"/>
<source src="http://www.WebsiteDevelopmentBook.com/
Chapter18/Hiker.flv" type="video/flv"/>
<source src="http://www.WebsiteDevelopmentBook.com/
Chapter18/Hiker.webm" type="video/webm"/>
<source src="http://www.WebsiteDevelopmentBook.com/
Chapter18/Hiker.mov" type="video/mov"/>
</video>
</body>
</html>
```

Letting YouTube Handle the Details

You may be thinking that video processing within a webpage is too challenging or too much effort. To simplify such processing, many users upload videos to You-Tube and then run the videos from there by embedding references to the video within their HTML file. Although YouTube simplifies the process, using YouTube may subject your videos to advertising.

Providing Multiple Audio Formats for Browsers

For years, inexperienced website developers would install background music within a site that automatically began to play when someone viewed the page. Unfortunately, most people did not like the fact that they suddenly had to adjust their computer's speaker volume to turn down the unexpected music. Instead, they wanted to control whether or not music is played.

Today, with the popularity of audio podcasts, developers often place audio files within webpages. To make it easier to embed such audio, HTML 5 provides the **<audio>** and **</audio>** tag pair, which is similar in use to the **<video>** and **</video>** tag pair. As you might suspect, different browsers support different audio file formats, which makes the process of integrating audio into a webpage more complex.

The following HTML file, AudioDemo.html, uses the **<audio>** and **</audio>** tag pair to place an audio control on a page. Within the tags, the file uses two **<source>** tags to specify one audio file in the .ogg file format and one in the .mp3 format. When a browser examines the tag, it selects the audio format that it supports:

```
<!DOCTYPE html>
<html>
<body>
<h1>Rock!</h1>
<audio controls="controls">
<source src="http://www.WebsiteDevelopmentBook.com/
Chapter18/Rock.mp3" type="audio/mp3"/>
<source src="http://www.WebsiteDevelopmentBook.com/
Chapter18/Rock.ogg" type="audio/ogg"/>
</audio>
</body>
</html>
```

In this case, the <**audio**> tag includes the **controls** attribute, which directs the browser to display control icons you can use to play, pause, and control the audio. Note that the tag also does not include the **autoplay** attribute, which directs the browser to start the audio automatically after the page downloads. When you view the file, the browser will display the audio controls shown in **FIGURE 18–5**.

Making Audio Files Work with Older Browsers

Not all browsers support the <**audio**> and </**audio**> tag pair. To support older browsers, you can use the <**object**> and <**embed**> tags to place audio within your

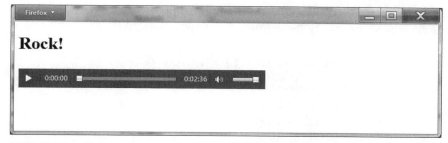

FIGURE 18–5 Displaying audio controls that allow a user to play, pause, and control an audio within a webpage

page. The following HTML file, OldStyleAudio.html, illustrates how to support various browsers:

```
<!DOCTYPE html>
<html>
<body>
<h1>Jazz!</h1>
<embed src="http://www.WebSiteDevelopmentBook.com/
Chapter18/jazz.mp3"></embed>
<object src="http://www.WebSiteDevelopmentBook.com/
Chapter18/jazz.mp3"></object>
</body>
</html>
```

As you can see, the file includes support for both the **<embed>** and **<object>** tags.

Using a Link to an Audio File

Another way to support audio in older browsers is to simply place a hyperlink to the audio file within your webpage, as shown in the following HTML file, AudioLink.html:

```
<!DOCTYPE html>
<html>
<body>
<h1>Groove!</h1>
<a href="http://www.WebSiteDevelopmentBook.com/
Chapter18/Groove.mp3">Click Here</a>
</body>
</html>
```

When the user clicks on the link to the audio file, the browser downloads the audio file and then uses a "helper" program to play the audio.

Background Audio the Old-Fashioned Way

As discussed, the use of audio within a webpage is not new to HTML 5. For years, developers have used the **<bgsound>** tag to direct a browser to download and automatically play an audio file in the background as the user viewed a page. The **<bgsound>** tag, however, is deprecated and may not be supported by all browsers. Instead, if you want background music or other audio for your site, you should use the **<audio>** tag.

Keep in mind that many users are annoyed by sites that play music or sounds when they load. Your page design should put the user in control of whether or not audio plays. That said, the following HTML file, AutoplayAudio.html, starts and loops background music as the page is viewed:

```
<!DOCTYPE html>
<html>
<body>
<audio src="http://www.WebSiteDevelopmentBook.com/
Chapter18/LoveStory.mp3" autoplay loop="true">
</audio>
<img src="http://www.WebSiteDevelopmentBook.com/
Chapter18/clouds.jpg">
</body>
</html>
```

As you can see, the <**audio**> tag specifies **autoplay** and then includes the **loop** attribute to repeat the music.

Real-World Web Design

As you have learned, including video and audio within a webpage can become complex if your goal is to support all browsers. To make the process easier, sites such as Yahoo! now provide Web-based **media players** that you can direct your browser to use to play back video or audio. The media players, in turn, support various video file formats, which simplify your work. The following HTML file, YahooMediaPlayer.html, uses the Yahoo! media player to play a video when you click on the corresponding video link:

```
<!DOCTYPE html>
<html>
<body>
<a href="http://www.WebSiteDevelopmentBook.com/
Chapter18/Sunset.mp4">Sunset Video</a><br/>
<a href="http://www.WebSiteDevelopmentBook.com/
Chapter18/Cold.mp3">Music Audio</a>
<script type="text/javascript" src="http://media-
player.yahoo.com/js"></script>
</body>
</html>
```

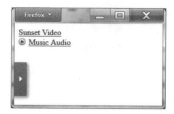

FIGURE 18-6 Clicking on the video link shown here will bring up the Yahoo! media player control.

Credit: © spotmatik/Shutterstock

When you view the file and click on the video link, the browser displays the Yahoo media player control, as shown in **FIGURE 18-6**, and plays the corresponding video.

Hands-On HTML

To view the HTML files or to experiment with the files presented in this chapter, visit this book's companion website at *http://www.websitedevelopmentbook.com/ Chapter18/TryIt.html.*

CHAPTER SUMMARY

You can make extensive use of phone-based video cameras to record content you later want to post on the Web. Likewise, audio-based podcasts that can play from a computer or mobile device have become very popular. As you design webpages, there will be times when you integrate video or audio content into your page. In an attempt to make such integration easier, HTML 5 introduced the **<video>** and **<audio>** tags.

Unfortunately, because not all browsers support HTML 5, and because different browsers support different audio and video file formats, the process of integrating audio and video into a webpage remains complex. In this chapter, you learned how to use the HTML 5 video and audio capabilities while continuing to provide support for older browsers.

KEY TERMS

Autoplay

Codec

Downloaded video

Media player

Streaming video

Video file format

CHAPTER REVIEW

1. Create an HTML file named VideoTest.html that uses the **<video>** and **<source>** tags to play one of the following video files:
   http://www.WebSiteDevelopmentBook.com/Chapter18/raft.mp4
   http://www.WebSiteDevelopmentBook.com/Chapter18/raft.ogg
   http://www.WebSiteDevelopmentBook.com/Chapter18/raft.webm

2. Modify the VideoTest.html file that you created in Question 1 to add controls the user can use to play, pause, and control the video.

3. Modify the VideoTest.html file to autoplay and to loop the video.

4. Use the **<embed>** and **<object>** tags to modify the VideoTest.html file to support common browsers.

5. Create an HTML file named AudioTest.html that uses the **<audio>** and **<source>** tags to play one of the following audio files:
   http://www.WebSiteDevelopmentBook.com/Chapter18/sitari.mp3
   http://www.WebSiteDevelopmentBook.com/Chapter18/sitari.ogg

6. Modify the AudioTest.html file that you created in Question 5 to add controls the user can use to play, pause, and control the audio.

7. Modify the AudioTest.html file to autoplay and to loop the audio.

8. Use the **<embed>** and **<object>** tags to modify the AudioTest.html to support common browsers.

HTML 5 Document Structure and Semantics

HTML, THE HYPERTEXT MARKUP language, has its origin in other markup languages that were used by publishers to format text pages. Years ago, for example, people using word processing software actually placed special codes within their documents to turn on bolding, italics, underlining, and so on. HTML 5 continues HTML's ties to document formatting by adding tags that devices can use to specify attributes for various document-based structures, such as headers, footers, figures, captions, sidebars, and more. In addition, HTML includes several tags that provide meaning, which developers refer to as **semantics**, to different items on a page.

Learning Objectives

This chapter examines the HTML 5 structural and semantic tags. By the time you finish this chapter, you will understand the following key concepts:

- How HTML 5 provides new tags you can use to define a document structure, such as its header, footer, figures, and captions
- How to create a document sidebar
- How to group and organize blogs, articles, and editorials
- How to organize a page section
- How to work with figures and figure captions
- How to identify document navigational links
- How to hide underlying content by displaying summary text
- How using the HTML 5 **<mark>** and **</mark>** tag pair allows you to highlight text within a document
- How to specify a word break

HTML 5's New Tags for Defining a Document Structure

When students create a paper-based document or report, they often use document headers and footers to specify information, such as the document's title, date, page numbers, and so on. In a similar way, many HTML pages present document-like content.

To help Web developers consistently present such page areas, HTML 5 provides **<header>** and **</header>** tag pairs as well as **<footer>** and **</footer>**. The following HTML file, HeaderFooter.html, illustrates each tag's use:

```
<!DOCTYPE html>
<html>
<body>
<header style="background-color:yellow">
Document Title</header>
<p style="background-color:lightblue">
Lorem ipsum dolor sit amet, consectetur
adipisicing elit, sed do eiusmod tempor incididunt
ut labore et dolore magna aliqua. Ut enim ad minim
veniam, quis nostrud exercitation ullamco laboris
nisi utaliquip ex ea commodo consequat. Duis aute
irure dolor in reprehenderit in voluptate velit
esse cillum dolore eu fugiat nulla pariatur.
Excepteur sint occaecat cupidatat non proident,
sunt in culpa qui officia deserunt mollit anim id
est laborum.
</p>
<footer style="background-color:orange">
Copyright (C) 2013, Somesite.com</footer>
</body>
</html>
```

As you can see, the page uses cascading style sheets to style the **<header>** and **<footer>** tags. If you view the file's contents, the browser displays the content, as shown in **FIGURE 19-1**.

Creating a Document Sidebar

Books, magazines, and newsletters make extensive use of sidebars to present information related to a document's main topic. To support similar webpage

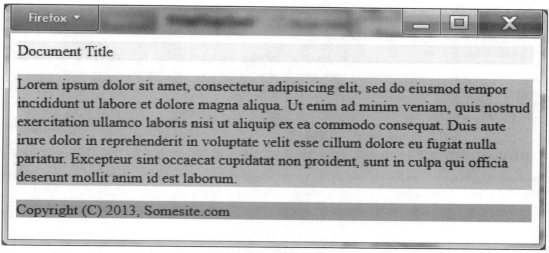

FIGURE 19-1 Formatting a page's header and footer regions

operations, HTML 5 provides the **<aside>** and **</aside>** tag pair. The following HTML file, Sidebar.html, illustrates the use of the tag pair:

```
<!DOCTYPE html>
<html>
<body>
<header style="background-color:yellow">
Document Title</header>
<aside style="width:200px; float:left;">
Sed ut perspiciatis unde omnis iste natus error sit
voluptatem accusantium doloremque laudantium, totam
rem aperiam, eaque ipsa quae ab illo inventore
veritatis et quasi architecto beatae vitae dicta
sunt explicabo.
</aside>
<div style="float:left; width:600px">
<p style="background-color:lightblue">
Lorem ipsum dolor sit amet, consectetur adipisicing
elit, sed do eiusmod tempor incididuntut labore et
dolore magna aliqua. Ut enim ad minim veniam, quis
nostrud exercitation ullamco laboris nisi utaliquip
ex ea commodo consequat.
</p>
```

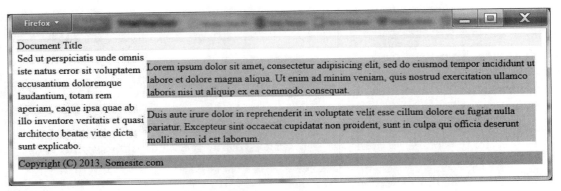

FIGURE 19-2 Displaying a sidebar within an HTML document

```
<p style="background-color:lightblue">
Duis aute irure dolor in reprehenderit in voluptate
velit esse cillum dolore eu fugiat nulla pariatur.
Excepteur sint occaecat cupidatat non proident,
sunt in culpa qui officia deserunt mollit anim id
est laborum.
</p>
</div>
<div style="clear:both;"></div>
<footer style="background-color:orange">
Copyright (C) 2013, Somesite.com</footer>
</body>
</html>
```

If you view the file's contents, the page will display the content shown in **FIGURE 19-2**.

Organizing Article Content

Many webpages consist of blogs, articles, and editorial content. To help Web developers group and organize such content, HTML 5 provides the **<article>** and **</article>** tag pair. You can think of an article within a webpage as a standalone content group, such as a blog. The following HTML page, ShowArticle.html, uses the tag pair to format page content:

```
<!DOCTYPE html>
<html>
<body>
```

```
<header style="background-color:yellow">
Document Title</header>
<aside style="width:200px; float:left;">
Sed ut perspiciatis unde omnis iste natus error sit
voluptatem accusantium doloremque laudantium,
totam rem aperiam, eaque ipsa quae ab illo
inventore veritatis et quasi architecto beatae
vitae dicta sunt explicabo.
</aside>
<div style="float:left; width:600px">

<article style="background-color:lightblue">
<p>
Lorem ipsum dolor sit amet, consectetur adipisicing
elit, sed do eiusmod tempor incididunt ut labore et
dolore magna aliqua. Ut enim ad minim veniam, quis
nostrud exercitation ullamco laboris nisi ut
aliquip ex ea commodo consequat.
</p>
<p>
Duis aute irure dolor in reprehenderit in voluptate
velit esse cillum dolore eu fugiat nulla pariatur.
Excepteur sint occaecat cupidatat non proident,
sunt in culpa qui officia deserunt mollit anim id
est laborum.
</p>
</article>

</div>
<div style="clear:both;"></div>
<footer style="background-color:orange">
Copyright (C) 2013, Somesite.com</footer>
</body>
</html>
```

If you view the file's contents, the browser will display the page contents, as shown in **FIGURE 19-3**.

Organizing Page Sections

As you just learned, within a webpage, an article is a complete content group, which can stand alone. In contrast, a section is a smaller piece of content that is

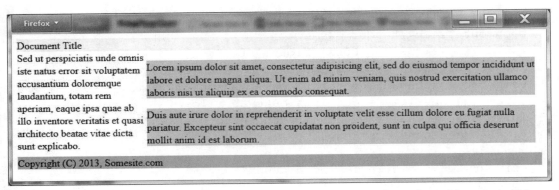

FIGURE 19-3 This image, the same screenshot as in Figure 19-2, also illustrates formatting article content within an HTML page.

not independent. To identify sections of content within a page, use the **<section>** and **</section>** tag pair. The following HTML file, SectionDemo.html, illustrates the use of the tags:

```
<!DOCTYPE html>
<html>
<body>
<header style="background-color:yellow">
Document Title</header>

<article>
<section style="background-color:lightblue">
Sed ut perspiciatis unde omnis iste natus error sit
voluptatem accusantium doloremque laudantium,
totam rem aperiam, eaque ipsa quae ab illo
inventore veritatis et quasi architecto beatae
vitae dicta sunt explicabo.
</section>

<section style="background-color:lime">
<p>
Lorem ipsum dolor sit amet, consectetur adipisicing
elit, sed do eiusmod tempor incididunt ut labore
et dolore magna aliqua. Ut enim ad minim
veniam, quis nostrud exercitation ullamco laboris
nisi ut aliquip ex ea commodo consequat.
</p>
```

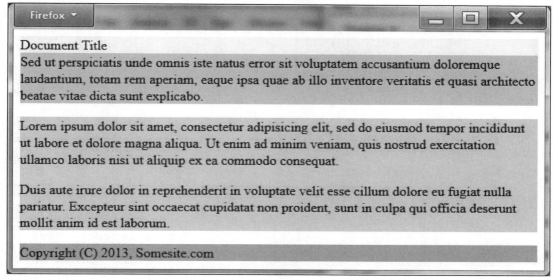

FIGURE 19-4 Using the **<section>** and **</section>** tag pair to group document sections

```
<p>
Duis aute irure dolor in reprehenderit in
voluptate velit esse cillum dolore eu fugiat nulla
pariatur. Excepteur sint occaecat cupidatat non
proident, sunt in culpa qui officia deserunt mollit
anim id est laborum.
</p>
</section>
</article>
<footer style="background-color:orange">Copyright
(C) 2013, Somesite.com</footer>
</body>
</html>
```

As you can see, the file defines two sections and assigns a different background color to each. If you view the file's contents, the browser displays the page, as shown in **FIGURE 19-4**.

Working with Figures and Figure Captions

Documents and webpages make extensive use of visuals. Within a paper-based document, authors often use figures and figure captions. To simplify similar processing with a webpage, HTML provides the **<figure>** and **</figure>** tag pair along with **<figcaption>** and **</figcaption>**. The following HTML file, Figure-Demo.html, illustrates the use of these tags:

```
<!DOCTYPE html>
<html>
<body>
<header style="background-color:yellow">
Document Title</header>

<article>
<section style="background-color:lime">
<p>
Lorem ipsum dolor sit amet, consectetur adipisicing
elit, sed do eiusmod tempor incididunt ut labore
et dolore magna aliqua. Ut enim ad minim
veniam, quis nostrud exercitation ullamco laboris
nisi ut aliquip ex ea commodo consequat.
</p>

<figure>
<img src="http://www.websitedevelopmentbook.com/
Chapter19/dog.jpg" />
<figcaption><b>Figure A: </b>My new dog
</figcaption>
</figure>

<p>
Duis aute irure dolor in reprehenderit in
voluptate velit esse cillum dolore eu fugiat nulla
pariatur. Excepteur sint occaecat cupidatat non
proident, sunt in culpa qui officia deserunt mollit
anim id est laborum.
</p>
</section>
</article>

<footer style="background-color:orange">
Copyright (C) 2013, Somesite.com</footer>
</body>
</html>
```

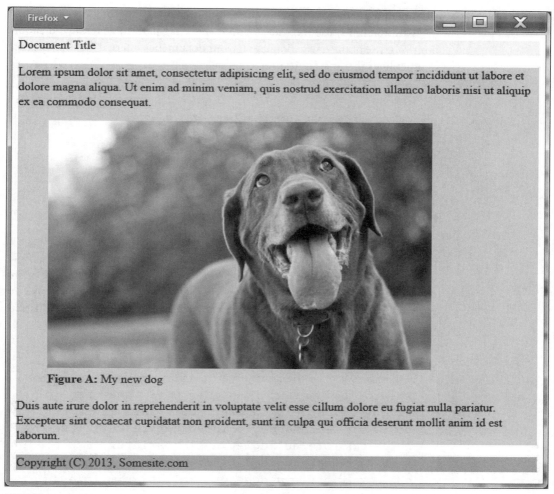

FIGURE 19-5 Using a figure and figure caption within an HTML page
Credit: © Eurobanks/Shutterstock

If you view the file's contents, your browser will display the content shown in **FIGURE 19-5**.

Identifying Document Navigational Links

As the length of a printed report increases, authors often integrate a table of contents to help the reader navigate the document. In a similar way, a Web-based document may consist of a set of related internal links. To group the document's navigational links, use the **<nav>** and **</nav>** tag pair. In general, you should limit your use of the navigation tags to your document's internal links, as opposed to other links that may appear on your page:

```
<nav>
<a href="#Chapter01">Chapter 1</a>
<a href="#Chapter02">Chapter 2</a>
<a href="#Chapter03">Chapter 3</a>
</nav>
```

Hiding Underlying Content

Depending on your document's contents, there may be times when, for page real estate purposes, you don't want to display all of the information about a topic. Instead, you can display summary text which, if the user is interested, he or she can expand to display the underlying specifics. In such cases, you can use the HTML 5 **<details>** and **</details>** tag pair. The following statements illustrate the tags' use:

```
<details>
<summary>This summary text will appear</summary>
The following text is hidden until the user
triggers the text content. Duis aute irure
dolor in reprehenderit in voluptate velit esse
cillum dolore eu fugiat nulla pariatur. Excepteur
sint occaecat cupidatat non proident, sunt in
culpa qui officia deserunt mollit anim id est
laborum.
</details>
```

In this case, the browser will display the summary text and hide the text that follows. Not all browsers support the **<details>** and **</details>** tag pair. Depending on the browser, the actual process the user must perform to expand and display the underlying content varies.

Highlighting Document Text

As readers read books and other text-based content, they often use a highlighter to mark key passages. Using the HTML 5 **<mark>** and **</mark>** tag pair, you can highlight content to which you want to draw the reader's attention. You might, for example, display text with a yellow background color. The following HTML file, MarkText.html, illustrates the tags' use:

```
<!DOCTYPE html>
<html>
<body>
<header style="background-color:yellow">
Document Title</header>

<article>
<section style="background-color:lime">
<p>
Lorem ipsum dolor sit amet,
<mark style="background-color:orange">
consectetur adipisicing elit,</mark>sed do eiusmod
tempor incididunt ut labore et dolore magna aliqua.
Ut enim ad minim veniam, quis nostrud exercitation
ullamco laboris nisi ut aliquip ex ea commodo
consequat.
</p>

<p>
Duis aute irure dolor in reprehenderit in
<mark style="background-color:orange">
voluptate velit esse cillum dolore eu fugiat nulla
pariatur. Excepteur sint occaecat cupidatat</mark>
non proident, sunt in culpa qui officia deserunt
mollit anim id est laborum.
</p>
</section>
</article>

<footer style="background-color:lightblue">
Copyright (C) 2013, Somesite.com
</footer>
</body>
</html>
```

If you view the page, the browser will display the highlighted content, as shown in **FIGURE 19-6**.

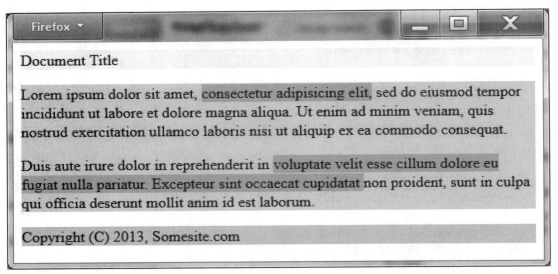

FIGURE 19-6 Highlighting document text using the **<mark>** and **</mark>** tag pair

Specifying a Word Break

By default, when a browser needs to wrap text, the browser does so at a whitespace location, such as a space character or tab. Depending on your page content, you may prefer that the browser break the text within a word. In such cases, you can use the **<wbr>** tag to specify a potential break location:

```
I like to play basket<wbr>ball.
```

Real-World Web Design: Supporting User Agents and International Pages

Across the Web, pages display date and time values in a variety of formats. To help user agent programs, such as search engine robots, find and process the date and time information, HTML provides the **<time>** and **</time>** tag pair. This type of tag pair is an example of semantic tags, discussed at the beginning of this chapter. Using the tags, you can present the date and time using a format most meaningful to the user and then include a **datetime** attribute, which the user agents can process:

```
The store opens at <time datetime="10-15-13
12:00am">Midnight on the 13th</time>
```

TABLE 19-1 TAGS USERS MAY WANT TO USE FOR TEXT USING LANGUAGES OTHER THAN ENGLISH	
Tag	**Purpose**
<ruby>	Defines a ruby annotation, which is frequently used for East Asian typography.
<rt>	Defines a pronunciation for a <ruby> annotation.
<rp>	Defines content for a browser to display if the browser does not support ruby annotations.
<bdi>	Groups text, which may be displayed from left to right or from right to left.

If the date you are referencing corresponds to the page's publication date, include the **pubdate** attribute within your **<time>** and **</time>** tag pair.

If you create pages that work with languages other than English, you may need to leverage the HTML 5 tags listed in **TABLE 19-1**. These are other examples of semantic tags.

Hands-On HTML

To view the HTML files or to experiment with the files presented in this chapter, visit this book's companion website at *http://www.websitedevelopmentbook.com/Chapter19/TryIt.html.*

CHAPTER SUMMARY

Across the Web, much of the page content is similar in appearance to a paper-based document; that is, the content has a header, footer, figures, captions, and so on. To help developers structure and format such content, HTML 5 provides several new tags. In addition, HTML 5 provides the **<time>** and **</time>** tags you can use to provide semantics or meaningful dates and times that appear in a document. These can be used by user agents in their processing of a webpage. Finally, this chapter presents several tags developers may need when they work with languages other than English.

KEY TERMS

Semantics

CHAPTER REVIEW

1. Create an HTML file that uses the following tags to define document sections:
   - <header> and </header>
   - <footer> and </footer>
   - <aside> and </aside>
   - <article> and </article>
   - <section> and </section>
   - <figure> and </figure>
   - <figcaption> and </figcaption>
2. Use CSS to format each tag so that each section stands out within the page.

Creating Scalable Vector Graphics Files

chapter

20

THROUGHOUT THIS BOOK, YOU have extensive use of bitmap-graphics files, normally stored in the .JPG file format. In this chapter, you will examine **scalable vector graphics (SVG)** files. These graphics are powerful and flexible in that they don't lose quality if they are resized. As it turns out, an SVG file consists of XML entries, which define the graphic. Across the Web, many sites offer SVG graphics that you can purchase and download and then use on your site. In addition, most vector-based drawing programs let you save the graphics you create as an SVG file.

Learning Objectives

This chapter introduces common SVG operations. By the time you finish this chapter, you will understand the following key concepts:

- How to embed a graphic stored within an SVG file in an HTML page
- How to use the **<svg>** and **</svg>** tag pair to specify common SVG shapes
- How to display text at a specific location, in a specific color, at a rotational angle, or even following a curved path
- How SVG provides advanced capabilities, including blurs, gradients, and more

Placing an SVG Image Within an HTML Page

There are two ways to place an SVG image within a webpage. First, if you have the image stored as an SVG file, with the .SVG extension, you can use the **<object>** and **</object>** tag pair to place the image within the webpage. The following HTML file, SVGDemo.html, places an SVG image file within a page:

```
<!DOCTYPE html>
<html>
<body>
<object data="http://www.websitedevelopmentbook.
com/Chapter20/FirstSvg.svg" type="image/svg+xml">
<embed src="http://www.websitedevelopmentbook.com/
Chapter20/FirstSvg.svg" type="image/svg+xml"/>
</object>
</body>
</html>
```

Depending on your browser type, you may have to install additional plugins to display the embedded SVG image. When you view the file's contents, the browser will display the page as shown in **FIGURE 20–1**.

FIGURE 20–1 Embedding an SVG graphic within a webpage
Credit: © hugolacasse/Shutterstock

The second way to place an SVG image within a page is to place the instructions that define the image within the **<svg>** and **</svg>** tag pair. The following HTML file, EmbedSVG.html, embeds SVG image instructions:

```
<!DOCTYPE html>
<html>
<body>
<svgxmlns="http://www.w3.org/2000/svg"
version="1.1">
<rect width="100" height="100"
style="fill:red;stroke-width:2;stroke:white"/>

<circle cx="100" cy="50" r="40" stroke="black"
stroke-width="2" fill="blue"/>

<ellipse cx="200" cy="50" rx="100" ry="50"
style="fill:yellow;stroke:black;stroke-width:2"/>
</svg>

</body>
</html>
```

As you can see, within the **<svg>** and **</svg>** tag pair, the file defines a rectangle, circle, and ellipse. When viewing the file's contents, the browser displays the image as shown in **FIGURE 20–2**.

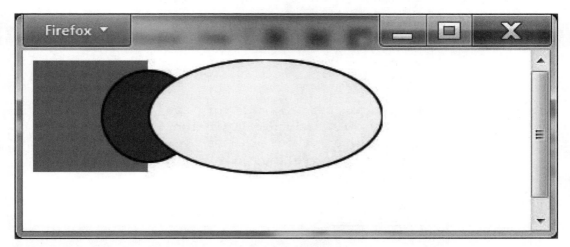

FIGURE 20–2 Embedding SVG image instructions within an HTML file

Creating Common Shapes

To help you create common shapes, such as a line, circle, ellipse, square, and rectangle, SVG defines specific shape elements. The following sections examine how to use these elements to create simple shapes.

Drawing an SVG Line

To draw a line using SVG, specify the line's start and end points and optional styles, such as the line color and width. The following HTML file, SVGLine.html, draws a line across a page:

```
<!DOCTYPE html>
<html>
<body>

<svgxmlns="http://www.w3.org/2000/svg"
version="1.1">
<line x1="0" y1="0" x2="200" y2="200"
style="stroke:black"/>
</svg>

</body>
</html>
```

When you view the file's contents, the browser will display the line as shown in FIGURE 20–3.

The following HTML file, SVGLineWidth.html, changes the previous graphic to include a line width:

```
<!DOCTYPE html>
<html>
<body>

<svgxmlns="http://www.w3.org/2000/svg"
version="1.1" width="300" height="300">
<line x1="0" y1="0" x2="200" y2="200"
style="stroke:yellow; stroke-width:20;"/>
</svg>

</body>
</html>
```

In this case, when you display the file's contents, the browser displays the contents as shown in FIGURE 20–4.

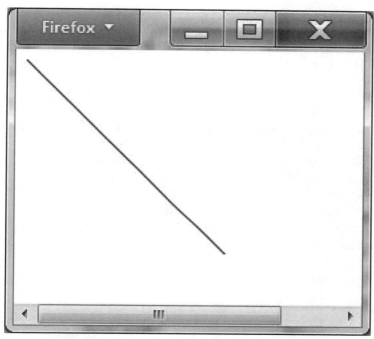

FIGURE 20-3 Drawing a line using SVG graphics

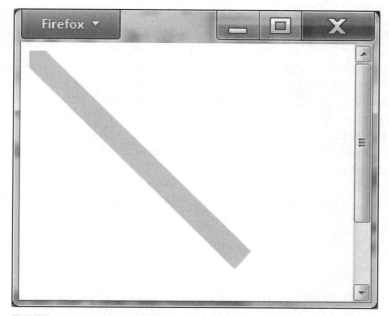

FIGURE 20-4 Drawing an SVG line with a color and width

Using only a line, you can create interesting graphics. The following HTML file, 3DSVGCube.html, draws a simple cube shape:

```
<!DOCTYPE html>
<html>
<body>

<svgxmlns="http://www.w3.org/2000/svg"
version="1.1" height="300" width="300">
<line x1="100" y1="100" x2="200" y2="100"
style="stroke:black; stroke-width:2;"/>
<line x1="100" y1="100" x2="100" y2="200"
style="stroke:black; stroke-width:2;"/>
<line x1="200" y1="100" x2="200" y2="200"
style="stroke:black; stroke-width:2;"/>
<line x1="100" y1="200" x2="200" y2="200"
style="stroke:black; stroke-width:2;"/>

<line x1="130" y1="70" x2="230" y2="70"
style="stroke:black; stroke-width:2;"/>
<line x1="100" y1="100" x2="130" y2="70"
style="stroke:black; stroke-width:2;"/>
<line x1="200" y1="100" x2="230" y2="70"
style="stroke:black; stroke-width:2;"/>

<line x1="230" y1="70" x2="230" y2="170"
style="stroke:black; stroke-width:2;"/>
<line x1="200" y1="200" x2="230" y2="170"
style="stroke:black; stroke-width:2;"/>
<line x1="100" y1="200" x2="130" y2="170"
style="stroke:black; stroke-width:2;"/>
<line x1="130" y1="70" x2="130" y2="170"
style="stroke:black; stroke-width:2;"/>
<line x1="130" y1="170" x2="230" y2="170"
style="stroke:black; stroke-width:2;"/>
</svg>

</body>
</html>
```

Note that in this case, the <**svg**> tag specifies the image's height and width. If you do not specify a width of at least 2, items that you specify, such as lines or shapes, may be clipped so that they do not appear.

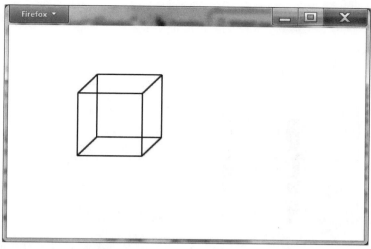

FIGURE 20-5 Drawing a 3-D cube using SVG lines

When you display the file's contents, the browser displays the shape shown in **FIGURE 20-5**.

Finally, the following HTML file, SVGChart.html, uses SVG lines to create a simple chart:

```
<!DOCTYPE html>
<html>
<body>

<svgxmlns="http://www.w3.org/2000/svg"
version="1.1" height="300" width="500">
<line x1="100" y1="100" x2="100" y2="300"
style="stroke:black; stroke-width:2;"/>
<line x1="100" y1="300" x2="500" y2="300"
style="stroke:black; stroke-width:2;"/>

<line x1="200" y1="300" x2="200" y2="120"
style="stroke:blue; stroke-width:20;"/>
<line x1="300" y1="300" x2="300" y2="140"
style="stroke:red; stroke-width:20;"/>
<line x1="400" y1="300" x2="400" y2="110"
style="stroke:green; stroke-width:20;"/>
</svg>

</body>
</html>
```

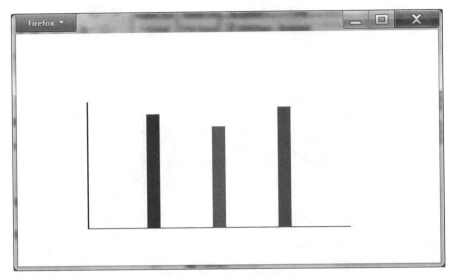

FIGURE 20-6 Using SVG graphics to create a simple chart

As you can see, the file draws an x and y axis and then draws three thicker colored bars. Later in this chapter, you will learn how to use text elements within a graphic. In this case, you might use a text element to label the data. When you view this file's contents, the browser will display the chart as shown in **FIGURE 20-6**.

Creating a Square or Rectangle

To create a square or rectangle using SVG, use the **<rect>** element. The following HTML file, SVGSquare.html, draws a square within a page:

```
<!DOCTYPE html>
<html>
<body>

<svgxmlns="http://www.w3.org/2000/svg"
version="1.1" width="120" height="120">
<rect width="100" height="100"
style="fill:orange;stroke-width:2;stroke:blue"/>
</svg>

</body>
</html>
```

When you view the file's contents, the browser displays the shape shown in **FIGURE 20-7**.

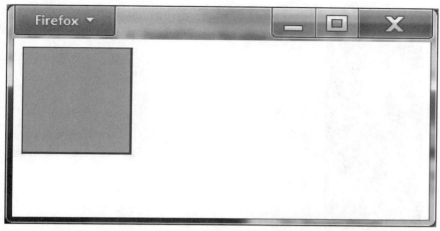

FIGURE 20-7 Using the SVG **<rect>** element to draw a square

In a similar way, the following HTML file, SVGRectangle.html, uses the <rect> element to draw a filled rectangle:

```
<!DOCTYPE html>
<html>
<body>

<svgxmlns="http://www.w3.org/2000/svg"
version="1.1" width="300" height="300">
<rect width="100" height="200"
style="fill:red;stroke-width:2;stroke:blue"/>
</svg>

</body>
</html>
```

When you view the file's contents, the browser will display the filled rectangle as shown in **FIGURE 20-8**.

Drawing a Circle or Ellipse

To draw an SVG circle, use the <**circle**> element. The following HTML file, SVGCircles.html, draws several circles:

```
<!DOCTYPE html>
<html>
<body>
```

FIGURE 20-8 Drawing a filled SVG rectangle

```
<svgxmlns="http://www.w3.org/2000/svg"
version="1.1" width="600" height="400">
<circle cx="100" cy="50" r="40" stroke="black"
stroke-width="2" fill="blue"/>
<circle cx="220" cy="100" r="80" stroke="black"
stroke-width="2" fill="red"/>
<circle cx="440" cy="150" r="120" stroke="black"
stroke-width="2" fill="green"/>
</svg>

</body>
</html>
```

As you can see, the file specifies each circle's x and y location as well as the radius. Then the file specifies a file color and surrounding line stroke.

When you view the file's contents, the browser displays the shapes as shown in **FIGURE 20-9**.

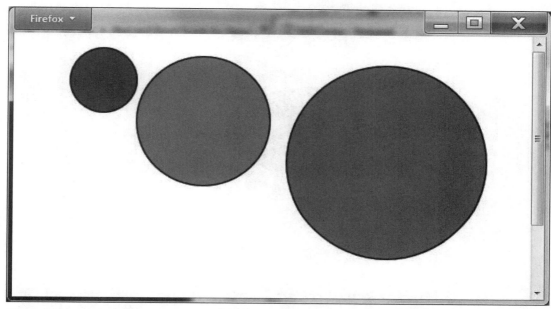

FIGURE 20-9 Drawing SVG circle shapes within a webpage

In a similar way, to draw an ellipse, use the SVG **<ellipse>** element. The following HTML file, SVGEllipse.html, draws an ellipse:

```
<!DOCTYPE html>
<html>
<body>

<svgxmlns="http://www.w3.org/2000/svg"
version="1.1" width="300" height="200">
<ellipse cx="120" cy="100" rx="100" ry="50"
style="fill:orange;stroke:black;stroke-width:2"/>
</svg>

</body>
</html>
```

When you view the file's contents, the browser displays the page shown in **FIGURE 20–10**.

Drawing a Polygon

With respect to SVG graphics, a polygon is a shape with at least three sides that you can close. To draw an SVG polygon, use the **<polygon>** element to specify the

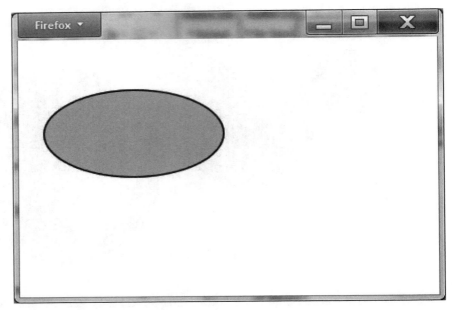

FIGURE 20-10 Drawing an SVG ellipse within a webpage

point coordinates. The following HTML file, SVGDrawPoly.html, draws to polygons:

```
<!DOCTYPE html>
<html>
<body>

<svgxmlns="http://www.w3.org/2000/svg"
version="1.1" width="300" height="200">
<polygon points="200,10 100,190 300,190" style="fil
l:red;stroke:black;stroke-width:1"/>
</svg>

</body>
</html>
```

As you can see, the image defines the coordinates of a triangle. When you view the file's contents, the browser will display the shapes as shown in **FIGURE 20-11**.

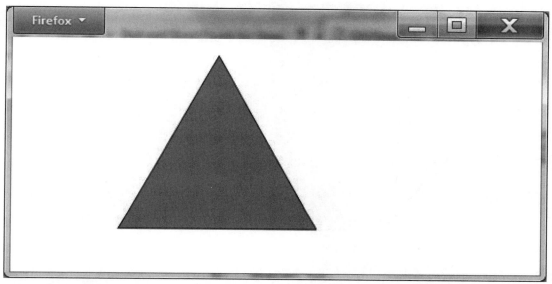

FIGURE 20–11 Drawing SVG polygons within a webpage

Drawing a Polyline

An SVG polyline is a line with several points. To draw a polyline using SVG, use the **<polyline>** element to specify the coordinates. The following HTML file, SVGDrawPolyline.html, draws a line with several segments:

```
<!DOCTYPE html>
<html>
<body>

<svgxmlns="http://www.w3.org/2000/svg"
version="1.1" width="300" height="200">
<polyline points="50,20 90,125 110,140 150,190
220,190" style="fill:none;stroke:blue;
stroke-width:2"/>
</svg>

</body>
</html>
```

When you view the file's contents, the browser will display the line shown in **FIGURE 20–12**.

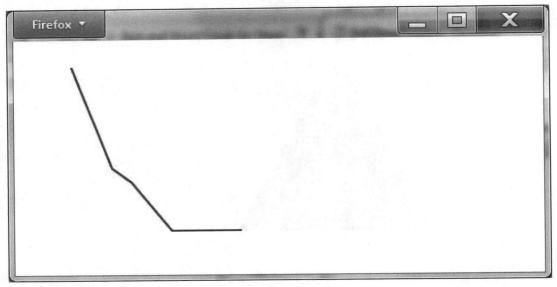

FIGURE 20-12 Drawing line segments using the SVG **<polyline>** element

Drawing a Path with Lines and Curves

The SVG **<path>** element lets you specify a series of movement and drawing commands:

- a = elliptical Arc
- c = curveto
- h = horizontal lineto
- l = lineto
- m = moveto
- q = quadratic Bézier curve
- s = smooth curveto
- t = smooth quadratic Béziercurveto
- v = vertical lineto
- z = closepath

The following HTML file, SVGPath.html, uses the **<path>** element to draw a complex line:

```
<!DOCTYPE html>
<html>
<body>
```

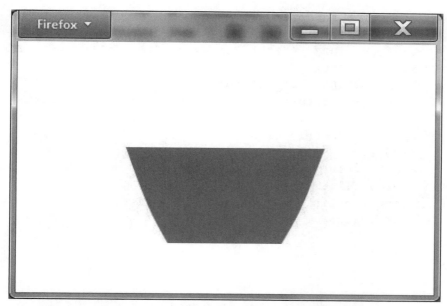

FIGURE 20-13 Using the SVG **<path>** element to draw a complex shape

```
<svgxmlns="http://www.w3.org/2000/svg"
version="1.1" width="300" height="200">
<path d="M100,100 Q200,400,300,100"
style="fill:red;stroke-width:2;stroke:white"/>
</svg>

</body>
</html>
```

When you view the file's contents, the browser will display the shape shown
in **FIGURE 20–13**.

Drawing Text in SVG

Using SVG, you can display text at a specific location, in a specific color, at a rotational
angle, or even following a curved path. To display text using SVG, use the **<text>** element. The following HTML file, SVGText.html, displays several SVG text elements:

```
<!DOCTYPE html>
<html>
<body>
```

```
<svgxmlns="http://www.w3.org/2000/svg"
version="1.1" width="800" height="300">
<text x="100" y="100" font-size="24" fill="red">SVG
is cool!</text>
<text x="300" y="100" font-size="24" fill="blue"
transform="rotate(90 300,100)">SVG is cool!</text>
<defs>
<path id="path1" d="M500,100 a1,1 0 0,0 100,0"/>
</defs>
<text x="10" y="100" font-size="24"
style="fill:red;">
<textPathxlink:href="#path1">SVG is cool!
</textPath>
</text>
</svg>

</body>
</html>
```

When you view the file's contents, the browser displays the text shown in
FIGURE 20–14.

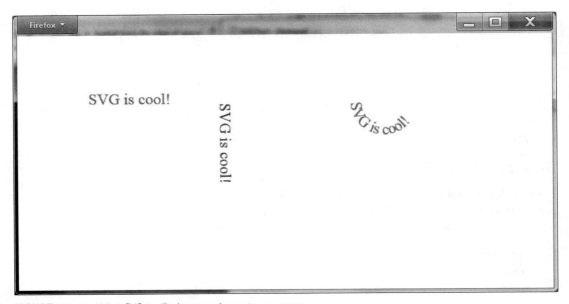

FIGURE 20-14 Using SVG to display text elements on a page

Advanced SVG Capabilities

Beyond drawing simple shapes, SVG provides the ability to filter, blur, apply gradients, drop shadows to images, and more. The following HTML file, AdvancedSVG.html, illustrates several such capabilities:

```
<!DOCTYPE html>
<html>
<body>

<svgxmlns="http://www.w3.org/2000/svg"
version="1.1" width="600" height="200">
<defs>
<linearGradient id="grad1" x1="0%" y1="0%"
x2="100%" y2="0%">
<stop offset="0%" style="stop-color:Yellow;
stop-opacity:1"/>
<stop offset="100%" style="stop-color:Green;
stop-opacity:1"/>
</linearGradient>
</defs>
<ellipse cx="100" cy="100" rx="100" ry="55"
fill="url(#grad1)"/>

<defs>
<radialGradient id="grad2" cx="50%" cy="50%"
r="50%" fx="50%" fy="50%">
<stop offset="0%" style="stop-color:blue;
stop-opacity:0"/>
<stop offset="100%" style="stop-color:orange;
stop-opacity:1"/>
</radialGradient>
</defs>
<rect x="300" y="50" width="100" height="100"
fill="url(#grad2)"/>

<defs>
<filter id="f1" x="0" y="0">
<feGaussianBlur in="SourceGraphic"
stdDeviation="15"/>
</filter>
</defs>
```

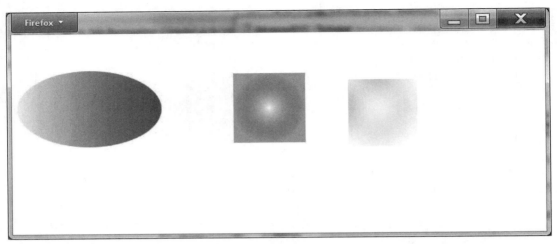

FIGURE 20–15 Advanced SVG image capabilities

```
<circle cx="500" cy="100" r="40" stroke="green"
stroke-width="3"

fill="yellow" filter="url(#f1)"/>
</svg>

</body>
</html>
```

In this case, the file uses a linear gradient, a radial gradient, and a blur. When you view the file's contents, the browser displays the shapes shown in **FIGURE 20–15**.

Real-World Web Design

The ability to scale SVG graphics makes them a great choice for clip art, logos, and other illustrations. This chapter introduced SVG processing. As you work with SVG images, you may want to utilize the SVG Reference, which you can find at the W3Schools website at *http://www.w3schools.com/svg/default.asp,* as shown in **FIGURE 20–16**.

Hands-On HTML

To view the HTML files or to experiment with the files presented in this chapter, visit this book's companion website at *http://www.websitedevelopmentbook.com/Chapter20/TryIt.html.*

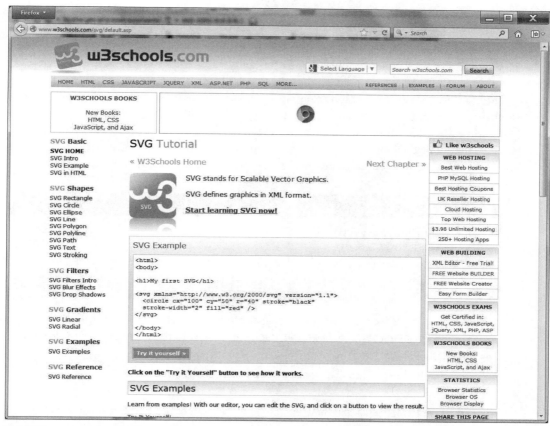

FIGURE 20-16 The SVG Reference at the W3Schools website

Reproduced with *permission of w3schools.com*

CHAPTER SUMMARY

Scalable vector graphics (SVG) are unique in that they do not lose quality when you scale them. Unlike pixel-based graphics, which contain specific color values for the dots that make up an image, a **vector graphic** contains XML-based instructions the browser uses to render the graphic. Because SVG graphics do not work in terms of dots, the browser can easily scale them. This chapter introduced the use of SVG graphics within a webpage. You can embed an existing .SVG file within a webpage or, using the **<svg>** and **</svg>**, place the actual instructions that draw the graphic. In Chapter 21, "Introducing the HTML 5 Canvas," you will learn how to program images that appear within a canvas object in an HTML 5 webpage.

KEY TERMS

Scalable vector graphic (SVG)
Vector graphic

CHAPTER REVIEW

1. Create an HTML file that uses the graphic at *http://www.websitedevelopmentbook.com/ Chapter20/sampleSVG.svg*. Allow the graphic to scale with the webpage. Size the webpage, and describe your findings.

2. Create an HTML file, ThreeSquares.html, that displays red, white, and blue squares using SVG.

3. Create an HTML file named BullsEye.html that uses SVG circles to create a bullseye-like graphic.

4. Create an HTML file, FirstInitial.html, that uses the SVG **<polyline>** element to draw your first initial.

5. Create an HTML file that creates a simple bar chart using the SVG **<rect>** element.

6. Create an HTML file that illustrates the use of SVG gradients.

7. Create an HTML file that displays the text "Hello, SVG!" at various angles using SVG.

Introducing the HTML 5 Canvas

ACROSS THE WEB, USERS expect webpage interactivity. For years, Web developers turned to Flash-based animations to provide such interactions. Unfortunately, not all browsers supported Flash—most specifically, those browsers running on the popular iPad and iPhone. This chapter introduces the HTML 5 **canvas**, which provides a region on the page where you can display text, graphics, and animations by using JavaScript programming. The canvas is ideal for dynamic content such as charts, graphs, and animations.

Learning Objectives

This chapter will introduce you to working with the HTML canvas. By the time you finish, you will understand the following key concepts:

- How to use the canvas for dynamic content
- How to test if a browser supports canvas operations
- How to create a canvas using the **<canvas>** and **</canvas>** tag pair
- How to position a drawing point and draw lines on the canvas using the **moveTo** and **lineTo** functions
- How to scale the canvas using the **onmouseover** and **onmouseout** event
- How to draw a square or rectangle using the **rect** function
- How to draw circles and arcs using the **arc** function
- How to integrate photos into the canvas
- How to display text within the canvas
- How to draw curved lines within the canvas

Ways to Use and Not Use the Canvas

The HTML 5 canvas is ideal for dynamic content, such as animations, performance dashboards, charts, and so on. Do not use the canvas to display traditional HTML graphics or text—doing so provides no benefit. Instead, if your page requires dynamic content, the canvas is for you.

Testing for Browser Canvas Support

As with most HTML 5 features, you should test the current browser to determine if it supports the canvas. The following HTML file, TestCanvas.html, tests whether or not the browser supports the canvas and then displays an **alert** dialog box so stating:

```
<!DOCTYPE html>
<html>
<head>
<script>

function TestCanvas()
{
  if (document.createElement("canvas"))
    {
    alert('Browser supports the Canvas');
    }
  else
    alert('Browser does not support the Canvas');
}
</script>

</head>
<body onload="TestCanvas()">
</body>
</html>
```

As you can see, the code tries to create a **canvas** object. If the object is created, the **if** statement evaluates as true, and the code will display the corresponding message.

Displaying a Canvas

A canvas is simply a region in a webpage where you can display dynamic text and graphics. The following HTML file, DisplayCanvas.html, draws a 200x200 canvas on the webpage. The file displays a red border around the canvas to better identify the region:

```
<!DOCTYPE html>
<html>
<body>
<canvas width="200" height="200" style="border:
2px solid red;"></canvas>
</body>
</html>
```

As you can see, to create a canvas region, simply use the **<canvas>** and **</canvas>** tag pair. When you view the file's contents, the browser displays a page similar to that shown in **FIGURE 21-1**.

In a similar way, the following HTML file, FillCanvas.html, assigns a yellow background color to a canvas region:

```
<!DOCTYPE html>
<html>
<body>
<canvas width="200" height="200"
style="background-color:yellow;"></canvas>
</body>
</html>
```

When you view this file's contents, your browser displays a screen similar to that shown in **FIGURE 21-2**.

Depending on your content needs, there may be times when you need multiple canvases within your page. The following HTML file, TwoCanvas.

FIGURE 21-1 Defining a canvas region within a webpage

FIGURE 21-2 Assigning a background color to a canvas

html, creates two canvases within the webpage, framing one and coloring the other:

```
<!DOCTYPE html>
<html>
<body>
<canvas width="200" height="200" style="border:
2px solid red;"></canvas>

<canvas width="200" height="200"
style="background-color: yellow;"></canvas>
</body>
</html>
```

When you view this file's contents, the browser displays the canvases as shown in **FIGURE 21-3**.

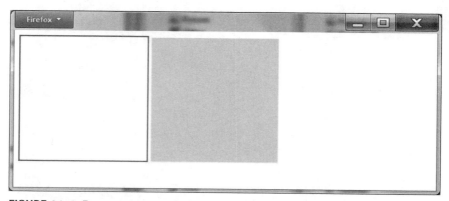

FIGURE 21-3 Two canvases on a single page, one framed and the other colored

Drawing a Line Within the Canvas

The canvas is an object and as such, it has several methods you can use JavaScript to call. To draw a line, for example, you use the **lineTo** function. Likewise, before drawing a line, you use the **moveTo** function to position the starting drawing point. The following HTML file, CanvasLine.html, creates a canvas object, moves to the location 50, 50, and then draws a line from that point to location 150, 150:

```
<!DOCTYPE html>
<html>
<head>
<script>
function drawLine()
{
var canvas = document.getElementById('myCanvas');
var context = canvas.getContext('2d');

context.beginPath();
context.moveTo(50,50);
context.lineTo(150,150);
context.stroke();
}
</script>
</head>
<body onload="drawLine()">
<canvas id="myCanvas" width="200" height="200"
style="border: 2px solid red;"></canvas>
</body>
</html>
```

As you can see, the **moveTo** function specifies the line's starting point. Then, the **lineTo** function specifies the endpoint. When you view the file's contents, your browser displays the contents shown in **FIGURE 21-4**.

In a similar way, the following HTML file, DrawSquare.html, uses the **lineTo** function to draw a simple square:

```
<!DOCTYPE html>
<html>
<head>
<script>
function drawSquare()
{
```

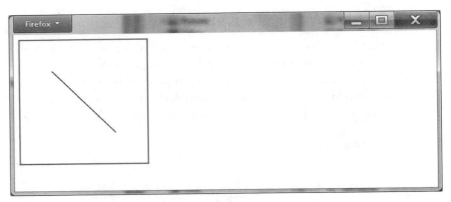

FIGURE 21–4 Drawing a line within an HTML 5 canvas

```
var canvas = document.getElementById('myCanvas');
var context = canvas.getContext('2d');

context.beginPath();
context.moveTo(50,50);
context.lineTo(50,150);
context.lineTo(150,150);
context.lineTo(150,50);
context.lineTo(50,50);

context.stroke();
}
</script>
</head>
<body onload="drawSquare()">
<canvas id="myCanvas" width="200" height="200"
style="border: 2px solid red;"></canvas>
</body>
</html>
```

In this case, the file moves to the square's starting point using the **moveTo** function. Then, the function simply calls the **lineTo** function four times to draw the square's sides. When you view the file's contents, your browser displays the square, as shown in **FIGURE 21–5**.

Next, the HTML file, ThickStar.html, increases the line width used by the **lineTo** function to draw a "thick" star, as shown in **FIGURE 21–6**:

```
<!DOCTYPE html>
<html>
```

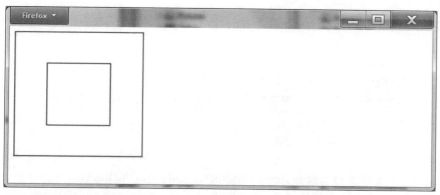

FIGURE 21-5 Using the **lineTo** function to draw a square

```
<head>
<script>
function drawStar()
{
var canvas = document.getElementById('myCanvas');
var context = canvas.getContext('2d');

context.beginPath();
context.moveTo(100,50);
context.lineTo(175,200);
context.lineTo(0,100);
context.lineTo(200,100);
context.lineTo(25,200);
context.lineTo(100,50);
context.lineWidth = 3;
```

FIGURE 21-6 Using the **lineWidth** property to adjust the line width

```
context.stroke();
}
</script>
</head>
<body onload="drawStar()">
<canvas id="myCanvas" width="200" height="200">
</canvas>
</body>
</html>
```

In this case, to specify the line width, the code uses the **lineWidth** property, which specifies the line thickness in pixels.

The following HTML file, FillStar.html, uses the **fillstyle** attribute and **fill** method to fill the sections of the star with red:

```
<!DOCTYPE html>
<html>
<head>
<script>
function fillStar()
{
var canvas = document.getElementById('myCanvas');
var context = canvas.getContext('2d');

context.beginPath();
context.moveTo(100,50);
context.lineTo(175,200);
context.lineTo(0,100);
context.lineTo(200,100);
context.lineTo(25,200);
context.lineTo(100,50);
context.lineWidth= 3;

context.fillStyle = '#FF0000';
context.fill();

context.stroke();
}
</script>
</head>
<body onload="fillStar()">
<canvas id="myCanvas" width="200" height="200">
```

FIGURE 21-7 Filling the sections of a star with color

```
</canvas>
</body>
</html>
```

As you can see, the code draws the files that create the star and then fills the shape with the color red using the **fillStyle** attribute and the **fill** function. When you view the file's contents, the browser displays the star, as shown in **FIGURE 21-7**.

Scaling a Canvas Object

As discussed, the canvas is ideal for applications that require dynamic content. The following HTML file, ScaleCanvas.html, uses the **onmouseover** and **onmouseout** events to scale the canvas image when the user moves the mouse on to or out of the canvas region. As shown in **FIGURE 21-8**, the file doubles the size of the image during a mouse over operation and then restores the image when the user moves the mouse out of the canvas:

```
<!DOCTYPE html>
<html>
<head>
<script>
function drawStar(scaleX, scaleY)
{
var canvas, context;
canvas = document.getElementById('myCanvas');
context = canvas.getContext('2d');
context.beginPath();
context.clearRect(0, 0, canvas.width, canvas.
height);
```

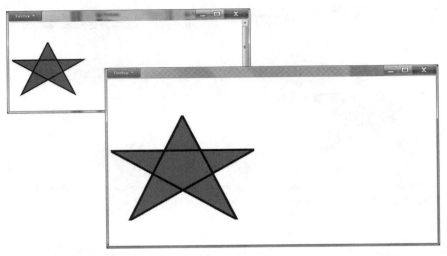

FIGURE 21-8 Scaling a canvas image with mouse events

```
context.scale(scaleX, scaleY);
context.moveTo(100,50);
context.lineTo(175,200);
context.lineTo(0,100);
context.lineTo(200,100);
context.lineTo(25,200);
context.lineTo(100,50);
context.lineWidth = 3;
context.fillStyle = '#FF0000';
context.fill();
ontext.stroke();
}
</script>
</head>
<body onload="drawStar(1, 1)">
<canvas id="myCanvas" width="400" height="400"
onmouseover="drawStar(2, 2);"
onmouseout="drawStar(0.5, 0.5);"></canvas>
</body>
</html>
```

As you can see, the code specifies the desired scale and then renders the shape. When using the **scale** function, the parameter value 1 corresponds to 100 percent, 2 to 200 percent, 0.5 to 50 percent, and so on.

Drawing and Filling Rectangles

As you have seen, using the **lineTo** function, you can draw a square or rectangle on the canvas. In addition to using **lineTo** function calls, you can use the canvas **rect** function:

```
context.rect(x, y, height, width);
```

The following HTML file, DrawRects.html, uses the **rect** function to display two rectangles:

```
<!DOCTYPE html>
<html>
<head>
<script>
function drawRects()
{
var canvas, context;
canvas = document.getElementById('myCanvas');
context = canvas.getContext('2d');

context.rect(100, 100, 100, 200);
context.fillStyle = '#FF0000';
context.fillRect(300, 100, 50, 100);
context.stroke();
}
</script>
</head>
<body onload="drawRects()">
<canvas id="myCanvas" width="400" height="400">
</canvas>
</body>
</html>
```

In this case, the page draws one rectangle filled and one not. When you view the file's contents, the browser will display the rectangles, as shown in **FIGURE 21-9**.

Drawing a Circle

To draw a circle on the canvas, use the **arc** function:

```
context.arc(x, y, radius, start angle, stop angle);
```

The following HTML file, CirclesAndArcs.html, uses the arc function to draw circles and partial circles, as shown in **FIGURE 21-10**.

FIGURE 21-9 Using the canvas object **rect** function to draw rectangles

The following statements implement the CirclesAndArcs.html file:

```
<!DOCTYPE html>
<html>
<head>
<script>
```

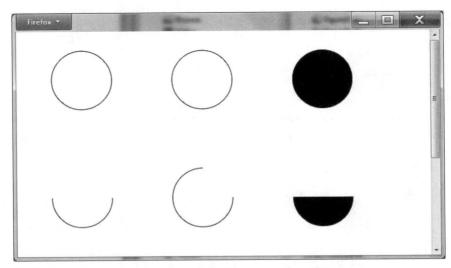

FIGURE 21-10 Using the **canvas** object **arc** function to draw circles and arcs

```
function drawCircles()
{
var canvas, context;

canvas = document.getElementById('myCanvas');
context = canvas.getContext('2d');

context.beginPath();
context.arc(100,75,50,0,2*Math.PI);
context.stroke();

context.beginPath();
context.arc(300,75,50,0,2*Math.PI);
context.stroke();

context.beginPath();
context.arc(500,75,50,0,2*Math.PI);
context.fill();
context.beginPath();
context.arc(100,275,50,0,1*Math.PI);
context.stroke();

context.beginPath();
context.arc(300,275,50,0,1.5*Math.PI);
context.stroke();

context.beginPath();
context.arc(500,275,50,0,1*Math.PI);
context.fill();
}

</script>
</head>
<body onload="drawCircles()">
<canvas id="myCanvas" width="600" height="600">
</canvas>
</body>
</html>
```

Drawing an Ellipse

To draw an ellipse on the canvas, scale the canvas after drawing a circle. The
following HTML file, CanvasEllipse.html, draws a circle and then scales the

canvas to stretch the circle into an ellipse. Then the code resets the scaling and repeats the process to draw an ellipse along the x axis:

```
<!DOCTYPE html>
<html>
<head>
<script>
function drawCircles()
{
var canvas, context;

canvas = document.getElementById('myCanvas');
context = canvas.getContext('2d');

context.beginPath();
context.scale(1, 2);
context.arc(100,75,50,0,2*Math.PI);
context.stroke();

context.scale(1, 0.5);
context.beginPath();
context.scale(2, 1);
context.arc(200,75,50,0,2*Math.PI);
context.stroke();
}

</script>
</head>
<body onload="drawCircles()">
<canvas id="myCanvas" width="600" height="600">
</canvas>
</body>
</html>
```

When you view the file's contents, the browser will display ellipses similar to that shown in **FIGURE 21–11**:

Working with Images

Using the canvas, you have a variety of functions you can use to draw lines and shapes. In addition, using the canvas, you can load and manipulate photo images.

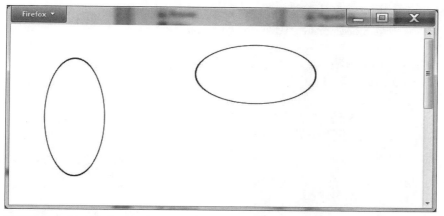

FIGURE 21-11 Drawing an ellipse by scaling a circle

The following HTML file, ScreenSaver.html, creates a canvas object and then
cycles through a series of image files to create a screen saver:

```
<!DOCTYPE html>
<html>
<head>
<script>

vari = 0;

function ShowSlide()
{
var canvas, context;
canvas = document.getElementById('myCanvas');
context = canvas.getContext('2d');
context.clearRect(0,0,600,600);

  if (i == 0)
    {
    context.drawImage(document.
    getElementById("dog"), 10, 10);
    i++;
    }
  else if (i == 1)
    {
```

```
      context.drawImage(document.
      getElementById("cat"), 10, 10);
      i++;
      }
   else
      {
      context.drawImage(document.
      getElementById("horse"), 10, 10);
      i = 0;
      }
   setTimeout (ShowSlide, 3000);
   }

</script>
</head>
<body onload="setTimeout (ShowSlide, 100);">
<canvas id="myCanvas" width="600" height="600">
</canvas>
<div style="visibility:hidden">
<img id="dog" src="dog.jpg">
<img id="cat" src="cat.jpg">
<img id="horse" src="horse.jpg">
</div>
</body>
</html>
```

As you can see, the file creates a division within which it places three images. To prevent the images from appearing, the code hides the division. Then, the code uses a timer to call the **ShowSlide** function to show a specific image. Within the function, the code first clears the rectangle area of the canvas in case one image is larger than another.

When you view the file's contents, your screen displays images as shown in **FIGURE 21-12**.

Displaying Text Within the Canvas

Often, when you display graphical content, you will need to label different elements with text. The canvas object supports a variety of text-based functions and properties. The following HTML file, HelloCanvas.html, creates a canvas and then displays a "Hello" message within it:

```
<!DOCTYPE html>
<html>
```

FIGURE 21-12 Using the canvas to create a slide show

Credit (from top): © Christian Mueller/Shutterstock; © Anastasija Popova/Shutterstock; © Melanie Hoffman/Shutterstock

```
<head>
<script>

function sayHello()
{
var canvas, context;
canvas = document.getElementById('myCanvas');
context = canvas.getContext('2d');

context.font = '72px Calibri';
context.strokeText('Hello canvas!', 100, 100);
}

</script>
</head>
<body onload="sayHello();">
<canvas id="myCanvas" width="600" height="600">
</canvas>
</body>
</html>
```

FIGURE 21-13 Displaying text within a canvas region

In this case, the font selected is a 72-pixel Calibri. The code then positions the message display area to ensure that the image fits within the canvas area.

When you view the file's contents, the browser displays the text message as shown in **FIGURE 21-13**.

Drawing Curved Lines

In previous examples, you used the lineTo function to draw a straight line. Often, you need to draw curved lines. For such cases, use the canvas Bezier or quadratic methods. The following HTML file, CurvedLines.html, illustrates the use of each:

```
<!DOCTYPE html>
<html>
<head>
<script>

function sayHello()
{
var canvas, context;
canvas = document.getElementById('myCanvas');
context = canvas.getContext('2d');

context.beginPath();
context.moveTo(50,50);
context.bezierCurveTo(50,100, 200, 100, 200,250);
context.stroke();
```

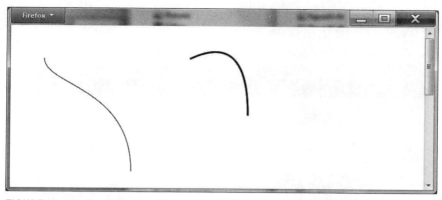

FIGURE 21-14 Drawing curved lines using the Bezier and quadratic methods

```
context.beginPath();
context.moveTo(300, 50);
context.quadraticCurveTo(400, 0, 400, 150);
context.lineWidth = 3;
context.stroke();
}

</script>
</head>
<body onload="sayHello();">
<canvas id="myCanvas" width="600" height="600">
</canvas>
</body>
</html>
```

When you view the file's contents, your browser displays the curved lines as shown in **FIGURE 21-14**.

Real-World Web Design

This chapter introduced the HTML 5 canvas object and how to use it to create dynamic content within a webpage. In Chapter 22, "Advanced Canvas Programming," you will learn how to create animations and program 3-D objects. If you plan to create real-world applications using the canvas, review the HTML 5 canvas specification on the W3Schools website at *http://www.w3schools.com/html/html5_canvas.asp*, as shown in **FIGURE 21-15**.

FIGURE 21-15 The HTML 5 canvas specification on the W3Schools website.
Reproduced with permission of w3schools.com

Hands-On HTML

To view the HTML files or to experiment with the files presented in this chapter, visit this book's companion website at *http://www.websitedevelopmentbook.com/Chapter21/TryIt.html*.

CHAPTER SUMMARY

To help Web developers create interactive content, HTML 5 provides a canvas object, which defines a region in the page where the developer can draw shapes, text, and images dynamically using JavaScript. This chapter introduced the canvas and simple drawing operations you can perform. In Chapter 22, "Advanced Canvas Programming," you will learn how to create animations and how to perform 3-D graphics within the canvas.

KEY TERMS

Canvas

CHAPTER REVIEW

1. Create an HTML file that uses the **moveTo** and **lineTo** functions to draw a triangle.
2. Modify the HTML file that you created in Question 1 to fill the triangle.
3. Modify the HTML file that you created in Question 2 to label the shape with the word "triangle."
4. Create an HTML file, Shapes.html, that draws a circle, ellipse, square, diamond, and rectangle.
5. Create an HTML file that uses the **moveTo** and **lineTo** functions to draw a 3-D cube.
6. Create an HTML file that draws similar curved lines using the Bezier and quadratic functions.

Advanced Canvas Programming

© Risto Viita/Shutterstock

chapter

22

IN CHAPTER 21, "INTRODUCING the HTML 5 Canvas," you learned the basics of programming the HTML 5 canvas using JavaScript. This chapter continues your examination of the canvas. You will learn several more advanced graphics programming techniques, such as gradients, drop shadows, moving and rotating objects, and working with pixel-based data.

Learning Objectives

By the time you finish this chapter, you will understand the following key concepts:

- How the HTML 5 canvas supports linear and radial gradients
- How to fill a shape with a pattern using an image
- How to apply drop shadows to text and graphics
- How to repeat or appear to move an image across the canvas using image translation
- How to rotate the canvas x and y axis coordinates using image rotation
- How the canvas provides functions that developers can use to directly access the pixels that make up an image

Applying Linear and Radial Gradients

In Chapter 21, you learned how to draw filled shapes using the **fillStyle** property. The following HTML file, SampleFills.html, draws three shapes using different colored fills:

```
<!DOCTYPE html>
<html>
<head>
<script>

function FillShapes()
{
  var canvas, context;

  canvas = document.getElementById('myCanvas');
  context = canvas.getContext('2d');
  context.beginPath();
  context.fillStyle = '#00FF00'
  context.fillRect(100, 50, 100, 100);
  context.stroke();

  context.fillStyle = '#FF0000';
  context.fillRect(300, 50, 50, 100);
  context.stroke();

  context.fillStyle = '#0000FF';
  context.moveTo(550, 100);
  context.arc(500,100,50,0,2*Math.PI);
  context.fill();
  context.stroke();
}

</script>
</head>
<body onload="FillShapes()">
<canvas id="myCanvas" width="600" height="400">
</canvas>
</body>
</html>
```

As you can see, before filling each shape, the page specifies the desired **fillStyle** color. If you view the file's contents, the browser displays the images shown in **FIGURE 22–1**.

FIGURE 22–1 Using the **fillStyle** property to select fill colors

With respect to graphics programming, a **gradient** specifies a range of location-dependent colors to fill a region. The HTML 5 canvas supports **linear gradients**, in which the colors change along a line that travels across the shape, and **radial gradients**, in which the colors change, radiating out from the center of a circle. To create a linear gradient, use the canvas object **createLinearGradient** method and the gradient object **addColorStop** method. The **createLinearGradient** method specifies the start and stop x and y coordinates for the gradient. The **addColorStop** method specifies a value between 0 and 1 and a color that specifies the color for a region of the gradient.

The following HTML, LinearGradient.html, draws three shapes, each with different gradients:

```
<!DOCTYPE html>
<html>
<head>
<script>

function FillShapes()
{
  var canvas, context, gradient;

  canvas = document.getElementById('myCanvas');
  context = canvas.getContext('2d');
  context.beginPath();

  gradient = context.createLinearGradient(100,50,
  200,50);
  gradient.addColorStop(0,"red");
  gradient.addColorStop(1,"white");
  context.fillStyle = gradient;
```

```
    context.fillRect(100, 50, 100, 100);
    context.stroke();

    gradient = context.createLinearGradient(300,50,
    300,150);
    gradient.addColorStop(0,"blue");
    gradient.addColorStop(1,"green");
    context.fillStyle = gradient;
    context.fillRect(300, 50, 50, 100);
    context.stroke();


    gradient = context.createLinearGradient(500,50,
    500,150);
    gradient.addColorStop(0,"yellow");
    gradient.addColorStop(1,"orange");
    context.fillStyle = gradient;
    context.moveTo(550, 100);
    context.arc(500,100,50,0,2*Math.PI);
    context.fill();
    context.stroke();
}

</script>
</head>
<body onload="FillShapes()">
<canvas id="myCanvas" width="600" height="400">
</canvas>
</body>
</html>
```

As you can see, the file draws three shapes, each with a different linear gradient.

If you view the file's contents, the browser displays the gradients shown in **FIGURE 22-2**.

With a linear gradient, the colors change along a line that travels across the shape. With a radial gradient, the color changes in a circular pattern from the center of the circle outward. You can use a linear or radial gradient with any type of shape that you want to fill.

To create a radial gradient, use the **createRadialGradient** and **addColor-Stop** methods:

```
createRadialGradient(circleStartx,circleStarty,radi
us,circleStopx,circleStopy, radius);
```

FIGURE 22–2 Drawing gradients on the HTML 5 canvas

The following HTML file, RadialGradient.html, creates three shapes filled with radial gradients:

```
<!DOCTYPE html>
<html>
<head>
<script>

function FillShapes()
{
  var canvas, context, gradient;

  canvas = document.getElementById('myCanvas');
  context = canvas.getContext('2d');
  context.beginPath();
  gradient = context.createRadial
  Gradient(100,50,100,150,100,25);
  gradient.addColorStop(0,"red");
  gradient.addColorStop(1,"green");
  context.fillStyle = gradient;
  context.fillRect(100, 50, 100, 100);
  context.stroke();

  gradient = context.createRadial
  Gradient(300,50,50,350,150,50);
  gradient.addColorStop(0,"yellow");
  gradient.addColorStop(1,"blue");
  context.fillStyle = gradient;
  context.fillRect(300, 50, 50, 100);
  context.stroke();
```

```
    gradient = context.createRadial
    Gradient(500,50,50,500,150,25);
    gradient.addColorStop(0,"yellow");
    gradient.addColorStop(1,"orange");
    context.fillStyle = gradient;
    context.moveTo(550, 100);
    context.arc(500,100,50,0,2*Math.PI);
    context.fill();
    context.stroke();
}

</script>
</head>
<body onload="FillShapes()">
<canvas id="myCanvas" width="600" height="400">
</canvas>
</body>
</html>
```

If you view the file's contents, the browser will display the images shown in
FIGURE 22–3.

FIGURE 22–3 Filling shapes with radial gradients

Using a Fill Pattern

In addition to letting you fill a shape using a color, the canvas also lets you specify
an image to use as a pattern to fill a shape, using the **createPattern** method. The
following HTML file, PatternShapes.html, fills shapes with several different
pattern images:

```
<!DOCTYPE html>
<html>
```

```
<head>
<script>

function FillShapes()
{
  var canvas, context, image, pattern;
  canvas = document.getElementById('myCanvas');
  context = canvas.getContext('2d');
  context.beginPath();
  image = document.getElementById("dog");
  pattern = context.createPattern(image,"repeat");
  context.fillStyle = pattern;
  context.fillRect(100, 50, 100, 100);
  context.stroke();

  image = document.getElementById("cat");
  pattern = context.createPattern(image,"repeat");
  context.fillStyle = pattern;
  context.fillRect(300, 50, 50, 100);
  context.stroke();

  image = document.getElementById("wine");
  pattern = context.createPattern(image,"repeat");
  context.fillStyle = pattern;
  context.moveTo(550, 100);
  context.arc(500,100,50,0,2*Math.PI);
  context.fill();
  context.stroke();
}

</script>
</head>
<body onload="FillShapes()">

<canvas id="myCanvas" width="600" height="400">
</canvas>
<img id="dog" style="visibility:hidden"
src="http://www.websitedevelopmentbook.com/
Chapter22/dog.jpg" />
<img id="cat" style="visibility:hidden"
src="http://www.websitedevelopmentbook.com/
Chapter22/cat.jpg" />
<img id="wine" style="visibility:hidden"
```

```
src="http://www.websitedevelopmentbook.com/
Chapter22/wine.jpg" />

</body>
</html>
```

As you can see, the file uses the image tag to load the images, but makes their visibility hidden so they do not appear outside of the canvas.

If you view the file's contents, the browser displays the shapes shown in **FIGURE 22–4**.

FIGURE 22–4 Using an image-based pattern to fill a shape

Credit (from top): © Christian Mueller/Shutterstock; © Anastasija Popova/Shutterstock; © Gts/Shutterstock

Applying Drop Shadows to Text and Graphics

Within the canvas, you can add a drop shadow to text or graphics that provides a highlight or dimension to an item. The canvas provides several properties you can use to specify the color, position, and sharpness of the shadow. The following HTML file, ShadowShapes.html, illustrates each of the shadow properties:

```
<!DOCTYPE html>
<html>
<head>
<script>
```

```
function FillShapes()
{
  var canvas, context;

  canvas = document.getElementById('myCanvas');
  context = canvas.getContext('2d');

  context.shadowColor = 'black';
  context.shadowOffsetX = 10;
  context.shadowOffsetY = 10;
  context.shadowBlur = 10;
  context.fillStyle = '#00FF00';
  context.fillRect(100, 50, 100, 100);

  context.fillStyle = '#FF0000';
  context.fillRect(300, 50, 50, 100);
  context.stroke();

  context.fillStyle = '#0000FF';
  context.moveTo(550, 100);
  context.arc(500,100,50,0,2*Math.PI);
  context.fill();
  context.stroke();
}

</script>
</head>
<body onload="FillShapes()">
<canvas id="myCanvas" width="600" height="400">
</canvas>
</body>
</html>
```

If you view the file's contents, the browser displays the shadows as shown in
FIGURE 22-5.

Moving an Image on the Canvas

To create animations, there will be times when you will need to move, or "translate,"
an image on the canvas. To do **image translation**, use the canvas object **translate**
method to specify a new drawing origin. The following HTML file, RepeatSquare.
html, uses **translate** to repeat the drawing of a square across the canvas:

```
<!DOCTYPE html>
<html>
```

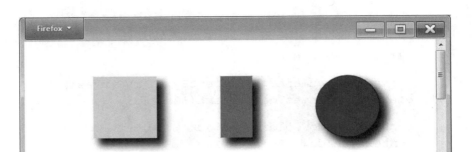

FIGURE 22–5 Applying drop shadows to canvas images

```
<head>
<script>

function FillShapes()
{
  var canvas, context;

  canvas = document.getElementById('myCanvas');
  context = canvas.getContext('2d');

  context.fillStyle = '#00FF00';

  for (i = 0; i < 500; i = i + 110)
    {
      context.fillRect(0, 50, 100, 100);
      context.translate(110, 0);
    }
}

</script>
</head>
<body onload="FillShapes()">
<canvas id="myCanvas" width="600" height="400">
</canvas>
</body>
</html>
```

In this case, the code uses a **for** loop to move the rectangle horizontally across the page. Within the **for** loop, the code uses the **context.translate** method to set the location of the object.

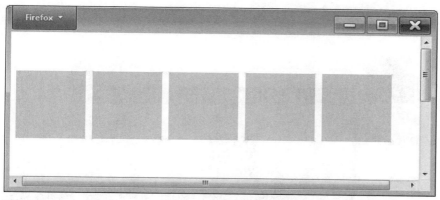

FIGURE 22-6 Using the canvas object **translate** method to move an image

If you view the file's contents, the browser displays the repeated squares, as shown in **FIGURE 22-6**.

The following HTML file, SlideSquare.html, creates a simple animation that slides the square across the canvas:

```
<!DOCTYPE html>
<html>
<head>
<script>

var i = 0;

function FillShapes()
{
  var canvas, context;

  canvas = document.getElementById('myCanvas');
  context = canvas.getContext('2d');

  context.fillStyle = '#FF0000';

  if (i < 400)
  {
    context.clearRect(i-1, 50, 100, 100);
    context.fillRect(i, 50, 100, 100);
    ++i;
    setTimeout(function() { FillShapes(); }, 10);
  }
}
```

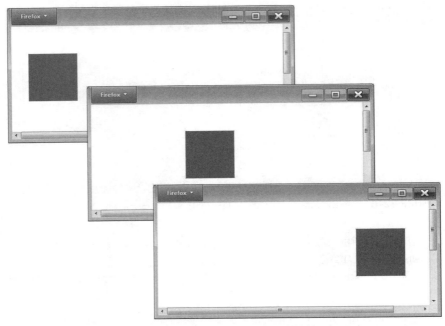

FIGURE 22-7 Creating a simple animation by translating a square across the canvas

```
</script>
</head>
<body onload="FillShapes()">
<canvas id="myCanvas" width="600" height="400">
</canvas>
</body>
</html>
```

In this case, the **FillShapes** function erases the previous square and then draws a new square one pixel to the right. The function uses a timer to call itself every 100 milliseconds.

If you view the file's contents, the browser displays the animation as shown in **FIGURE 22-7**.

Rotating the Canvas

In addition to translating the canvas origin as just shown, you can use the **rotate** method to rotate the canvas. The following HTML file, RotatedSquare.html, rotates the canvas and then draws a square:

```
<!DOCTYPE html>
<html>
```

```
<head>
<script>

function RotateSquare()
{
  var canvas, context;
  canvas = document.getElementById('myCanvas');
  context = canvas.getContext('2d');

  context.fillStyle = '#FF0000';
  context.translate(75, 50);
  context.rotate(Math.PI/180*45);
  context.fillRect(100, 0, 100, 100);
}

</script>
</head>
<body onload="RotateSquare()">
<canvas id="myCanvas" width="600" height="500">
</canvas>
</body>
</html>
```

If you view the page content, the browser displays the square image rotated at a 45-degree angle, as shown in **FIGURE 22-8**.

The following HTML file, TumbleSquare.html, changes the previous animation slightly to rotate the square as it moves and creates the illusion of a tumbling square:

```
<!DOCTYPE html>
<html>
<head>
<script>

var i = 0;
var Degree = 0;

function FillShapes()
{
  var canvas, context;

  canvas = document.getElementById('myCanvas');
  context = canvas.getContext('2d');
  context.save();
  context.fillStyle = '#FF0000';
```

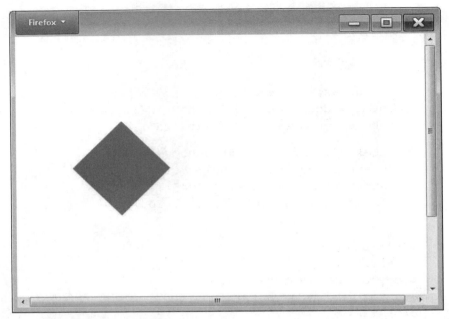

FIGURE 22-8 Rotating the HTML 5 canvas

```
if (i < 700)
  {
    context.clearRect(0, 0, 800, 400);
    context.translate((100+i)/2, 100);
    context.rotate(Math.PI/180*Degree);
    context.fillRect(-50, -50, 100, 100);
    i = i + 10;
    Degree = Degree + 15;
    setTimeout(function() { FillShapes(); }, 100);
  }
  context.restore();
}

</script>
</head>
<body onload="FillShapes()">
<canvas id="myCanvas" width="600" height="400">
</canvas>
</body>
</html>
```

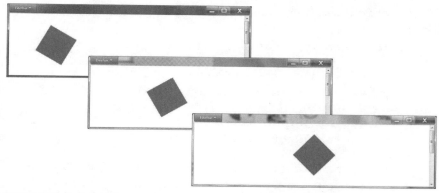

FIGURE 22-9 Combining rotation and translation to create a "tumbling" square

In this case, as the page moves the square across the page, it translates the origin to the center of the square and then rotates it. By using the **context. save** and **context.restore** methods, the page can save the original drawing context and later restore it, which simplifies the determination of the square's center.

If you view the file's contents, the browser will tumble the square across the canvas, as shown in **FIGURE 22-9**.

Manipulating Pixel Data

At the end of the day, images that appear on the HTML 5 canvas are simply pixel values that have corresponding red, green, blue, and opacity values. To create animations, developers often work directly with pixels. To help you perform such operations, the canvas provides three methods:

```
context.getImageData(x, y, width, height);
context.putImageData(dataArray, x, y);
context.createImageData(width, height);
```

The following HTML file, GetPut.html, displays a 50x50 rectangle. The file then uses the **getImageData** method to create an array that holds the image data. The page then puts the image at a different location using the **putImage-Data** method:

```
<!DOCTYPE html>
<html>
<head>
<script>
```

```
function GetImageData()
{
  var ImageData, canvas, context;

  canvas = document.getElementById('myCanvas');
  context = canvas.getContext('2d');

  context.fillStyle='#ff0000';
  context.fillRect(10,10,50,50);

  ImageData = context.getImageData(10, 10, 50, 50);
  context.putImageData(ImageData, 200, 200);
}

</script>
</head>
<body onload="GetImageData()">
<canvas id="myCanvas" width="600" height="500">
</canvas>
</body>
</html>
```

If you view the file's contents, the browser will display the two rectangles as shown in **FIGURE 22-10**.

Accessing Alpha Values to Change Image Transparency

After you use the **getImageData** method to create an array of red, green, blue, and alpha values, you can manipulate those values directly. The following HTML file, ChangePixels.html, displays a red rectangle image. The page repeatedly loops through the image reducing the image's red and green values while maximizing the blue values to create a blue square. The file then puts that data to the canvas:

```
<!DOCTYPE html>
<html>
<head>
<script>

function GetImageData()
{
  var ImageData, canvas, context;

  canvas = document.getElementById('myCanvas');
  context = canvas.getContext('2d');
```

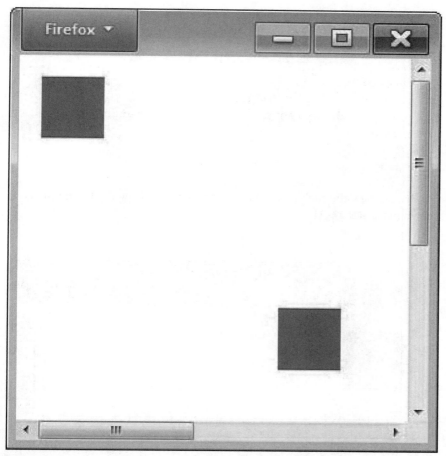

FIGURE 22-10 Rotating an image across the screen using image data

```
context.fillStyle='#ff0000';
context.fillRect(10,10,50,50);

ImageData = context.getImageData(10, 10, 50, 50);

var imageData = ImageData.data;
var i;
for(i = 0; i < imageData.length; i+= 4 ) {
    imageData[i] = 0;  // red
    imageData[i+1] = 0; // green
    imageData[i+2] = 255; // blue
  }
```

```
        context.putImageData(ImageData, 200, 200);
}

</script>
</head>
<body onload="GetImageData()">
<canvas id="myCanvas" width="600" height="500">
</canvas>
</body>
</html>
```

If you view the file's contents, the browser will show the fading image as shown in FIGURE 22-11.

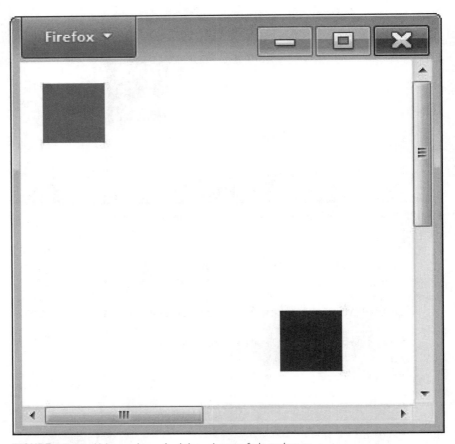

FIGURE 22-11 Using an image's alpha values to fade an image

Real-World Web Development

At the time of this writing, the HTML 5 canvas supports only 2-D graphics. In the future, it will support 3-D graphics as well. If your application requires 3-D graphics, use WebGL, which provides a free JavaScript-based API of 3-D graphics functions. For specifics on WebGL, visit the *http://www.khronos.org/webgl/* shown in **FIGURE 22-12**.

Hands-On HTML

To view the HTML files or to experiment with the files presented in this chapter, visit this book's companion website at *http://www.websitedevelopmentbook.com/Chapter22/TryIt.html*.

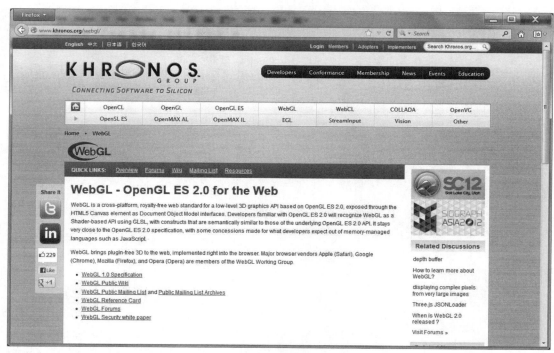

FIGURE 22-12 The WebGL library provides support for 3D graphics.
Reproduced with permission of the Khronos Group

CHAPTER SUMMARY

This chapter examined more advanced graphics programming capabilities, such as drop shadows, gradients, image rotation and translation, and direct access to an image's pixel data. Using the concepts this chapter presents, you can animate the display of a wide range of images.

KEY TERMS

Gradient

Image translation

Linear gradient

Radial gradient

CHAPTER REVIEW

1. Create an HTML file that fills a variety of squares and rectangles with linear gradients.
2. Create an HTML file that fills a variety of squares and rectangles with radial gradients.
3. Create an HTML file that fills a variety of shapes with different patterns.
4. Create an HTML file that slides a triangle across the canvas.
5. Create an HTML file that shows a shape with three copies of the shape to the right. Within the first copy of the image, display only the image's red color values by zeroing out the green and blue color values. Within the second image copy, show only the green color values. Within the third copy, show only the blue colors.
6. Research the WebGL library, and report your findings.

CSS Transformations and Rotations

THROUGHOUT THE LAST SEVERAL chapters, you have examined a wide range of graphics operations—from text and image translations to rotations. With those operations in mind, it makes sense to revisit the capabilities cascading style sheets provide to support similar text and image manipulation.

Learning Objectives

This chapter examines the movement, rotation, scaling, and skewing of text and graphics using CSS. By the time you finish this chapter, you will understand the following key concepts:

- How to use the CSS **transform** property to translate or move, rotate, skew, or scale an HTML element
- How to use the **transform** property **rotate** function to rotate an HTML element on a page
- How to use the **transform** property **translate** function to move an HTML element on a page
- How to use the **transform** property **scale** function to increase or decrease the size of an HTML element on a page
- How to use the **transform** property **skew** function to skew an HTML element on a page along the object's x or y axis

The CSS Transform Property

The CSS **transform** property provides several functions you can use with CSS styles to translate or move, rotate, skew, or scale an HTML element. Depending on your browser, the name of the **transform** property may differ:

```
-moz-transform:

-ms-transform:

-o-transform:

-webkit-transform:

transform:
```

Rotating an Object

Using the **transform** property **rotate** function, you can rotate an element a specified number of degrees on the page. The following HTML file, ImageRotate.html, displays two columns of photos. The first column rotates the photos at 15 degrees and the second at 345, as shown in **FIGURE 23-1**:

```
<!DOCTYPE html>
<html>
<head>
<style type="text/css">

.right {
-moz-transform: rotate(345deg);
-ms-transform: rotate(345deg);
-o-transform: rotate(345deg);
-webkit-transform: rotate(345deg);
transform: rotate(345deg);
}

.left {
-moz-transform: rotate(15deg);
-ms-transform: rotate(15deg);
-o-transform: rotate(15deg);
-webkit-transform: rotate(15deg);
transform: rotate(15deg);
}
```

FIGURE 23-1 Using the **rotate** function to rotate images within a page
Credit (clockwise from top left): © Christian Mueller/Shutterstock; © Gts/Shutterstock;
© Vaclav Volrab/Shutterstock; © Anastasija Popova/Shutterstock

```
</style>
</head>
<body>
<img class="left" width="300" height="200"
src="http://www.websitedevelopmentbook.com/
Chapter23/dog.jpg" />
<img class="right" width="300" height="200"
src="http://www.websitedevelopmentbook.com/
Chapter23/wine.jpg" />
<br/>
<img class="left" width="300" height="200"
src="http://www.websitedevelopmentbook.com/
Chapter23/cat.jpg" />
<img class="right" width="300" height="200"
src="http://www.websitedevelopmentbook.com/
Chapter23/cigar.jpg" />
```

```
</body>
</html>
```

As you can see, the file simply defines **right** and **left** classes within which it select rotations of 15 degrees and 345 degrees.

Depending on your page design, you also may want to rotate text and possibly background colors within a page. The following HTML file, RotateDivs. html, changes the previous HTML file slightly to include text and background colors for each image, as shown in **FIGURE 23-2**. The file rotates each of the page objects by rotating the containing <**div**> tags:

```
<!DOCTYPE html>
<html>
```

FIGURE 23-2 Rotating text and image contents within a webpage

Credit (clockwise from top left): © Christian Mueller/Shutterstock; © Gts/Shutterstock;
© Vaclav Volrab/Shutterstock; © Anastasija Popova/Shutterstock

```
<head>
<style type="text/css">

.right {
-moz-transform: rotate(345deg);
-ms-transform: rotate(345deg);
-o-transform: rotate(345deg);
-webkit-transform: rotate(345deg);
transform: rotate(345deg);
float:right;
}

.left {
-moz-transform: rotate(15deg);
-ms-transform: rotate(15deg);
-o-transform: rotate(15deg);
-webkit-transform: rotate(15deg);
transform: rotate(15deg);
float:left;
}

h1 { text-align:center; }
</style>
</head>
body>
<div class="left" style="width:300px; height:300px;
background-color: blue;">
<img width="300" height="200" src="http://www
.websitedevelopmentbook.com/Chapter23/dog.jpg" />
<h1>Dogs Rule</h1>
</div>
<div class="right" style="width:300px;
height:300px; background-color: red;">
<img width="300" height="200"
src="http://www.websitedevelopmentbook.com/
Chapter23/wine.jpg" />
<h1>Cheeers!</h1>
</div>
<div style="clear:both;"></div>
<br/>
<div class="left"style="width:300px; height:300px;
background-color: green;">
```

```
<img width="300" height="200" src="http://www
.websitedevelopmentbook.com/Chapter23/cat.jpg" />
<h1>Meow!</h1>
</div>
<div class="right" style="width:300px;
height:300px; background-color: yellow;">

<img width="300" height="200" src="http://www
.websitedevelopmentbook.com/Chapter23/cigar.jpg" />
<h1>Relax!</h1>
<div>
</body>
</html>
```

As you can see, the file uses CSS classes for the right and left columns, which rotate each column's images. The page then assigns the corresponding class to each division to rotate the corresponding content.

Combining JavaScript and CSS to Spin an Object

Depending on your page content and purpose, there may be times when you will want to spin an object on the page, either to get the user's attention or possibly to implement a screen saver image effect. The following HTML file, SpinImage.html, repeatedly spins an image 360 degrees by combining JavaScript and CSS, as shown in **FIGURE 23-3**:

```
<!DOCTYPE html>
<html>
<head>
<script>
var i = 0;

function SpinImage() {

document.getElementById("body").innerHTML =
  '<img ' +
  'style="-moz-transform: rotate(' + i + 'deg); ' +
  '-ms-transform: rotate(' + i + 'deg); ' +
  '-o-transform: rotate(' + i + 'deg); ' +
  '-webkit-transform: rotate(' + i + 'deg); ' +
  'transform: rotate(' + i + 'deg); "' +
  'src="http://www.websitedevelopmentbook.com/
  chapter23/spiral.jpg">';
i = i + 1;
```

FIGURE 23-3 Combining JavaScript and CSS to spin an image
Credit: © marinini/Shutterstock

```
}
</script>
</head>
<body id="body" onload="setInterval(function()
{ SpinImage(); }, 25)">
</body>
</html>
```

In this case, when the page loads, the browser calls the **SpinImage** function, which rotates the image based on the degrees contained in the variable **i.** The function is then called every 25 milliseconds to rotate the image one degree at a time.

Translating an Object

As you have learned, developers often refer to moving objects on the screen as "translating" them. Using the **transform** property **translate** functions, you can move an object along the x and y axis:

```
transform: translateX(value);

transform: translate(value);

transform: translate (value, value);
```

The following HTML file, MoveDiv.html, moves page content up and down the left-hand side of the window, as shown in **FIGURE 23–4**. The page again combines JavaScript and CSS:

```
<!DOCTYPE html>
<html>
<head>
<style type="text/css">

.top {
-moz-transform: translateY(10px);
-ms-transform: translateY(10px);
-o-transform: translateY(10px);
-webkit-transform: translateY(10px);
transform: translateY(10px);
}

.middle {
-moz-transform: translateY(200px);
```

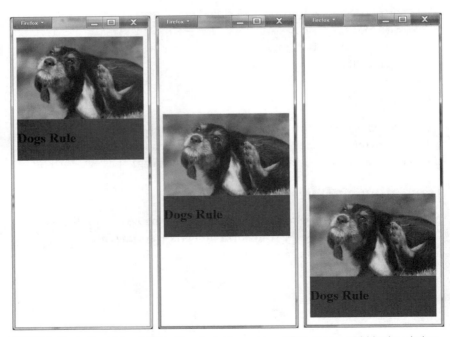

FIGURE 23–4 Combining CSS and JavaScript to move an HTML element within the window
Credit: © Christian Mueller/Shutterstock

```
-ms-transform: translateY(200px);
-o-transform: translateY(200px);
-webkit-transform: translateY(200px);
transform: translateY(200px);
}

.bottom {
-moz-transform: translateY(400px);
-ms-transform: translateY(400px);
-o-transform: translateY(400px);
-webkit-transform: translateY(400px);
transform: translateY(400px);
}

</style>
<script>
var i = 0;
var direction = 'Down';

function moveDiv()
{
  if ((i == 0) && (direction == 'Down'))
    {
      document.getElementById('dog').className=
        'middle';
      ++i;
    }
  else if ((i == 1) && (direction == 'Down'))
    {
      document.getElementById('dog').className =
        'bottom';
      ++i;
    }
  else if ((i == 2) && (direction == 'Down'))
    {
      document.getElementById('dog').className =
        'middle'; direction = 'Up';
      --i;
    }
  else if ((i == 1) && (direction == 'Up'))
    {
      document.getElementById('dog').className = 'top';
      --i;
    }
```

```
      else if ((i == 0) && (direction == 'Up'))
        {
          document.getElementById('dog').className =
            'middle'; direction = 'Down';
          i = 1;
        }
    }
</script>
</head>
<body onload="setInterval('moveDiv()', 3000)">
<div id="dog" class="top" style="width:300px;
height:300px; background-color: blue;">
<img width="300" height="200" src="http://www
.websitedevelopmentbook.com/Chapter23/dog.jpg" />
<h1>Dogs Rule</h1>
<div>
</body>
</html>
```

In this case, the page calls the **moveDiv** function every three seconds and then moves the division based on its current location and direction.

Scaling an Object

Using the **transform** property **scale** function, you can increase or decrease an object's size. The following HTML file, GrowAndShrink.html, uses the scale function to repeatedly increase and decrease an image's size, as shown in **FIGURE 23-5**:

```
<!DOCTYPE html>
<html>
<head>
<script>
var i = 1.0;
var direction = 'Grow';

function GrowAndShrink() {

  document.getElementById("body").innerHTML =
    '<img ' +
    'style="-moz-transform: scale(' + i + ', ' + i
    + '); ' +
```

FIGURE 23-5 Using the **scale** function to increase and decrease an image's size
Credit: © marinini/Shutterstock

```
        '-ms-transform: scale(' + i + ', ' + i + ');' +
        '-o-transform: scale(' + i + ', ' + i + '); ' +
        '-webkit-transform: scale(' + i + ', ' + i
        + '); "' +
        'transform: scale(' + i + ', ' + i + '); "' +
        'src="http://www.websitedevelopmentbook.com/
        chapter23/spiral.jpg">';

        if (direction == 'Grow')
          i = i + 0.25;
        else
          i = i - 0.25;

        if (i == 1.0)
          direction = 'Grow';
        else if (i == 2.0)
          direction = 'Shrink';
      }
    </script>
  </head>
  <body id="body" onload="setInterval(function()
  { GrowAndShrink(); }, 500)">
  </body>
</html>
```

In this case, when the page loads, it calls the function GrowAndShrink every 500 milliseconds to grow and shrink the image using the scale function.

Flipping an Object

In the previous example, you used the **transform** property **scale** function to change an image's size. As it turns out, if you pass the value -1 to the **scale** function, you can flip the element, as shown in **FIGURE 23-6**.

The following HTML file, FlipImage.html, flips two images—one along the x axis and one along the y axis, as shown in **FIGURE 23-7**.

```
<!DOCTYPE html>
<html>
<head>
<style>
.flip {
```

FIGURE 23-6 Using the **scale** function to flip an item across the x or y axis
Credit: © Gts/Shutterstock

FIGURE 23–7 Flipping images using the **scale** function

Credit (from left): © Christian Mueller/Shutterstock; © Anastasija Popova/Shutterstock

```
-moz-transform: scaleY(-1);
-ms-transform: scaleY(-1);
-o-transform: scaleY(-1);
-webkit-transform: scaleY(-1);
transform: scaleY(-1);
}
</style>
</head>
<body>
<imgsrc="http://www.websitedevelopmentbook.com/
chapter23/dog.jpg">
<img src="http://www.websitedevelopmentbook.com/
chapter23/cat.jpg"><br/>
<img class="flip" src="http://www
.websitedevelopmentbook.com/chapter23/dog.jpg">
```

```
<img class="flip" src="http://www
.websitedevelopmentbook.com/chapter23/cat.jpg"><br/>
</body>
</html>
```

Skewing an Object

The **transform** property **skew** function lets you display page elements at an angle along the x or y axis:

```
skewX(value);

skewY(value);

skew(value, value);
```

The following HTML file, SkewImage.html, uses the **skew** functions to display an image at different orientations, as shown in **FIGURE 23-8**:

```
<!DOCTYPE html>
<html>
<head>
```

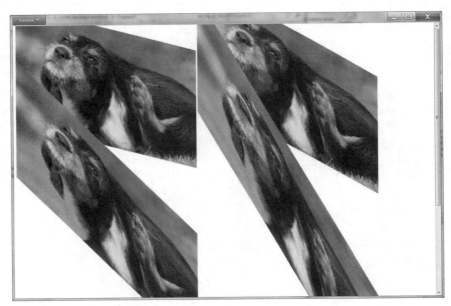

FIGURE 23-8 Skewing image content within a webpage
Credit: © Christian Mueller/Shutterstock

```
<style>
.skew15 {
-moz-transform: skewY(15deg);
-ms-transform: skewY(15deg);
-o-transform: skewY(15deg);
-webkit-transform: skewY(15deg);
transform: skewY(15deg);
}

.skew30 {
-moz-transform: skewY(30deg);
-ms-transform: skewY(30deg);
-o-transform: skewY(30deg);
-webkit-transform: skewY(30deg);
transform: skewY(30deg);
}

.skew45 {
-moz-transform: skewY(45deg);
-ms-transform: skewY(45deg);
-o-transform: skewY(45deg);
-webkit-transform: skewY(45deg);
transform: skewY(45deg);
}

.skew60 {

-moz-transform: skewY(60deg);
-ms-transform: skewY(60deg);
-o-transform: skewY(60deg);
-webkit-transform: skewY(60deg);
transform: skewY(60deg);
}

</style>
</head>
<body>
<img class="skew15" src="http://www
.websitedevelopmentbook.com/chapter23/dog.jpg">
<img class="skew30" src="http://www
.websitedevelopmentbook.com/chapter23/dog.jpg"><br/>
<img class="skew45" src="http://www
.websitedevelopmentbook.com/chapter23/dog.jpg">
```

```
<img class="skew60" src="http://www
.websitedevelopmentbook.com/chapter23/dog.jpg"><br/>
</body>
</html>
```

Real-World Web Design

This chapter examined CSS operations that perform rotation, translation, scaling, and skewing in two dimensions. Depending on your page content, there may be times when you need to perform such operations in 3-D. To get started with such operations, read the CSS 3D Transforms Module on the W3 website at *http://dev .w3.org/csswg/css3-3d-transforms/,* as shown in **FIGURE 23-9**. Again, depending on your browser, the steps you must perform to use the 3-D operations may differ.

Hands-On HTML

To view the HTML files or to experiment with the files presented in this chapter, visit this book's companion website at *http://www.websitedevelopmentbook.com/ Chapter23/TryIt.html.*

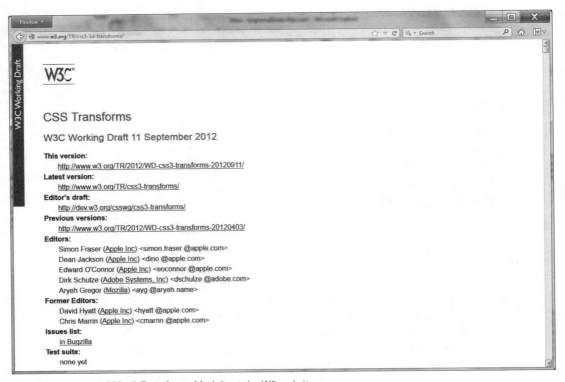

FIGURE 23-9 The CSS 3D Transforms Module at the W3 website

CHAPTER SUMMARY

Using JavaScript, CSS, and jQuery, you have learned a variety of ways to manipulate HTML elements on a page. In this chapter, you examine ways to perform text and image translations rotations using CSS as well as scaling and skewing operations. In Chapter 24, "Performing CSS Transitions and Animations," you will look at advanced ways to animate webpage elements using CSS.

CHAPTER REVIEW

1. Create an HTML file that displays an image at different degrees of rotation.
2. Create an HTML file that skews an image in different ways.
3. Create an HTML file that moves text content around the window to different locations.
4. Create an HTML file that uses the **scale** function to flip text-based content.
5. Create an HTML file that combines JavaScript and CSS to move an image across the window from the top-left corner to the bottom-right corner.

Performing CSS Transitions and Animations

THROUGHOUT THIS BOOK, YOU have used JavaScript, jQuery, and the HTML 5 canvas to create dynamic text and graphics-based animations. In this chapter you will learn how to perform animations using **CSS transitions**, which specify the properties you desire for an element's starting and ending state. The browser, in turn, applies the transitions to create an animated effect. In this way, you do not need to use JavaScript or jQuery.

Learning Objectives

This chapter explains how to use CSS transitions to specify an HTML element's ending properties. By the time you finish this chapter, you will understand the following key concepts:

- How to use CSS transitions to specify an HTML element's ending state, as defined by CSS property values
- How to use a timer as a transition trigger

Getting Started with CSS Transitions

To create a CSS transition, specify ending state property values for an HTML element, such as color, opacity, or location. When you change one of the specified property values, you trigger the browser's application of the transition.

The following HTML file, ImageOpacity.html, uses a CSS transition to fade an image into view. The page initially displays a button, which you can click to start the transition. Actually, the button will call code that changes the image **opacity** property value, which in turn, directs the browser to apply the transition. The browser then fades the image into view, as shown in **FIGURE 24-1**.

```
<!DOCTYPE html>
<html>
<head>
<style>
img {
-moz-transition: opacity 5s;
-ms-transition: opacity 5s;
-o-transition: opacity 5s;
```

FIGURE 24-1 Using a CSS transition to fade an image into view
Credit © Gts/Shutterstock

```
-webkit-transition: opacity 5s;
transition: opacity 5s;
}
</style>
<script>
function ShowImage()
{
  document.getElementById("wine").style.opacity = 1;
}
</script>
</head>
<body>
<img id="wine" style="opacity:0"
src="http://www.websitedevelopmentbook.com
/chapter23/wine.jpg"><br/>
<button onclick="ShowImage()">Click Here</button>
</body>
</html>
```

In this case, the file originally sets the image **opacity** to 0. When the user clicks the button, the page calls the **ShowImage** function, which changes the **opacity** to 1. This triggers the transition.

Looking at a Second Transition Example

The following HTML file, ExtendBox.html, increases the width to a square, colored page division across the window. As the box increases in width, its color also changes from blue to yellow. As such, the transition actually involves two CSS properties: the location and the color.

```
<!DOCTYPE html>
<html>
<head>
<style>
div {
-moz-transition: width 5s, background-color 5s;
-ms-transition: width 5s, background-color 5s;
-o-transition: width 5s, background-color 5s;
-webkit-transition width 5s, background-color 5s;

transition: width 5s, background-color 5s;
}
</style>
```

```
<script>
function SlideBox()
{
  document.getElementById('box').style.width =
  '500px';
  document.getElementById('box').style
  .backgroundColor = '#FF0000';
}
</script>
</head>
<body>
<div id="box" style="background-color:blue;
position:relative; width:200px; height:200px;">
</div><br/>
<button onclick="SlideBox();">Click Here</button>
</body>
</html>
```

In this case, the file defines two transitions, one for the width and one for the background color. The page separates the time for each transition with a comma. If you view the file's contents, the browser will move the box, as shown in **FIGURE 24–2**.

FIGURE 24–2 Applying multiple CSS transitions to an element

Using a Timer as a Transition Trigger

The previous examples have used a button to trigger the CSS transitions. The following HTML file, SlideBothDirections.html, uses a JavaScript-based timer to repeatedly move a box back and forth across the window. After the page loads, the browser calls the **StartAnimation** function, which begins to move the box. The page then sets a timer, which occurs after the five-second transition to start the shape moving in the opposite direction. The page repeats this processing, indefinitely changing the box's direction across the page:

```
<!DOCTYPE html>
<html>
<head>
<style>
div {
-moz-transition: width 5s, background-color 5s;
-ms-transition: width 5s, background-color 5s;
-o-transition: width 5s, background-color 5s;
-webkit-transition width 5s, background-color 5s;
transition: width 5s, background-color 5s;
}
</style>
<script>
var direction = "right";

function CloseBox()
{
  document.getElementById('box').style.width =
  '200px';
  document.getElementById('box').style
  .backgroundColor = '#0000FF';
  setTimeout(function () { SlideBox(); }, 6000);
}

function SlideBox()
{
  document.getElementById('box').style.width =
  '500px';
  document.getElementById('box').style
  .backgroundColor = '#FF0000';
  setTimeout(function () { CloseBox(); }, 6000);
}
```

```
</script>
</head>
<body>
<div id="box" style="background-color:blue;
position:relative; width:200px; height:200px;">
</div><br/>
<button onclick="SlideBox();">Click Here</button>
</body>
</html>
```

A Final Transition Example

The following HTML file, Welcome.html, displays a small "welcome" message in the middle of the page. The page then uses a CSS transition to expand the message, as shown in **FIGURE 24-3**.

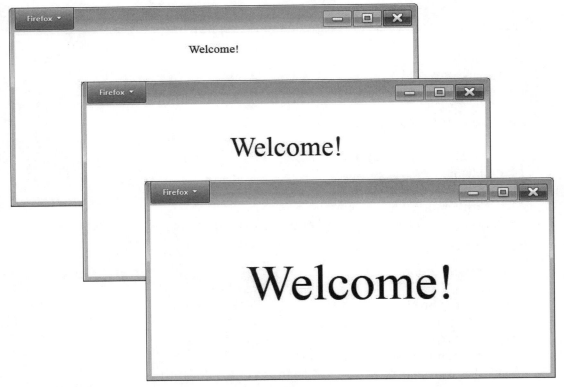

FIGURE 24-3 Using a CSS transition to enlarge a text message

```
<!DOCTYPE html>
<html>
<head>
<style>
p {
-moz-transition: font-size 8s;
-ms-transition: font-size 8s;
-o-transition: font-size 8s;
-webkit-transition font-size 8s;
transition: font-size 8s;
}
</style>
<script>
function GrowFont()
{
  document.getElementById('welcome').style
  .fontSize = '500%';
}
</script>
</head>
<body onload="GrowFont()">
<div>
<p id="welcome" style="text-align:center;">
Welcome!</p>
</div>
</body>
</html>
```

In this case, when the page loads, it calls the **GrowFont** function, which increases the paragraph's text, the welcome message, by 500 percent. This triggers the transition.

Getting More Specifics on CSS Transitions

The previous examples introduced you to CSS transitions. If you plan to use such transitions within the pages you create, read the Transitions Module on the W3 website at *http://www.w3.org/TR/css3-transitions/*, as shown in **FIGURE 24-4**.

Real-World Web Design

As you have learned, when using **CSS transitions**, specify how an element will change from a starting state to ending state through the use of CSS properties. The browser, in turn, determines the transition process. A **CSS animation**, in contrast,

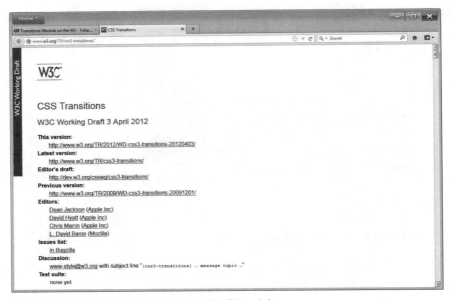

FIGURE 24-4 The Transitions Module on the W3 website

Reproduced with permission of the World Wide Web Consortium (W3C)

defines intermediate states within the transition process called **keyframes**, which the browser uses as it performs the transition. In other words, a **CSS animation** is essentially a collection of CSS transitions.

To specify a CSS animation, create a named animation that specifies the **keyframes** using syntax similar to that shown here:

```
@keyframe 'TurnRed' {
  33% { background-color: green; }
  66% { background-color: blue; }
 100% { background-color: red; }
}
```

After you define the animation, you can assign it to an HTML element as follows:

```
div { animation-name: Turn-Red; }
```

Today, browser support for CSS animations varies. Test your browser to determine its level of support as well as any changes to the syntax you must perform, such as preceding names with **moz-**, **o-**, and so on.

For specifics on CSS animations, read the Animation Module on the W3 website at *http://dev.w3.org/csswg/css3-animations/*, as shown in **FIGURE 24-5**.

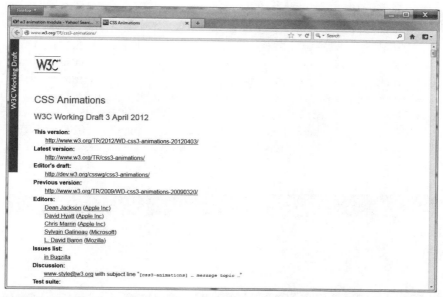

FIGURE 24-5 The Animation Module on the W3 website
Reproduced with permission of the World Wide Web Consortium (W3C)

Hands-On HTML

To view the HTML files or to experiment with the files presented in this chapter, visit this book's companion website at *http://www.websitedevelopmentbook.com/Chapter24/TryIt.html.*

CHAPTER SUMMARY

Throughout this book, you have performed text- and graphics-based animations using JavaScript, jQuery, and the HTML 5 canvas. In this chapter, you learned how to use CSS transitions to specify an HTML element's ending properties. When you trigger a transition, the browser changes the element from its current state to your specified ending state. This chapter also introduced CSS animations, which are essentially a collection of transitions developers call "keyframes." As you have learned, the browser plays a major role in the CSS transition process. Before you use transitions or animations within your webpages, make sure you have the browser support you need.

KEY TERMS

CSS animation
CSS transition
Keyframe

CHAPTER REVIEW

1. Create a CSS transition that changes the color of an <h1> heading from black to red over a three-second period. Use a button to trigger the transition.

2. Create a CSS transition that moves an image across the page (using the image x position) over a five-second period.

3. Create an HTML file that displays a large "welcome" message. The message should then shrink out of view over an eight-second period.

4. Research CSS animations at the W3 website, and report your findings. Try to find a browser that supports animations, and create a simple example.

Utilizing Web Storage

FOR YEARS, COOKIES WERE the only option available to most Web developers for storing temporary information. Using a cookie, a developer could store up to 4KB of data. A website might, for example, use a cookie to track the items in a your shopping cart from one site visit to the next or track your preferences while traversing a site. HTML 5 expands beyond the storage capabilities that cookies provide to allow session-based storage and long-term storage. The session-based storage exists until you leave the site or close the window. In contrast, the long-term storage persists until you or the application deletes the data. The HTML 5 Standard provides session and long-term storage support up to 5MB.

Learning Objectives

This chapter examines the HTML 5 data-storage capabilities. By the time you finish this chapter, you will understand the following key concepts:

- How to create, store, retrieve, and delete cookies using JavaScript
- How to store and retrieve session-based data using the **sessionStorage** object and increase the amount of data stored
- How to store and retrieve long-term data using the **localStorage** object

Data Storage the Old-Fashioned Way

As discussed, for years Web developers have made use of temporary storage locations called **cookies**, which reside on your disk. The cookie-based storage is temporary in that you can delete the cookies, or an application can delete cookies that it previously created. A cookie is domain dependent; that is, it relates to a specific site. When you later visit that site and request a page, your browser will send the related cookies, too, as shown in FIGURE 25-1.

Using JavaScript, an HTML page can set or retrieve cookies. The following HTML file, SetCookie.html, uses JavaScript to create a cookie named **FirstCookie** that contains the value Chapter 25. In this case, the cookie expires in 10 days:

```
<!DOCTYPE html>
<html>
<head>
<script>
function CreateCookie()
{
  var CookieExpirationDate = new Date();
  var Days = 10;

  CookieExpirationDate.setDate(CookieExpirationDate
  .getDate() + Days);

  document.cookie="FirstCookie" + "=" + escape
  ("Chapter 25") +
  ";expires="+CookieExpirationDate.toUTCString();
```

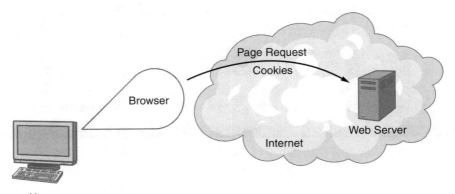

FIGURE 25-1 When a user visits a website, the browser sends the data contained in cookies for that site with the page request.

```
  alert('Created the cookie: FirstCookie with the
  value Chapter 25');
}

</script>
</head>
<body onload="CreateCookie()">
</body>
</html>
```

To create a cookie, you must specify the cookie name, the cookie value, and the date at which the cookie will expire.

Using JavaScript, you can also retrieve data stored within a cookie. The following HTML file, ShowCookie.html, first creates a cookie named **FirstCookie**. Then, the JavaScript looks up and displays the value of that cookie:

```
<!DOCTYPE html>
<html>
<head>
<script>

function CookieOperations()
{
  CreateCookie();
  DisplayCookie();
}

function DisplayCookie()
{
  var CookieArray = document.cookie.split(";");
  var value, name;

for (i=0; i<CookieArray.length; i++)
{
  name = CookieArray[i].substr(0,CookieArray[i]
  .indexOf("="));
  value = CookieArray[i].substr(CookieArray[i]
  .indexOf("=")+1);

  while (name.indexOf(' ') == 0) // delete
  leading spaces
    name = name.substr(1);
```

```
  if (name == 'FirstCookie')
    alert('Retrieved cookie, FirstCookie,
    Value: ' +value);
 }
}

function CreateCookie()
{
  var CookieExpirationDate = new Date();
  var Days = 10;

  CookieExpirationDate.setDate(CookieExpirationDate
  .getDate() + Days);

  document.cookie="FirstCookie" + "=" + escape
  ("Chapter 25") +
  ";expires="+CookieExpirationDate.toUTCString();

  alert('Created the cookie: FirstCookie with the
  value Chapter 25');
}
</script>
</head>
<body onload="CookieOperations()">
</body>
</html>
```

Normally, a webpage that uses cookies checks to see if a cookie is defined and, if not, it creates the cookie. The following HTML file, ShowPageCookies. html, checks to see if a cookie named DemoCookie exists. If it does not, the JavaScript creates the cookie and assigns it the current date and time. If you revisit the page, it looks up the cookie and tells you the date and time of your first visit:

```
<!DOCTYPE html>
<html>
<head>
<script>
function DisplayCookie(cookieName)
{
var CookieArray = document.cookie.split(";");
var value, name;
```

```
for (i=0; i<CookieArray.length; i++)
{
  name = CookieArray[i].substr(0,CookieArray[i]
  .indexOf("="));
  value = CookieArray[i].substr(CookieArray[i]
  .indexOf("=")11);

  while (name.indexOf(' ') == 0) // delete
  leading spaces
    name = name.substr(1);

  if (name == cookieName)
    alert('Retrieved cookie, your first visit
    was: ' + value);
 }
}

function CheckIfCookieExists(cookieName)
{
var CookieArray = document.cookie.split(";");
var value, name;

for (i=0; i<CookieArray.length; i++)
{
  name = CookieArray[i].substr(0,CookieArray[i]
  .indexOf("="));
  value = CookieArray[i].substr(CookieArray[i]
  .indexOf("=")+1);

  while (name.indexOf(' ') == 0) // delete
  leading spaces
    name = name.substr(1);

  if (name == cookieName)
    return(true);
}

return(false);
}

function CreateOrDisplayCookie()
{
if (CheckIfCookieExists("DemoCookie") == false)
```

```
    {
    var CookieExpirationDate = new Date();
    var Days = 10;

    CookieExpirationDate.setDate(CookieExpirationDate
    .getDate() + Days);

    document.cookie="DemoCookie" + "=" + new Date()
    .toString() +
    ";expires="+CookieExpirationDate.toUTCString();

    alert('Created the cookie—this is your
    first visit');
    }
else
    DisplayCookie("DemoCookie");
}

</script>
</head>
<body onload="CreateOrDisplayCookie()">
</body>
</html>
```

Should you later want to delete a cookie, set the cookie's expiration date to a date in the past. Note that some browsers will not immediately delete the cookie and instead wait until the browser restarts.

Using cookies, a Web developer can store 4,096 bytes of data. Depending on the browser, the number of cookies a page can create may differ. As you might guess, handling a large number of cookies can increase an application's complexity.

Storing Temporary Data in HTML 5

A **session**, with respect to a browser, is the period during which you have a window open on a specific domain, such as *www.yahoo.com*. If you close the window or move to a new domain, the session ends. Session data, therefore, is data that exists during a browser session.

To store temporary data within HTML 5, your pages use JavaScript to access the **sessionStorage** object. To determine if a browser supports the HTML storage capabilities, your code can test whether or not the **window.sessionStorage** object is defined.

Note: Some browsers will not define the object for pages opened from the current disk using the file:// protocol. For those browsers, you must perform the storage operations from a Web server-based page.

The following HTML file, CheckStorage.html, displays an alert dialog box stating whether or not the browser supports HTML 5 storage facilities:

```
<!DOCTYPE html>
<html>
<head>
<script>

function CheckStorage()
{
  if (window.sessionStorage != null)
    alert("Storage supported");
  else
    alert("Storage not supported");
}
</script>
</head>
<body onload="CheckStorage()">
</body>
</html>
```

To store data using the **sessionStorage** object, use the **setItem** method to specify a lookup key and a value:

```
sessionStorage.LookupKey = "Data Value";
```

For example, the following entry creates a key called **UserVisit** and assigns the current date to the key:

```
sessionStorage.UserVisit= new Date().toDateString();
```

The following HTML file, SessionStorage.html, prompts you for your name and then stores the name within a session variable:

```
<!DOCTYPE html>
<html>
<head>
<script>
```

```
function StoreName(name)
{
  if (window.sessionStorage != null)
    {
      window.sessionStorage.Name = name;
      alert('Stored the name: ' + sessionStorage
      .Name);
    }
  else
    alert("Storage not supported");

}
</script>
</head>
<body>
Name: <input id="nameField" type="text"></input>
<button onclick="StoreName(document
.getElementById('nameField').value)">Store
Name</button>
<button onclick="alert('The stored name: ' +
sessionStorage.Name);">Show Name</button></body>
</html>
```

Within the page, you can click the ShowName button to display the current name value. Experiment with the page by entering your name, viewing the name, closing the window, and then redisplaying the page. As you will find, when you return to the page later, the name is undefined because the session ended.

Storing Multiple Values

Using the **sessionStorage** object, your pages can store many data values. The following HTML file, UserInfo.html, prompts you for a name, age, e-mail, and phone number. When you later click the ShowInfo button, the page uses JavaScript to retrieve the corresponding data values for display:

```
<!DOCTYPE html>
<html>
<head>
<script>

function StoreInfo(name)
{
  if (window.sessionStorage != null)
```

```
    {
    window.sessionStorage.Name = document
    .getElementById('nameField').value;
    window.sessionStorage.Age = document
    .getElementById('ageField').value;
    window.sessionStorage.Phone = document
    .getElementById('phoneField').value;
    window.sessionStorage.Email = document
    .getElementById('emailField').value;
    }
  else
    alert("Storage not supported");
}

function ShowInfo()
{
  alert(sessionStorage.Name + ' ' + sessionStorage
  .Age + ' ' +
  sessionStorage.Phone + ' ' + sessionStorage
  .Email);
}
</script>

</head>
<body>
Name: <input id="nameField" type="text">
</input><br/>
Age: <input id="ageField" type="text">
</input><br/>
Phone: <input id="phoneField" type="text">
</input><br/>
Email: <input id="emailField" type="text">
</input><br/>
<button onclick="StoreInfo()">Store Data</button>
<button onclick="ShowInfo();">Show Info</button>
</body>
</html>
```

In this case, the JavaScript code assigns four values, each with a unique key name, to the **sessionStorage** object. Later, when you click the **ShowInfo** button, the JavaScript code retrieves those specific values.

Clearing Data from the Session Storage

As you have learned, the browser's session data is lost when you close the browser window or move it to a different domain. In addition, there may be times when an application wants to delete the data itself. In such cases, the application can call the **removeItem** function to clear one item, or it can use the **clear** function to remove all of its session variables.

The following HTML file, ClearSession.html, prompts you for information. The page contains a Show Info button that displays the user-entered data. The page also contains a Clear Info button that directs the application to clear the temporary storage:

```
<!DOCTYPE html>
<html>
<head>
<script>
function StoreInfo(name)
{
 if (window.sessionStorage != null)
  {
  window.sessionStorage.Name = document
  .getElementById('nameField').value;
  window.sessionStorage.Age = document
  .getElementById('ageField').value;
  window.sessionStorage.Phone = document
  .getElementById('phoneField').value;
  window.sessionStorage.Email = document
  .getElementById('emailField').value;
  }
 else
  alert("Storage not supported");
}

function ShowInfo()
{
alert(sessionStorage.Name + ' ' + sessionStorage
.Age + ' ' +
sessionStorage.Phone + ' ' + sessionStorage.Email);
}
</script>

</head>
<body>
Name: <input id="nameField" type="text"></input><br/>
```

```
Age: <input id="ageField" type="text"></input><br/>
Phone: <input id="phoneField" type="text">
</input><br/>
Email: <input id="emailField" type="text">
</input><br/>
<button onclick="StoreInfo()">Store Data</button>
<button onclick="ShowInfo();">Show Info</button>
<button onclick="sessionStorage.clear();">Clear
Info</button></body>
</html>
```

Again, take time to experiment with the application by adding, displaying, clearing, and then attempting to display the data.

Storing Long-Term Data

There may be times, such as if you have an e-commerce shopping cart, when you will want to keep data from one user session to the next. In such cases, your pages should use the **localStorage** object. The use of the **localStorage** object is identical to that of the **sessionStorage** object, with the exception that the data you store persists until it is deleted.

The following HTML file, LongTermStorage.html, checks for previously stored data and, if found, displays that data and prompts you to update it. The file uses a **localStorage** object to store the data from one session to the next:

```
<!DOCTYPE html>
<html>
<head>
<script>
functionStoreName(name)
{
 if (window.localStorage != null)
  {
  window.localStorage.Name = name;
  alert('Stored the name: ' + localStorage.Name);
  }
 else
  alert("Storage not supported");
}

</script>
</head>
<body>
```

```
Name: <input id="nameField" type="text"></input>

<button onclick="StoreName(document.getElementById
('nameField').value)">Store Name</button>
<button onclick="alert('The stored name: ' +
localStorage.Name);">Show Name</button>
</body>
</html>
```

Experiment with the file by storing data, closing the browser window, and then opening a new window with the page. As you will find, your data persists across sessions.

Real-World Web Design

Normally, by using the **sessionStorage** or **localStorage** objects, you can meet most client-side data-storage requirements. That said, there may be times when

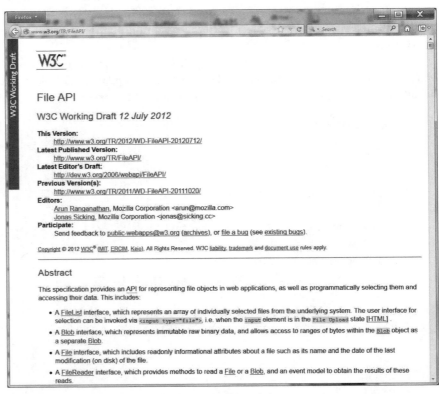

FIGURE 25-2 The File API specification at the W3 website.

Reproduced with permission of the World Wide Web Consortium (W3C)

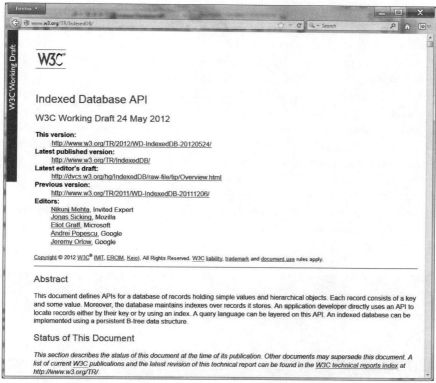

FIGURE 25-3 For specifics on the IndexedDB database API, visit the W3 website.
Reproduced with permission of the World Wide Web Consortium (W3C)

your applications need to access a file that resides on the client side. You might, for example, want to create a photo gallery that features pictures from the user's local machine. In such cases, your applications can use the File API, which the W3 website discusses in detail at *http://www.w3.org/*, as shown in **FIGURE 25-2**.

In addition, many browsers are now implanting or have implemented support for the IndexedDB database API, which JavaScript code can use to store and retrieve data from a client-side database. Using such a database, an application might download, for example, a copy of an online catalog. Then, as you traverse the catalog, the code can retrieve items from the local copy as opposed to performing slower server-based data requests. For specifications on the IndexedDB database API, visit the W3 website at *http://www.w3.org/TR/IndexedDB/*, as shown in **FIGURE 25-3**.

Hands-On HTML

To view the HTML files or to experiment with the files presented in this chapter, visit this book's companion website at *http://www.websitedevelopmentbook.com/Chapter25/TryIt.html*.

CHAPTER SUMMARY

For years, developers have made extensive use of cookies to store temporary data on a user's system. Using a cookie, an application can store up to 4KB of data. When you later visit a website and request a page, the browser sends any related cookies to the site.

To simplify client-side data storage operations and increase the amount of data an application can store, HTML provides a session-based storage object and a long-term storage object. A session is the period of time when you interact with a site. If you close the browser window or move to a new site, the session ends. Using the **sessionStorage** object, applications can store session-based data. In a similar way, the **localStorage** object lets you store data from one session to the next. Data you store using the **localStorage** object remains on the system until you or the application delete the data.

Using the **localStorage** and **localStorage** objects, your applications can store up to 5MB of data. If you need to store more data than that, consider using the File API or IndexedDB database API.

KEY TERMS

Cookie
Session

CHAPTER REVIEW

1. Create an HTML file that uses JavaScript to create two cookies, one that contains the time of the last visit and a second that includes the date.

2. Create an HTML file that displays the cookies that you created in Question 1.

3. Create an HTML file that uses the **sessionStorage** object to store the user's browser type when the file first loads (use the **<body>**tag **onload** event). Provide a button on the page that displays the saved data.

4. Create an HTML file that uses the **localStorage** object to store the date and time of the last visit to the site. Display the information when the site is revisited.

5. Research the File API, and discuss the capabilities it provides.

6. Research the IndexedDB API, and discuss the capabilities it provides.

Creating Location- Aware Webpages Using Geolocation

AROUND THE WORLD, USERS now make extensive use of mobile phones and hand-held devices to access pages on the World Wide Web. Most phones now have a **geopositioning system (GPS)** to provide information about the phone's current location. Such GPS capabilities change the way you interact with the Web. With a few clicks, you can find nearby restaurants, retailers, and other services; you can get driving directions from your current location; and you can instantly summon a cab or emergency vehicle.

Learning Objectives

This chapter examines the steps to perform to create location-aware webpages. By the time you finish this chapter, you will understand the following key concepts:

- How geopositioning services determine a device's location and the related accuracy of the result
- How to enable geopositioning support
- How to test if a browser supports geolocation
- How to support callback functions within an application
- How to track movement using the geoposition API
- How to integrate Google Maps
- How to use the Google Maps API to map a location

How Geopositioning Identifies Your Location

How geopositioning determines location and with what accuracy it does so depend on the device type. To start, as shown in **FIGURE 26-1**, if you are using a mobile phone or hand-held device with GPS capabilities, the GPS system uses satellites to triangulate your location. Satellite triangulation is extremely accurate; however, it may take time due to the slow satellite communication.

Second, if you are using an Internet-connected computer, the geopositioning software uses your Internet Protocol (IP) address to determine the location. Unfortunately, as shown in **FIGURE 26-2**, the IP address normally corresponds to the location of your Internet service provider, which could be hundreds or even thousands of miles away.

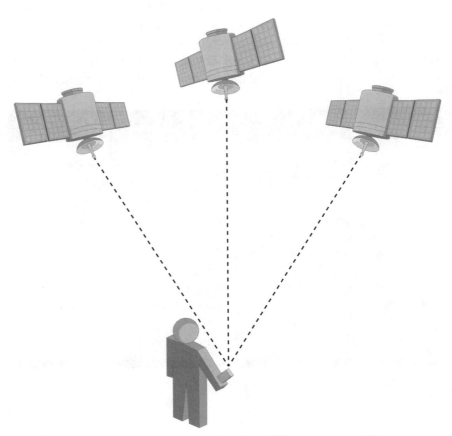

FIGURE 26-1 To determine a user's phone location, a GPS system uses satellites to triangulate the location.

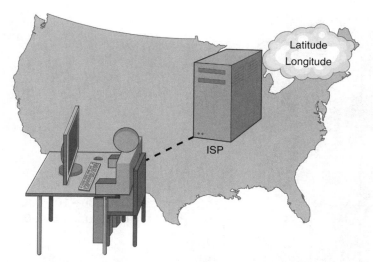

FIGURE 26-2 To determine the location of a computer user, geopositioning software uses the computer's IP address.

Finally, if the user has a Wi-Fi connection within a city that provides access points, the geopositioning software triangulates your position from the locations of known access points, as shown in **FIGURE 26-3**.

Working with Latitudes and Longitudes

As you will learn, geolocation software normally specifies locations in terms of latitude and longitude. These are expressed in terms of degrees, minutes, and seconds, as shown in **FIGURE 26-4**.

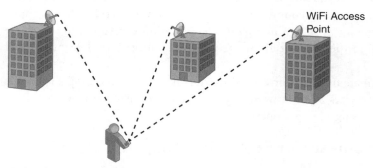

FIGURE 26-3 To determine the location of a Wi-Fi user, geopositioning software triangulates the position from the known location of Wi-Fi access points.

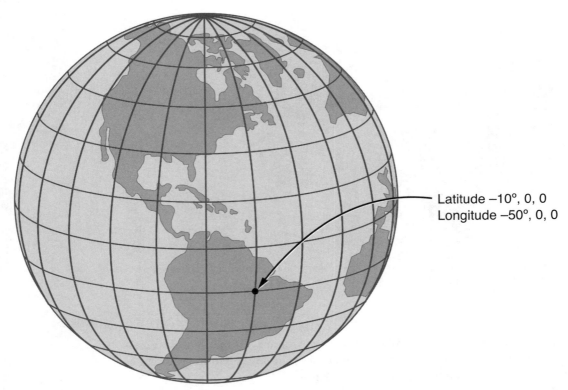

Latitude −10°, 0, 0
Longitude −50°, 0, 0

FIGURE 26-4 Geolocation software reports positions in terms of latitudes and longitudes.

Enabling Geolocation Capabilities

As you might expect, many users are not thrilled by having applications that "know" where they are or can track their movements. Therefore, to protect your privacy, browsers require you to enable geolocation services for an application. Normally, as shown in **FIGURE 26-5**, you must respond to a browser prompt before the browser allows geolocation software to determine your position.

To eliminate the need for you to continually respond to prompts to enable geolocation services, many browsers and phones allow you to permanently enable such services using a setup property.

Testing a Browser for Geolocation Support

Although newer browsers provide geolocation support, older ones do not. To determine if a user's browser supports geolocation, use JavaScript to test whether

FIGURE 26-5 Before an application can determine your location, geolocation software must ask you for permission.

the **navigator.geolocation** object is defined. The following HTML file, Test-Geolocation.html, illustrates how to test for browser geolocation support:

```
<!DOCTYPE html>
<html>
<head>
<script>

function DisplaySupport()
{
  if (navigator.geolocation)
    alert("Geolocation supported");
  else
    alert("No geolocation support");
}

</script>

</head>
<body onload="DisplaySupport()">
</body>
</html>
```

As you can see, the file simply tests if the **navigator.geolocation** object is defined and then displays a statement message.

Understanding Callback Functions

Browsers implement geolocation services as an **application program interface (API)**, which is a set of software routines an application can use to accomplish a specific task. To use the API, place JavaScript statements within your HTML files that call specific functions that are built into the API. Often, as shown in **FIGURE 26–6**, the API functions perform their processing and then pass back the result to your code by calling a function that you define, which developers refer to as a **callback function**.

In the case of the geolocation API, your JavaScript code calls the **getCurrentPosition** function, passing to the function the names of two callback functions. The **getCurrentPosition** function calls one when it successfully obtains a location and the other should an error occur:

```
navigator.getCurrrentPosition(NameofSuccessFunction,
NameofErrorHandlingFunction);
```

The following HTML file, ShowMyPosition.html, uses the **getCurrentPosition** function to determine the user's current location:

```
<!DOCTYPE html>
<html>
<head>
<script>
function ShowPosition()
{
  if (navigator.geolocation)
    navigator.geolocation.getCurrentPosition
    (DisplayResult, DisplayError)
  else
    alert("Browser does not support geolocation");
}
```

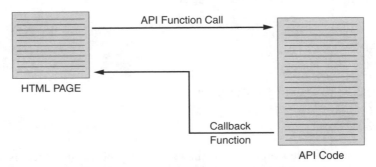

API Function Call

HTML PAGE

Callback Function

API Code

FIGURE 26–6 HTML files use JavaScript to call the geolocation API, which performs processing and then "calls back" a function in your code to resume your program's processing.

```
function DisplayResult(Position)
{
  var message = "Latitude: " + Position.coords.
  latitude;
  message += "Longitude: " + Position.coords.
  longitude;
  message += " Accuracy: " + Position.coords.
  accuracy + " meters";
  alert(message);
}

function DisplayError(Error)
{
  var message;

  switch(Error.code) {
    case 0: message = "Error retrieving location
    information";
      break;
    case 1: message = "User prevented location
    access";
      break;
    case 2: message = "Browser could not retrieve
    data";
      break;
    case 3: message = "Browser timed out during
    data retrieval";
      break;
  }

  alert(Message);
}

</script>
</head>
<body onload="ShowPosition()">
</body>
<html>
```

In this case, the page will display a message box that contains your current location in terms of latitude and longitude. In addition, the page displays an "accuracy" value, which provides an estimate, in meters, of the result's accuracy.

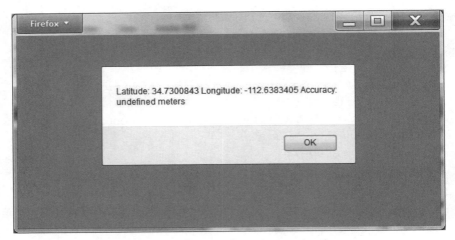

FIGURE 26-7 Using geolocation software to determine your location

When you view the file's contents, your browser displays output similar to that shown in **FIGURE 26-7**.

Tracking a User's Position

Many phones now support built-in applications that provide real-time driving directions. Rather than repeatedly calling the **getCurrentPosition** function to implement such processing, simply direct the geolocation software to monitor the user's location, and then notify the application of location changes by using, instead, the **watchPosition** API function. After you call the **watchPosition** function, the API will continue to call back a function within your code as their location changes. To turn off the callback processing, your code must call the **clearWatch** API method.

The following HTML file, WatchMyPosition.html, illustrates the use of the **watchPosition** function:

```
<!DOCTYPE html>
<html>
<head>
<script>

var id;

function ShowPosition()
{
  if (navigator.geolocation)
    id = navigator.geolocation. watchPosition
    (DisplayResult, DisplayError)
```

```
  else
    alert("Browser does not support geolocation");
}

function DisplayResult(Position)
{
  var message = "Latitude: " + Position.coords.
  latitude;
  message += " Longitude: " + Position.coords.
  longitude;
  message += " Accuracy: " + Position.coords.
  accuracy + " meters";
  alert(message);
}

function DisplayError(Error)
{
  var message;

  switch(Error.code) {
    case 0: message = "Error retrieving location
    information";
      break;
    case 1: message = "User prevented
    location access";
      break;
    case 2: message = "Browser could not
    retrieve data";
      break;
    case 3: message = "Browser timed out during
    data retrieval";
      break;
  }

  alert(Message);
}

</script>
</head>
<body onload="ShowPosition()">
<button onclick="navigator.geolocation.
clearWatch(id)">Clear Watch</button>
</body>
<html>
```

As you can see, the JavaScript simply calls the **watchPosition** API function. The function, in turn, monitors the device movement and reports on changes in location. The page includes a button to turn off the geolocation position monitoring.

Take time to experiment with the code using a mobile phone or hand-held device that has GPS capabilities.

Integrating Google Maps

Across the Web, users make extensive use of the Google Maps website to obtain driving directions. As it turns out, Google provides a JavaScript-based interface that your HTML files can use to integrate the maps into the pages you create. Although Google Maps are not part of HTML 5, they are presented here because they fit nicely into the geopositioning processing.

Integrating Google maps into an HTML file is easy. To start, link in Google's JavaScript code that provides their interface to the API:

```
<scriptsrc="http://maps.google.com/maps/api/
js?sensor=false"></script>
```

Then, use a **<div>** and **</div>** tag pair to specify a location in your page where you want the map to appear.

The following HTML file, MapWhiteHouse.html, uses the address of the White House, 1600 Pennsylvania Avenue, Washington, D.C., to display a map to the location:

```
<!DOCTYPE html>
<html>
<head>
<script src="http://maps.google.com/maps/api/
js?sensor=false"></script>
<script>

var map;

function DisplayMap()
{
var geocoder;

geocoder = new google.maps.Geocoder();

var mapOptions = {
    zoom: 8,
mapTypeId: google.maps.MapTypeId.
ROADMAP,streetViewControl:true
   }
```

```
map = new google.maps.Map(document.
getElementById("mapLocation"), mapOptions);var
address = "1600 Pennsylvania Ave, Washington, D.C.";

geocoder.geocode( { 'address': address },
ResultsCallBack);
}

function ResultsCallBack (results, status)
{
  if (status == google.maps.GeocoderStatus.OK)
    {
    map.setCenter(results[0].geometry.location);
    var marker = new google.maps.Marker
    ({ map: map, position: results[0].geometry.
    location});
    }
  else
    alert("Geocode was not successful:"+ status);
}
</script>

</head>
<body onload="DisplayMap()">
<div id="mapLocation" style="width: 640px; height:
480px;"></div>
</body>
</html>
```

In this case, the page uses JavaScript to pass the address of the desired location, the White House, to the **geocode** method. Then, the page uses the **Marker** API function to draw a location marker on the map.

When you view the file's contents, your browser displays a street map similar to that shown in FIGURE 26-8.

Using the plus/minus bar on the left side of the map, you can zoom the map display in or out. If you select Satellite view, your screen displays a photo image of the area, as shown in FIGURE 26-9.

Finally, if you drag the person icon onto the street, you can view a street-level view of the location, provided Google has such photos within its database.

Take time to experiment with the webpage by entering addresses of locations that you know.

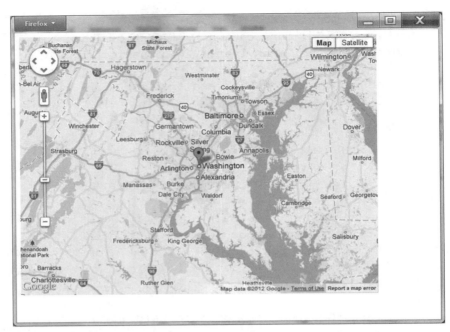

FIGURE 26–8 Using the Google Maps API to display a street map within a webpage
© 2012 Google

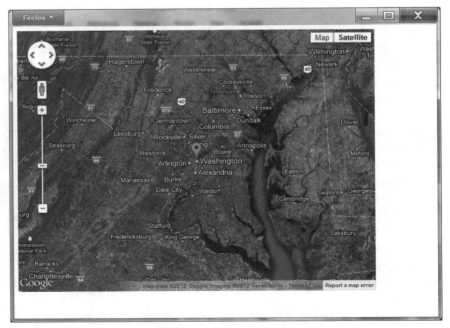

FIGURE 26–9 Using the Google Maps API to display a satellite image of an address
Map data © 2013 Google Imagery © 2013 TerraMetrics, Inc. www.terrametrics.com

Mapping Your Current Location

Earlier in this chapter, you learned how to use the geolocation API to determine a user's current location. The following HTML file, MapMyLocation.html, determines the user's current location and then displays a corresponding map:

```
<!DOCTYPE html>
<html>
<head>
<script src="http://maps.google.com/maps/api/
js?sensor=false"></script>
<script>

var map;
function DisplayMap()
{
  if (navigator.geolocation)
    navigator.geolocation.getCurrentPosition
    (DisplayResult, DisplayError)
  else
     alert("Browser does not support geolocation");
}

function DisplayResult(position)
{
var geocoder;

geocoder = new google.maps.Geocoder();

var mapOptions = {
  zoom: 8,
  mapTypeId: google.maps.MapTypeId.ROADMAP,
  streetViewControl:true
  }

  map = new google.maps.Map(document.
  getElementById("mapLocation"), mapOptions);

  var latlng = new google.maps.LatLng(position.
  coords.latitude, position.coords.longitude);

  geocoder.geocode('latLng': latlng},
  ResultsCallBack);
}
```

```
function ResultsCallBack (results, status)
{
  if (status == google.maps.GeocoderStatus.OK)
    {
    map.setCenter(results[0].geometry.location);
    var marker = new google.maps.Marker({ map: map,
    position: results[0].geometry.location });
    }
  else
    alert("Geocode was not successful: " + status);
}

function ShowPosition()
{
  if (navigator.geolocation)
   navigator.geolocation.getCurrentPosition(Display
   Result, DisplayError)
  else
    alert("Browser does not support geolocation");
}

function DisplayError(Error)
{
  var message;

  switch(Error.code) {
    case 0: message = "Error retrieving location
    information";
      break;
    case 1: message = "User prevented
    location access";
      break;
    case 2: message = "Browser could not
    retrieve data";
      break;
    case 3: message = "Browser timed out during
    data retrieval";
      break;
  }

  alert(Message);
}
</script>
```

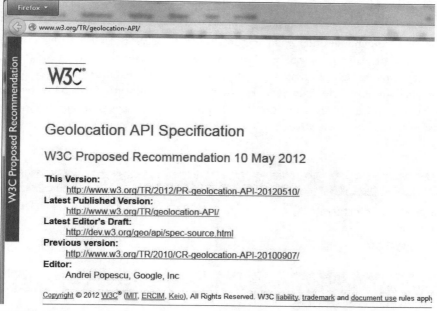

FIGURE 26–10 For specifics on geolocation processing, refer to the Geolocation API Specification. *Reproduced with permission of the World Wide Web Consortium (W3C)*

```
</head>
<body onload="DisplayMap()">
<div id="mapLocation" style="width: 640px;
height: 480px;"></div>
</body>
</html>
```

In this case, the file first uses the geolocation API to determine your latitude and longitude. Then, the JavaScript passes those values to the Google Map API to render the street map.

Real-World Web Design

This chapter provides an introduction to using the geolocation API. For more specifics on the API, read the Geolocation API Specification at the W3 website at *http://www.w3.org/TR/geolocation-API/*, as shown in **FIGURE 26–10**.

Hands-On HTML

To view the HTML files or to experiment with the files presented in this chapter, visit this book's companion website at *http://www.websitedevelopmentbook.com/Chapter26/TryIt.html*.

CHAPTER SUMMARY

The use of geolocation changes how webpages interact with users. By determining a user's location, a page can display more meaningful information, such as nearby stores, restaurants, and more. Today, most mobile phones and hand-held devices provide GPS support. To make it easy for webpages to use geolocation data, HTML provides a geolocation API. This chapter introduces the use of the API. In addition, this chapter presents ways to integrate Google Maps into your pages to provide street maps, satellite photos, and even street-level views of locations.

KEY TERMS

Application program interface (API)
Callback function
Geopositioning system

CHAPTER REVIEW

1. Modify the MapWhiteHouse.html file presented in this chapter to map the Eiffel Tower.

2. Using a mobile phone or hand-held device with GPS capabilities, use theWatchMyPosition .html file presented in this chapter to monitor your movement. Discuss your findings.

3. Create an HTML file named CityHighlights.html that provides a pull-down list of cities, such as Seattle, New York, and so on. When the user selects a city, display a map of an interesting site within that city.

Drag-and-Drop Processing

TODAY, MOST COMMON APPLICATIONS, such as word processors, e-mail, and file utilities, support drag-and-drop operations. With HTML 5, such operations are extending to webpages. Using drag-and-drop operations within a webpage, you might drag objects that you want to purchase into a shopping cart, toppings onto a pizza before placing an online order, and more. In addition, you will soon be able to drag-and-drop content from an application onto a webpage or vice versa.

Learning Objectives

This chapter introduces the HTML 5 drag-and-drop capabilities. By the time you finish this chapter, you will understand the following key concepts:

- How a drag-and-drop operation works
- How to create a draggable element within a webpage
- How to respond when a drag operation starts
- How to specify that an area allow an object to be dragged into it and dropped
- How to perform the drop operation

FIGURE 27-1 Dragging the Google graphic within the Google homepage
Google and *the Google logo are registered trademarks of Google Inc., used with permission.*

How "Drag-and-Drop" Works

Many of the webpages you use on a regular basis may already support some forms of **drag-and-drop operations**. These mouse-based operations allow you to click on an object and then, while holding down the mouse button, move it to a new location. When you release the mouse button, the software drops the object at the new location. **FIGURE 27-1**, for example, shows the Google homepage. If you drag the Google graphic using your mouse, you will find that the graphic can be moved around the page. In addition, you may even be able to drop the graphic onto your desktop.

Creating a Draggable Webpage Element

Under HTML 5, you make virtually any element draggable by assigning the **draggable="true"** attribute to the element. The following HTML file, DogCat.html, displays two images, one of a dog and one of a cat, as shown in **FIGURE 27-2**. The image of cat has the **draggable="true"** attribute and is thus draggable, whereas the image of the dog is not. As such, using your mouse, you can drag the cat image around the page. The dog image, in contrast, will not move.

FIGURE 27-2 Creating a draggable element within an HTML 5 page
Credit © Marjanneke de Jong/Shutterstock; © eurobanks/Shutterstock

The following statements implement the DogCat.html file:

```
<!DOCTYPE html>
<html>
<body>
<img src="dog.jpg" draggable="false" id="dog"
width="400" height="300" />
<img src="cat.jpg" draggable="true" id="cat"
width="400" height="300"/>
</body>
</html>
```

In this case, you can drag the image around the page, but you cannot yet drop it.

Handling a Drag Operation

After you make an HTML element draggable, the browser needs to be told what it should do with the dragged data. In this case, simply store the ID of the corresponding image element. Later, use the ID to move the data to a target location.

The following HTML file, SpecifyDragElementId.html, shows Step 2 of the drag-and-drop process—Step 1 was making the element draggable. As you will see, the file responds to the **ondragstart** event by assigning the ID of the cat image to the drag event:

```
<!DOCTYPE html>
<html>
<head>
<script>
function drag(event)
{
  event.dataTransfer.setData("Text", event.target.id);
}
</script>
</head>
<body>
<img src="dog.jpg" draggable="false" id="dog"
width="400" height="300" />
<img src="cat.jpg" draggable="true" id="cat"
width="400" height="300" ondragstart="drag(event)"/>
</body>
</html>
```

Making an Area "Droppable"

By default, a webpage will not allow content to be dragged or dropped onto it. To specify that an area allow content to be dragged into it, turn off the element's default behavior. The following HTML file, ProvideTarget.html, creates a division within the page that is capable of storing dragged data:

```
<!DOCTYPE html>
<html>
<head>
<script>
function permitdrop(event)
{
  event.preventDefault();
}
```

```
function drag(event)
{
  event.dataTransfer.setData("Text", event.target.id);
}
</script>
</head>
<body>
<img src="dog.jpg" draggable="false" id="dog"
width="400" height="300" />
<img src="cat.jpg" draggable="true" id="cat"
width="400" height="300" ondragstart="drag(event)"/>
<br/>
<div ondragover="permitdrop(event)"
style="background-color: yellow; width:400px;
height:300px"></div>
</body>
</html>
```

As you can see, when an **ondragover** event occurs, the page calls the **permit-Drop** function, which enables the drag-and-drop operation.

Allowing the Drop Operation to Occur

Just as an area within a webpage normally does not allow objects to be dragged into the area, the area also does not allow an object to be dropped. The last step to providing drag-and-drop support is specifying the processing that should occur when you drop an object. The following HTML file, CatDragAndDrop.html, allows you to drag and drop the cat image from the top of the page to the area at the bottom of the page:

```
<!DOCTYPE html>
<html>
<head>
<script>
function drop(event)
{
  event.preventDefault();
  var data=event.dataTransfer.getData("Text");
  event.target.appendChild(document.get
  ElementById(data));
}
```

```
function permitdrop(event)
{
  event.preventDefault();
}

function drag(event)
{
  event.dataTransfer.setData("Text", event.target.id);
}
</script>
</head>
<body>
<img src="dog.jpg" draggable="false" id="dog"
width="400" height="300" />
<img src="cat.jpg" draggable="true" id="cat"
width="400" height="300" ondragstart="drag(event)"/>
<br/>
<div ondragover="permitdrop(event)"
ondrop="drop(event)" style="background-color:
yellow; width:400px; height:300px"></div>
</body>
</html>
```

As you can see, the code handles the **ondrop** event for the division by calling the **drop** function. Within the **drop** function, the code disables the element's default processing to allow the drop and then appends the element to the end of the division's current contents (which was empty to start).

When you view this file's content, you can drag the cat image, as shown in **FIGURE 27-3**.

A Second Example

In a similar way, the following HTML file, Shopping.html, displays several photos of items that you can drag into a shopping cart, as shown in **FIGURE 27-4**. In this case, after you place an item into the cart, you can change your mind and remove the item by simply dragging it out of the cart and back into the group.

The following statements implement the Shopping.html file:

```
<!DOCTYPE html>
<html>
<head>
<script>
function drop(event)
```

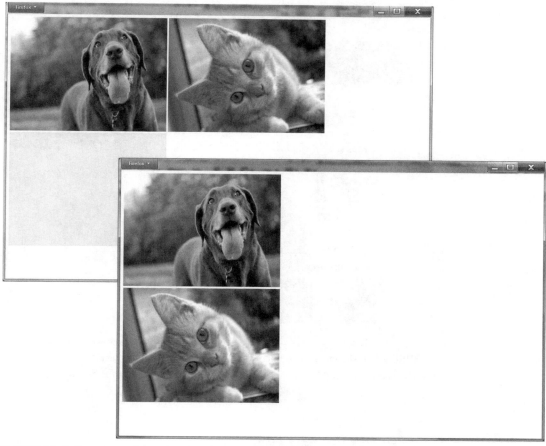

FIGURE 27-3 Dragging and dropping a cat image within an HTML page
Credit © Marjanneke de Jong/Shutterstock; © eurobanks/Shutterstock

```
{
  event.preventDefault();
  var data = event.dataTransfer.getData("Text");
  event.target.appendChild(document.
  getElementById(data));
}

function permitdrop(event)
{
  event.preventDefault();
}
```

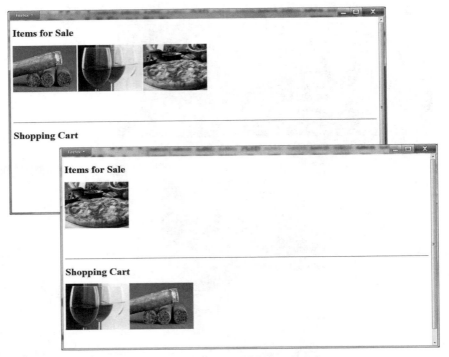

FIGURE 27-4 Dragging and dropping items to and from a shopping cart
Credit © Vaclav Volrab/Shutterstock; © Gts/Shutterstock; © Daniel Cozma/Shutterstock

```
function drag(event)
{
  event.dataTransfer.setData("Text", event.target.id);
}
</script>
</head>
<body>
<div style="height:300px; width:800px;" ondragover=
"permitdrop(event)" ondrop="drop(event)" >
<h1>Items for Sale</h1>
<img src="cigars.jpg" draggable="true" id="cigars"
width="200" height="150"
ondragstart="drag(event)"/>
<img src="wine.jpg" draggable="true" id="wine"
width="200" height="150" ondragstart="drag(event)"/>
```

```
<img src="pizza.jpg" draggable="true" id="pizza"
width="200" height="150"
ondragstart="drag(event)"/></div>
<hr/>
<div style="height:300px; width:800px;" ondragover=
"permitdrop(event)" ondrop="drop(event)">
<h1>Shopping Cart</h1></div>
</body>
</html>
```

As you can see, the page simply makes all of the images draggable and then allows each division to support track-and-drop operations.

Real-World Web Design

This chapter introduced Web-based drag-and-drop operations. If you plan to develop real-world applications that use drag and drop, first read the Drag-and-Drop Specification on the W3 website at *http://www.w3.org/TR/2011/WD-html5-20110525/dnd.html,* as shown in **FIGURE 27-5**.

Hands-On HTML

To view the HTML files or to experiment with the files presented in this chapter, visit this book's companion website at *http://www.websitedevelopmentbook.com/Chapter27/TryIt.html.*

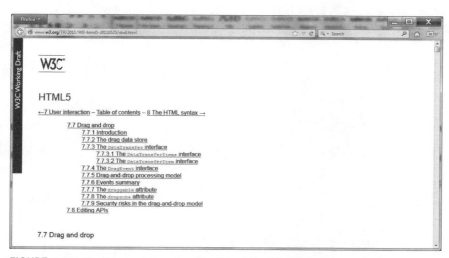

FIGURE 27-5 The Drag-and-Drop Specification at the W3 website
Reproduced with permission of the World Wide Web Consortium (W3C).

CHAPTER SUMMARY

Drag-and-drop operations are common within most application programs today. HTML 5 provides drag-and-drop support for webpage elements. Using HTML 5 drag-and-drop, you might, for example, be able to drag items from a catalog into a shopping cart. In the near future, the ability will exist to drag items from a page into other applications or vice versa. This chapter introduced drag-and-drop operations. In Chapter 28, "Integrating Web Workers," you will learn how to perform concurrent processing within your webpages.

KEY TERMS

Drag-and-drop operation

CHAPTER REVIEW

1. Create an HTML file that lets you drag an image from the top of the page to the bottom.

2. Create an HTML file that contains two side-by-side tables. The left table should contain photos of your favorite items. Allow the user to drag the items from the table on the left to the table on the right side.

Integrating Web Workers

FOR YEARS, OPERATING SYSTEMS have allowed multiple programs to run at the same time. Today, applications also take advantage of multiple threads of execution to perform concurrent tasks. Using HTML Web workers, webpages can now use similar threads to perform concurrent processing. A webpage might, for example, use a background task to spell-check content or to parse a large collection of JSON data, as you learned about in Chapter 14, "Processing JavaScript Object Notation." Developers use JavaScript to define the processing a Web worker performs.

Learning Objectives

This chapter introduces the use of HTML 5 Web workers. By the time you finish this chapter, you will understand the following key concepts:

- How a Web worker is essentially a JavaScript routine that performs concurrent processing within the background
- How to create and use a Web worker within an HTML page
- How to start, stop, and terminate a Web worker
- Which objects a Web worker can and cannot access

Understanding Web Workers

In general, to perform concurrent processing, an operating system quickly switches between tasks, giving the perception that multiple actions are occurring at the same time. Given that today's processors are often multicore, the operating system can assign each core processor a task to perform. Developers refer to such tasks as a **thread of execution**. Each thread contains the instructions the processor executes to accomplish a specific task.

A **Web worker** is not a person but a JavaScript routine that allows a webpage to perform similar concurrent processing. In general, a webpage uses a specific JavaScript file that contains the code the worker performs to accomplish a task. The webpage that uses the worker creates a worker object, which begins to perform its processing within the background. As the worker completes its processing, it sends a message to the webpage. The webpage, in turn, can use the message as appropriate. The Web worker does not impact the webpage performance because it runs in the background.

Testing a Browser for Web Worker Support

To test if your browser supports Web workers, you can test if the **Worker** object is defined. The following HTML file, TestWorkerSupport.html, tests for the **Worker** object and then displays an **alert** dialog box as to whether Web workers are supported:

```
<!DOCTYPE html>
<html>
<head>
<script>

function testWorkerSupport()
{
  if (typeof(Worker) != "undefined")
    alert("Web Workers Supported");
  else
    alert("Web Workers Not Supported");
}

</script>
</head>
<body onload="testWorkerSupport();">
</body>
</html>
```

Note: For security reasons, you cannot run a webpage that uses a Web worker from a file:// connection. You must upload your HTML file and JavaScript file to a Web server. To run the examples presented in this chapter, see the "Try It" section at the end of the chapter, which lets you run the files from the book's companion website.

Creating a Web Worker Script

A Web worker is essentially a JavaScript routine that performs specific processing as a **background task**. A background task is a thread of execution the processor executes during its "free time" or using an available core processor. The following JavaScript file, Time.js, defines a function that wakes up every second to determine the current time. The code then uses the **postMessage** function to send the time back to the webpage that is using the worker:

```
function myTimer()
{
  var date = new Date();
  vartimeStr = date.toLocaleTimeString();
  postMessage(timeStr);
  setTimeout(myTimer,1000);
}
setTimeout(myTimer,1000);
```

As you can see, the code provides the **myTimer** function that gets the date and time and then posts a message containing the time. The code then resets the timer.

Using the Web Worker

The following HTML file, UseWorker.html, displays a photo and two buttons, which you can use to turn the worker on or off. In addition, the page defines a space that it uses to display the current time:

```
<!DOCTYPE html>
<html>
<head>
<script>

var worker;
```

```
function startWorker()
{
if (typeof(Worker) != "undefined")
{
  worker = new Worker("time.js");
  worker.onmessage = function(event)
  {showTime(event); };
}
else
  alert("Web Workers Not Supported");
}

functionshowTime(event)
{
  document.getElementById('clock').innerHTML =
  event.data;
}

function StopWorker()
{
  if (worker)
    {
      worker.terminate();
      worker = null;
    }
}

function StartWorker()
{
  if (! worker)
    startWorker();
}

</script>
</head>
<body onload="startWorker();">
<div id="clock" style="font-size:100px"></div>
<img src="hourglass.jpg">
<br/>
<button onclick="StopWorker()">Stop Worker</button>
<button onclick="StartWorker()">Start Worker</button>
</body>
</html>
```

FIGURE 28-1 Using a Web worker to obtain the current system time
© *Valerie Potapova/Shutterstock*

When you view this page, the browser will display the controls in **FIGURE 28-1**.

Within the HTML file, the code first tests if the browser supports Web workers. If it does, the file then creates a worker object. After the worker object exists, the page can send messages to or receive messages from the worker. In this case, the file receives the current time as a message. Each time the worker sends a message, the **onMessage** function displays the received time within the page region that is reserved for the clock:

```
<!DOCTYPE html>
<html>
<head>
<script>

var worker;

function startWorker()
{
  if (typeof(Worker) != "undefined")
```

```
  {
    worker = new Worker("time.js");
    worker.onmessage = function(event)
    {showTime(event); };
  }
  else
    alert("Web Workers Not Supported");
}

function showTime(event)
{
    document.getElementById('clock').innerHTML
    = event.data;
}

function StopWorker()
{
  if (worker)
  {
    worker.terminate();
    worker = null;
  }
}

function StartWorker()
{
  if (! worker)
    startWorker();
}

</script>
</head>
<body onload="startWorker();">
<div id="clock" style="font-size:100px"></div>
<img src="hourglass.jpg">
<br/>
<button onclick="StopWorker()">Stop Worker</button>
<button onclick="StartWorker()">Start Worker</button>
</body>
</html>
```

When you click the Stop Worker button, the page calls a function that terminates the worker:

```
functionStopWorker()
{
  if (worker)
    {
      worker.terminate();
      worker = null;
    }
}
```

As you can see, the code tests to ensure the worker exists, in case it was previously terminated, and then calls the **terminate** function to stop it.

In contrast, if you click the Start Worker button, the code again checks if a worker is already running, and if not, creates a new one:

```
functionStartWorker()
{
  if (! worker)
    startWorker();
}
```

Looking at a Second Example

The following HTML file, FamousQuotes.html, displays a photo, a name, and a quote, as shown in **FIGURE 28-2**. Every 10 seconds, the file changes its content based on the worker input.

The following code implements the Quotes.js worker file:

```
var index = 0;

var quotes = new Array('Lincoln; Lincoln.jpg;
Better to remain silent and be thought a fool than
to speak out and remove all doubt.',
        'Washington; Washington.jpg; Be courteous
to all, but intimate with few, and let those
few be well tried before you give them your
confidence.');

function myTimer()
```

FIGURE 28-2 A webpage that receives a photo, name, and quote from a Web worker
Credit (both images): © Cory Thoman/Shutterstock

```
{
  postMessage(quotes[index]);
  index += 1;
  if (index == 3)
    index = 0;
  setTimeout(myTimer,10000);
}
```

```
setTimeout(myTimer,500);
```

As you can see, the script uses an array of character strings that define the person's name, a corresponding image file, and a quote. Every 10 seconds the timer triggers, which causes the function to send the next quote data. The script continues to repeat through the array elements.

The following statements implement the FamousQuotes.html file:

```
<!DOCTYPE html>
<html>
<head>
<script>

var worker;

function startWorker()
{
  if (typeof(Worker) != "undefined")
    {
      worker = new Worker("Quotes.js");
      worker.onmessage = function(event)
      {showQuote(event); };
    }
    else
      alert("Web Workers Not Supported");
}

function showQuote(event)
{
  var name = event.data.substring(0, event.data
  .indexOf(';'));
  document.getElementById('name').innerHTML = name;

  varimagefile = event.data.substring(event.data
  .indexOf(';')+1, event.data.lastIndexOf(';'));
  document.getElementById('photo').src = imagefile;

  var quote = event.data.substring(event.data
  .lastIndexOf(';')+1);
  document.getElementById('quote').innerHTML = quote;
}
```

```
function StopWorker()
{
  if (worker)
    {
      worker.terminate();
      worker = null;
    }
}

function StartWorker()
{
  if (! worker)
    startWorker();
}

</script>
</head>
<body onload="startWorker();">
<div id="name" style="font-size:100px"></div>
<img id="photo" src="lincoln.jpg">
<div id="quote" style="font-size:48px"></div>
<br/>
<button onclick="StopWorker()">Stop Worker</button>
<button onclick="StartWorker()">Start Worker</button>
</body>
</html>
```

In this case, when the file receives a message from the worker, the file uses JavaScript parsing functions to extract the name, image file, and quote. The file then updates its display using the components.

Objects a Web Worker Can and Cannot Access

Web workers are meant to perform complex processing within the background. Web workers cannot access the following objects because they reside in an external JavaScript file:

- window object
- document object
- parent object
- localStorage or sessionStorage

Web workers can, however, access the following:

- location object
- navigation object
- application cache
- XMLHTTP Request

Real-World Web Design

This chapter introduced Web worker processing. If you plan to develop real world solutions that use Web workers, refer to the Web Worker Specification that the W3 website provides at *http://www.w3.org/TR/workers/,* as shown in **FIGURE 28-3**.

Hands-On HTML

To view the HTML files or to experiment with the files presented in this chapter, visit this book's companion website at *http://www.websitedevelopmentbook.com/Chapter28/TryIt.html.*

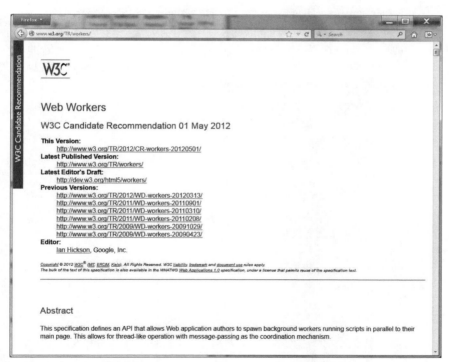

FIGURE 28-3 The HTML 5 Web Worker Specification at the W3.org website
Reproduced with *permission of the World Wide Web Consortium (W3C)*

CHAPTER SUMMARY

With many computers now using multicore processors, the use of threads to implement concurrent processing is becoming quite common. In this chapter, you learn how to use Web workers to perform background processing for a webpage. As you learned, a Web worker is essentially a JavaScript routine that performs specific processing. Because the Web worker performs its processing in the background, the worker does not impact the webpage performance. In Chapter 29, "Communicating via WebSockets," you will learn how to create webpages that can communicate with a server using WebSockets.

KEY TERMS

Background task
Thread of execution
Web worker

CHAPTER REVIEW

1. Create an HTML file that uses a Web worker to provide a random graphic image every 30 seconds, which the page displays as a screen saver.

2. Modify the UseWorker.html file presented in this chapter to send a "stop" message to the Web worker to suspend its processing rather than terminating the worker. Then, the Start Worker button should send a "start" message to resume the worker's processing.

3. Search the Web for applications that use Web workers, and report on your findings.

Communicating via WebSockets

USERS TODAY MAKE EXTENSIVE use of texting and instant messaging to communicate. Websites often integrate text-based chats to allow them to exchange messages with technical support staff or sales team members. To make it easier for developers to integrate such capabilities, HTML 5 introduces a WebSocket application program interface (API). Admittedly, the API is still in its infancy. Over time, however, you can expect it to grow to support greater capabilities, such as **peer-to-peer communication**. This is communication between two applications without the use of a server as an intermediary.

Learning Objectives

This chapter introduces the WebSocket API. By the time you finish this chapter, you will understand the following key concepts:

- How to understand sockets as endpoints and the communication channel
- How to test for browser support for the WebSocket API
- How to use a socket for data communication
- How to use the WebSocket API to send and receive messages to and from a remote server

Understanding Sockets

To communicate across the Web, two programs must establish a connection, normally using TCP/IP, across which they send and receive messages. You can think of a **socket** as an endpoint to the connection. Developers use the term sockets to describe the endpoints and the communication channel between them. This chapter examines the use of the WebSocket API to open, use, and later close a communication channel.

Testing Browsers for WebSocket Support

To begin, test your browser's support for the WebSocket API. Your code can test to see if the **window.WebSocket** object is defined. The following HTML file, Test-Socket.html, illustrates how you might perform such processing:

```
<!DOCTYPE html>
<html>
<head>
<script>
function testSocketSupport()
{
  if (window.WebSocket)
    alert("Sockets Supported");
  else
    alert("Sockets Not Supported");
}
</script>
</head>
<body onload="testSocketSupport()">
</body>
</html>
```

As you can see, the file uses an **if** statement to test if the object is defined and then displays a corresponding message using an **alert** dialog box.

Exchanging Messages with a WebSocket Server

To perform server-based WebSocket communication, you need a server application that supports such communication. Across the Web, you can find WebSocket servers written in PHP, Python, Java, and more. Several of the servers let you run them on your own local host.

To make it easy for you to get started, the WebSocket.org website provides an "echo server," which echoes back messages it receives from a client. The following

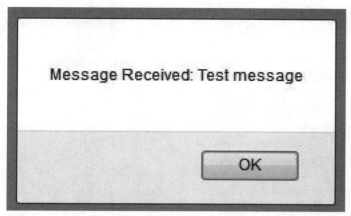

FIGURE 29-1 Using WebSockets to communicate with a remote server

HTML file, SocketEcho.html, connects to the server and sends a text message. When the server receives and echoes the message back, the webpage displays the received message within an **alert** dialog box, as shown in **FIGURE 29-1**:

```
<!DOCTYPE html>
<html>
<head>
<script>

varwebsocket;
function testSocketSupport()
{
  if (window.WebSocket)
    {
      varServerURL = "ws://echo.websocket.org/";
      websocket = new WebSocket(ServerURL);
      websocket.onopen = function(evt)
        { openFunction(evt) };
      websocket.onclose = function(evt)
        { onClose(evt) };
      websocket.onmessage = function(evt)
        { onMessage(evt) };
      websocket.onerror = function(evt)
        { onError(evt) };
    }
```

```
    else
      alert("Sockets Not Supported");
}

function openFunction(event)
{
  sendMessage("Test message");
}

function onMessage(event)
{
  alert("Message Received: " + event.data);
}

function onClose(event)
{
  alert(event.data);
}

function onError(event)
{
  alert(event.data);
}

function sendMessage(msg)
{
  websocket.send(msg);
}
</script>
</head>
<body onload="testSocketSupport();">
</body>
</html>
```

In this case, the code calls the **testSocketSupport** method, which determines if **sockets** are supported, and if so, creates a **WebSocket** object. Sockets are abstractions of a pipe connection to which a program can connect in order to send and receive messages across a channel. As part of the object creation process, the code opens the connection. As a result, the code's **openFunction,** which is an event handler for the WebSocket's **open** event, is called. In turn, it sends the message. After the server receives and echoes the message, the **onMessage** message handler receives and displays the message.

Expanding the Example

The following HTML file, AskMessage.html, prompts you for a message. When you click the Send button, the page uses a WebSocket to send the message to the server. The page then displays the message it receives back within the form, as shown in **FIGURE 29–2**:

```
<!DOCTYPE html>
<html>
<head>
<script>
var websocket;

var socketsSupported = false;

function Initialize()
{
  if (window.WebSocket)
    {
      var ServerURL = "ws://echo.websocket.org/";
      websocket = new WebSocket(ServerURL);
      websocket.onopen = function(evt)
        { openFunction(evt) };
      websocket.onclose = function(evt)
        { onClose(evt) };
      websocket.onmessage = function(evt)
        { onMessage(evt) };
      websocket.onerror = function(evt)
        { onError(evt) };

      alert('Establishing Connection');
      while (websocket.readyState == websocket.
        CONNECTING); // wait until socket is
        connected
      socketsSupported = true;
    }
  else
    alert("Sockets Not Supported");
}

function Send(msg)
{
  Initialize();
```

```
        if (socketsSupported)
            websocket.send(msg);
    }

    function onMessage(event)
    {
        document.getElementById('response').innerHTML =
            event.data;
    }

    function onClose(event)
    {
        alert(event.data);
    }

    function onError(event)
    {
        alert(event.data);
    }

    </script>
    </head>
    <body>
    Message: <input id="msg" type="text"></input>
    <button onclick="Send(document.
    getElementById('msg').value)">Send Message</button>
    <br/><br/>

    Response: <div id="response"></div>
    </body>
    </html>
```

FIGURE 29-2 Using a WebSocket to send and receive messages between a client and server

When you establish a WebSocket connection, there is some network overhead that occurs as the client and server prepare to communicate. In this case, the code displays a message stating that it is establishing a connection. The code then loops until the connection occurs.

Real-World Web Design

As discussed, the WebSocket API is still developing. Before you start using the WebSocket API, review the API specification at the W3 website at: *http://www.w3.org/TR/2009/WD-websockets-20091029/*, as shown in **FIGURE 29-3**.

Hands-On HTML

To view the HTML files or to experiment with the files presented in this chapter, visit this book's companion website at *http://www.websitedevelopmentbook.com/Chapter29/TryIt.html*.

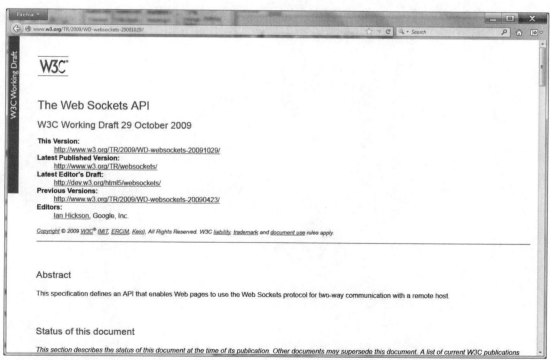

FIGURE 29-3 The WebSocket API specification at the W3 website
Reproduced with *permission of the World Wide Web Consortium (W3C)*

CHAPTER SUMMARY

As you surf the Web, you undoubtedly have seen sites that let you "chat with a representative" in real time using a text-based chat. To make it easier for developers to integrate such capabilities into the sites they create, HTML 5 provides a WebSocket API. This chapter introduced the API and the way you can use it to communicate with a remote server. Over time, we can expect the API to continue to provide new capabilities, such as peer-to-peer communication, communication between two applications without the use of a server as an intermediary.

KEY TERMS

Peer-to-peer communication
Socket

CHAPTER REVIEW

1. Search the Web for applications that use the HTML WebSocket API and report your findings.
2. Search the Web for a WebSocket server that you can install on your system's local host or on a remote server. Modify the SocketEcho.html file presented in this chapter to use your server.

HTML 5 Forms Processing

IN CHAPTER 6, "GETTING USER INPUT WITH FORMS," you examined these operations in detail. The processing presented in Chapter 6 uses standard HTML. In this chapter, you examine new form-based features provided through HTML 5. As you will learn, many of these features are still evolving; but they indicate significant capabilities for the future. That said, it is important to test each of the features this chapter presents using a variety of browsers to ensure that your browser provides the support you need.

Learning Objectives

This chapter examines the new form-based features of HTML 5. By the time you finish this chapter, you will understand the following key concepts:

- What the three form elements are
- How to use the HTML 5 **<datalist>** tag to specify a list of words form fields to assist with autocompletion
- How to use the HTML 5 **<keygen>** tag to generate a private and public encryption key pair
- How to use the HTML 5 **<output>** tag to integrate the result of a calculation into a form's display
- How to use the HTML 5 form attribute values
- What the HTML 5 input values are

HTML 5 Form Elements

A form element is a tag or tag pair that you can place within the **<form>** and **</form>** tag pair. HTML 5 adds three form elements to examine: **<datalist>**, **<keygen>**, and **<output>**.

Creating a Data List

A **data list**, in HTML 5, is a list of entries, similar to entries within a pull-down list, but without the pull-down. The browser uses the list to **autocomplete** user input as you type. **Autocompletion** is an input technique where a program, such as a browser, attempts to anticipate a user's remaining input. If, for instance, you go to the website of your favorite pizza place and order "pepperoni" for the fifth time, you may not have to enter more than "pep" before the autocomplete function kicks in. To create a datalist, you must specify options within the **<datalist>** and **</datalist>** tag pair:

```
<datalist id="states">
<option>Alabama</option>
<option>Arizona</option>
<option>Arkansas</option>
<option>California</option>
<option>Nevada</option>
</datalist>
```

The following HTML file, StatesDatalist.html, for example, builds a data list of several state names and then uses the list within an **<input>** tag:

```
<!DOCTYPE html>
<html>
<body>
<form action="http://www.WebsiteDevelopmentBook.
com/Chapter06/FileUploader.php" enctype="multipart/
form-data" method="post">
<datalist id="states">
<option>Alabama</option>
<option>Arizona</option>
<option>Arkansas</option>
<option>California</option>
<option>Nevada</option>
</datalist>
```

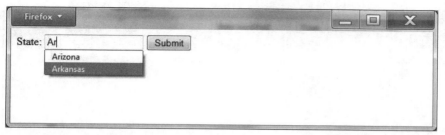

FIGURE 30-1 Using an HTML 5 data list to direct the browser to autocomplete a form's field

```
State: <input type="text" list="states"/>
<input type="submit" value="Submit"/>
</form>
</body>
</html>
```

As the user types a state name, the browser will suggest matching state names, as shown in **FIGURE 30-1**.

Creating a Private and Public Key Pair

By default, unless you are using an https:// connection, the content that a form sends to a remote server is unencrypted. To move toward encrypted content, HTML 5 has introduced the <**keygen**> tag, which directs the browser to create and store a private key and to send a public key to the server. At the time of this writing, the <**keygen**> tag is still in flux with varied browser support:

```
<keygen name="keyname"/>
```

Using the Output of a Calculation

The HTML 5 <**output**> and </**output**> tag pair lets you display the result, or output, of a calculation. The following HTML file, OutputDemo.html, illustrates the tag's use:

```
<!DOCTYPE html>
<html>
<body>
<form oninput="add.value = parseInt(x.value) +
parseInt(y.value)">
x <input type="text" name="x" value="0"/>
y <input type="text" name="y" value="0"/>
<br/><br/>
```

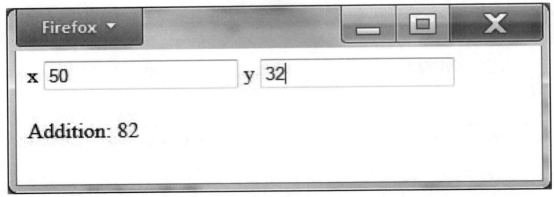

FIGURE 30-2 Using the HTML 5 **<output>** tag to display the result of a calculation

```
Addition Result: <output name="add" for="x y">
</output><br/>
</form>
</body>
</html>
```

As you can see, the page displays two input fields. After you type values for each field, the form will display the results of an addition of the two values, as shown in **FIGURE 30-2**. Again, it may be that not all browsers support the **<output>** tag.

HTML 5 Form Attributes

In addition to providing three new form elements, HTML 5 provides several attributes for either the **<form>** or **<input>** tags. The sections that follow examine each attribute. Again, before you use these attributes within a real world application, take time to test your code within a variety of browsers.

Directing the Browser to Autocomplete a Field or Form

As you surf the Web, there may be times when your browser attempts to autocomplete text in fields as you type, based on your previous responses. Under HTML 5, you can enable or disable such processing for an entire form or for fields on a field-by-field basis:

```
<form autocomplete="off">
<input type="text" name= "username"
autocomplete= "off">
```

Disabling Form Validation

By default, when you use different HTML 5 field types and attributes, your browser tries to validate form fields. Depending on the form's purpose, you may want to disable such validation using the **<form>** tag **novalidate** attribute:

```
<form novalidate>
```

Specifying a Field to Receive the Input Focus Within a Form

By default, when you create an HTML form, the browser assigns the first field in the form with the keyboard focus. Using the HTML 5 **autofocus** attribute, you can specify the field that you desire to first receive the focus:

```
Username: <input type="text" name= "username">
</input/><br/>
Password: <input type="password"
name="UserPassword"/><br/>
Nickname: <input type="text" name="nickname"
autofocus/>
```

In the statements above, the browser first assigns the keyboard focus to the nickname field.

Using the <Input> Tag Form Attribute

Normally, developers group a form's **<input>** tags within the **<form>**and **</form>** tag pair. If, for some reason, you have an **<input>** tag that resides outside a form, you can use the **form** attribute to specify the tag's corresponding form:

```
Nickname: <input type="text" name= "nickname"
form="formName"/>
```

Overriding a Form's Submit-Method Attribute

As you have learned, when a browser submits a form's data, the browser performs either a **get** or **put** operation:

```
<form action="http://www.WebsiteDevelopmentBook.
com/FormEcho.php" method="post">
```

Depending on the processing you are performing, there may be times when you will want to override a form's specified submission method. In such cases, use the **<input>** tag **formmethod** attribute:

```
<input type="submit" formmethod="get"/>
```

Overriding a Form's Validation Processing

As you have learned, HTML 5 provides the **<form>** tag **novalidate** attribute that specifies whether or not the form's contents should be validated. Depending on your form's processing, there may be times when you will want to provide a button that allows submission without validation. In such cases, use the **<input>** tag **formnovalidate** attribute:

```
Field: <input type="email" formnovalidate/>
```

Controlling the Display of a Server's Response

When you submit a form to a remote server, should the server send a response, the page displays the response. Depending on your form's purpose, there may be times when you will want to display the server response within a different window. To do so, use the **formTarget** attribute. The following HTML file, FormTarget.html, uses the FormEcho script on this book's companion website. The page provides a submit button, which uses the attribute to display the script's results in a new window:

```
<!DOCTYPE html>
<html>
<body>
<form action="http://www.WebsiteDevelopmentBook
.com/FormEcho.php" method="post">
Value: <input type="text" name="UserEntry"/><br/>
<br/>
<input type="submit" value="Back"/>
<input type="submit" formTarget="new"
value="New window"/>
</form>
</body>
</html>
```

If you view the file's content and then submit a result to the form, the browser displays the server's result in a separate window, as shown in **FIGURE 30-3**.

Specifying an Input Tag's Height and Width

As you have learned, using an element's **height** and **width** attributes, you can specify the item's size within an HTML page. When you specify the HTML 5 **type="image"** attribute, you can specify an **<input>** tag's height and width. The following HTML file, InputSize.html, specifies the size of an **<input>** element:

```
<!DOCTYPE html>
<html>
<body>
```

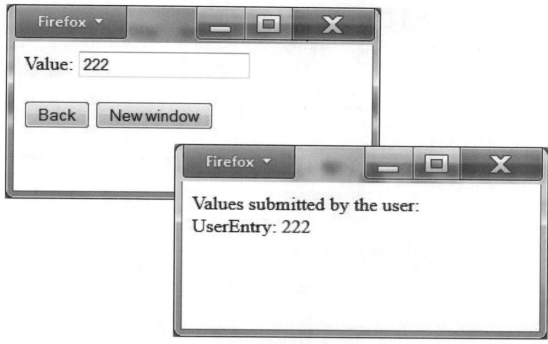

FIGURE 30-3 Displaying a form's server response in a separate window

```
<form action="http://www.WebsiteDevelopmentBook
.com/FormEcho.php" method="post">
<input type="image" src="pickme.jpg" width="100"
height="50"/>
<input type="image" src="cool.jpg" width="100"
height="50"/>
</form>
</body>
</html>
```

When you view the file's contents, the browser displays the page, as shown in **FIGURE 30-4**. When you click on a button, the browser submits the x and y locations of the mouse click.

Using a Data List Reference

As you have learned, an HTML 5 data list defines a list of entries the browser uses to match keyboard input for a field. Using the **list** attribute, you can refer to a pre-existing data list:

```
State: <input type="text" list="states"/>
```

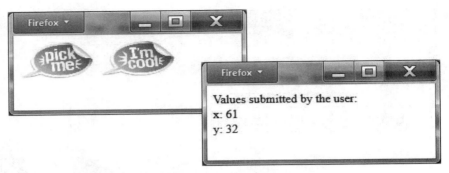

FIGURE 30-4 Sizing an **<input>** tag under HTML 5

Credit © Olena Pantiukh/Shutterstock

Specifying Min and Max Values

Often, a field will prompt a user for a numeric or date field for which you want to restrict the user to a range of values. Using the **min** and **max** attributes, you can specify the ranges, as shown here:

```
Age: <input type="number" min="0" max="120"/>
```

The **min** and **max** attributes also can be used with the HTML range input type:

```
Age: <input type="range" min="0" max="120"/>
```

Specifying Multiple Values for a File-Upload Operation

In Chapter 6, you learned that using the **<input>** tag **type="file"** attribute, you can allow the user to select a file for an upload operation. Using the HTML 5 **multiple** attribute, you can allow the user to select multiple files:

```
File(s):<input type="file" name="file" id="file"
multiple/>
```

The script that receives your submission also needs the ability to process multiple files.

Specifying a Regular Expression Pattern for Text Input

Often, when you prompt users for input using a form, such as a phone number or e-mail address, you will want them to put the data within a specific format. Using the HTML 5 **pattern** attribute, you can specify a **regular expression** the user's input must meet in order to be considered valid. A regular expression is a sequence of characters that can be used to match an entry based upon predefined rules. The following statements, for example, illustrate how you might use the attribute for a phone number:

```
<!DOCTYPE html>
<html>
<body>
<form action="http://www.WebsiteDevelopmentBook
.com/FormEcho.php" method="post">
Phone <input name="phone" type="text"
pattern="^[2-9]\d{2}-\d{3}-\d{4}$"/><br/><br/>
<input type="submit"/>
</form>
</body>
</html>
```

Your browser may display an error message if the value you enter does not match the format specified.

Specifying a Field Placeholder

Normally, when a page displays a form, the browser displays blank values for each text field. The HTML 5 **placeholder** attribute lets you specify a value that the browser initially displays within a field. The value might, for example, show a sample of the data format the field expects. The following HTML file, UsePlaceholder.html, uses two placeholder values:

```
<!DOCTYPE html>
<html>
<body>
<form action="http://www.WebsiteDevelopmentBook
.com/FormEcho.php" method="post">
Default: <input type="text"/><br/>
Placeholder: <input type="text" placeholder="(###)-
###-####"/><br/>
<input type="submit"/>
</form>
</body>
</html>
```

When you view the file's contents, the browser displays the values, as shown in **FIGURE 30-5**.

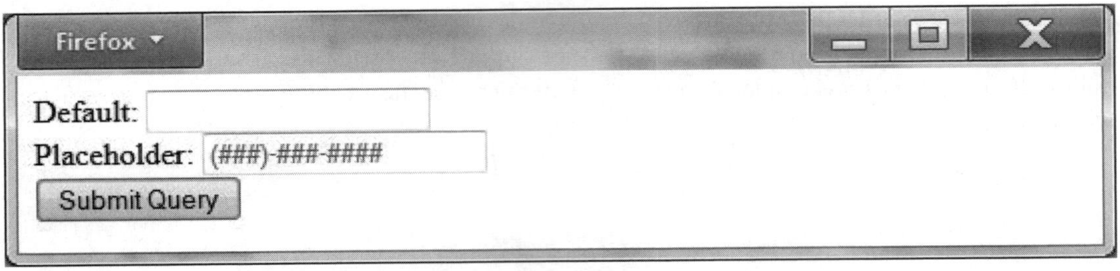

FIGURE 30-5 Displaying placeholder values within an HTML 5 form

Specifying That a Field Is Required

Many forms have one or more required fields, for which the user must provide values. Normally, after the user submits the form, a JavaScript routine on the page detects missing fields and notifies you to provide them. HTML 5, in contrast, provides the required attribute, which tells the browser that a field is required. The following HTML 5 file, UseRequired.html, uses a required field:

```
<!DOCTYPE html>
<html>
<body>
<form action="http://www.WebsiteDevelopmentBook
.com/FormEcho.php" method="post">
Default: <input type="text"/><br/>
Placeholder: <input type="text"
required/><br/><br/>
<input type="submit"/>
</form>
</body>
</html>
```

Depending on your browser, if you omit a required field, the browser displays a message stating you must provide a value, as shown in **FIGURE 30-6**.

Specifying a Step Attribute

Depending on the type of values for which your form is prompting, there may be times when you want to specify a list of numbers separated by a specific value, such as 0, 5, 10, 15, and so on. Only a few browsers currently support the step attribute:

```
<input type="number" name="Fives" step="5">
```

FIGURE 30-6 Using the HTML 5 **required** field to specify required fields to the browser

You may also use the **step** attribute with the **range** input type:

```
<input type="range" name="sales" min="50" max="100"
step="5">
```

Understanding HTML 5 Input

As you have learned in Chapter 6, within an **<input>** tag you can use the **type** attribute to specify the kind of value a field accepts, such as text, password, radio buttons, check boxes, and so on. HTML 5 adds the following **<input>** tag types, as specified in TABLE 30-1.

Today, many browsers still do not fully support the various types. Instead, the browsers simply treat the fields as **text** fields. Take time to experiment with different browsers to determine their level of support.

Real-World Web Design

To help you get started with HTML 5 form attributes and elements, the W3Schools website provides two excellent tutorials. The first, at *http://www.w3schools.com/ html/html5_form_elements.asp*, examines HTML 5 form elements. The second, at *http://www.w3schools.com/html/html5_form_attributes.asp*, presents form attributes introduced with HTML 5.

Hands-On HTML

To view the HTML files or to experiment with the files presented in this chapter, visit this book's companion website at *http://www.websitedevelopmentbook.com/ Chapter30/TryIt.html*.

TABLE 30-1   NEW <INPUT> TAG TYPE ATTRIBUTES SUPPORTED BY HTML 5

Input Type	Purpose
color	Prompts the user for a color. Some browsers may display a color-picker dialog box.
date	Prompts the user for a date. Some browsers may display a date-picker dialog box.
datetime	Prompts the user for a date and time. Some browsers may display a date and time dialog box with a time zone.
datetime-local	Prompts the user for a date and time. Some browsers may display a date and time dialog box without a time zone.
e-mail	Prompts the user for a string in e-mail format.
month	Prompts the user for a month.
number	Prompts the user for a numeric value.
range	Prompts the user for a value within a specified range. Some browsers may display a slider.
search	Prompts the user for search text. Most browsers will implement the field as a text field.
tel	Prompts the user for a string in a phone number format.
url	Prompts the user for a valid URL.
week	Prompts the user for a week.

Chapter Summary

Across the Web, sites make extensive use of forms to prompt you for input. Chapter 6, "Getting User Input With Forms," examined form processing and user input operations in detail. This chapter introduced the form-based features provided in HTML 5. Unfortunately, many of these features are still evolving, and their support is varied. That said, the features provide you with insights to browser capabilities in the future. Should you use the techniques this chapter presents, it is important that you test each with a variety of browsers to ensure that your browser provides the necessary support.

Key Terms

Autocompletion
Data list

Regular expression

Chapter Review

1. Create an HTML file that uses a data list of computer terms within the webpage.
2. Discuss a scenario for which you would use the **<keygen>** tag.
3. Create an HTML file that demonstrates the use of the HTML 5 **<output>** tag.
4. Create an HTML file that demonstrates the use of the **autofocus** attribute.
5. Discuss when you might need to change a form's encoding technique.
6. Search the Web for three different regular expressions you might use within a webpage, and demonstrate their use.
7. Create an HTML file that demonstrates the use of the HTML 5 **placeholder** attribute.
8. Create an HTML file that demonstrates the use of the HTML 5 form validation.

Browser Identification

© Risto Viita/Shutterstock

chapter

31

AS THE CAPABILITIES YOU include within a webpage increase, you may want to determine a user's browser type so that you can process accordingly. For example, you might want to customize the code you are using to integrate video, or you may want to format page content differently for a Web and mobile browser.

Learning Objectives

This chapter examines a few techniques you can use to determine a browser's capabilities. By the time you finish this chapter, you will understand the following key concepts:

- What "hacks" are, and why Web developers try to avoid them
- How to determine a browser's user-agent setting using JavaScript
- How to determine a user's browser type
- What ways exist to identify a mobile browser

A Word on "Hacks"

If you speak with Web developers, you will encounter a variety of opinions with respect to whether or not one should perform browser-specific processing within the pages they create. Many developers will refer to an example of such processing as a **hack**, because it can lead to code that is difficult to understand and hard to maintain. Other developers, in contrast, will criticize the common browsers for not yet providing across-the-board standards. In either case, before you perform browser-specific processing, ask yourself if there is another approach that may produce code that will work now and in the future.

Understanding the User Agent

A **user agent** is a program that performs one or more tasks for the user. When a user surfs the Web, the browser is the user agent. One of the ways to determine a user's browser type is to ask the browser to specify its user-agent value. The following HTML file, UserAgent.html, uses JavaScript to request the user-agent value and then uses an alert dialog box to display the corresponding value:

```
<!DOCTYPE html>
<html>
<body>
<script type="text/javascript">

alert("User-agent header sent: " + navigator.
userAgent);

</script>
</body>
</html>
```

When you view the file's contents, the browser will display a dialog box similar to that shown in **FIGURE 31-1**, which displays the value stored for the browser's user-agent value.

To access the user-agent value, the code uses the **navigator** object built into JavaScript and then selects the **userAgent** field.

By parsing the user-agent value, your code can determine the specific browser type. The following HTML file, BrowserType.html, uses a series of if-else statements to display the current browser type:

```
<!DOCTYPE html>
<html>
```

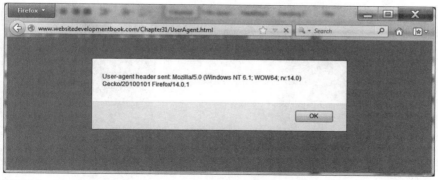

FIGURE 31-1 Displaying a browser's user-agent value

```
<body>
<script type="text/javascript">

if (navigator.userAgent.indexOf("Safari") !=-1)
  alert("Safari");
else if (navigator.userAgent.indexOf("Chrome") !=-1)
  alert("Chrome");
else if (navigator.userAgent.indexOf("Opera") !=-1)
  alert("Opera");
else if (navigator.userAgent.indexOf("MSIE") !=-1)
  alert("Internet Explorer");
else if (navigator.userAgent.indexOf("Firefox") !=-1)
  alert("Firefox");
else
  alert("Other browser");

</script>
</body>
</html>
```

The code, in this case, uses the **indexOf** function to test if the user-agent field contains a specific word. If the word is found, the **indexOf** function returns the starting character location. If the string is not found, the function returns the value -1. By testing the value the **indexOf** function returns, the code can determine if a specific string (browser type) is specified in the user-agent value.

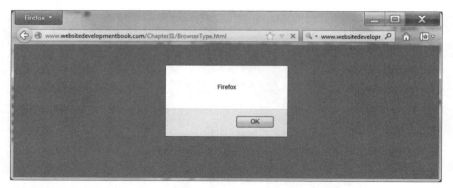

FIGURE 31-2 Parsing the user-agent value to determine a browser type

When you view the file's contents, the browser displays a dialog box similar to that shown in **FIGURE 31-2** that displays the browser type.

In a similar way, the following HTML file, BrowserSpecifics.html, uses the **navigator** object **appName** and **appVersion** fields to display the browser name and version:

```
<!DOCTYPE html>
<html>
<body>
<script type="text/javascript">

alert(navigator.appName + "-- " + navigator.
appVersion);

</script>
</body>
</html>
```

When you view the file's contents, your browser displays a dialog box similar to that shown in **FIGURE 31-3**, which displays the browser name and version number.

Determining the Browser Type on the Web Server

The previous examples used JavaScript on the client (user) side to determine browser specifics. If you are writing server-side applications, you can use a scripting language, such as PHP, to determine the browser type and then download appropriate content dynamically.

FIGURE 31-3 Using the JavaScript **navigator** object **appName** and **appVersion** fields to identify specifics about a browser

The following PHP script, BrowserType.php, which you can access at *http://www.websitedevelopmentbook.com/Chapter31/BrowserType.php*, uses server-side processing to display browser specifics:

```php
<?php
print $_SERVER['HTTP_USER_AGENT'];
?>
```

When you view the page contents, your browser displays output similar to that shown in **FIGURE 31-4**.

Other Navigator Object Fields

Depending on your processing needs, there may be other **navigator** object fields your code can leverage. **TABLE 31-1** briefly summarizes the object fields.

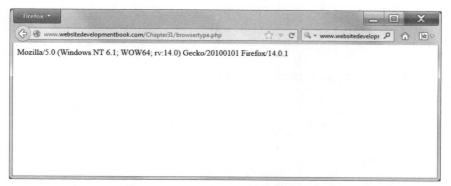

FIGURE 31-4 Using a scripting language to determine browser specifics on the server side

TABLE 31-1	ADDITIONAL OBJECT FIELDS YOUR CODE CAN LEVERAGE
Field	**Purpose**
appName	Returns the browser name
appVersion	Returns the browser version
cookieEnabled	Returns true or false based on whether cookies are enabled in the browser
platform	Returns browser platform
ppCodeName	Returns the browser code name
userAgent	Returns the browser user-agent

Identifying a Mobile Browser

Many developers use the same page content for Web-based and mobile browsers. As you know, mobile devices have a much smaller screen display than their PC-based counterparts. Therefore, for a mobile browser, a developer may need to display content that is more compact or less extensive.

One way to detect a mobile browser is to use a technique similar to those just shown to determine and parse the user-agent setting. Unfortunately, there are many different mobile agents, which makes such processing hard to understand and difficult to maintain. Worse yet, the number of agents changes.

As an alternative, some developers use the JavaScript **screen** object to determine the browser's screen settings (height and width). The following HTML file, BrowserScreenResolution.html, displays an **alert** dialog box that contains the browser screen width and height:

```
<!DOCTYPE html>
<html>
<body>
<script type="text/javascript">

alert ("Browser resolution: " + screen.width +
" x " + screen.height);

</script>
</body>
</html>
```

FIGURE 31–5 Displaying the browser's screen resolution

When you display the file, the browser will display the resolution settings, as shown in **FIGURE 31–5**.

Let Others Do the Mobile Device Detection Work

As you might guess, the ability to detect a mobile browser has become very important to many companies. Across the Web, several sites, such as *http://Detect MobileBrowsers.com*, provide code snippets you can use to accurately detect a mobile browser. The advantage of using such a site's code is that most sites like this one do a good job of keeping the browser list current.

Real-World Web Design

Depending on the processing your webpages perform, sometimes you need to know the user's Internet Protocol or IP address. You might need such information for advertisement processing and billing, or you may have sites that you want to prevent from accessing your content (a blacklist). Often, you will perform such IP-address processing on the server side. The following PHP script, which you can access at *http://www.websitedevelopmentbook.com/Chapter31/IPAddress.php*, displays the user's IP address, as shown in **FIGURE 31–6**:

```php
<?php
print $_SERVER['REMOTE_ADDR'];
?>
```

To create a blacklist of sites you want to prevent from seeing your page, create a similar server-side script that determines the user's IP address, and compare it to a list of prohibited sites.

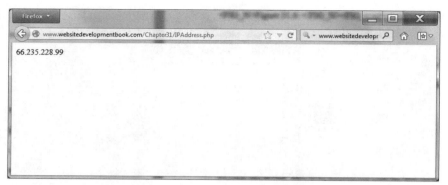

FIGURE 31-6 Determining and displaying a user's IP address

Hands-On HTML

To view the HTML files or experiment with the files presented in this chapter, visit this book's companion website at *http://www.websitedevelopmentbook.com/Chapter31/TryIt.html.*

CHAPTER SUMMARY

Depending on the processing your webpages perform, there may be times when you need to know specifics about a user's browser. You might use such information, for example, to customize the display for a mobile device or control how your page integrates audio or video. In this chapter, you learned how to determine a user's browser type using JavaScript as well as server-side scripts. Before you perform such processing on your own pages, however, keep in mind that such code can be difficult to understand and hard to maintain.

KEY TERMS

Hack
User agent

CHAPTER REVIEW

1. Create an HTML file that identifies common mobile devices, such as the iPhone and Android.
2. Create an HTML file that retrieves and displays the value of the **navigator** object platform field.
3. Modify the HTML file you created for Question 1 to display one image for a computer-based Web browser and a different image for a mobile device.

GLOSSARY OF KEY TERMS

Absolute URL A uniform resource locator (Web address) that begins with http:// and then specifies a website, possibly a folder, and then a filename.

Ad network A company that will deliver advertisements to a webpage from multiple sources.

Animated GIF An image file that contains a simple animation.

Application program interface (API) A set of software routines an application can use to accomplish a specific task.

Array A variable capable of storing multiple values.

Asynchronous Not occurring at the same time (as something else). When a program calls an asynchronous function, it does not know when the processing is complete. When the processing is done, the browser normally calls a special callback function to process the result.

Asynchronous JavaScript and XML (AJAX) A technique that lets JavaScript exchange messages within a remote server.

Autocompletion An input technique for which a program, such as a browser, attempts to anticipate a user's remaining input.

Autoplay A setting that directs the browser to "play automatically" a video or audio after a page is loaded.

Background task A thread of execution that the processor executes during its "free time" or using an available core processor.

Browser A program with which users view content on the World Wide Web.

Callback function A function within a webpage, which an API can call to resume processing within the page.

Canonicalization The process of converting data into one standard form. With respect to webpages, canonicalization would mean having one standard page.

Canvas A region within an HTML 5 webpage where JavaScript can be used to display shapes, images, and text.

Cascading style sheet (CSS) A file recording style detail, such as fonts and colors, that is read by browsers so that style is consistent over multiple webpages.

Cell padding An attribute, specified by the `<table>` tag **cellpadding**, that defines the number of pixels between cell content and the surrounding cell border.

Cell spacing An attribute, specified by the `<table>` tag **cellspacing**, that defines the pixel space that appears between table cells.

Checkbox A small square on a computer screen that a user can click on to register a choice.

Codec A compression technique used to optimize video or audio quality or file size. Three common video codecs are H.264, Theora, and V8.

Conditional processing A kind of decision-making processing, supported by JavaScript, which lets programs make decisions using the **if**, **if–else**, and **switch** statements.

Content delivery network A collection of Web servers distributed across a geographic area that developers can rent space upon to hold webpage resources in order to reduce webpage download times.

Cookie A data storage facility resident on a disk. An application can use it to store up to 4KB of data. When you visit a website, the browser sends the corresponding cookies to the website. The application or the user can delete the cookie.

Cost per click (CPC)   The amount advertisers pay for one user click upon an advertisement.

Cost per thousand impressions (CPM)   The amount advertisers pay for 1,000 user viewings of an advertisement

CSS animation   A collection of CSS transitions, specified as keyframes, which the browser applies to an HTML element.

CSS class definition   A style a Web developer assigns to a class name, which the developer can then apply to specific tags using the **class** attribute.

CSS transition   A browser-performed transition of an HTML element from a starting state to an ending state, as specified by CSS property values.

Data list   An HTML 5 list of entries defined by the <datalist> tag that specifies terms the browser uses to autocomplete an input field.

Definition list   A list of terms and their meanings. To create a definition list in HTML, use the **<dl>** and **</dl>** tag pair.

Deprecated tag   An older HTML tag that browsers may discontinue using in the future. Developers should avoid the use of deprecated tags within the pages they create.

Document Object Model (DOM)   A model that browsers use to track the elements that make up a webpage.

Domain name   A name of a website, such as *www.Microsoft.com.*

Dots per inch (DPI)   A measure of an image's resolution. Most digital cameras provide high-resolution images at 300 DPI. To reduce the file of image files on the Web, in order to speed up their download time, most Web images are 72 DPI.

Downloaded video   Video that, in contrast to streaming video, must download completely to the user's system before it can play.

Drag-and-drop operation   A mouse-based operation within which a user can click on an object and then move the object, while holding down the mouse button, to a new location. When you release the mouse button, the software drops the object at the new location. HTML 5 supports drag-and-drop operations with webpage elements.

Embedded style   A CSS style that a developer defines within the **<style>** and **</style>** tag pair, which applies to an HTML tag select, a class definition, or is id-based in relation to an HTML element's **id** attribute. Developers use embedded styles to apply formatting to an entire HTML page.

External style   A CSS style that a developer defines within a text file, which applies to an HTML tag select, a class definition, or is id-based corresponding to an HTML element's **id** attribute. Developers then link the CSS file into HTML pages using the **<link>** tag. Because all of the pages that make up a website can use the same CSS file, the site maintains a consistent look and feel, and developers can easily make changes to style definitions that instantly apply throughout the site.

External style sheet   A text file containing CSS style definitions that developers can link into one or more webpages.

File Transfer Protocol (FTP)   The standard network protocol for transferring files across the Internet to remote Web servers.

Geopositioning system (GPS)   A system that combines hardware and software to determine a user's or a device's current location.

Global variable   A variable that is known throughout every function within a file.

Gradient   A graphic programming technique that specifies a range of location-dependent colors used to fill a region.

Hack   A term Web developers use to describe code a developer puts into a webpage that solves one problem, but may cause other problems if it is difficult to understand and hard to maintain.

Hyperlink   Text or an image within a webpage that a user clicks on in order to jump to or display a specific page of content.

Hypertext markup language (HTML)   The tags Web developers use to format webpages.

Id–based style   A style a Web developer assigns to a name (identifier), which the developer can later apply to one tag based on that tag's **id** attribute.

Image map   A map that defines coordinates within an image that a Web browser will associate with a specific Web address. If the user clicks a mouse within the coordinates, the browser will display the corresponding Web content.

Image padding   Placing space around an image to separate it from other content within a webpage.

Image translation   The process of moving an image across the canvas.

Inline style   A CSS style that a developer places within an HTML tag to specify one or more formatting directives to the browser. Developers specify inline styles by applying a value to a tag's **style** attribute.

InnerHTML   The content that appears between a tag's starting and ending tags, such as ****innerHTML here****.

Iterative processing   Program processing that repeats one or more statements a specific number of times or while a specific condition is met.

JavaScript   A scripting language whose instructions are executed by the browser—a process called client-side processing. Developers often use JavaScript, for example, to validate the contents of a form before sending the contents to a remote server for processing.

JavaScript Object Notation (JSON)   A format application used to represent objects within a file or data transmission.

JQuery   A library of JavaScript functions your page can use to manipulate items on your webpage.

Keyframe   One of the intermediate steps within a CSS animation.

Keyword   A word that is reserved by a programming language, such as **if** or **function**, that has special meaning to the language and cannot be used for a variable name.

Linear gradient   A gradient in which the colors change along a line that travels across the shape.

List item   An entry within an ordered or unordered list. To specify a list item in HTML, you use the **<li>** and **</li>** tag pair.

Local variable   A variable that is known only to the function within which the variable is declared.

Lorem ipsum   An industry-standard placeholder (or dummy) text that graphics designers can use within the pages they design until the actual content is available.

Media player   Software that can play a media file, such as an audio or video file. To simplify the integration of audio and video within a webpage, companies across the Web are now offering media players that developers can integrate into their webpages using JavaScript.

Nested list   A list of items that appears within another list of items. To create a nested list in HTML, place an ordered or unordered list within a **<li>** and **</li>** tag pair of a surrounding (outer) list.

Nested table   A table created within the **<td>** and **</td>** tag pairs of another table.

Opacity   A measure of the amount of light that can pass through an object.

Ordered list   Also called a numbered list; a list of items that appears in alphabetical or numerical order. To create an ordered list in HTML, use the **<ol>** and **</ol>** tag pair.

Page divisions   Webpage containers within which a developer can place and style related HTML tags. Developers create a page division using the **<div>** and **</div>** tag pair.

Password field   A text box that does not display the content a user types, but rather, asterisks or other placeholder characters.

Peer-to-peer communication   Communication between two applications without the use of a server as an intermediary.

Program   A set of instructions that accomplish a specific task.

Property   An attribute value within a style definition, such as **background-color** or **font-family**, to which a developer can assign a specific value.

Pseudo class   A predefined CSS selector that applies styles based on a dynamic state, such as having a user's mouse hover over the element or the element receiving the keyboard focus; or based upon the object's position within a page, such as the first item within a list. CSS pseudo class names are preceded by a colon, such as **:hover**.

Pseudo element   A predefined CSS selector that applies to part of a tag's contents, such as the first line or character of a paragraph or the space above or below the element.

Pull-down list   A user-input control that restricts the user to selecting only entries from within the list.

Radial gradient   A gradient for which the colors change, radiating out from the center of a circle.

Radio buttons   User-input controls that a form will display in a group for which the user can only select one of the buttons within the group, as with the station-selection buttons on the front of a radio. Web developers place radio buttons within a form using the **<input>** tag **type="radio"** attribute.

Regular expression   A sequence of characters that can be used to match an entry on the basis of predefined rules. Web developers use regular expressions to validate form fields such as e-mail addresses and phone numbers.

Relative URL   A uniform resource locator (Web address) that is relative to the current HTML page location.

Resolution   A measure of the number of pixels a computer screen uses to display content or an image file uses to represent a photo. In general, the higher the resolution, the sharper the image.

Robots   Special programs that examine webpage content to determine a website's focus so the page can be appropriately indexed within a search engine.

Royalty-free image   An image that you can use on a webpage without having to pay the owner a fee (royalty) each time the image is displayed.

Rules   The lines that surround cells within an HTML table, the appearance of which is controlled by the **<table>** tag rules attribute.

Scalable vector graphic (SVG)   A powerful and flexible type of graphic file, which consists of XML-based directives that define the graphic; SVG graphics do not lose quality when scaled.

Screen reader   Software that "reads" aloud the contents of a webpage aloud using a voice synthesizer. Screen reader software allows users with visual disabilities to experience a webpage.

Script   Programming instructions normally written in a language such as PHP, Perl, or Python and executed by a remote server to perform specific processing. Browsers normally submit a form's contents to a remote script.

Search engine optimization (SEO)   The steps Web developers perform to increase a site's ranking within a search engine's query results.

Semantics   The study of meaning or relationship of words and content. HTML 5 provides new features developers can use to provide greater semantics for the webpages they create.

Session   The period of time in which you interact with a site. If you close your browser window or move to a new site, your session ends.

Socket   An abstraction of a pipe connection to which a program can connect in order to send and receive messages across a channel.

Streaming video   A video whose file format allows a browser to start playing it after it has been only partially downloaded. In contrast, a "downloaded video" must be downloaded in its entirety before the browser can start to play it.

Style   A collection of formatting attributes applied to an HTML tag. Using a style for text, a developer may specify a font family, font size, text color, text alignment, and so on.

Syntax   Rules that define a language, the way words are put together into sentences. In JavaScript, the syntax requires that a statement end with a semicolon.

Table caption   Text that defines an HTML table's contents specified by the **<caption>** and **</caption>** tag pair.

Table header   Text that appears at the top of a table column that describes the column's contents, specified by the **<th>** and **</th>** tag pair.

Tag-specific classes   A class definition that applies only to a specific selector. Developers create a tag-specific class definition by preceding the class name with a selector and a dot, such as **p.className**.

Text area   A user-input control within which users can type a large amount of text, such as comments about a website or even the text that makes up their résumé. Unlike a textbox, which has a fixed length, a text area supports an unlimited number of characters. Web developers create a text area using the **<textarea>** and **</textarea>** tag pair.

Textbox   A user-input control within which a user can type text. Web developers create a text box using the **<input>** tag **type= text"** attribute.

Text editor   A program, such as the Windows Notepad Accessory, that lets a user create and edit a text file.

Thread of execution   A series of instructions the CPU executes to perform a specific task.

Transparent background   An image of the background of which is transparent (as opposed to a white square) so that when the image is displayed on a webpage, the webpage background will appear as the image background.

Unordered list   A bulleted list; a list of items, normally proceeded by a circular bullet, that appear in no particular order. To create an unordered list in HTML, use the **<ul>** and **</ul>** tag pair.

User agent   A program that performs one or more tasks for the user. When a user surfs the Web, the browser is the user agent.

Variable   A named location within memory that programs use to temporarily store data as they execute.

Vector graphic   A graphic image that is defined by a series of instructions that draw vectors to create an illustration.

Video file format   A file type that specifies how a video file was saved. Common video file formats include MP4, ogg, FLV, and WebM.

Web-development software   Special software that allows a developer to create webpage content using a drag-and-drop and visual user interface. A common Web-development program is DreamWeaver.

Web Hypertext Application Technology Working Group (WHATWG)   The group that helped drive the HTML 5 specification.

Web server   A special computer on the Web from which users can use their browser to request and view Web content. Web developers normally create HTML files on their own PC and then use FTP to upload the files to a Web server.

Web worker   A JavaScript routine the browser executes as a background task.

Whitespace   Space characters, tabs, and blank lines used by programmers to improve the readability of their code.

World Wide Web Consortium (W3C)   The group that oversees many Web initiatives, including the development of the HTML 5 specification.

Index